Information Processing Management

SECOND EDITION

RALPH A. SZWEDA
Monroe Community College

D. VAN NOSTRAND COMPANY
New York Cincinnati Toronto London Melbourne

TO RUTH, ERIC, AND DAD
for their patience, understanding, and support

D. Van Nostrand Company Regional Offices:
New York   Cincinnati

D. Van Nostrand Company International Offices:
London   Toronto   Melbourne

Copyright © 1978 by Litton Educational Publishing, Inc.
Library of Congress Catalog Card Number: 78-56964

ISBN: 0-442-80509-8

Published by D. Van Nostrand Company
135 West 50th Street, New York, N.Y. 10020

10 9 8 7 6 5 4 3

CONTENTS

INTRODUCTION

In our first edition, we stressed the growing need for a data processing manager who was an administrator and only to a limited degree a technician. The need for administrative skills continues to grow, while the required technical expertise on the job is decreasing. That is not to say that a data processing manager no longer requires a working knowledge of data processing tools and technology. Subject-matter knowledge is still a requisite, but now the manager must determine how best to utilize data processing and an organization's resources to support the user's decision-making needs. The manager must constantly view the user's needs in terms of the overall objectives of the entire organization—a multi-functional rather than mono-functional perspective.

In this edition, we are incorporating the changes that are affecting the management process in a data processing organization. The data processing manager must be more of a planner and less a practitioner of the data processing art. Traditionally, the manager has limited the idea of planning to a specific system or programming project. Though this level of planning is still necessary, the data processing manager must also engage in intermediate and long-range planning for utilization of data processing. Long-range planning involves the use of a five-year plan to anticipate user demands for services. The projections are translated into hardware, software, and other resource needs and become the basis of subsequent priority decisions. In a large organization, for example, the manager must determine the impact and possible application of distributed networks of small processors linked to a large computer.

Budgetary practices long neglected or abused by the data processing manager must either be initiated, improved on, or reinstituted to ensure the optimal use of data processing resources in an organization. The ever-increasing costs of data processing services are forcing organizations to realistically use feasibility studies, cost-benefit analyses, and assessment and selection of hardware and software.

The use of teams and other variations in organizational structures places a greater emphasis on the concept of participative management. The manager must learn to delegate more, consider suggestions, and take criticism seriously. In addition, the formation of teams and other organizational units requires more thought, planning, and control. These variations also place greater emphasis on personnel training and career development schemes.

In this text, we cover the management principles that are most applicable to the data processing organization. We also deal with numerous other topics that affect or are affected by the management principles. More emphasis has been placed on the concepts of planning, project management, organization structures, dealing with users, development of data processing personnel, security, and the use of steering committees. In addition, the innovations in documentation and performance standards have been adapted to the text.

The need to select and design successful systems permeates every organization. The data processing manager must use feasibility studies, perform cost-benefit analyses, select and evaluate hardware and software, and implement controls to ensure the development and implementation of beneficial systems. These topics have been provided with an in-depth coverage in the text.

Each chapter is supplemented by a case study that is based on an actual situation.

HOW TO USE THIS TEXTBOOK
a guide for the Data Educator

There are several options available to the instructor utilizing *Information Processing Management* in the classroom environment. The option used may depend on the course objectives, the background and experience of the students, and the time-frame for the course.

The options are as follows:

1. If the students have had a previous management course, the instructor may choose to review the management process in chapter 1 or begin with a study of the feedback concept in that chapter. The instructor may then proceed with a study of the structural organization, staffing, the budget process, and design and layout of data processing facilities in chapters 2, 3, 6, and 7 respectively. In addition the instructor may use the case studies at the end of the chapters. The instructor may also wish to include the relevant segments on documentation and performance standards, and controls from chapters 4, 5, and 10.

2. If the students have had no prior management course, the instructor will most definitely wish to begin with the management process in chapter 1. The instructor may then proceed with a study of the structural organization, staffing, the budget process, design and layout of data processing facilities in chapters 2, 3, 6 and 7. In addition, the instructor may extract the relevant segments on documentation and performance standards, and controls in chapters 4, 5, and 10. Case studies are also available for reinforcement.

3. For an operations management course the instructor will wish to begin with the management process in chapter 1. The instructor may then include a study of the structural organizations, staffing, documentation and performance standards, the budget process, design and layout of facilities, and management controls in chapters 2, 3, 4, 5, 6, 7 and 10. In addition, the instructor may extract relevant material from chapter 9, which is concerned with hardware/software selection.

4. In a combined management and systems course, the instructor may wish to deal with the management segment initially and then go on to a study of the relevant systems material. Or the instructor may wish to begin with the systems material and then a study of the management area. This type of course would require two semesters or quarters.

The related management material would be the management process, structural organization, staffing, performance standards, and the budget process in chapters 1, 2, 3, 5, and 6 respectively. The systems segment would be concerned with the documentation standards, survey and feasibility studies, and hardware/software selection and management controls in chapters 4, 8, 9, and 10 respectively.

5. For an advanced systems course, the instructor would include a study of documentation and performance standards, the budget process, the survey and feasibility studies, hardware/software selection, and management controls in chapters 4, 5, 6, 8, 9, and 10 respectively.

In each option the instructor may wish to extract other relevant information from or minimize the content of any of the suggested chapters. In addition, case studies are available for class discussion and reinforcement purposes.

CHAPTER 1

The Management Process

INTRODUCTION / Management is an activity that is evident in all organizations, irrespective of whether they are industrial, commercial, governmental, educational, professional, or religious. Its existence becomes more meaningful to us when we consider that it is management that is responsible for the efforts and achievements of each organization.

As an activity, management within any one organization may be strongly influenced by the organization's stockholders (or members), employees, competitors, and public. To maintain an effective level of harmony among all of these groups ranks as a most difficult management task.

MANAGEMENT DEFINED

Management is a problem-solving and decision-making process executed by the manager in supporting the data and information needs of the overall organization. The manager skillfully applies the available resources to the management process in order to achieve the desired goal or goals. The term "management" should be regarded as an activity rather than as the managerial personnel within an organization. Such personnel should be described by the general term "managers." Managers are the administrators and supervisors, at all levels of an organization, who make things happen by effectively utilizing the available human, hardware, software, time, budget, and material resources. A manager can be the chief administrator; manager of data processing; director of information services; systems analysis and applications programming manager; tabulating operations supervisor; data control supervisor; lead systems analyst; data entry supervisor; and so on.

What Does a Manager Do?

A manager is responsible for the application of the five management functions—planning, organizing, coordinating, directing, and controlling—to an operation or activity. In this role he formulates the proper mix of managerial efforts by raising certain basic questions regarding the meaning and purpose of his activity. As he develops the answers to these questions he begins to execute the management process.

The first two of the six basic questions involve knowing *what* is to be done and *why* it is to be done; these questions must be answered before definition of the specific goals and planning for the goal-attainment process can be initiated. The third question is concerned with the *how* of the operation; this means determining the optimal application of the available resources—of manpower, material, budget, time, hardware, and software. The fourth question is *who* will actually do the work; here the personnel requirements must be determined. Logically we now move on to the fifth question of *when* will the work be done; this implies the necessity of a schedule for all related events and identification of response time requirements. The final and most important basic question is *where*. (It should be realized that this deals with the setting of an operation or activity in the organizational environment, not with the room location in which the goal must be accomplished.) To answer this basic question involving where, the manager must determine how other organizational activities affect and relate to his own objective. For example, the manager must gauge the contribution to be made by these activities, the types of communications channels that must be established and maintained, and their demands on the services of the information processing activity.

In order for the manager to answer successfully each of the six basic questions in management, he must be capable of envisioning the total operation and its interrelated activities. It is not enough for him simply to display professional technical competence in the management of an information processing activity. The information processing manager also has to have the ability to apply the management functions to the development and maintenance of an operationally effective activity.

APPROACHES TO MANAGEMENT ACTIVITY

There are two approaches to management activity within an organization. These are the dynamic approach and the static approach.

The static approach is a simple approach because it places each situation in an ideal environment. This doctrinal approach to the management process is based on the belief that all situations and problems are similar in nature, and that all work either flows logically in a straight line or can be arranged to operate in such a manner. Consequently, it utilizes solutions that have already been developed in other situations and in response to other problems.

Figure 1.1 Static approach to management

The static approach includes no provision for monitoring programs because no acceptable norms or deviation parameters are established during the planning stage. The lack of monitoring simplifies the controlling function, but also makes it unsuitable for use by the information processing manager who must know what is happening. Figure 1.1 illustrates the static approach.

Using the dynamic approach, the manager evaluates each problem or situation in its environmental setting to develop a relevant goal-attainment plan. He applies realistic attitudes to the existing situation, to the resources available, and to the possible courses of action. This enables the manager to design, develop, direct, and control an operationally effective activity. Such an approach provides for the evaluation of actual results and their comparison with the desired goals, as well as for the realignment or adjustment of activities as needed in order to achieve the objective.

Figure 1.2 illustrates the dynamic approach to management activity. After the objective has been defined and the plan of action developed and imple-

Figure 1.2 Dynamic approach to management

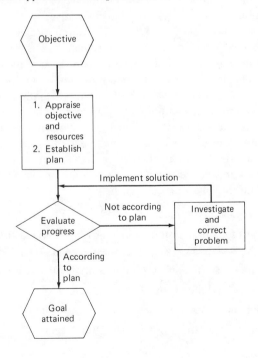

mented, the progress of the operation is continuously monitored and evaluated. The evaluation process involves comparing the actual results in terms of results, time, budget, personnel utilization, and output quality; with the planned ones at preestablished assessment points. If a deviation is found at any such point, the manager must then consider and implement the best course of action to insure that the operation will continue to move toward the desired end result.

It is the need for constant monitoring that can dampen a manager's enthusiasm for the dynamic approach. But the information processing manager must be willing and able to deal with any unexpected condition that may arise during the management process. An operationally effective manager must know what is happening, be willing to evaluate the operation, and be able to interrupt it at any point or step to implement any necessary corrections.

THE ROLE OF OBJECTIVES IN MANAGEMENT

Every managerial action must be geared to the achievement of a desired goal. However, before any effort is expended on goal attainment, the manager should know and understand the specific purpose of the objective and why he is striving to achieve it. Subsequently, he must determine the scope of the objective not only in relation to the total concept of his responsibility, but also in terms of its relative importance to the overall organization. Consequently, if it seems that the proposed objective will have an unfavorable effect on the organization's current policies, plans, or profit, the manager will have to either seek a restatement of the original objective or suggest a viable alternative.

The objectives to be achieved are generally communicated to the information processing manager by an upper-echelon manager or a user organization manager through a memorandum or a special-purpose form requesting information processing services. If an objective is communicated in an oral manner, the information processing manager must secure a written confirmation of the objective to prevent any misunderstanding or misinterpretation of the goal(s).

Figure 1.3 illustrates a memorandum that an information processing manager may receive from a user organization. To understand the nature of the request, determine the feasibility of such a request and to subsequently develop the requested system, the information processing manager and/or his subordinate(s) must raise the following questions:

Why is this request being made? *what need do we have for it?*

Is this a request for a new system or modification of an existing system or subsystem? *a whole new job or some sort of maintenance. Could be enhansement*

Is the requested system a subsystem of an interrelated system? *Take into consideration if one change will effect the other impact of the system*

What is the expected life of the requested system?

What internal and external influences affect the system?

What functional areas are to be affected by this request?

Resource will need will be different for each case. what will be the impact be the entire system.

```
MEMORANDUM

TO: Data Processing Manager

FROM: Chief Accountant

SUBJECT: New System

    We need to develop and implement a new interactive billing and collection
system for the organization.
```

Figure 1.3 Memorandum requesting data processing services

What are the expected performance requirements for the system or subsystem? *accuracy, response times for reporting (performance)*

What are the user's response time requirements?

What resource limitations have been imposed on the requested system?

What time-frame has been allocated for the completion of the request, or what is the expected completion date?

From the responses to these questions, the information processing manager will be able to identify the specific goals that are implied in the memorandum. For example, the requested billing and collection system may include the following required functions:

An accounting for the charges, allowances, credits and adjustments.

The capability of preparing a follow-up on overdue accounts.

The ability to retrieve open accounts.

The ability to prepare various management reports, such as a daily trial balance, aging of accounts by stated periods, etc.

These items represent but a partial listing of the required functions in a simple billing and collection system. Yet, these and other requirements are not immediately evident from the information contained in the request by the user organization. The required items must be further defined to provide additional specific information on the major activities, applicable performance requirements, and the environmental influences affecting the system. For example, if we were to partially expand the first item in the list—"An accounting for the charges, allowances, credits, and adjustments"—the following specific requirements may be identified:

To prepare a customer-account master record prior to the actual sales transactions.

To post charges and adjustments to the master sales record within 20–30 minutes after the transaction has occurred.

To post payments to the account master record within 10–30 minutes after receipt of the payment.

To provide a daily statement for all customer charges, adjustments, and payments prior to the opening of business on the next business day.

To provide a completed statement of charges, adjustments, and payments to the customer within 24 hours after the customer's account has been closed.

To provide a monthly statement of all sales transactions and payments to each customer within 3 business days of the closing month.

To maintain an accuracy rate of $\pm$ 1 percent on all accounts.

To ensure that the means of accounting is consistent with all standard bookkeeping and accounting practices.

The information gathered during this goal-definition process will enable the information processing manager to determine the hierarchy of objectives, the interdependence of the many steps in the goal-attainment process, and the priority that is to be allocated to each objective and step.

Review Questions: Group 1A

1. Define the term "management."
2. How would you describe the role of a manager?
3. If you were the manager of an information processing activity, why would you choose the dynamic approach to management and not the static approach?
4. Why is a complete understanding of an objective regarded as an important part of the management process?

THE PHASES AND FUNCTIONS OF MANAGEMENT

Management activity in every operation is divided into two distinct phases. These are the pre-executory phase and the executory phase.

The pre-executory phase is activated after the manager has clearly defined the objective. It is during this phase of management activity that the manager initiates the preliminary proceedings necessary to implement the steps toward achievement of the desired goal. These proceedings are three of the five basic management functions: planning, organizing, and coordinating.

One of the manager's first steps in the pre-executory phase is to communicate the broad and specific objectives to his subordinates, as well as to any other people who may be affected by the operation. In addition, he is responsible for selecting the best course of action and establishing a network of interdependent procedures. The results of the manager's preparatory planning, organizing, and coordinating efforts will be made operational during the executory phase of management.

In the second phase of management activity, the executory phase, the manager oversees the implementation of the prepared plan of action in order to

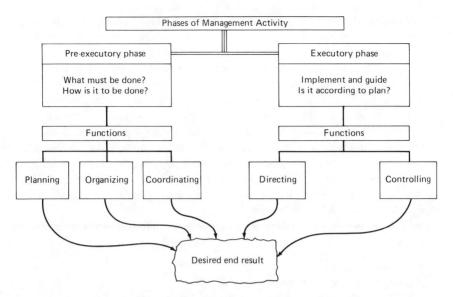

Figure 1.4 The phases and functions of management activity

achieve the desired objective. In doing this, he performs the remaining two basic management functions: directing and controlling. With the assistance and cooperation of his subordinates, he activates all resources, guides them and keeps them flowing in a goal-attainment pattern.

Although there is an imaginary boundary between the pre-executory and the executory phases of management activity, the manager should be ready at all times to replan, reorganize, and recoordinate in order to maintain the operation on course.

Figure 1.4 illustrates the pre-executory and executory phases of management activity. It also shows how these phases relate to the five basic management functions.

The Pre-Executory Phase

After the objective has been defined, the manager turns his attention to the steps that will enable him to accomplish the objective. Although it is conceivable that some objectives can be attained with little or no preplanning effort by the manager, it is unlikely that he would receive many, if any, such assignments. Therefore, the manager responsible for achieving a certain objective can expect to use the basic management functions of planning, organizing, and coordinating.

THE PLANNING FUNCTION

Planning may be defined as the technique used by the manager to design and develop a functional operation. It is the foundation from which all future management activity will be generated. During the planning process, the manager defines the broad objectives; formulates the specific objectives; visualizes how the operation will function and how the operation will affect the entire organization; determines the resource requirements and control specifications; and assigns priorities.

UNDERSTANDING THE OBJECTIVE. The manager's first step in any planning activity is to successfully interpret his assignment. In addition to defining the broad objective, he has to determine the specific objectives and their relationship to one another. This knowledge will enable the manager to ascertain the resources required and whether the broad objective is indeed attainable. Having formulated the specific objectives, the manager must identify the necessary tasks to be performed, the interdependency required by each to achieve the desired goals, and the performance targets.

1. EVALUATING THE SITUATION. In evaluating the situation, the manager resolves or answers three basic questions. These are:

 a) What is currently being done?
 b) What is the span of time involved?
 c) What is the objective's relationship to the organization?

a) *What is currently being done?* It is necessary for the manager to study what is currently being done because the existing situation or operation is already accomplishing certain objectives. These objectives must be compared with the proposed ones to determine whether the effect of realizing the new goals will result in the same problem-riddled situation or whether it will alleviate the condition. This is a most difficult task for the manager because very often the effect is not evident until a planned activity has been initiated or completed. A manager must have the foresight to analyze the past, present, and future and consequently ascertain the probable effectiveness of the objective.

The manager also faces a dilemma when he evaluates an objective for a proposed operation. The proposal has been made to either alleviate an existing problem or to avoid any possible future problems.

Every objective affects the overall organization structure in which a manager must operate. Therefore, the manager has to determine the extent to which other elements of the organization will be involved. After he ascertains which organizational groups will have an influence on the end result, he determines the degree and extent of their contribution to the accomplishment of that desired result. The difficult aspect of the manager's task here is that he must communicate with all levels of the organization as clearly and as objectively as possible.

Company policies and procedures also affect the setting of a situation. Consequently, the manager needs to establish how they relate to his operation because they are responsible for the conduct of all operations within the organization.

The manager's appraisal of the current situation makes him aware of the existing organizational structure, the role of the groups within it, the existing policies and procedures, and the organizational resources that are available to him. This knowledge gives the manager an understanding of the kind of system he must design and develop in order to achieve the desired goal.

b) What is the span of time involved? In planning, a manager becomes involved in a span of time which may range from a short-term period to a relatively long-term period. He has to consider the time element because he has the responsibility for developing an overall schedule for the proposed plan, as well as a detailed one for the sequence of operations.

Plans for the immediate future or for a period of time within two years of the present are regarded as short-term plans. Many data processing activities fall within this time interval. Such activities as processing one-time reports or preparing holiday or summer-vacation schedules are typical examples of short-term planning.

In contrast, such important activities as the design and development of a new data base management system or the conversion to new computer hardware systems require long-term planning. This kind of planning is concerned with a time interval that begins about two years from the present and extends to an indeterminable date in the future. However, the manager has to deal with immediate as well as future goals within this framework. This is why he needs to have the capability to execute short-term objectives within the context of a long-term plan. To do this successfully, he has to learn to adjust the schedule in response to changes that may occur in any of the immediate, intermediate, or future objectives. He must particularly consider the development of policies, procedures, and contingency actions to offset future changes in the organizational setting.

The manager quickly discovers that it is easier to consider short-term planning than long-range planning. This is because although all kinds of planning can be influenced by changes in hardware, software, organizational goals, or business conditions, the effect of such changes can be measured and anticipated much more accurately on a short-term basis. Consequently, there is a tendency for the manager to overemphasize immediate goals at the expense of the development of adequate long-range objectives. The manager must integrate the short-term and long-term goals into a plan in which the former will blend and contribute to attaining the long-range objectives.

Whether he is dealing with short-term or long-term plans, the data processing manager finds it useful, when considering the time element in planning, to make use of a GANTT chart (see Figure 1.5), or a PERT network diagram.

c) What is the objective's relationship to the organization? Many managers fail to perceive the proper role of an objective in relation to the needs of the overall organization. Quite frequently a project's development and/or operations' schedule becomes cluttered with tasks or jobs that provide little or no rate of return on investment. The attention given to these kinds of "jobs" tends to "crowd out" the truly meaningful and important "jobs."

The manager must evaluate the importance of an objective and its level of priority within the overall organizational structure. This can be a difficult task

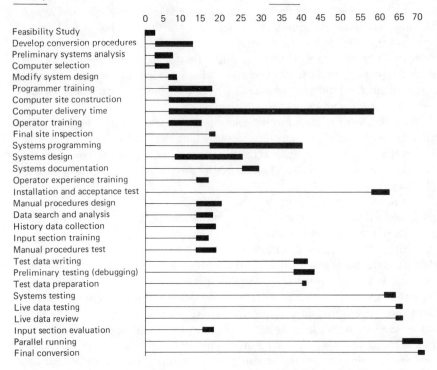

Figure 1.5 Sample of a Gantt chart used in computer installation project

because the manager is not always aware of an organization's long-term plans. Upper-echelon involvement in the activities of the information processing function and/or the use of steering committees (see chapter 2) can correct this deficiency in the organization's management process.

The plan that is developed will be affected by the priority and relative significance attributed to the specific objectives and the time span involved.

2. SELECTING THE BEST COURSE OF ACTION. After the manager has acquired a thorough understanding of the objective and has evaluated the situation so that he knows what resources he has available, the time span involved, and the setting in which he must function, he is ready to move on to the next stage of planning. Drawing on his knowledge of the strengths and weaknesses of a given situation, he formulates several courses of action for investigation and consideration.

After the manager has developed several such alternatives, he then tests each hypothesis to select a course of action that will produce either the best results or the most appropriate solution to a problem. Each possible course of action is tested for:

a) Acceptability
b) Flexibility
c) Cost-benefit
d) Time
e) Resource application

a) *Acceptability.* To be acceptable a manager's plan of action must be capable of functioning effectively within its own environmental setting. The manager's plan must carefully consider all of the external and internal influences and the parameters and constraints imposed on the originally stated objectives. Failure to perceive the setting in the same terms as the manager's superiors, subordinates, and the users may result in a plan that is unacceptable or unworkable. For example, a manager's plan must not negatively affect the profit picture; violate any contractual agreements; be the source of labor grievances; result in violation of federal, state, or local laws; and so on. Nor should it be an ill-conceived plan containing many extraneous steps and operations that make it very difficult for users and equipment operators to interact easily with the system. As a result, an implemented plan of action may become obsolete very quickly or lose its operational effectiveness.

b) *Flexibility.* The plan must make provisions for recognizing and effecting change. Though a manager begins with the assumption that he has developed a perfect plan, he must also realistically recognize that some corrective-action planning may also be necessary. The need for corrective action may be especially necessary when the plan is tested, debugged, and initially implemented. During the life of the plan, it is conceivable that other changes may also be necessary. Therefore, each plan must include some provision for monitoring, evaluation and corrective action to effect any changes that may be necessary. Also, each plan must contain some provision for actual or potential growth.

c) *Cost-benefit.* The manager must realistically assess the costs and benefits to be derived from developing and implementing the proposed plan. An information processing manager, just like any manager in the organization, must realistically assess the costs and the benefits of the proposed plan to determine their impact on the organization's profit picture. Though costs may be nominal, the benefits may be very superficial, and the impact on the survival profit quite substantial. (The survival profit is a nominal sum that is earned by the organization beyond the break-even point.)

d) *Time.* The manager must determine whether the proposed plan of action can be developed and implemented within the time-frame proposed for the project. The time estimates are developed by applying the organization's performance standards to the required tasks and operations in the proposed plan.

e) *Resource application.* The proposed plan must make optimal use of the available human, hardware, software, time, budget, and material resources. The information processing manager must initially determine if the resources available for the project are adequate. If not, the manager must make the upper-echelon manager aware of the kinds and types of resources needed to successfully achieve the desired objectives.

Operational effectiveness of a plan is measured by the results obtained; therefore, it cannot be rigid because data processing operations are performed within a dynamic framework. In essence, each plan is tentative and subject to modification and to implementation of alternative actions. The manager needs to visualize the total operative system and the relationship of interdependent activities, as well as the effect of change on the organization. It is a desirable quality for a manager to have the ability to see ahead and plan within the long-term context.

Many of the actions performed by the manager as part of the planning function are also an inherent part of a feasibility study (see chapter 8). These activities will be conducted by information processing specialists under the direction and control of the manager.

THE ORGANIZING FUNCTION

After the manager has selected his plan of action, he then establishes the framework within which the objective is to be attained. Setting up such a framework represents the organizing function, which is basically concerned with the establishment of an organizational structure, development of procedures, determination of resources, and the allocation of resources.

It is important to note that organizing is a dynamic activity. Good results cannot be guaranteed simply as a result of applying a well-ordered pattern. Therefore, a manager must employ periodic monitoring to determine whether his organizational concept is meeting present and future needs. The concept must be designed to reflect proper balance among all functions, for an improper balance in the design of the organizational structure can result in a disproportionate weighting of elements. This, in turn, may give the lesser elements more consideration than they should be given; or it may mean that some major elements are overlooked or incorrectly analyzed. Either way, an improper balance invariably results in the creation of problems.

It must be emphasized and noted that, in most instances, the manager is not able to develop an organizational concept rapidly. This lack of speed is useful, because to rush into a pattern without approaching the situation realistically could well result in a disastrous predicament for the manager (see chapter 2).

1. INTERRELATING THE VARIOUS RESPONSIBILITIES. The primary function of an organization structure is to establish a framework through which decisions can be made and initiated. It is through this structure that the scope and extent of responsibilities are defined and the functional interrelationships are identified. Within the organizational framework, there are two patterns of relationship that the manager needs to develop and recognize. These patterns are identified as the formal and informal structures.

The formal structure delineates the various organizational positions, together with their responsibilities, functions, and lines of authority. An informal structure develops within the framework of the formal one as a result of close relationships among certain personnel in the group. These informal groups can have a marked effect on the formal structure because they involve human emotions, interests, and personal feelings.

It is obvious, therefore, that the manager needs to consider the effects of such informal groups while he is developing his organizational structure. These groups exist in every organization where people are banded together for attainment of a common goal. Their influence stems largely from the data bits and pieces they derive from the operation and the manner in which they disseminate the information throughout the organization. For example, data on a pending computer conversion or system innovation may be freely exchanged at the luncheon table in the company cafeteria or at a social affair; the circulation of such information could have a positive or negative effect on the organization. The significant influence that these informal groups can bring to bear, directly and indirectly, on the activity of the entire group must be given consideration in the formulation of the organizational concept.

Within the structural aspects of organization underlying the formal structure, there are four basic points to consider. These are:

a) Unity of command
b) Span of control
c) Assignment of effective personnel
d) Delegation of authority

a) *Unity of command.* The unity of command means that authority and responsibility for directing and controlling the actions aimed at are vested in a single manager at each supervisory level in an organization. The chief administrator at the top of the managerial hierarchy retains overall authority and responsibility for the objective. It is important, however, that he delegate authority and responsibility throughout the organization from one manager to another, so that each may accomplish his assigned tasks. The amount of authority and responsibility decreases with each successively lower level.

As a result of the delegation of authority and responsibility, there is a need for a network of clearly defined supervisory channels. Each such channel provides for the effective flow of communications from the top to the bottom, and back. The two-way flow of information through the network allows for instructions and orders to move downward and for feedback on progress and problems to flow upward.

The downward communications should be simple and direct, so that there is little or no demand for interpretation and clarification from the subordinate levels. Any such call for interpretation and clarification implies the possibility of distortion of meaning and intent, which could delay or hamper goal attainment. Thus, in preparing communications, the manager must not only strive for clarity, but must also remember that his subordinates have a variety of backgrounds and experiences. Handled effectively, downward communications can also help to create a satisfying and cooperative attitude among the manager's subordinates.

The upward communications provide a flow of information from the subordinate levels concerning the status of the progress being made on the operation, as well as any problems that may have arisen. This reverse flow of information, frequently referred to as feedback, is evaluated and utilized by the upper echelon in directing and controlling the activity. The manager must not, at any cost, block the flow of data and ideas from those involved in the operation, because such an action hampers the decision-making process and could result in failure to achieve the objective.

b) Span of control. The concept of span of control is concerned with the number of subordinates who can be effectively supervised at given levels within an organizational structure. In many organizations, this is determined by applying a mathematical figure to the number of individuals each manager should control. Such ratios generally vary from 14:1 to 18:1. In some organizations, though, the number of subordinates reporting to a manager is increased, in an effort to reduce operating costs. The number of subordinates reporting to any one manager may fluctuate above or below the ratio during a given time span. A particular manager may control 14, 5, or 18 subordinates, for the 14:1 ratio is simply a corporate average that can be used as a basis of comparison for cost purposes.

There is no predetermined formula that can be applied to every organizational level and manager. Each level of activity has to be analyzed independently to determine the number of subordinates needed. It is important to note that each manager can be limited in the number of subordinates he can effectively manage with his own personal experience, the time available to give subordinates, and the ability of his subordinates to carry out their assignments.

Simply stated, there is a point of diminishing returns which is reached if the organizational unit is expanded to a size that will dilute the operational effectiveness of the manager. A major factor in determining that point has to do with the fact that as people are added to an organizational unit, the number of organizational relationships increases. Consider, for example, a manger who supervises two subordinates, A and B. He is directly involved in two relationships—himself and A and himself and B. But he is also concerned with the relationship between A and B. If another person is added to the unit, the relationships increase from three to six, even though there has been only one personnel addition.

Often, as part of the feasibility study, a manager and his staff will be called on to make recommendations to the chief administrator regarding the span of control for a particular organizational unit (see chapter 8). The proposals should be made only after an evaluation of the operational effectiveness of such a unit has been made. The impact of suggested personnel changes on the organization has to be made known to the chief administrator.

c) Effective assignment of personnel. In order for an organizational unit to attain maximum operational effectiveness, its manager must evaluate and select the proper personnel; in each case, he must assign the right person to the right job (see also chapter 3). Making such assignments is a difficult task for the manager, because neither jobs nor people are the same. Each job requires particular skills or abilities of the person performing it. And each individual has his own hopes, ambitions, capabilities, likes, and dislikes. Therefore, in addition to having full knowledge of each job, the manager must learn about and assess each member of his organization and then effectively match each person with the right job.

The most dynamic aspect of any organization is its human element, so the manager most willing to focus on his working relationship with his subordinates is the manager who stands to reap the greatest rewards. An interactive manager encourages his subordinates to assist him in the detection, identification, and solution of problems. To secure such cooperation, the manager needs to carefully appraise the capabilities, desires, and motivations of his personnel. Furthermore, he finds it important to help develop the capacities of the subordinates and to stimulate their levels of performance. At the same time, he treats his personnel as people, not machines, for he recognizes that they are all different and that they do not pursue their own interests with the same degrees of determination, motivation, or consistency. Therefore, it is important psychologically as well as operationally for the manager to express a continued willingness to know his subordinates and take an interest in their well-being.

d) *Delegation of authority.* After being assigned a position of responsibility in an organizational unit, the manager then begins to delegate authority to his own subordinates in the hierarchical structure. This is no simple matter, for it involves a great deal more than merely drawing blocks on the organization chart or completing generalized job descriptions.

The delegation of authority is a very necessary and important part of the organizing function because it can have either a positive or negative effect on the manager's operational effectiveness. If a typical manager appraises his position realistically, he finds that nearly one-half of his time is devoted to routine work. Delegation of some or all of such work would enable him to devote more time to the active direction and control of his operation. A manager can also improve the morale of his subordinates and provide training and experience by giving them certain managerial responsibilities. It has been estimated that a manager who spends 75 percent of his time in applying the management functions to an activity can lead his organizational unit to high productivity. In contrast, a manager who spends two-thirds of his time in helping to do the routine work and only one-third in management activity finds that the unit is low in productivity. To offset this negative effect, such a manager will spend many hours beyond his normal workday helping to do the work. This condition is really acceptable only for short-term emergency periods, for any prolonged activity of this type results in a state of fatigue that will greatly reduce the mental and physical effectiveness of the manager.

There are many people outside of the profession who wonder why there are data processing managers who pursue such a suicidal course. There are at least three common reasons—or excuses—and not one of them is really defensible or logical.

The most common excuse is phrased in various ways, such as: "It is easier for me to do it than to have to tell somebody and wait for him to give me what I want," or "I don't have time to explain this to somebody or write it out for him." This type of thinking obviously stems from the fact that the manager is confident of his ability as a technician, but uncertain of himself as a leader.

A second excuse is: "It will be my head that rolls if he goofs!" Here the manager feels that he knows the technical side of the job and is capable of achieving the objective, but that he is uncertain about his personnel's reliability. If a manager is unable to determine the capabilities of his personnel, he will never be able to effectively assign any responsibility to anyone. And this, in turn, can lead to disastrous results and weaken the organization. The dynamic aspects of the data processing field make it impossible for anyone to become an autocratic individualist and also be successful in operating an organizational unit.

A third common excuse is that the manager lacks the manpower or the qualified manpower. Although it is true that the industry is currently suffering from a shortage of qualified technicians, managers are at least partly responsible for this condition because many of them are reluctant or unwilling to train people to alleviate the shortage. The *training* of personnel, no less than the supervision of subordinates, ranks as an essential part of the management process. (The training function is discussed in detail in chapter 3.)

The manager's willingness to delegate responsibility is only the first step toward putting the principle into practice. He soon discovers that some subordinates are unwilling to accept authority, that some are leaners or followers, and that some simply cannot supervise. That is why the manager very often has to train people to accept responsibility.

It is also important for the manager to realize at the very beginning that some of his subordinates may be able to perform certain functions as well, if not better, than he can. Accepting the fact that every person has certain strengths and weaknesses, the manager should strive to delegate authority in a way that capitalizes on the strengths of his subordinates. He may have to settle for an output or a job performance of slightly lower quality than if he had personally accomplished the task. However, this is a compromise he must be willing to make. It gets him away from the routine work. At the same time, the subordinate will gain experience in accomplishing the task—experience that will be reflected in his future performance.

Before actually delegating authority, the manager makes certain that the subordinate has the capability and the personality to accept such responsibility. After this has been determined, the manager then decides upon the limits to be set on the delegated authority. In establishing such limits, the manager must clearly stipulate the following:

1. The Goal or Objective
2. The Chain of Command
3. The Progress Reports Required
4. The Time Span

5. The Span of Control
6. Budget Limitations

1. The Goal or Objective. The manager must pinpoint and state in writing the goal or objective that the subordinate is expected to achieve.

Such a specification will enable the subordinate to plan and organize his own operation or assignment to achieve the desired end.

2. The Chain of Command. Who will be the immediate superior to whom the subordinate will report his progress and from whom he will seek assistance if required? It is vital that an open communications channel be maintained in order to report the subordinate's progress and to prevent his overextending the scope of his authority and responsibility.

Looking at this matter from the subordinate's point of view, it can be stated that the subordinate wants and needs to receive clear and understandable instructions so that he knows what is expected of him and what the manager will and will not permit him to do.

3. The Progress Reports Required. The manager should state clearly the type and frequency of progress reports to be made by the subordinate. To determine the progress being made, the manager may require statistical, oral, or written reports.

Statistical reports are generally in the form of charts, graphs, or numerical tabulations. Figure 1.6 is an example of the kind of statistical report used to indicate the progress being made by the programming group in preparing for installation of new computing equipment. Such a report form provides statistical information on the manning strength of an activity, the number of programs written in different languages, and the stages of completion. This type of presentation may or may not be adequate to indicate the results achieved. If the manager requires additional information, he must contact the project leader or programming manager. Brevity may prove to be an advantage, because only specific information will be collected and there will be no need to filter the feed-

Figure 1.6 Sample of statistical report

Personnel Assigned				Programs by Languages					Percent of Programs					
Senior program analyst	Program analyst	Programmer	Programmer trainee	RPG	BAL	COBOL	FORTRAN IV	PL/I	Defined	Coded	Desk checked	Tested	Completed	Documented

back. Also, the specific data categories facilitate the updating of existing status information. Depending on the length and importance of the project, the statistical reports may be required on a daily or weekly basis.

Oral reports tend to be biased or may be inaccurate because of the subordinate's inability to communicate with his immediate supervisor. Yet they can be effective if the manager is able to perceive and understand any such bias or to recognize any communications difficulties. Not only are oral reports personal and immediate, but they also help to give the subordinate the feeling that he is not merely an errand boy. In addition, the manager can directly query the subordinate individual to determine if any problems have arisen. Furthermore, the two men may be able to resolve any such difficulties at the time the report is being made. If oral reports are made frequently, they can serve as an excellent monitoring device through which evaluation and adjustments can be made.

Written reports may be used to provide information on the progress or status of an activity or operation. Such reports are generally used to provide some feedback on special or extended projects. For example, daily written reports may be prepared to give the status of a data conversion project; preliminary reports may be prepared on the status of construction of a data processing facility; and interim reports may be prepared and issued from time to time on the progress in a long-term conversion from one type of computing hardware to another. Written reports are also used to convey the results of problem-solving or other investigative work. Figure 1.7, for example, is a written report prepared by a systems analyst as a result of an investigation to determine the reasons for preparation of erroneous reports by a functional activity.

Written reports represent, in most cases, an after-the-fact type of reporting, so they can be only of limited value in quickly changing situations; too much time may be spent in their preparation and too little gained from the time and energy expended.

On the other hand, there is also the danger that written reports may be

Figure 1.7 Sample of written report

A major problem which has caused the delay in the maintenance of records, especially for mechanized systems, is the lack of understanding by the personnel involved with the use of data processing techniques. Personnel are not aware of how data processing systems function or what can be obtained from such systems. Therefore, more training for clerical personnel is needed. The role of clerical personnel in input preparation and providing accurate source data for the system is not clearly understood. The outgrowth of this has been that the transcription of information has been performed on a "when the time is available" basis. Consequently, there has been a lack of continuity and a high incidence of error in the processing of data. The lack of personnel partially attributes to the error rate and lack of continuity. However, the lack of importance accorded to data processing within the department is also a significant factor.

prepared too quickly; hastily prepared reports may lack valid or complete data and consequently be of little or no value in decision-making.

4. Time Span. The subordinate must be aware of the time period involved or available so that he may plan and schedule his own operation accordingly.

5. Span of Control. Just as the manager knows his span of control, it is important for the subordinate to know the number and caliber of persons who will come under his supervision during the assignment.

6. Budget Limitations. When a budget is allocated to a particular project, the subordinate should be made aware of this fact to assist him in deciding when and what action to initiate. The subordinate should be told the actual dollar value involved, what resources may be funded, and who must authorize the expenditures.

2. THE DEVELOPMENT OF PROCEDURES. The other major component of the organizing function (after interrelating the various responsibilities) is the development of procedures that will prescribe the manner or techniques to be used in achieving the objective. These procedures will become the focal point of the operation during the executory phase, for the manager will use them to direct and coordinate the effort of the organization unit.

Figure 1.8 Sample of an operating procedure

TITLE: Special Education Student File Maintenance Procedure

GENERAL:

The purpose of this procedure is to prescribe the necessary manual and automated steps that must be accomplished in the maintenance of the punched card file for Special Education Students.

PROCEDURE:

1. When both the SE1 and SE2 forms have been received within the Special Education Branch, the data entry clerk will transcribe the necessary data elements to the Special Education Input coding sheet.
2. The Special Education Input coding sheets will be forwarded to the Computer Services–Input Preparation Section for key punching and key verification.
3. The Computer Services–Input Preparation Section will arrange for the keying operations and return the Special Education Input coding sheets to the Special Education Branch.
4. The resulting punched card records will be sorted in pupil number sequence and listed to produce a "New Special Education Students Report." The report will be submitted to the Special Education Branch for verification and processing.
5. Following verification of the "New Special Education Students Report" by the Special Education Branch, the Computer Services–Input Preparation Section will forward the punched card records to the Operations Center for merging with the existing Special Education Student Master File.

Each procedure is developed as a result of breaking down an operation into its component steps. These are then carefully analyzed to determine the most efficient and effective way of accomplishing the desired task. The details are documented to provide for uniformity and standardization in the operation (see chapter 4).

Figure 1.8 illustrates a typical information processing procedure. The procedure directs the most effective use of the organization's human, hardware, and material resources. The information contained in the procedure can also be used to establish a machine-loading schedule and make personnel assignments (see chapter 5). Following this procedure will ensure that each time the personnel manager requests this report, the desired end result will be produced for him.

THE COORDINATING FUNCTION

This is the third and last management function in the pre-executory phase of the management process.

The coordinating function cannot be initiated until the manager has gained a clear understanding of the overall setting. The setting must be understood because no operation can be executed in a vacuum; data processing activity cuts across all organizational lines, so that it influences other activities or is influenced by them.

Coordination is the process of establishing effective communications with those organizational elements not under the direct control of the manager, but which influence or are influenced by the manager's operation. It necessitates the smooth blending of all integral parts to provide for maximum output.

To help understand the coordination required in an operation, it is useful to examine a situation in which the data processing manager is responsible for the production of remittance advices and drafts for an accounts payable application. For this type of application the network of coordination would have to include the accounts payable section of the accounting department, together with the treasury, inspection, receiving, and purchasing departments. Together, these groups are responsible for the order entry, receival of the goods, verification of quantity and condition, verification of payment amounts and discounts, authorization of payment, and the transmittal of the drafts to the vendors. Furthermore, there may also be by-products of the application, such as various journal entry reports, billing to subsidiaries or other plants, and input for an inventory control application; this would necessitate coordination between the financial, results accounting, and inventory control functions.

In this example, the data processing manager must employ measures to ensure that the inputs from the purchasing, accounts payable, inspection, and receiving groups are correct, and that any adjustments made to any purchase or invoice order are correct and properly applied (see chapter 10). In addition, the manager must abide by the rulings of the treasury department on draft amount limits and national contract payments. And where the output becomes input for by-product reports, the manager must ensure that it is correct and properly entered into the system. The data processing manager is dependent upon all of these other organizations for meeting his time schedules, for corrections and adjustments, and for relevant output for decision making. Therefore, it becomes imperative that he establish close coordination between his operation and those activities which affect it.

1. PROBLEMS. The manager must consider the expectations and needs of users and subordinates in preparing for and executing the coordination function. The users are frequently unhappy with the data processing organization because they feel the systems do not perform as expected or fail to provide the necessary decision-making support. Data processors may be unhappy because they feel the users fail to cooperate, may not adequately communicate their needs, or are unreasonable in their demands for information services and systems.

To improve the rapport with user functions, the data processing manager/administrator must consider the following needs and expectations:

Maintain and monitor an effective operations schedule to ensure the production of accurate and timely outputs.

Maintain an optimally effective production facility capable of collecting and transcribing the data and reporting the processed outputs within a desired time-frame.

Maintain good quality controls to ensure the accurate capture, transcription, processing, storage, and reporting of data and information.

Maintain adequate back-up and recovery procedures to ensure minimal or no disruptions of vital data and information systems and services.

Assign qualified personnel and properly staff the functional activities within data processing to ensure the proper design, implementation, and production of necessary systems.

Establish and maintain effective testing procedures to ensure that all new and revised systems and programs are completely tested and debugged prior to implementation. Also, make sure that periodic audits will be conducted to ensure that the systems and/or programs maintain their operational effectiveness.

Maintain accurate, current, and relevant documentation for user and operations personnel for each system. The user documentation should be simple, easy to use, and devoid of "computerese."

Maintain an open channel of communication between data processing and the user by encouraging feedback on problems encountered, dissemination of information on events affecting the user, and encouraging the use of a steering committee (see chapter 2).

Ensure that in the design and development of systems and programs, provision for actual or potential growth is made. This will enable the data processing function to service user requests for modification to existing systems or programs without a major redesign effort.

2. THE CATEGORIES OF COORDINATION. The operational category of coordination involves coordinating the various activities of a manager's function and the activities of persons in other functions involved in a system or project. This form of coordination is necessary in order to implement and maintain a multi-functional approach to the use of data processing services. Coordinating the activities of a manager's own function is not difficult because much of it can be achieved through the delegation of authority. Coordination with those external functions involved in a manager's operations, however, is more challenging but necessary. It is necessary for the development of systems which will enjoy both utility and durability.

The informational category of coordination provides for a broad band of communications efforts—keeping the executive committee, managers, subordinates, and other personnel fully informed. It is not intended that this form of coordination be used to pay lip service to other functions. Informational coordination provides a means of resolving conflicts, securing clearances, disseminating ideas, and for developing and maintaining organizational contacts. For data processors, informational coordination can be a highly effective mechanism for disseminating ideas and information about the capabilities and uses of data processing techniques. Subsequently, this may facilitate the development and/or maintenance of inter-system cooperation.

The two patterns of coordination are interwoven to help provide for a smooth functioning of operations, facilitate development of broader systems, and rectify any problems which may arise. The patterns provide the ways and means for maximizing the operational effectiveness of the data processing organization.

Review Questions: Group 1B

1. Why should a manager have to concern himself with the pre-executory phase in the management process?
2. What would happen (if anything) if a manager chose to ignore evaluating a situation?
3. It is important for a manager to clearly define the supervisory channels in an organizational structure. Explain why.
4. One of the difficulties encountered in many organizations is the inability of a manager to effectively supervise all of his subordinates. Why is this a problem? How does this type of problem occur?
5. Why are some managers unwilling or hesitant about delegating authority to their subordinates?
6. If you, as a manager, were assigned a particular goal to achieve, what would you want to know initially?
7. Why must a data processing manager be concerned with the coordination of activities?

The Executory Phase

It is during the execution phase that the manager implements and oversees the prepared plan of action that has been developed during the pre-executory phase by application of the planning, organizing, and coordinating functions. At this stage the manager is concerned with utilizing the directing and controlling functions of management in order to bring the plan to fruition. However, the pre-executory functions do not cease so that the new management functions can be initiated. Rather, all five functions are incorporated into the executory phase of management, for the manager has to be ready at all times to replan, reorganize, and recoordinate as needed. Nevertheless, his principal emphasis is on giving direction and control.

THE DIRECTING FUNCTION

The directing function is sometimes referred to as the execution, or action, function. In the broadest sense, direction is the manipulation of the available resources according to the formulated plan in order to achieve the objective. This requires day-to-day evaluations and decisions by the manager to keep the operation effective and moving according to plan.

This management function consists of three major elements. The first of these is the communications element, which involves the transmission of the policies, objectives, and procedures to all those persons who are connected with the operation. The second element is the training of personnel, which involves the development and education of personnel so that they can carry out their assigned responsibilities related to goal achievement. The third element is the establishment of a pattern of operations; this requires the development of ways and means to guide the operation.

Traditionally, the term "directing" has been limited by various writers on the subject to mean the "direction of people." In a dynamic environment, however, directing involves the total operation. This means that the manager has to be concerned with directing both people and procedures. In an actual operation, the manpower resource is concerned with the utilization of the other available resources—materials, time, hardware, software, and money. For the manager to put all of these resources into action, in definite relation to one another, requires the use of procedures, which provide the linkage in a series of interrelated steps to produce the desired end result. Personnel and procedures are not independent of each other; rather, they are interdependent, for it is only through the combined interaction of them that the manager can be fairly certain that the desired end result will actually be achieved.

1. THE DIRECTION OF PERSONNEL. People, the most dynamic element in any operation, must be given careful consideration because they are unlike any other resource at the disposal of the manager. And the manager has to carefully integrate this unique resource into his operating plan.

The success of the manager in achieving teamwork among his subordinates depends on the degree of understanding and interest which he has in his people. The following statements are some valid generalizations that apply directly to this issue of teamwork. It can be said of the people in an organizational unit that:

They work best when they know that the manager is interested in them and recognizes their wishes.

They make every attempt to fulfill the complete expectations of the manager.

They work more effectively when they know that the manager is attempting to make good use of their talents, abilities, and suggestions.

They work best for a manager whom they can trust and respect, and who lets each subordinate know how he fits into the total spectrum.

They work best when kept informed about all matters that concern or affect them.

Undoubtedly, there are many other generalizations that could be added to this list; these, though, are probably the most important ones.

2. THE DIRECTION OF PROCEDURES. As important as the directing of people is the directing of procedures. The procedures, oral or written, for a particular operation will, in answer to five of the six basic questions in management, specify: what is to be done, how it is to be done, who will do it, where will it be done, and when it is to be done.

The procedures are aimed at putting into motion the plan that has been developed in the pre-executory phase. They cover the general and interdepartmental policies, departmental matters, and technical instructions. In addition to being focused on the main objective, they are designed to achieve several other specific purposes:

To provide the performance standards against which the output can be effectively measured with application of the control function.

To assist in the training of personnel.

To ensure uniform application of company policies and administrative rules.

To ensure that each operation will be performed uniformly.

To ensure a smooth operation and provide for a control of progress.

a) Auditing procedures. Procedures are essential to every operation for the maintenance of its effectiveness. Consequently, the procedures need to be periodically reviewed for removal, revision, or replacement, and for their retaining as much simplicity as possible. Furthermore, whenever changes are made to a procedure, the information about these changes needs to be conveyed to all affected parties. Unfortunately, this very important procedure is all too often overlooked within a data processing activity, with the ultimate result of chaos or mismanagement of an operation, project, or installation. To deal with this mistake, many firms implement an annual procedural audit. The data processing procedure illustrated in Figure 1.8 is the kind of procedure that should be audited annually.

The reviewer-auditor determines if the procedures are current, relevant, clear, and compatible. If a procedure is current, it reflects all changes that had been effected since the previous audit. If it is relevant, it contributes to the effectiveness of the current operation. If it is clear, it is easy to read and understand. If it is compatible, it is comparable with other procedures within the system, which, in turn, reduces the chances of conflict in the goal-attainment process.

CONTROLLING

The controlling function is a continuous monitoring activity. It is used to compare the current status and condition of resources from an ongoing operation with the planned criteria that had been formulated during the pre-executory phase and that had been implemented with the directing function. The controlling function also makes provision for problem detection, identification, and correction if necessary.

The ability to monitor an activity requires that the manager understand clearly the objective to be reached and the setting in which the operation is to be performed. It also requires that he be aware of the acceptable standard of performance and the allowable parameters for deviation from that standard. In monitoring an activity, the manager can gain a clear and graphic understanding of progress-versus-plan by making use of PERT network diagrams, or GANTT charts (see chapter 5).

1. THE FEEDBACK CONCEPT. The feedback concept is a technique applied repeatedly during the controlling function to evaluate the performance of an operation. The operation's progress is monitored to determine if current performance conforms with planned performance. This comparison provides a status indicator (deviation or normal), which is then evaluated by the manager to determine if corrective action is necessary or potentially beneficial. Any corrective input is fed into the operation, where, once again, it will be monitored and evaluated. This monitor-evaluate-correct process has become universally known as the feedback concept.

Figure 1.9 provides the diagrammatic basis for a fuller understanding of the feedback control mechanism in operation within an organization. This mechanism is often referred to simply as the feedback loop.

The function of the feedback loop begins after the initiation of the operation being directed toward the attainment of a desired goal. Current performance or output is compared with the plan at point A on the diagram. If the actual progress and the planned result are the same at this point, then the status of the operation is registered as normal and the operation continues until monitored again at point F. However, if, at point B, the actual progress is above or below the planned result, the status of the operation is indicated as a deviation. It is at this point and time that the feedback of information becomes extremely important and that the series of steps beginning at point B are initiated.

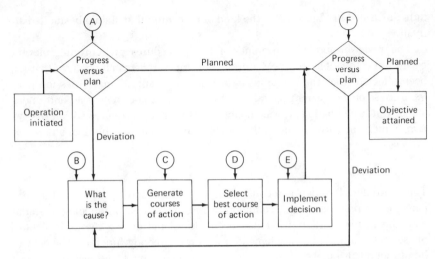

Figure 1.9 Feedback control concept

It is important to note that in a real operation (rather than an idealized sample such as this), several checkpoints are included at which the actual-versus-planned comparison is made. Should a deviation be detected at any of these points, then the alternate path is immediately taken so that the problem analysis can begin at point B.

At point B, the actual feedback loop is initiated with the analysis of the problem. The deviation must be investigated to recognize the problem and to specify the deviation. The analysis of the deviation, or variance, should reveal: what the deviation is, where the deviation actually occurred, and when the deviation occurred. *What* the deviation is must be known to determine the deviation's seriousness and its possible effects on succeeding phases of the operation. If the manager does not understand the problem, he can hardly hope to correct the cause and remedy the effect. If there are several problems involved, the manager must be able to recognize and identify them individually and to assign a priority for analysis and solution. *Where* the deviation actually occurred must be known in order to help isolate the event and to provide critical information for the problem-solving phase. *When* the deviation occurred must be known in order to pinpoint the occurrence and to reduce the amount of probing time required for problem analysis.

When each of these three factors is known, the manager's task is to uncover the possible causes of the deviation. The difficulty here is to recognize how the various events or activities in a total operation are interrelated and how the process of change affects this interrelationship. It is imperative that the manager fully understand the setting and the objective because this understanding will enable him to envision this interrelationship of factors, which, in turn, will help him to isolate the most important cause or causes.

Because the significant cause or causes are sometimes difficult to find, the manager has to be prepared to initiate some careful probing and analysis. He must, at the same time, recognize the possible dangers inherent in hasty judgments or conclusions about the cause. His best approach, therefore, is to use the facts uncovered to develop a hypothesis and then test it.

The best way for the manager to test his hypothesis is to tear apart the explanation. This is not a very simple task because the manager may have to explode his own theory in order to avoid reaching a false conclusion—an activity that is not very flattering to his ego. However, it is a useful method for recalling the hard-to-find reasons for a deviation in an operation.

When the manager has determined the significant cause or causes, he is ready to move on to the next stage of the feedback control mechanism, marked by point C in the illustration. At this point in the loop, the manager determines whether or not he needs to take corrective action. If he does need to, he then considers the possible courses of action that will enable him to correct or modify the situation.

At point D in the loop, the manager selects the best course of action. He assesses each course of action for acceptability, flexibility, cost-benefit, time, and resource application (the same basic tests that the manager applies in the planning function of the pre-executory phase).

It is at this stage in the feedback control mechanism that the manager usually begins to feel pressed for time. His difficulty is that, while still committed to completing the objective within a specified time period, he has much less allowable time for replanning than he had for the initial planning. This time limitation may well force him to select the most expedient course of action rather than the best one. Furthermore, he has to be more specific in assessing his revised course of action so that he will be able to determine very quickly any actual or potential problems that may arise from its implementation. This means he needs to initiate controls to serve as an early warning system. Such a system requires dependable feedback so that the manager can begin to cope as soon as possible with the problem. In addition, he also needs to set up some contingency plans for dealing with the problem once it has been identified by the early warning system. Without these various forms of preplanning, the manager cannot hope to operate successfully within a dynamic environment.

Having selected the best or most expedient course of action, the manager then implements this plan in order to modify or correct the operation in which the deviation occurred. Implementation takes place at point E in the diagram.

Again, at point F, the manager monitors the activity to determine that the operation is proceeding according to the original or modified plan. If the actual results meet the planned results, then the operation will terminate successfully. If, however, another deviation is found to exist, the feedback control mechanism is reactivated by branching back to point B where the problem-solving process must be reinstituted.

To see how the feedback works in reality, it is useful to examine the following practical example. A programming manager learns that there has been a schedule slippage on a programming project. The next major event in the project's schedule is to perform a combined test on the three interrelated modules. However, the second module has not yet been completely tested and debugged.

The programming manager must identify the cause of the problem, and when and where the problem occurred. The slippage may be due to such factors as a lack of computer time, poor design specifications, a change in objectives, a lack of manpower, poor test data, a bad test plan, or faulty documentation. It is possible that there may be one cause or a combination of causes in this instance.

From his analysis of the situation, the programming manager learns that the reason for the slippage is due to poor test data generated by an inexperienced programmer. To correct the problem, the programming manager must assign a senior programmer to the test data generation process. In addition, the manager must determine what action can be executed to minimize the impact of the slippage on the overall schedule and if alteration of the complete schedule may be necessary.

In this instance, the manager determines that there will be an additional delay in the schedule due to the redesign and redevelopment of the test data. But, in reviewing the schedule, he feels that he has some slack time in the plan and this will not necessitate complete revision of the schedule. His premise will be checked when the feedback loop is again applied to the schedule.

Review Questions: Group 1C

1. Discuss the comment "He is a good manager because he rolls up his sleeves and pitches right in to get the job done."
2. The direction of procedures is considered to be as important in the management process as the direction of personnel. Why?
3. Explain the controlling function as it is used in the management process.
4. In what ways does the feedback concept affect all of the managerial functions?

SUMMARY

In this chapter, we have discussed the basic concepts of the management process. This material provides a fundamental understanding of the framework within which a data processing manager must act. In addition, it defines and describes the various major aspects of the management process that affect the manager.

Management is an activity that provides for the interactive application of available resources to achieve a desired goal. This activity is defined and guided by a manager, who strives to develop an optimal mix of his manpower, machine, material, and money resources in order to attain the stated objective. The manager conducts his activity utilizing either the static or dynamic approach to management. The static approach deals with the activity in terms of an ideal environment in which the application of predefined rules and procedures will produce the desired end result. The dynamic approach recognizes that conditions relating to an operation can and do change. Therefore, it requires that a manager evaluate the setting first and then formulate his plan of action. It also requires that the manager constantly monitor and evaluate the progress of his activity to determine how the actual results compare with the planned ones. Any deviation from the plan must be identified, evaluated, and promptly corrected if necessary. Whether a manager selects the static approach or the dynamic approach depends on his own training, background, and experience, as well as on the approach preferred by his supervisor.

Before a manager activates the management process, he begins by resolving a broad objective into a specific objective, and subsequently into the detailed steps that must be accomplished to achieve the desired end result. Having properly defined his objective and its components, the manager implements the basic management functions of planning, organizing, and coordinating. These three functions constitute the pre-executory phase of the management process, during which the manager decides what and how the objective is to be accomplished and with what human and material resources he will be working.

Having formulated his procedures and assembled his resources, the manager moves into the executory phase of the management process. During this phase, he implements the procedures and guides the resources in the goal-attainment process, using the basic management functions of directing and controlling. In the directing function, the manager is responsible for activating the operation, which involves directing both people and procedures. During the controlling function, he compares and evaluates the actual results of the operation with those established during the pre-executory phase. This activity involves the feedback concept, which is an integral part of the dynamic approach to management. Feedback control provides the manager with an excellent technique for problem detection, identification, and correction, which enables him to maintain progress as planned and to achieve the desired goal.

CASE STUDY 1.1

The Raleric Toy Company

The Raleric Toy Company has a medium-sized information processing center. The function has twenty employees that are principally divided into an operations group and a programming group. The director of data processing has assigned the responsibility for data entry, computer operations, data control, and tape and disk library to the supervisor of operations. The assistant director is responsible for the computer center operations in the absence of the director and for the programming group. In addition, the assistant director is responsible for advanced planning and systems development.

The director prides himself on being a friendly person and attempts to maintain a very close personal relationship with each of the center's employees. He also urges each of the employees to come to his office and discuss their problems, whatever they may be.

Quite frequently, the director will direct a programmer or equipment operator to lay aside a current task and undertake a different assignment. The director feels that such interruptions are necessary and justified in order to "service" the users. The assistant director has become visibly upset with the director's actions and has attempted to discuss these episodes with the director, but to no avail. The director defends his actions by saying, "We have a job to do and it is our job to service the user's needs."

If a subordinate disagrees with the assistant director, he will approach the director, who will quite frequently override the wishes or desires of the assistant director. The director has frequently chastised his assistant for failing to maintain a good rapport with the subordinates. The director has advised the assistant to improve on the human relations aspect of the job.

On occasion, the director will perform some minor program writing so that he doesn't become "rusty" and so that his staff knows that he can "still do it." These programs are usually for special requests submitted by the director's friends. Sometimes, he will have one of the programmers assist him on the project to get the job done faster.

Discussion Questions

1. The director has been described by some as a "manager who makes things happen." Would you agree or disagree with the statement? Why?
2. Has the director properly delegated authority and responsibility to the assistant director and to the supervisor of operations? If not, why not?
3. Does the director's dedication to "users" conflict with the overall objectives for the data processing function? Why or why not?
4. Is it necessary for the director to prove his technical competence? Why or why not?

CHAPTER 2

The Structural Organization
of Data Processing

INTRODUCTION / It is evident today that many organizations still view data processing simply as a means of reducing clerical activity; as providing a recordkeeping capability for vast amounts of historical data; as providing an automated means for performing repetitive tasks; as a tool for the accounting department; or as a way to support the reporting needs of an organization.

The more forward-looking managers are recognizing that this point of view is counterproductive to the needs of the overall organization. These managers have come to realize that the processing of data is not the primary function of the data processing organization. A data processing organization can contribute significantly to the profit picture of an organization, help to improve its competitive position or industry ranking, and provide the kinds of information services that are an intrinsic part of the decision-making process.

The more-advanced managers have restructured their data processing organizations to make them more responsible for the definition and development of organization-wide information processing systems; for the investigation of innovative techniques and their application to the organization as a whole; and for the design, development, and implementation of user-systems that will contribute directly to the organization's profit.

These forward-looking organizations have also become more involved in providing direction and control for the data processing organization.

THE ROLE OF THE EXECUTIVE COMMITTEE

The activities of the data processing function serve to support the goal-attainment efforts of other elements in the organizational environment. Due to the increasing complexity and importance of the various data processing systems and applications, it is more important that the plans and activities of the data processing function be consistent with the goals of the overall organization. To minimize the risks and increase the value of the information processing services, the data processing function must be included in the short-range and long-range planning for an organization. The data processing manager must be made aware of the organization's long-range and short-range goals and the schedules for accomplishing the stated objectives.

In many organizations, the data processing manager is not provided with an in-depth awareness of the organization's goals, but is expected to "react" to the organization's demands. The need to react to a demand may prove very time-consuming and result in a misutilization of the hardware, software, human, and material resources. To ensure that an organization maximizes its rate of return from the investment in a data processing function requires direct involvement by the executive committee in the plans and activities of the data processing function.

The immediate effect of such involvement is that the data processing manager will become aware of the organization's long-range and short-range goals, major constraints, and schedules. An awareness of these facts will enable the data processing manager to provide for a long-range planning effort that will be consistent with the organization's overall objectives. To facilitate this entire process of interaction and involvement, forward-looking organizations are establishing a data processing steering committee and requiring the development of a five-year plan for information processing systems, hardware, software, and staffing.

The data processing steering committee is generally headed by the organization's chief executive officer and includes the managers of the major user organizations, the data processing manager, and several senior data processors. The steering committee will approve the long-range plans for the data processing function; oversee the development of a contingency plan; oversee the development and implementation of data processing systems that will contribute to the effectiveness and profit of the overall organization; monitor the performance and effectiveness of the data processing function; help to develop a realistic budget for the data processing function; and secure the necessary resources to provide the required levels of support for an organization.

Effective operation of a steering committee will help to ensure that wherever necessary, multi-functional systems will be developed and implemented to support the organization's goal-attainment process and that these systems and other implemented systems will prove to be cost-effective. Also, that the group can oversee the development of a formal contingency plan for the data processing function. The members of the steering committee, due to its composition, can recognize the impact of a disruption in information processing on the overall organization. Based on this analysis, the steering committee can formulate a policy that provides the data processing manager with some guidelines for the development of a contigency plan.

The initial development of a five-year plan for the data processing function will be a time-consuming but necessary effort. The information contained in the plan will provide the executive committee with an indicator of how the data processing manager expects to react to a dynamic environment. Acceptance of this long-range plan by the executive committee indicates its commitment to the goals and activities of the data processing organization. (The plan must be periodically evaluated to determine its relevance to the growth patterns of the overall organization and the need for modifying or updating the plan.)

The information systems segment of the plan must identify the currently operational systems, the planned systems, and the systems that may potentially be automated. The estimated life of each current system must be identified, along with any proposed changes or improvements, a time-frame for effecting changes or improvements, and the potential cost of any changes or enhancements. The planned systems segment will identify those systems that are currently under development or scheduled for development. To facilitate understanding of these systems by the executive committee, the data processing manager must include a brief description of each system; how these systems will affect the organization; the organizational elements affected by the system; the development and implementation costs (see chapter 6); a development and implementation schedule; the proposed payback; and the projected processing requirements in terms of the resources needed. The potential systems segment will identify those systems that merit future development and implementation. In this segment, the manager includes a brief description of the proposed system, identifies the impact on the overall organization, potential cost-benefit, and proposed development and implementation time-frame.

The hardware/software segment of the five-year plan will indicate the current status of the hardware and software used by the organization, the proposed replacements and enhancements, the current and future costs, and the current and projected utilization. The hardware/software needs of the organization should be related to the current systems, those under development, and future systems.

The staffing segment of the five-year plan should reflect the current and proposed staffing for the data processing function. Realistically, it may be difficult to project the human resource needs beyond two or three years, but the manager must attempt to identify the kinds and types of personnel that may be needed to support the growth needs of the organization. This information could be used for developing the career pathing plans (see chapter 3) for an organization. The staffing segment should also include current and projected staffing costs.

Much of the detailed information to support the five-year plan will be an integral part of the documented survey maintained by the data processing manager (see chapter 8).

RESPONSIBILITY FOR ADMINISTRATION
AND CONTROL

Because data processing is a management tool of great depth and breadth, its capability should not and cannot be limited to one functional activity within the organization. This is why the overall responsibility for the administration and control of a data processing function lies with the upper echelon of the organization.

The authority and responsibility for the data processing function should be delegated to an executive who is capable of determining total organizational requirements. Preferably, the administrator or manager of the data processing function should also be a member of the executive committee.

The responsibilities of a data processing administrator or manager include the following:

Defining the broad objectives and developing the specific objectives for the function.

Developing the sequence of steps, operations, procedures, and tasks to accomplish the stated objectives.

Defining and developing the organizational structure for the data processing function.

Developing the lines of authority and responsibility.

Establishing criteria for the recruitment, selection, appraisal and training of personnel.

Establishing and maintaining the proper liaison and communications channels with those functions directly and indirectly involved with the data processing function.

Developing the means for evaluating the progress and effectiveness of the data processing function.

Developing the necessary controls for accuracy, quality, and costs.

Assisting in the procurement of the necessary resources.

Advising the executive committee about failures as well as success.

Review Questions: Group 2A

1. Why must a multi-functional approach to the use of data processing services be developed in each organization?
2. Why should the executive committee become involved in the direction of the data processing activity?
3. One of the primary responsibilities of a data processing administrator is to define the feedback control system. Explain why this is an important responsibility.

LINE AND STAFF ACTIVITIES

In most organizations, the people can be classified in terms of two basic structural types or activities. These are the line activity and the staff activity.

The line activity, the one most closely connected with the actual operation, is very often referred to as the "doer" or operating activity because it is instrumental in attaining the objective. It is at the line level in the hierarchical structure that the basic management functions of directing and controlling are applied to any plan developed at the staff level.

The staff activity provides advice and support for strengthening the line activity. This level is manned by people who are specialists with a breadth of knowledge, skills, and experience. The abilities of the staff specialists relieve the line manager of detailed technical chores, which he himself either may not be capable of dealing with or may not have the time to do. A staff specialist cannot generally direct outside of his own realm, so his plans, suggestions, or recommendations must be carried out through the line activity. This lack of authority to direct others sometimes creates problems because staff specialists may exceed their delegated authority. However, in many organizations, they produce tangible output rather than mere talk—an output that a line activity can implement.

Figures 2.1 and 2.2 illustrate two different line-staff relationships. In Figure 2.1 the planning and development group and the systems group are placed on a staff level to serve in an advisory and planning capacity for the director of data

Figure 2.1 Example of line-staff structure

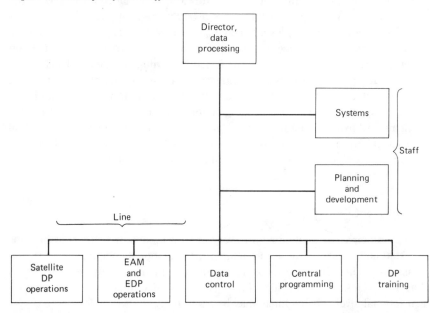

The Structural Organization of Data Processing

35

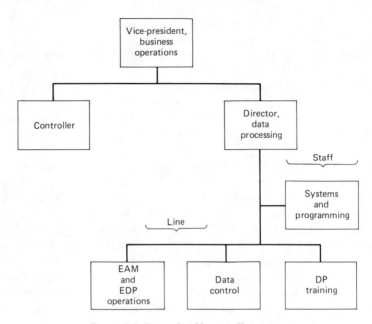

Figure 2.2 Example of line-staff structure

processing. The planning and development group is placed at the staff level because one of its primary functions is to evaluate the overall effectiveness of the various data processing functions. At this level, it is not competing with any other functional group, so it will be more objective in its appraisal. The systems group is placed at the staff level to add objectivity to its operations. At this level, it has the additional leverage to ensure that the systems that are designed and developed will be implemented by the functional groups at the line level.

In Figure 2.2, the systems and programming personnel are placed at the staff level to produce the technical documentation for the training, data control, EDP and EAM operations groups. The tangible output produced at the staff level is implemented by the operating services at the line level. Generally, in this type of a structural arrangement, the systems and programming group is small and the personnel often perform both systems and programming functions.

Easing the Conflict

Some problems inevitably arise in every organizational structure that has line and staff activities, and these can hamper the operational effectiveness of the organization. Therefore, the data processing administrator/manager must work diligently to resolve the conflict and to gain the maximum output from each organizational level. The conflicts may be eased by:

An explicit delegation of authority for both levels.

Balancing the opportunities for the education and training for both line and staff.

Limiting the line-level "empires."

Reducing the budget disparities, wherever possible, between line and staff.

Providing a clear definiton of advisory roles and tasks for the staff-level group.

Review Questions: Group 2B

1. What are the causes of conflict between the staff and line-level activities within the data processing function?

THE FUNCTIONAL ORGANIZATION

As the organizational structure expands, it becomes more complex. To simplify this structure, many organizations employ the process of divisionalization in order to break down a major function into its component parts or activities. This process is frequently applied to the data processing function.

Figure 2.3 Divisionalization of the data processing function

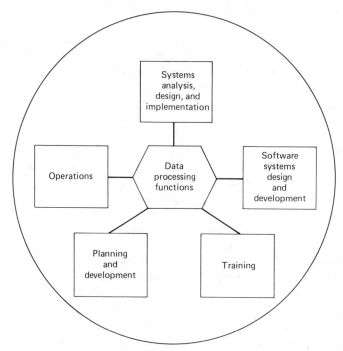

The five component activity groups of the data processing function are:

1. Systems Analysis, Design, and Implementation Group
2. Software Systems Design and Development
3. Planning and Development Group
4. Operations Group
5. Training Group

This divisionalization is illustrated in Figure 2.3.

The Systems Analysis, Design, and Implementation Group

A system can be described as a detailed plan or arrangement for utilizing the available hardware, software, human, time, budget, and material resources to accomplish a given goal. The system must be guided by a well-defined procedure and the activities monitored and evaluated to ensure goal attainment. To develop a rationalization of the interdependence of these activities involves analysis and design. The analysis phase is concerned with determining the following factors:

The source of the data elements

The process required to maintain the development and flow of these data elements

The steps and operations required to produce a useful output

The type of output required

The design phase is concerned with the development of a procedure or system that will include the above-mentioned requirements and accomplish a given task or objective. The system needs to provide for the collection, classification, and manipulation of data; to utilize the available resources; and to lead to meaningful reports. It is such systems that represent the foundation of the data processing activity.

The systems analysis, design, and implementation group—commonly referred to simply as the systems group—is very often maintained as a staff-level agency. This means that the group has to implement its ideas, concepts, and designs through the programming group and/or the operations group. The structural and functional arrangements vary from organization to organization. The detailed organizational format of the data processing function is developed by upper-echelon executives who base their decision on organizational objectives, as well as on the function's relationship to the existing structure and its contribution to the overall effectiveness of the organization.

After a problem has been defined, requirements established, and the solution developed, the systems group must implement the approach. For the systems personnel, the implementation process is primarily one of coordination. Prior to the actual implementation, the analyst must conduct a readiness review to ensure that all of the interacting elements and factors are ready for cut-over. The analyst must evaluate the status of user and operation's documentation, physical facilities for installation of new equipment, computer programs, personnel training, and so forth. When actual implementation occurs, the analyst must monitor the affected activities to ensure that all operations are proceeding according to plan. If any problems are detected, the analyst must coordinate with the personnel responsible for that segment to initiate remedial action. Within a reasonable period of time after implementation, the analyst must conduct a follow-up, which is made to determine that all problems have been resolved, that the implemented plan is achieving the stated objectives, and that the previously stated savings and benefits have been achieved.

RESPONSIBILITIES

In most data processing activities, a systems group has six major responsibilities. These are:

1. The analysis of existing manual systems
2. The analysis of existing punched card systems
3. The analysis of computerized systems
4. The analysis of proposed systems
5. The analysis and design of changes in existing (operational, manual, punched card, and computerized) systems
6. The design of systems for manual, punched card equipment, and computerized operations

1. EXISTING MANUAL SYSTEMS. In any organization, manual systems must be investigated to determine whether or not it is feasible to convert them to an automated process. All manual systems do not readily lend themselves to automation, so it is useful to use the following three good tests, which should be applied to the evaluation of any manual system:

a) Can it be done better mechanically? This first test implies that the information can be provided more readily and more accurately than it can under the manual system.

b) Can it be done more economically? Economic feasibility should be based primarily on tangible savings and only secondarily on the intangibles. Automated systems are very often justified on the basis that the information will be made available more readily, thereby enabling the manager to make decisions more quickly. This is a loaded statement because it implies that the manager must have quick access to the information at any cost. It may be very nice to have the information sooner, but is it really necessary and does it warrant the extra cost involved?

c) Can the same type of information be provided? This third test is one that must be thoroughly applied to any manual system. It is made to ensure that the user can receive the information he needs to do the job with and in the format that will increase and not impede his productivity.

A common complaint among many users of data processing services is that they do not now receive all of the pertinent information that was formerly available to them. Another complaint is that they now have to use two different reports to assemble the desired information. Maintaining an open communications channel between the systems group and the user during the analysis phase can reduce or eliminate such conditions. If such a condition becomes unbearable, it will eventually have to be changed, thereby incurring additional development expenses.

2. EXISTING PUNCHED CARD SYSTEMS. An analysis of punched card systems will most generally be made when an organization is either converting to or considering computerized operations. This is a necessary step in order to take full advantage of computer equipment. Converting from a punched card system to a computerized system without making significant changes will result in uneconomical runs and the need to develop additional controls.

Some organizations attempt to reduce their initial development cost for systems and programming by converting from unit-record applications to computerized unit-record applications. The computerized unit-record applications are direct conversions of EAM control panels to computer programs, written most generally in a report program generator (RPG) or assembler language. No real attempt is made to integrate or analyze the operations; rather, all that is done is to convert each control panel in its existing form to a computer run. Inevitably, this results in a multitude of programs, with each of them performing a separate function, such as listing, tabulating, calculating, etc.

The author has personally observed an organization equipped with a medium-scale computer with four tape drives using a computerized unit-record approach to processing. For three years the organization continued to process the hourly rated employees payroll by utilizing the computer only as a high-speed printer and calculator. It is conceivable that the entire payroll for approximately five thousand employees could be processed in approximately ten hours. In this instance, the tangible savings would exceed the development costs incurred for systems and programming effort.

3. COMPUTERIZED SYSTEMS. Some experts estimate that no computerized system lasts more than two years without a major or significant change. This view is based primarily on the fact that changes in organizational objectives are bound to occur and that systems personnel become more sophisticated in their approach to the computer. For example, when an organization initially converts to disk-oriented hardware from unit-record equipment or a card-oriented computer, the early applications continue to utilize serial rather than random access techniques and continue to lack good data management practices. As the personnel gain operating experience and confidence, they revise their applications to utilize the random access techniques.

In any conversion, the systems personnel apply the methods and the hardware and/or software that are most familiar to them, and they tend to continue doing so until they develop a sense of security and an adequate level of confidence about the new approach. Such conservatism cannot prevail for any prolonged period of time because it tends to reduce or eliminate any tangible savings to be gained from the conversion.

In organizations that insist on a definite conversion or installation schedule, the personnel tend to choose the approach that will yield the fastest, though not necessarily the most efficient, results. This practice is undertaken with the stated understanding that the application will be modified at a later date, when more time is available. However, some organizations never reach the point when time is available. Consequently, optimal results are never achieved, tangible savings are never maximized, and the desired objectives are only partially attained. No computerized system, however good, is infinitely perfect; therefore, changes can and should be made as frequently as needed in order to improve the system's operational effectiveness.

4. PROPOSED SYSTEMS. A typical organization experiences change: new ideas evolve, changes in organizational objectives and needs arise, legal requirements are imposed that affect the existing operation, potential users are found, and numerous other situations develop. Such changes invariably give rise to proposals for new systems. In addition, the organization receives a stream of vendor announcements about new or improved hardware and software. These announcements must all be analyzed to determine their potential operational effectiveness and economic feasibility. The analyses may indicate that certain proposals lack economic or practical justification, or that advances in the state of the art are still not sufficiently developed to permit practical design and implementation. The analyses may also show that a current proposal is definitely valid, but that the organization would be wise to wait for further technological developments in the field before making any decision. For example, some current proposals for the use of data collection or data communications devices could well be affected by the progress being made in laser technology. Similarly, current proposals for expediting the input into a data processing system may change with the continuing development of optical character recognition (OCR) devices.

The OCR and other proposals may not be economically feasible because the cost of the hardware currently available may still be prohibitively expensive for the organization. Or, they may be technically unsatisfactory; for example, the volume of source documents may be low, the quality of paper or impressions unacceptable, or the documents may be either too large for the equipment or incorrectly designed. Such economic and technical factors can weigh heavily in the evaluation of a proposal.

When a proposal is found to have merit, the systems group should initiate a feasibility study to determine the proposal's practical and economic justification. The feasibility study will critically investigate the impact of a proposal on the organization, its present and future objectives, the existing system, and its cost effectiveness. If there is justification for proceeding with development of the proposal, then the design of the system will be initiated. It is possible, however, that a change to an existing system may also facilitate the user's needs.

The analysis of proposed systems also includes comparative assessments. The current operation is studied and evaluated and then compared with the proposed approach in order to determine the advantages and disadvantages of each operation. This kind of comparison can be effectively made only by conducting a feasibility study. (The subject of feasibility studies is discussed in detail in chapter 8.)

5. CHANGES IN EXISTING SYSTEMS. The need for new information, shifts in emphasis regarding objectives, and other organizational changes commonly give rise to the necessity of changing an existing system. In these cases, as in those relating to proposals for new systems, the systems group must analyze the situation, determine what should be done, and then implement the changes wherever possible. The systems group uses the same basic methods of analysis. It studies and evaluates the current operation, investigates the possible changes, examines the possibilities of using improvements in hardware and software, and initiates feasibility studies as needed.

The following is a good example of changing an existing system. An organization is currently receiving accounting data for the general ledger from its subsidiaries through the mail. The competition of business has forced the headquarters accounting organization to advance the closing of the books by two days. Consequently, the submission schedule of the subsidiary reporting units must be altered to reflect the new requirements. The first thought of the subsidiaries would be to advance their operating schedules. Investigation by the systems group may reveal that such a step may not be possible and that a revision in the mode of data transmission to the headquarters accounting organization may be required. The systems group would then initiate a feasibility study to decide upon an expeditious and economical mode of data transmission.

6. DESIGN OF SYSTEMS. The design of systems is one of the most important responsibilities of the systems group. In the previously mentioned responsibilities, there is a limited amount of design work performed by the analyst when considering possible alternatives. The preliminary design specifications must be subsequently detailed and finalized to produce a solution to the problem. The design of systems is concerned with development of procedures necessary for the processing of data and the establishment of management controls to ensure the attainment of a given objective. The specifications developed by the group must optimize the input, output, processing, storage, and communications characteristics to produce a well-designed data processing system. These specifications include such items as source document, form, card, and record layouts; system flowcharts; operating instructions; and other essential documentation for the programming, operations, and training groups of the data processing function. (The subject of documentation is discussed in detail in chapter 4.)

Review Questions: Group 2C

1. How may a data processing activity be structured by function?
2. Which tests should be applied in evaluating a manual system when it is being considered for conversion to an automated process?

3. Why must the systems group be concerned with existing manual, punched card, and computerized systems?

Software Systems Design and Development Group

Software systems include such products as the computer's operating system, application programs, utilities, job control language, file management, supervisory control, statistical recording programs, algorithms, data base administrators, debugging aids, modules, telecommunications control programs, management science programs, compilers and macros. The design and development of software systems is not unlike the process involved in the design and development of information processing systems. The design process is particularly important because it will affect development and testing costs; the adaptability, maintainability, reliability, and efficiency of a program or module; and program portability.

In larger organizations, the software personnel may be placed into several occupational categories: business (applications) programmers, scientific and technical programmers, systems (software) programmers, and maintenance programmers. In addition, we may have telecommunications and data base programming specialists.

In many organizations, the software group is referred to as the programming group. This group, like the systems group, is very often maintained as a staff-level activity. However, in some instances, it is a line-level function.

RESPONSIBILITIES

A software group usually has the following major responsibilities:

1. The design and development of programs for computerized data systems
2. The development of modules and generalized programs
3. The writing of utility and media conversion programs
4. Maintenance of existing programs
5. Maintenance of the operating system, program library, and specialized software

1. PROGRAMS FOR COMPUTERIZED DATA SYSTEMS. Generally, the primary responsibility of the software group is the design of computer programs to facilitate the development and implementation of computerized data systems. These programs are generally referred to as applications programs. In some instances, the software group may be charged with the responsibility for adapting or modifying a software package for use in a given information processing system. The programmer must structure a solution that will make optimal use of the hardware, software, and storage.

The software personnel must interact with the users and system personnel to identify the programming requirements and data flows. Having gained an understanding of what is to be done, the programmer will subdefine the information processing system into programs and subsequently into modules, if feasible. In designing the programs and modules, the programmer must determine the optimal storage arrangements and requirements, select an optimal language, and optimize the data handling and computational procedures. This information is then translated into narratives, flowcharts, decision tables, outlines, and/or top-down structures to describe the logic of the programs and modules needs. The software personnel must then check these logic structures for effectiveness before any program coding is initiated. The coding sheets are then desk checked for clerical and logical accuracy. Test data ("artificial" and "live"), a test plan, and documentation must be prepared for the testing and debugging sessions. Once the programs and modules are working properly, the instructions, specifications, and graphics for the users and equipment operators, and the documentation package must be finalized.

2. MODULES AND GENERALIZED PROGRAMS. Generalized programs are those programs that have been specially designed to facilitate the production of a variety of user-requests based on different constraints and parameters. Generalized programs can be written to support a variety of applications. An organization may develop a generalized program that may be used to perform file maintenance and updating on a variety of source files. The programming manager must determine if one of the report writer or report program generator packages could be acquired to perform the same software functions. It may be possible to purchase the packaged software at a significant savings in software development costs.

Modular programming is currently viewed by many as a panacea to solve all software development problems for the programming and data processing managers. Modular programming can and does facilitate the software development process, if properly executed. The proper execution of modular programming must begin with the design phase before any program coding is undertaken. The software designer must subdefine the program into modules (small segments of code) that will ultimately be linked into a workable program through predetermined calling sequences.

Modules can also be produced in the form of reusable code. These types of modules can be linked from an existing program or a module library to another program. Modules in this category can be used for performing such repetitive functions as code checking, page-header routines, tests for alphabetic data in a numeric field, or numeric data tests on an alphabetic field.

The modules can be used to reduce software development costs and the need for machine time, and to improve program efficiency and programmer productivity.

3. UTILITY AND MEDIA CONVERSION PROGRAMS. Media conversion programs are written to move data from one media form to another. Input data may be converted to a different medium in order to expedite the input process into the central processing unit. Similarly, data may be written on a mass storage device like disk and then, in an off-line operation, written on a different medium. The media forms most commonly affected are punched cards, magnetic tape, magnetic disk, printer, plotter, or computer output microfilm (COM). File dumps for

security or data transfer purposes are common examples of media conversion programs. Some of the media conversion programs may be very sophisticated and include such items as editing and formating.

Utility programs are written to handle a great many repetitive computer operations requiring software for such functions as ditto, tape copy, traces, and test generators. Utility programs may also be written for use as part of the operating system software. Included in this category may be editors and loaders and input/output routines.

4. PROGRAM MAINTENANCE. The maintenance of existing computer programs is an essential but time-consuming responsibility. Many data processing organizations estimate that from 15 to 20 percent of the programming group's budget is expended on the maintenance task.

The time required for maintenance can be reduced significantly through the application of sound design concepts during original planning and development. It can be further reduced by the subsequent application of program and documentation standards.

As part of its maintenance responsibility, the programming group has to deal with the modification and alteration of existing programs that result from changes made in a computerized system, tax factors, parameters, hardware, or software. These program changes must be analyzed and inserted; then the revised programs have to be thoroughly tested, debugged, and documented before they are operational for productive processing.

One of the most common difficulties at this stage is that the documentation of changes is very often overlooked by the maintenance programmer. Consequently, future maintenance activity is delayed until he becomes aware of the reason for, and the degree of change or modification in, prior maintenance operations. (The subject of program documentation is discussed further in chapter 4.)

In some organizations, the responsibility for program maintenance is relegated to a relatively inexperienced programmer, such as a junior programmer or trainee, in the belief that performance of this task requires very little practical experience. This assumption may be somewhat valid in organizations where good programming design concepts and documentation standards are stressed. However, because of the differences in program logic, an inexperienced programmer may well expend more time and effort than a more-experienced person would have in performing the maintenance function.

5. OPERATING SYSTEM, PROGRAM LIBRARY, AND PACKAGED SOFTWARE MAINTENANCE. In many organizations, the responsibilities for the operating system, program library, and packaged software are assigned to the systems (software) programmers. The systems programmers must work with the applications programmers, users, and software and hardware vendors to determine the best programming languages, library routines, operating systems, data structures, and strategies to employ. The systems programmers may also design compilers, operating systems, telecommunications and data base management software for an organization.

The systems programmers must also code, maintain, and debug modifications and corrections to the operating systems, utilities, and software package tests. In this capacity, the systems programmers will perform the "SYSGEN"—updating the operating system and its associated software to reflect the latest vendor modifications (releases). These software personnel are also responsible for analyzing and tracing problems in applications programs, software packages, operating systems, hardware, and/or operating personnel.

Review Questions: Group 2D

1. Why should a manager encourage and enforce good design practices in programming?
2. In what ways do program modules play an important part in increasing the productivity of the programming personnel?
3. Should the manager of a small data processing function be concerned with program maintenance? Explain your answer.

Planning and Development Group

This group is primarily responsible for evaluating and initiating new uses of data processing within an organization. The group also audits the operational effectiveness of the organization's data processing function.

The planning and development group is responsible for such items as long-range planning, evaluating new services for the organization, evaluating non-computerized systems, purchase of hardware and/or software, and feasibility studies for special projects.

RESPONSIBILITIES

The major responsibilities of the planning and development group are:

1. Auditing the overall effectiveness of the data processing function
2. Auditing the effectiveness of existing information processing systems
3. Evaluating and initiating new uses of information processing systems for an organization
4. Evaluating and preparing recommendations on new hardware and/or software developments
5. Validating performance and documentation standards

1. OVERALL FUNCTIONAL EFFECTIVENESS. The planning and development group has become a watchdog group in many organizations. In this capacity, the group is responsible for evaluating the operational effectiveness of a data processing function. For example, a data processing function may express desires to expand its hardware capability to provide greater computing and processing power. An investigation of use, however, may prove that the CPU is utilized only 40 percent of the available productive time.

2. EFFECTIVENESS OF EXISTING SYSTEMS. The group is responsible for auditing the effectiveness of the existing information processing systems in the orga-

nization. Each system must be audited periodically to determine its support level to the needs of the user function. Some systems may be found to be obsolete, unresponsive, incomplete, and/or inadequate to meet the needs of the user function in its goal-attainment activity. Systems that are failing to meet their objectives must either be revised or replaced to prevent or minimize the waste of an organization's resources.

3. EVALUATE AND INITIATE NEW USES. The group must conduct feasibility studies (see chapter 8) to determine the economic, technical, and operational feasibility of new information processing systems for an organization. The systems would be evaluated in terms of meeting the long-term needs of the organization, to improve its competitive position in an organization, to improve the organization's profit picture, and/or to improve the decision-making capability of the organization. For example, an organization may consider the merit of developing a corporate data base or developing a distributed network. Noncomputerized systems, such as mail handling systems, may also be evaluated by this group.

In forward-looking organizations, the planning and development group may establish task forces or steering committees in conjunction with user functions to determine the need for new information processing systems. The information gathered by these task forces or steering committees may be used to develop currently needed systems or to identify systems that will be required in the future to support the needs of the overall organization.

4. INVESTIGATION OF NEW HARDWARE AND/OR SOFTWARE. The dynamic nature of the information processing field requires that an organization develop specialists in evaluating the cost-benefit of new developments in hardware and/or software. For example, the availability of point-of-sale (POS) devices may be very important to a retailing organization. Or, new computer performance measurement software may be very beneficial in identifying bottlenecks in computer productivity or poor programming.

5. VALIDATION OF STANDARDS. Evaluation of the operational effectiveness of the data processing function requires the existence of documentation and performance standards to provide some measure of actual progress. The planning and development group is responsible for the development of, implementation of, and follow-up on documentation standards (see chapter 4) and performance standards (see chapter 5) for evaluating the progress of the data processing function.

The Operations Group

The operations group is responsible for the production of decision-making information. As such, it is the focal point of data processing activity—the point where the output of the systems, software, training, and planning and development groups must be integrated in order to provide for an optimal productive process. The interaction of these functional resources must be carefully coordinated by the chief administrator and manager of the data processing function.

In many organizations, the operations group is harassed, maligned, and forced into the role of "goof-guilty" scapegoat. This negative attitude stems from the attribution of human characteristics to data processing equipment. Consequently, the equipment is deemed responsible for all human failings and all errors actually committed by data processing and non-data processing personnel. An operations group that is constantly under such stress will undoubtedly be failing to meet a large percentage of its objectives.

To provide for and maintain an effective activity, the operations manager must be fully aware of the factors of time, quality, quantity, and cost—each of which forms an essential part of the responsibilities delegated to the operations group.

RESPONSIBILITIES

The group's primary responsibilities are:

1. To establish and maintain an effective production schedule
2. To establish data control
3. To provide for the conversion of source data and/or control data entry
4. To establish and maintain communications channels with satellite operations and/or distributed processing networks
5. To establish a records control system

1. THE PRODUCTION SCHEDULE. Establishing a production schedule is a very difficult task. The schedule must be flexible enough to allow for production runs, special reports, reruns, preventive and unscheduled maintenance, program and system testing, and the compilation and assembly of programs. It must be constructed in such a manner as to give due consideration to each of the influencing factors and, at the same time, to provide for an optimal utilization of all available resources. The operations manager must monitor his schedule closely in order to ensure adherence to the stipulated times, as well as to detect, identify, and correct any scheduling problems that may occur. Failure to develop and maintain a realistic operating schedule will serve only to create a variety of problems, which may result in a waste of valuable human, hardware, software, material, time, and budget resources. The operations manager may make use of computer performance measurement software, that may identify bottlenecks in computer productivity, to improve upon computer setup and productivity. (The subject of scheduling is covered in chapter 5.)

2. DATA CONTROL. Because information used in the decision-making process must be accurate, management controls (see chapter 10) must be developed and utilized to ensure high quality of input, processing, and output. In order to maintain accuracy and operational effectiveness, the operations manager generally concerns himself with the establishment of document, accounting, procedure, and output controls. In addition, the manager must adapt performance and documentation standards to provide for more effective utilization of resources and for realistic scheduling.

3. DATA CONVERSION AND DATA ENTRY. The operations manager must give a great deal of attention to the conversion of data from human-sensible to machine-sensible language. Furthermore, the volume of transactions and source document formats affects the conversion rate. At present, most of the conversion is performed through the process of keypunching data elements into punched cards from the source documents; however, this process is comparatively slow and very often causes a production backlog. Some data conversion is performed through the use of such data recording devices as key-to-tape and key-to-disk. There is an increase in the number of installations utilizing this form of data conversion as an alternative to the keypunching process. Optical scanning devices and other alternatives to keypunching such as POS, badge readers, magnetic strip readers, cathode-ray tube terminals or the emerging technology of voice data entry are also being used for distributed data entry and data conversion.

The fact that more data will be entered by the users or as a by-product of an event or transaction, eliminating the keypunching operation, will place a greater need on input control. The operations manager must ensure that there will be the needed data editing and data validation processes to ensure a high quality of input and to facilitate correction of any exceptions identified.

4. COMMUNICATIONS WITH SATELLITE OPERATIONS AND DISTRIBUTED PROCESSING NETWORKS. Satellite operations can be very important because often they supply the input for many of the reports processed by the operations group. In many instances, the operations manager does not have direct control of the satellites, so he must establish and maintain a communications channel to permit a free flow of information and resources.

The trend toward distributed processing—a decentralization of the processing capabilities throughout the entire organization—will also require that the operations manager develop and maintain an effective communications channel. In most instances, the operations manager will maintain control over the distributed processing networks, but he may have to utilize his resources differently to maximize the effectiveness of the concept.

5. RECORDS CONTROL SYSTEM. In many organizations, the operations manager has acquired a new responsibility in recent years. This is the responsibility for retention and maintenance of the data elements stored on punched cards, paper tape, magnetic tape, magnetic disk packs, and other media used in the information processing cycle. This activity has become necessary because preparation of many of the management reports now requires historical data ranging in age from a few months to several years for comparison purposes in decision-making. The maintenance of such data creates storage and processing problems for the operations manager. He must establish a file retention system to protect these records against accidental destruction or deliberate alteration, as well as to maintain their processing quality. (Retention safeguards are discussed as part of management controls in chapter 10.)

The Training Group

Many organizations cling to the mistaken belief that training is a simple task, claiming that training involves no more than merely showing others how to perform a job or how a job is performed. Seeing this as a relatively simple task that requires very little time and no formal structure or plan, such organizations ignore the development and implementation of sound training programs. The function of training may sound simple in principle, but it never is in practice.

The effectiveness of any operation can be measured in part by the quality of the personnel assigned to the function responsible; such quality is developed by providing competent training and experience for the personnel involved in the process. Operational effectiveness can also be measured in part by the volume of requests for the function's services; such requests represent a gauge of how well the function is understood and valued by its present and potential users, and that in turn depends largely on how well the personnel are trained.

It is clear that an operationally effective organization is dependent on a well-structured training program. Because the training group serves such an essential function, its importance must not be minimized nor its responsibilities diluted. (Training is discussed more fully in chapter 3.)

RESPONSIBILITIES

A training group customarily has the responsibility to provide:

1. Technical training for data processing personnel
2. Technical and informational training for user organization personnel
3. Informational training for managers at all levels of the organization structure
4. Informational training for other members of the organization

1. TRAINING FOR DATA PROCESSING PERSONNEL. The training group will coordinate the use of training services offered by vendors, management consultants, colleges and universities, and professional educational services for the data processing personnel. Some of these sources may also be used to provide in-house training. If training is not available from these sources, is too limited, or is too costly, it is particularly important that a training capability be developed and maintained by the training group within the organization that will provide general orientation or detailed operating instructions. Software training programs teach program language syntax of a given language, use of a programming language for problem solving, and the application of software techniques or packages. Software training is generally very detailed and is provided primarily for programming personnel or subject-matter specialists.

However, a training group may be required to provide modified forms of software training. For example, the group may develop a special software course for systems and planning personnel in order to provide a balance between orientation and detailed information.

The training group should also have the capability to provide data processing personnel with training in simulation, direct access methods, programming for the use of inquiry units, and so on. Similarly, it should be able to teach the use of such applications as information retrieval, computer-assisted instruction, data base management, or sort-merge. The depth and breadth of knowledge provided by the training group for data processing personnel should lead to a handsome rate of return on investment through well-designed systems and programs that optimize the use of available resources.

2. TRAINING FOR USER PERSONNEL. Training is as essential for users as it is for data processing personnel because the users in an organization operate equipment, write programs, and submit input and/or utilize the output. Engineering and technical personnel are often provided with software training that emphasizes problem-solving techniques. In educational organizations, teaching personnel are taught the use of programming languages such as FORTRAN and/or BASIC as a tool for test item analysis, a form of computer-assisted instruction.

There is a general fallacy about hardware training that, to become an "expert," an operator simply needs to learn which buttons to push, to become aware of a few do's and don'ts (if the instructor is that generous), and to acquire some actual experience. Very often the end result of such informal training is faulty input data, equipment breakdown, excessive equipment downtime, the development of bad operating habits, and so on.

Vendors generally provide some limited hands-on or orientation-type training upon initial installation of the device. However, the operating manuals they provide are very general and include few, if any, examples. Therefore, to offset the possibility of any serious problems, the training group needs to develop practice workbooks that give detailed instructions—complete with proven examples—for dealing with various types of situations, conditions, and problems. Development of such workbooks must be a primary responsibility of the training group.

Users who write their own programs need to be provided some level of instruction regarding the various languages implemented for problem solving. This training program must cover the use of those computer instructions that facilitate the efficient use of computer storage, reduce translation and processing time, and simplify debugging. The user must also be made aware of any submission standards required by the operations group, such as job control card formats, priority or storage allocation codes, use of account numbers, etc. Figure 2.4, an excerpt from a user's manual published by an educational institution, details the job control card format required of all users submitting a program for translation or a production run. This type of training procedure enables the data processing function to provide high-quality service for the users and to make optimum use of its resources.

The training group is also responsible for making sure that any changes in the requirements are communicated to the users. Many organizations publish periodic newsletters to make the users aware of changes and modifications, or of the availability of any new software capabilities. Figure 2.5 consists of two extracts from such a newsletter intended for programming users.

Columns	Content
1–2	/ /
3	Blank
4–6	"JOB"
7	Blank
8–12	Account number (assigned)
13	Blank
14–23	Name of user (last name first)
24	Blank
25–27	User's own program number
28	Blank
29–31	Department number (faculty and staff use only)
32	Blank
33–35	Course identification (alpha prefix)
36–39	Course identification number
40–41	Course/Section number
43	Blank
44–60	Name of instructor (student must include)
61	Blank
62–67	Date (mo., day, yr. sequence in numeric form only)

Figure 2.4 Example of user job control card format

Figure 2.5 Extracts from a computer services newsletter

Loading Programs from Tape Files

A number of users have experienced some difficulty because of the tape loading technique required by the RAS Operating System. To circumvent the problems until a new loader system is released, the following is recommended:
Copy your files on disk utilizing the standard copy functions, and load from the disk file.

New Feature for SNOBOL 4 Users

1. The reserved words ?ABEND, ?ANCHOR, ?DUMP, ?FTRACE, and ?TRACE only accept integers as values.
2. ?TRACE is automatically decremented by 1 after tracing action as an aid in eliminating endless trace loops. The trace should be initialized to the number of traces desired. When ?TRACE has been decremented to zero, the tracing option is turned off.

Frequently neglected by data processing managers is training for users who are responsible for input preparation, utilization of output, data origination, coding or conversion. Some organizations have prepared documentation regarding completion of forms, types of forms to use, etc. Figure 2.6 consists of an excerpt from a standards manual detailing the standard procedure for completion of a

Figure 2.6 Example of standard procedure for completing a form

RALERIC FREIGHTWAYS	DATA PROCESSING MANUAL 10.1 December 15, 19 ____	
STANDARD PROCEDURE		
Subject INSTRUCTIONS FOR PREPARATION OF AIR SHIPPING LABEL		Application no.
Performed by	Action	
Warehouseman	1. After the appropriate entries have been made on the shipping document, the warehouseman will prepare a shipping label for each piece. The following information must be entered on the shipping label. a. *Consignor:* Enter the name of the organization making the shipment. b. *Destination:* Enter the final destination of the shipment. The destination is derived from the shipping document. c. *Document Number:* Enter the document number from the shipping document. d. *Weight:* Enter the weight of this piece *only.* e. *Piece Count:* Indicate the number of this piece and the total number of pieces in the shipment. For example, piece 1 of 10 pieces would be coded as 1/10. 2. Affix firmly each shipping label to each piece in the shipment. 3. Forward the shipping document to the traffic control clerk. 4. Place the cargo in the appropriate storage area.	
Prepared by	Approved by	Approval date

form. Some organizations include within the documentation the procedure for interpreting the output and its manipulation.

Many organizations imprint frequently used codes on the reverse side of a punched card or printer form. Some incorporate explanations of the columnar data on the reverse side of a printer form to simplify interpretation of the output in view of the user. This can be an inexpensive and effective way of providing necessary data in a convenient form to the user. Figure 2.7 illustrates the front and reverse sides of a punched card used as input for an off-the-job injury reporting system. The codes on the reverse side are used to identify the physical location where the reported injury occurred, the contributing cause, and the anatomical part affected.

Figure 2.7 User instruction: example of off-the-job injury reporting system punched card

DEPT.		E-NUMBER	NAME				OCCUP. CODE	SERVICE DATE	PERIOD ENDING	

		DAYS ABSENT	SICKNESS ABSENCE	PERSONAL ABSENCE	OTHER		HOURS WORKED			NOTES	

Record of Attendance:

PAID THIS YEAR				DAY	STD.	O.T.	NIGHT BONUS	This card is for calendar reporting roll only.
NOT PAID THIS YEAR				MON				If absence involves off-the-job injury, complete reverse side of this form.
				TUES				Rules are prescribed in M.D.I. 9.14.2.
TO BE PAID THIS PERIOD				WED				
				THUR				
APPROVALS				FRI				
EMPLOYEE	MGR.	SUPT.	OTHER					
				SAT				
APPROVALS PRESCRIBED IN M.D.I. 9.14.1				SUN				

IF ABSENCE WAS CAUSED BY OFF-THE-JOB INJURY,
CHECK ONE BOX IN EACH COLUMN BELOW:

DATES OF ABSENCE
FROM _____
TO _____

LOCATION	CAUSE	PART AFFECTED
☐1. HOME	☐1. SLIP, FALL	☐1. HAND
☐2. PUBLIC	☐2. LIFTING	☐2. ARM
☐3. SPORTS	☐3. HAND TOOLS, SHARP OBJECTS	☐3. FOOT
☐4. PRIVATE CAR	☐4. STRUCK, STRUCK BY	☐4. ANKLE OR LEG
☐5. PUBLIC TRANSPORTATION	☐5. MACHINE (POWER EQPT. OR AUTO)	☐5. EYE
☐6. PEDESTRIAN	☐6. ELECTRICITY	☐6. HEAD
☐7. OTHER	☐7. HEAT, COLD, EXPLOSION	☐7. BODY (TRUNK)
	☐8. CHEMICALS, POISONING	☐8. INTERNAL
	☐9. ANIMALS, INSECTS, OR PLANTS	☐9. COMBINATION
	☐0. OTHER	☐0. OTHER

If there are two or more occasions of absence within one pay period due to off-the-job injuries, complete and attach Form RAS 1819 for the second and subsequent absences.

When a system or application is implemented or modified, the training group is responsible for providing the users with the training and orientation necessary to ensure operational effectiveness. This task also affords the group an opportunity to test the documentation for accuracy and effectiveness. It can also serve to expose any difficulties or problems inherent in the design or documentation.

3. TRAINING FOR MANAGERIAL PERSONNEL. A practical awareness of the subject matter on the part of managerial personnel greatly helps to promote total management involvement, as well as implementation of a multi-functional approach to data processing service. Several organizations have developed in-house programs to provide different types and levels of training for managerial personnel. Nevertheless, such instruction remains the one aspect of training most often overlooked in an organization.

4. TRAINING FOR OTHER MEMBERS OF THE ORGANIZATION. The data processing activity must be regarded as a service function. Its growth and increased effectiveness is dependent upon both existing and potential users. The potential users may be responsible for proposing the development of new systems or applications that eventually result in massive cost reduction and improved operating efficiency. However, potential users are very often unaware of the capabilities of data processing as a management tool, so they fail to make any proposals or suggestions. This is the organization's loss. It is also the reason why training, even of a general kind, is needed for other members of the organization.

Some organizations are now making it a practice to conduct special orientation seminars for their personnel. These seminars, presented with the hope of stimulating employee thought and action, provide information about hardware, software, systems, and applications. The practice appears to be successful and gaining in popularity. For example, an executive of a blue-chip firm has advised the author that his organization has recorded substantial savings since implementing such seminar programs.

Review Questions: Group 2E

1. Explain why the planning and development group of the data processing function is very often referred to as a watchdog group.
2. What benefit, if any, would a data processing manager derive from recommending and implementing training for user personnel?

VARIATIONS IN ORGANIZATIONAL STRUCTURES

As stated earlier, the data processing function may be organized and reorganized in various ways. The manager must determine what type of organizational structure will provide the best support for users and make optimal use of the available data processing resources.

Currently, there are several variations in organizational structures that are applied to the systems and software personnel in the data processing function. The variations include the following formats:

1. The applications structure
2. The functional structure
3. The matrix organization
4. Chief programmer team
5. Egoless programming team

1. THE APPLICATIONS STRUCTURE. Using this type of format, the manager organizes the systems and software personnel into groups or teams according to major application areas, i.e., financial, marketing, engineering, and so forth. The assigned personnel become specialists and are responsible for all analysis, design, development, implementation, and maintenance of systems and programs in a given application area.

The chief advantage of this format is that it is user-oriented and minimizes the communications problems between users and data processors. One major disadvantage is that personnel may be periodically idle when there is no activity within an applications area. This situation would not provide for an optimal use of systems and software personnel. Also, it is difficult to apply this format to an organization that moves from mono-functional to multi-functional systems to support the decision-making needs of the overall organization.

2. THE FUNCTIONAL STRUCTURE. Using this type of format, the manager organizes the systems and software personnel by functional specialty. The systems personnel are organized into groups or teams according to the functional activities in the systems cycle—analysis, design, development, implementation, and maintenance. A systems person becomes a specialist in analysis or one of the other functions in the systems cycle.

The software personnel are also organized by a functional specialty, such as analysis, design, testing and debugging, implementation, and maintenance. These personnel may then be organized within the categories of commercial, scientific/technical, and systems programming.

The format enables a manager to develop highly skilled specialists in each of the functional specialties, but it may be very difficult to keep the systems and software personnel busy 100 percent of the time. Also, to be effective, this type of organizational format requires strict adherence to the organization's documentation and performance standards to minimize communications, control, and scheduling problems. There is also a need for intensive coordination by the manager to ensure that the necessary continuity exists as the workflow passes from one functional specialty to another. For example, it is essential that all the necessary data is passed from the specialists in analysis to the design specialists, and so forth. This same situation applies whether we consider systems or programming effort for new or maintenance tasks.

3. THE MATRIX ORGANIZATION. This type of format is an attempt to make optimal use of the organization's systems and software personnel. Software and systems personnel with a particular skill or set of skills are assigned to various applications or projects as the needs arise. This approach tends to overcome or minimize the problem of underutilizing experienced personnel. But it also generates a problem for the assignment of inexperienced personnel with no identifiable skills. This problem can be overcome by providing training for the inexperienced personnel and making a conscious effort to identify their strengths and weaknesses.

Managers using the matrix format sometimes tend to proliferate the number of project teams to handle the various needs of the organization. But the proliferation of teams may generate span of control problems for the data processing manager and/or the subordinate managers in the programming and systems functions.

4. CHIEF PROGRAMMER TEAM. This type of format is an attempt to increase programmer productivity and effectiveness by having senior software personnel primarily concerned with problem definition and description, and design of a solution. The so-called "mechanical" functions, such as test data generation, program coding, finalizing documentation, or submission of programs for compilation and testing, are performed by other personnel on the team.

The chief programmer is responsible for the detailed design and development of the software system. He is supported by a back-up programmer and other programmers on the team. The back-up programmer would serve as team leader in the absence of the chief programmer and would assist in the performance of other programming tasks. The team is also supported by a programming librarian who may be a specially trained secretary or programming technician. The low-level responsibilities for such functions as keypunching, submission of test runs, and listing of files are relegated to the programming librarian.

The chief programmer concept can provide for optimal use of the talents of senior software personnel. But it may also generate some other types of problems for the data processing manager. The back-up programmer must be willing to work in the shadow of the chief programmer. Also, it may make job advancement for other programmers on the team difficult because all programming effort seemingly revolves around the chief programmer and his assistant.

5. EGOLESS PROGRAMMING TEAM. This type of structure is based on the assumption that the entire programming team is equally involved in the problem definition, program design, coding, development, test plan development, testing and debugging, and software implementation. Having all members of the team involved in the various processes eliminates the communication problems and a waste of valuable resources.

There may be a problem of integrating new personnel into a team. Also, an organization's facilities may not provide for a conference room or work area where group discussions and debates on a software project may be conducted.

THE PROJECT MANAGEMENT CONCEPT

Project management is a formalized technique used by the manager to ensure the completion of a project on time, within the budget, and having achieved the desired results. The technique is considered to be the most efficient method for allocating, scheduling, and controlling an organization's resources in a given project. The efficiency may result from the need for continuous monitoring of a project and the generation of feedback on the project's actual status. This information gives the manager an opportunity to allocate and reallocate resources, and adjust the situation as necessary.

To utilize the concept, the manager must begin with well-defined objectives for the project. The definitions provide the manager with a clear understanding of what is to be done, why the project is being done, and with a definite starting and ending point for the project. The manager uses this information to identify the various tasks and subtasks to be performed, and the relationship between the tasks and subtasks in the overall project.

Based on time estimates secured from the users and the organization's own performance standards, the manager must establish realistic time estimates for each work unit (some combination of tasks and subtasks). The time estimates for the work units must fit into a realistic completion schedule for the project and be coupled with completion criteria for each work unit. The feedback on the monitored work units will then enable the manager to determine the actual progress and the quality of results achieved.

The manager must then outline his plan for the project. In preparing the plan, the manager will determine the specific work assignments that are to be delegated to the project's personnel. Wherever possible, the manager will attempt to balance the workload to improve on time estimates and effort requirements. The plan may be illustrated on a GANTT chart or PERT network diagram. The illustrated plan should enable the manager to visually monitor the project's status and view the effect of change on the project because the interrelated and concurrent activities are readily displayed.

FEEDBACK NEEDS

The personnel involved in a project must submit periodic reports on their activities. The feedback should indicate:

1. What the person has worked on
2. What the person plans to do next
3. What problems the person foresees that may require the manager's assistance

The manager must review the reports and evaluate their impact on the project. Based on the feedback, the manager may find it necessary to consider an alternative course of action to keep the project on target.

Project planning may not be very successful if:

1. There is no clear definition of what must be done
2. Adequate funding (see chapter 6) for the project is not available
3. Insufficient time is allowed for the project
4. The project leader is not a good administrator
5. The manager relies on word-of-mouth feedback rather than structured feedback
6. The project does not have upper-echelon involvement
7. The data processing manager and his subordinates do not believe in the project management concept
8. There is no quality review in the project
9. There are no performance standards for project scheduling
10. There are no documentation standards

Review Questions: Group 2F

1. Discuss one of the alternative types of organizational structure that may be used by a data processing manager in order to maximize the use of the human resource.
2. What are the benefits to be derived from utilizing the project management concept in an organizational structure?

SUMMARY

In this chapter, we have discussed the structural organization of data processing, together with the role of data processing in the overall organizational framework. If the data processing function is to be successful, it must be guided by the executive committee. It must also have a specific set of objectives and a particular setting within the organization. The interest in the data processing activity cannot be temporary; rather, it should be a continuing, active, and meaningful involvement because data processing sweeps vertically and horizontally across all functional activities.

Despite the importance of data processing, there is no clear-cut or magical way of structuring the function. Consequently, the structural format of each individual data processing function can vary; however, it should include the basic divisionalization into the systems analysis, design and development, software systems, planning and development, operations, and training groups. To make optimal use of the organization's resources, the data processing manager may also establish other functional structures, such as an applications group, a functional group, matrix organization, chief programmer and/or egoless programming teams, on a temporary or permanent basis.

The decision to adopt and/or implement a particular structural format involves consideration of the organizational objectives, size of the organization, budgets, available hardware, software, and personnel expertise.

Project management may also be used to help achieve a desired goal. However, the concept requires involvement by the executive committee, a dynamic project manager, adequate resources, a definable goal, and good controls. All projects do not readily lend themselves to this approach. It would not be feasible for an organization to concentrate its resources on a simple, relatively short-term project.

CASE STUDY 2.1

The Raleric Manufacturing Company

You have been employed by the Raleric Manufacturing Company as the data processing manager. In this capacity, you will report directly to the controller who is a member of the executive committee. The executive committee has delegated to you the responsibility for developing a structural format that will contribute to the overall effectiveness of the Raleric organization.

At present, the data processing operations group is a line activity directed and controlled by the manager of payroll services. The manager of payroll services reports directly to the superintendent of accounting, whose position places him at the staff level but not on the executive committee. The superintendent reports to the controller through the assistant controller.

The systems and procedures group, consisting of a systems analyst and three programmers, reports to the manager of industrial engineering. The manager, in a line-level position, reports directly to the director of engineering and manufacturing operations. The director's position is on the same level as that of the controller and is also an executive committee position.

There is also a satellite unit-record equipment operation, which is primarily concerned with the printing of merchandise shipping tickets, shipping notifications, and shipping releases. Data from these applications becomes input for the daily sales analysis report and for the weekly billing produced by the operations group. The operations manager is responsible for the satellite operation's personnel and equipment, but not for its operating schedule. That schedule is controlled by the manager of merchandise operations.

Training is presently limited to implementation of new systems and modifications. It is conducted by the systems analyst in conjuction with a personnel department member, who is concerned primarily with recruitment of personnel and, only secondarily, with organizational training.

A clerk in the payroll group is responsible for preparing and maintaining attendance reporting statistics. She keypunches her own input cards and has these verified by the data processing operations group. The data is used for a variety of weekly, monthly, quarterly, and annual reports, which are processed by the operations group. The operations manager is also responsible for the keypunch machine and for the storage of the source documents and input used in the absence-reporting application.

The engineering organization contracts with a local university for computer program writing, testing, debugging, and processing.

Discussion Questions

1. What structural format would you, as the data processing manager, recommend for the data processing activity? Be prepared to illustrate and defend your answer.
2. What type of structural format would you recommend for the programming function? Why? EGOLESS ⟹ MATRIX.
3. Do you agree with the split-responsibility arrangement for the satellite operation? If so, what are the advantages and disadvantages of such an arrangement? If not, how and why would you alter the arrangement?
4. Would you recommend that the training function be wholly absorbed by the personnel department in order to free your systems analyst for other responsibilities? Explain.
5. Would you recommend terminating the contract with the university and having the data processing function take on all of the programming activity needed for the engineering and technical operations? Explain.
6. Would you recommend the reassignment of the attendance statistics clerk to the data processing operations group? Explain.
7. Do you feel that the functional activity title "systems and procedures" has any pronounced influence upon the type of organizational format established? Explain.

CHAPTER 3

Staffing—

Personnel Selection,

Training, and Appraisal

INTRODUCTION / Before any operation can be initiated, a careful analysis of the manpower resource requirements must be undertaken. This analysis is concerned with both the goals and the manpower resources that are required and available.

After the manager has completed his definition of the broad objective, he should have a complete understanding of his specific objectives and tasks and a reasonable estimate of the resources available within a given time-frame. He can then inventory the available human resources to determine their experience, educational background, and trainability. This manpower is then matched with the draft of the organizational structure in order to study the relationships of the various positions and the strengths and weaknesses of each employee. Any defects in the organizational plan will be exposed at this time. Correction of them may require the creation of new or additional positions, elimination of positions, and/or the recruitment of additional personnel. When the organizational format has been made reasonably firm, the manager devotes his attention to the preparation of detailed job descriptions and related matters, together with the selection of personnel, the training of personnel, and the appraisal of personnel performance.

JOBS: DESCRIPTIONS, ANALYSIS, FACTORS, AND CLASSIFICATION LEVELS

Job Descriptions

A job description is a written statement about an individual position. It delineates the tasks, duties, and responsibilities associated with the position. It is the manager who prepares a job description for each position within the data processing structure. These descriptions become the basis for recruitment, selection, training, and appraisal of personnel.

Most job descriptions cover the following ten basic topics:

1. Job title
2. Wage rate, salary, and salary range
3. Tasks and duties
4. Reporting to whom
5. Relationship to total structure
6. Number of subordinates
7. Equipment involved
8. Working conditions
9. Physical demands
10. Specialized qualifications

1. JOB TITLE. The job title is used to identify the position within the structure. It is relevant only to the organization in which this classification has been made; it cannot be used readily to identify a position in another organization because titles and their descriptions differ greatly from organization to organization. Therefore, any inter-organizational comparison must be coupled with a description of the position's tasks, duties, responsibilities, and other requirements.

2. WAGE RATE, SALARY, SALARY RANGE. The remuneration specification for the position indicates whether the employee is paid on an hourly, weekly, monthly, or annual basis. If a salary range is included, it indicates the lower and upper compensation values for the position. The description should also indicate whether the amount is incremented either on a progression scale (in which case the step structure should be included) or merit basis. Due to the sensitivity of this topic, some organizations will not include the wage or salary on the job description.

3. TASKS AND DUTIES. The listing of tasks and duties defines the specific responsibility for the position. These specifications give the employee a clear understanding of what is expected of him and provide a basis for managerial evaluation of performance. In addition, they are particularly useful for indicating the training requirements for a given position.

4. REPORTING TO WHOM. There must be a clear designation of the supervisory position to which this position is subordinate. This identifies the immediate relationship to the chain of command. And it makes it clear to the employee as to whom he should notify or consult when problems or questions arise. It also indicates where instructions originate, as well, and the extent of the delegated authority.

5. RELATIONSHIP TO TOTAL STRUCTURE. The channels of communication that need to be established and/or maintained are delineated by indicating the relationship of the employee's position to the overall organizational structure.

6. NUMBER OF SUBORDINATES. The job description for a managerial position

must indicate the number of subordinates included in the span of control. It must also specify the number and type or types of personnel to be directed and controlled by the manager.

7. EQUIPMENT INVOLVED. In data processing occupations, specialized equipment is involved in most job positions, particularly in the programming and operations areas. The equipment involved in these jobs should therefore be specified for all positions, especially for newly created ones. Such specifications are particularly important in the recruitment, selection, and training of personnel. The type of equipment also indicates the training, background, and experience required of an employee in order to successfully perform the tasks and duties associated with each position.

8. WORKING CONDITIONS. These are concerned with environmental factors, legal requirements, and schedules. Noise and temperature are two common environmental factors to which an employee may be subjected in data processing occupations. The number of hours in a work week, the shift work requirements, and frequency of overtime are affected by the operating schedule. An employee should be made aware of these schedule requirements before he agrees to accept the position.

There may also be certain contractual obligations with a labor union which may require working on a rotating shift basis. This specification should be included in the job description.

9. PHYSICAL DEMANDS. For most data processing occupations, the physical demands are the same as for typical office positions. In some installations, limited walking may be required, or perhaps the need to physically transport cards and other materials. In punched card installations, though, the positions may well involve a considerable amount of standing, moving, and lifting. It is obvious that the proper planning and layout of the equipment and traffic patterns in an installation or organization generally have a strong influence on the physical demands required of the employees. (Installation planning and layout are discussed further in chapter 7).

10. SPECIALIZED QUALIFICATIONS. Some positions require that an employee possess specialized training and experience in order to cope with the demands of particular jobs. In upper-level positions, such as those in the systems, programming, and planning areas, these specialized requirements may be exacting. For example, such a position may require a university or college degree in a particular subject-matter field; an advanced degree plus managerial, planning, or programming experience in a subject-matter or functional area; or successful completion of specialized programming or subject-matter courses.

Figure 3.1 illustrates a job description used by one organization. Note that some of the previously discussed topics have not been included on the form. It is a practice of this organization to include only so-called necessary information on the form for managerial positions. The salary, for example, is deleted because it is considered confidential information. The job description forms for the subordinate personnel would include all of the previously discussed topics.

JOB DESCRIPTION

Job Title: Associate Director of Information Systems

Department: Information Systems

Reporting to: Director of Information Systems

Responsible for: Computing Resources Planning and Management Group

Major Duties: Will analyze and prepare the budget requests of an eight-campus distributed network supporting educational data systems and instruction; analyze the computing requirements for preparing and maintaining a master network plan; review and evaluate the hardware, software and other facility requirements; recommend the organizational staffing patterns for the network facilities; audit the resource requirements and actual utilization and make recommendations to the Director, when necessary; administer and manage the resource procurement process for the network; direct and control a professional and technical staff that will perform planning, evaluate and select hardware, software and supplies, and perform the necessary coordinations with user facilities.

Specialized Qualifications: Knowledge of cost-benefit analysis and budgeting. The ability to prepare vendor specifications and criteria for the procurement, evaluation and selection of hardware, software, and supplies. Requires a bachelor's degree and five years experience, two at the management level, in a computing facility with a batch and time-sharing operation.

Figure 3.1 Sample job description

Job Analysis

The requirements and specifications for managerial or nonmanagerial positions are determined as the result of a job analysis. This process involves the collection of data elements regarding the position and integrating the elements into a narrative format that results in a job description.

For a newly created position, the manager must ascertain all of the mental, physical, and manual factors. These specifications and requirements will be only temporary, as should be clearly indicated on the job description form. When the position has been filled, it must then be restudied to determine the adequacy or inadequacy of the original requirements and specifications. Initially, then, the job description offers a set of guidelines to assist in the recruitment and selection of personnel, and in the direction and control of an activity.

A position currently authorized and manned must be studied in detail by the manager or a trained job analyst. This audit will determine the tasks and duties being performed, as well as the accuracy and relevancy of the job requirements and specifications.

There are various ways of undertaking the analysis of a job, but it is important to emphasize that each way requires that the employee be advised of the purpose and extent of the study. This is essential for maintenance of good employee relations because job analyses are conducted for purposes of promotion, training, and performance evaluation, as well as for establishment of new positions and the development or evaluation of current job descriptions.

Job Factors

In each job analysis method, selected job factors must be given consideration. These factors represent certain basic requirements in a position and are subsequently used as a basis of wage rate or salary determination and job classification level assignment. The factors are arbitrarily established by each organization and depend on the activity requirements for a given position.

The factors most frequently considered in connection with data processing occupations are:

Education

Experience

Training

Physical demands

Working conditions

Equipment

Mental attitude

Ability to work with others

Ability to communicate

Technical skills

Job Skills (flowcharting, coding, documentation, testing, and debugging)

Speed

Accuracy

Varying degrees of importance or worth are accorded to each of these factors, based on job requirements. The education factor in a job analysis is used to determine the level of mental development needed to understand and perform the related tasks. In performing the job analysis, the manager or job analyst determines the level of mental development required for the position. This determination is compared against a previously established scale. The scale indicates the mental requirement for a given level on the scale and the worth of that level. For example, the lowest level for mental development on the scale may require the ability to read and write, add and subtract numbers. The upper end of the scale may require the technical knowledge to deal with much more complex problems. Subsequently, a value or worth must be assigned to each of these levels on the scale for wage and salary determination and job-level classification assignment.

Job Classification Levels

Jobs can be graded or classified with respect to levels of relative importance. At present, nearly every position in the data processing field falls into one of the three following categories:

1. The specialist level
2. The skilled level
3. The trainee level

1. THE SPECIALIST LEVEL. This level applies to positions normally regarded as key technical positions in the organization. Each such position requires that the job holder has full technical knowledge, plus the competency to operate effectively at the highest level. People qualify for specialist rating by virtue of training and experience in one or more subject-matter areas and by demonstrating their ability to coordinate, direct, and control others, with minimal supervision of their own activities. Such people include project coordinators, directors and leaders, together with senior systems analysts, senior systems analyst/programmers, senior information systems planners, senior systems programmers, senior applications programmers, senior computer operators, data control group leaders, user liaisons, and work process schedulers. In many organizations, job titles with an "A" suffix may also be considered in this classification, i.e., Systems Programmer A.

2. THE SKILLED LEVEL. Positions at this level require average knowledge of a subject-matter specialty, plus the ability to perform under an average-to-minimal amount of supervision. Generally, people in this category are capable of working on several phases or projects with enough self-direction so that they need only general direction. In some instances, skilled personnel are delegated minor direction and control responsibility. Included in this category are systems analysts, junior systems analysts, applications programmers, systems programmers, computer operators, and data control clerks. Also, included in this category may be job titles with "B" and "C" suffixes, e.g., Systems Analyst/Programmer B.

3. THE TRAINEE LEVEL. Included in this category are people employed at the base or entry level, as well as those being trained or developed in a particular skill or subject-matter specialty for ultimate progression to the skilled level. The trainees perform routine functions requiring constant direction and control. Among the people in this category are trainees for management, software, systems, planning, operations, and training, together with program coders, coding clerks, data control clerks, and tape and disk handlers.

Figure 3.2 illustrates the application of the classification method to the programming activity, as well as possible progression or career paths through the three levels within that occupational grouping. (Of course, the actual progression or career paths vary from organization to organization.)

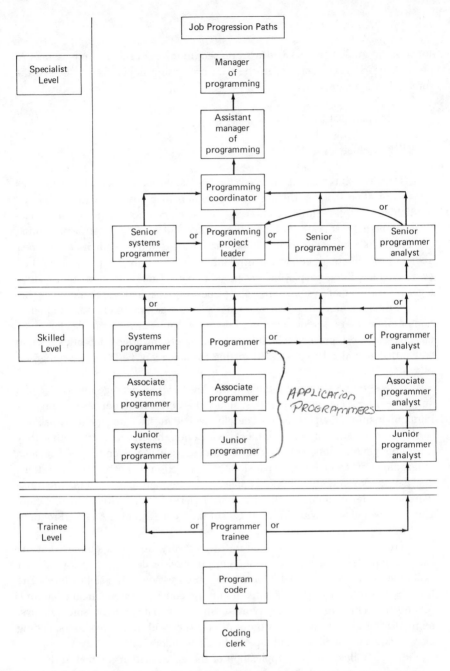

Figure 3.2 Job classification levels and job progression paths in programming activity

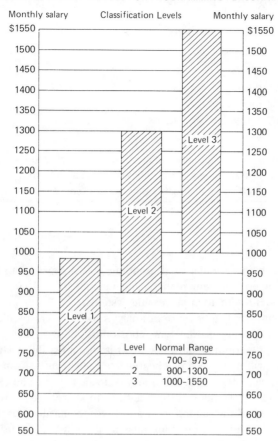

NORMAL SALARY RANGES FOR PROGRAMMING PERSONNEL

Level	Normal Range
1	700– 975
2	900–1300
3	1000–1550

Figure 3.3 Sample chart of classification levels and salary ranges

The effect of classification levels on salary ranges is illustrated in Figure 3.3. Each level has a normal range with a stated upper and lower salary parameter. The job factors and the classification levels are used to establish the monetary worth of each position.

Review Questions: Group 3A

1. What are the ten basic topics included in a job description?
2. Discuss one of the job classification levels particularly relevant to data processing personnel. What job titles may be included at that level?

OCCUPATIONAL GROUPINGS

There are five major occupational groupings in the data processing activity. These are:

1. Systems analysis
2. Programming
3. Computer operations
4. Peripheral equipment operations
5. Data control

Within each of these occupational groupings are included the manager, specialist, skilled, and trainee levels. As to specific positions, there are a variety of titles based upon individual or organizational preferences, as well as external influences.

Systems Analysis

The personnel in this occupational grouping are responsible for the analysis, design, development, implementation, and maintenance of computerized and non-computerized information processing systems.

The entire process begins with an analysis of the users requirements. The requirements, problems, parameters, constraints, performance criteria, costs and benefits are determined and evaluated through a feasibility study. The systems personnel will make recommendations to the executive committee. Based on these recommendations, a decision may be made to design an alternative system. The systems personnel will then develop an alternative approach that will support the needs of the organization and be economically, operationally, and technically feasible. Again, a decision must be made by the executive committee to determine if detailed development of a system should be undertaken. If a "go" decision is made, the systems personnel will then prepare the necessary specifications and coordinate the detailed development and testing of the alternative system. In addition, the systems personnel will prepare the necessary documentation (see chapter 4) and training for all personnel that will be interacting with the system. The system must then be implemented for productive use. After some period of time, a system evaluation is performed to determine if the system is functioning as expected and performing the needed tasks.

Periodically the systems personnel must perform maintenance on existing systems to implement any changes that may be required in an operationally effective system.

Programming

The traditional business and scientific programmer job categories have been expanded into the business (applications) programmers, scientific programmers, systems (software) programmers, maintenance programmers, telecommunications (on-line) specialists, and data base specialists. In order to provide some clarity to the tasks and duties performed by software personnel, the American Federation of Information Processing Societies conducted a survey in 1974 that resulted in a broad list. These were narrowed down into standard tasks and published in the *Computer Programmer Job Analysis Reference Text* (see bibliography).

The tasks of the software systems personnel are not unlike the tasks performed by the systems analysts. The software personnel must begin every project with an understanding of the requirements and data flows. This information is communicated to the software group by the systems analysts and user personnel. In addition, the software personnel must understand the data descriptions, file layouts, processes to be performed, performance criteria, and exception processing requirements.

From the planning and analysis stages, the software personnel embark on a design of programs, modules, and routines that will provide the desired end result. The design may be illustrated and/or described by using flowcharts, decision tables, narratives, outlines, and top-down or bottom-up structures. In developing the design, the software personnel must optimize processing time, perform storage trade-off analyses, and develop optimal data handling and computational procedures. The designs are discussed with the systems analyst and user personnel to make them aware of the required data designs and program flows in the overall information processing system.

Having gained the necessary approvals, the software personnel must then select a program language that will most effectively execute the job and begin to code the programs from the formal design. The coding is then desk checked for clerical and logical accuracy, and proper linkages to modules and/or subprograms. The software personnel must also develop "artificial" test data and a test plan to facilitate testing and debugging of the complete program and all interfaces. The program must then be tested with "live" data to ensure compliance with the formal specifications and desired objectives.

The software personnel must also develop the necessary documentation for user, operations, data control, and systems personnel.

There would be some refinements of these tasks and perhaps inclusions of other tasks for covering all of the duties and responsibilities of the software personnel. For example, the systems (software) programmers would also be responsible for designing and developing hardware, software, operating systems, and specialized software, package tests and/or trouble-shooting problems with the operating system software.

Computer Operations

This occupational grouping primarily includes those personnel that are responsible for maintaining the operation of the computer. In a large computer center, or data center as it is sometimes referred to, the computer operations personnel are assisted by tape and disk librarians and peripheral equipment operators.

The role of the computer operator is more than just pushing buttons, changing magnetic tapes or disk packs, loading card files into the card reader, and/or unloading the stackers of the card reader/punch unit. The computer operator must review the documentation of each job, determine the necessary equipment setup for each job, secure the necessary data files, prepare the job control, execute the proper error and recovery procedures, maintain a log of operations, and report all malfunctions to the operations supervisor.

In larger computer centers, the computer operator will direct and control the activities of other operations personnel and will maintain control for manipulating and actuating controls for the central processing unit (CPU). The sophistication of operating systems software requires that the computer operator be an "alert" person because the position requires considerable responsibility as mistakes can be very costly and time-consuming.

The position of tape and disk librarian is also included in this occupational category. Many organizations require that the computer operator work as a librarian to learn the importance of proper file handling procedures. The tape and disk librarian is responsible for maintaining control over disk packs, magnetic and paper tape, and magnetic cassettes. The responsibility includes recordkeeping for the classification, cataloging and storage of the various media used in the operations.

In addition, the librarian is responsible for inspection for wear and damage, scraping, cleaning and cutting of magnetic tapes, cleaning of magnetic disk packs, and splicing of paper tape to increase their effective utilization. In organizations utilizing computer-output microfilm, the librarian is also responsible for maintaining control over processing, cataloging, storage, and distribution of that medium.

Peripheral Equipment Operations

The personnel in this occupational grouping are responsible for the operation of such peripheral equipment as sorters, collators, high-speed printers, optical scanning units, data communications units, computer-output microfilm units, and so on.

The peripheral equipment operators may also be used to assist computer operators in data handling, changing of tape and disk drives, and securing the necessary input files and storage of data and output files. The title may also be used to include the data entry occupations such as keypunching or operating other key-driven devices such as key-to-tape, key-to-disk, or cathode-ray tube terminals.

Data Control

The personnel in this occupational grouping are involved with scheduling; preparation of records for data entry; maintaining various control records and source data for recurring reports; coding of source data for data entry purposes; decollation, bursting, binding, and distribution of reports; distribution of output media, such as microfilm; and maintenance of files and records.

Many organizations have a formal group to facilitate data entry and distribution of outputs. Most organizations have at least one person in this occupational grouping. Smaller organizations may include the responsibilities for the tape and disk library in this job category.

SELECTION OF PERSONNEL

The effectiveness of an organization is dependent upon the availability of personnel that are able to efficiently and successfully complete the necessary duties and responsibilities of the data processing function. The problem for the data processing manager is to locate and develop the kinds of personnel that will meet the organization's needs. The problem is that the data processing manager may select personnel that are either underqualified or overqualified. Personnel in the former category may not be able to complete the necessary tasks and, as a result, the organization may design, develop, and implement information processing systems that may fail to meet the stated objectives. Also, there may be much trial-and-error activity and this will result in missed schedules and a waste of budget, time, hardware, software, and material resources. The underqualified personnel may also become very frustrated by their efforts and leave the organization. Overqualified personnel may also become frustrated because they are being underutilized and their efforts may also result in poorly implemented information processing systems. Such persons may subsequently leave the organization and create turnover problems for the data processing manager and the organization.

Desirable Personality Traits and Job Skills

The data processing manager must search for the proper combination of personality traits and job skills when evaluating prospective and current personnel. It is important to recognize that these attitudes and characteristics should not be limited to the recruitment and selection process. Identification of the personality traits and job skills is also important for personnel development and performance appraisal.

The desirable attitudes and characteristics include the following:

Attention to detail
Ability to look critically at one's own work
Ability to reason and draw conclusions
Ability to develop meaningful test data and test plans
Ability to work well with and through other people
Ability to communicate orally and in writing

DEPENDABLE!

Adaptability to rapid change

Ability to handle multiple assignments

Ability to tolerate stress and work under pressure

Dependability

Ability to describe a problem and solution in graphic and/or narrative form

Ability to maintain organized work habits

Ability to produce work with a minimum number of errors

Ability to produce large amounts of usable work (coding, documentation, forms) in a limited amount of time

Ability to define a problem into its component parts and determine the relationships between the parts

Education Levels

A data processing manager must realistically appraise the educational requirements for each position within the data processing organization. There is a general tendency to overstate the educational requirements for a given position. For example, an organization may stipulate that the position for Computer Operator A must be staffed by a computer science graduate of a four-year program. This is a rather obvious overstatement of actual need for the position. One must question the need for knowledge of calculus and subjects like discrete structures to operate the console of a computing system. There is also a tendency to overstate the educational requirements for applications programmers, in many organizations.

Overstatement of requirements may lead to personnel morale and turnover problems. A person that is overqualified for a position may feel underutilized because the tasks assigned represent no challenge. Also, if the salary is not commensurate with the educational requirements, the person may express dissatisfaction with the arrangement and search for a new and more satisfying position.

Sources of Employees

Personnel recruitment and selection is a very costly activity. An organization may spend between $1500 and $5000 to hire an employee. Included in this cost are such items as advertising, interviewing, testing, travel, agency fees, and telephone charges. Although the high cost may result largely or exclusively from the use of outside placement services, the cost of using an in-house personnel-seeking group may well be comparable. So it behooves an organization to investigate each available source and to gain access to the best possible candidates available. This may help to reduce personnel turnover and the associated costs.

There are several basic kinds of sources from which to recruit candidates for the various occupational groupings. These include:

1. Other organizations
2. Colleges and universities
3. Professional associations
4. Specialized employment agencies
5. Management consultants
6. Other units within organization

1. OTHER ORGANIZATIONS. These constitute the most common source for recruiting experienced personnel, particularly when a specialized skill or a specific experience background is required. Personnel in data processing are nomadic by reputation and willing to move for a promotion, increase in salary, new challenge, or a chance to acquire new or more experience. These wanderers are generally recruited as a result of personal contact by the manager, one of his colleagues, or a subordinate. Sometimes they are found through advertising.

2. COLLEGES AND UNIVERSITIES. There are a number of community and junior colleges as well as some four-year colleges offering two- and four-year degree programs in machine operation, programming, systems, computer sciences, and related subjects. They provide personnel for entry at the trainee and skilled levels. Graduates of four-year institutions who show an aptitude for programming may be employed and trained at the equipment vendor's school or in the organization's own facility. They may then be assigned to programming at the trainee or skilled level. Many business administration majors are accepted as systems trainees. Mathematics majors are generally accepted as programmer trainees; experience has proven that other majors can also qualify for this position.

Many organizations send professional recruiters or members of their personnel department to the campuses to screen potential employees. Or they notify the college placement centers about positions available. Students who have registered with the placement centers are then notified about these availabilities.

In some communities, college students preparing to graduate are interviewed during the Christmas vacation period at a centralized location established either by the local chamber of commerce or a professional business group. Such an arrangement gives an organization an excellent opportunity to screen a large number of potential candidates.

3. PROFESSIONAL ASSOCIATIONS. Professional associations such as the Data Processing Management Association have formal or informal placement committees at the chapter level. These committees are able to provide organizations leads or résumés on potential candidates. Generally, a manager must be a member of such an association in order to participate in the placement service and thereby gain access to potential candidates.

4. SPECIALIZED EMPLOYMENT AGENCIES. There are a number of specialized employment agencies, sometimes called personnel consultants, that recruit potential candidates on a fee basis paid by the employers. The fees for most data processing positions range from 10 percent to 22 percent of the annual salary. The effectiveness of such an agency is very dependent upon the skill of the

recruiter and the reputation of the agency. The difficulty with utilizing many of these agencies is that they only direct or refer candidates to the employer; it becomes the employer's task to do the actual screening. However, some agencies do effectively screen out candidates within a given set of parameters.

5. MANAGEMENT CONSULTANTS. Like hardware vendors, management consultants also have an opportunity to observe potential candidates. In addition, they may also serve as screening agencies for the employer; in fact, some of them will actively recruit personnel for clients.

6. OTHER UNITS WITHIN ORGANIZATION. An organization—especially a large organization—can turn out to be an excellent but frequently overlooked source of personnel for itself. It provides an opportunity for employees to move up from within—a form of promotion that can be used to reward an employee for being conscientious, aggressive, and loyal. Non-data processing employees who are subject-matter-oriented can be trained in data processing techniques. Furthermore, as a result of their familiarity with company policies and practices, they can require less training time and can become productive sooner.

Many organizations have developed and maintained a skills inventory to facilitate employee selection. The inventories will generally contain data on experience with programming languages, operating systems, type of equipment, file structures, telecommunications, and data base techniques. The inventory may also include a self-evaluation of expertise and in some instances the data processing manager's assessment of an individual's expertise. The inventory will also include data on an individual's education with emphasis on courses that particularly relate to the job.

The information gained from a skills inventory can be used by the data processing manager for selection of personnel, upgrading to a more responsible position, to determine training and personnel development needs, and for determining the kinds of resources that are available for future development of information processing systems.

The Interview Process

The interview process should begin with an initial screening of potential candidates by reviewing the employment applications and résumés. The screening process determines the suitability or unsuitability of the candidates by comparing their skills, experience, and education levels to stated organization needs. Those candidates that are found to be suitable are selected for the next step in the interview process. The next step in the process may involve testing of the potential candidate. If the candidate is successful he then continues with the interview process. In many organizations, the testing procedure is not conducted until the employee has undergone several interviews and is found to be an acceptable potential candidate.

Some organizations employ a pre-interview technique to determine the applicant's suitability for the position. The pre-interview process is not an in-depth process. It is meant to clarify the organization's requirements for the benefit of the candidate and to determine if the candidate is still interested in the position. The pre-interview process may also uncover some personality flaws in a potential candidate that may be unacceptable to the organization.

The candidates for the position are now given an opportunity for a face-to-face meeting with the manager. In some organizations, the candidates will actually interview with several managers and possibly some senior data processing personnel on an individual or collective basis. This process enables the interviewer or interviewers to become personally acquainted with the candidate, to observe the candidate's motivation, appearance, ideas, reactions, and ability to express himself; and to discuss and explore the candidate's background, education, experience, and training. In turn, the candidate has an opportunity to learn more about the position in detail, as well as working conditions, salary, fringe benefits, and appraisal practices. Some of the latter information may actually be discussed and covered in the pre-interview.

Candor in the interview process is very important. The lack of candor may result in losing a suitable candidate or a new employee may become a turnover statistic because of dissatisfaction with the position.

The interviewer or interviewers must prepare themselves for the interview process. A potential candidate will form his impressions about an organization from his interviewers, the appearance of the setting in which the interview is conducted, and the kinds of questions that are asked. Many organizations have prepared a list of questions to be asked during the interview and an interview results form, for standardization purposes. This action may be particularly important to organizations that are involved in Affirmative Action employment programs.

It is also very important that the interviewers are aware of the position for which the candidate is being interviewed. The job factors vary and these must be considered in the interview process. For example, the job requirements for a systems analyst are very different from those for an applications or software programmer. The questions must be framed in such a manner as to determine if the candidate meets the minimum technical expectations of the position. Also, the interviewers must determine if this candidate will fit into the data processing organization; what are the candidate's strengths and weaknesses; and what special personality traits and job skills the candidate possesses.

It is important that the interviewer place the candidate at ease during the interview session. This may be accomplished initially by asking basic questions regarding the candidate's orientation with a particular hardware device, program language, operating system, or data gathering technique. It is important that the interviewer keep the candidate talking in order to make observations about the interviewee's ability to communicate, discuss technical matters, and so on. But it is also important that the interviewer control the interview session to gather the needed decision-making data about the potential candidate.

On conclusion of the interview, it is essential that the interviewer record his observations on the interview results form. After interviewing all of the candidates, the interview results forms can be reviewed by the manager to select the most suitable candidate or group of candidates. In some organizations, additional interviews may be conducted to select the most suitable candidate.

Because of the threat of a possible discrimination suit for an organization, the data processing manager must conduct uniform interviews. The manager may be forced to prove the validity and fairness of the interview process and techniques.

References

References are still included in the selection process, but their value is questionable. Many organizations will not respond to a reference inquiry beyond some very basic questions about term of employment, salary history, or whether the employer would rehire a former employee. The reluctance has resulted from damage suits instituted by former employees after having received adverse references. Some organizations are asking potential employees to sign waivers permitting the organization to secure a reference and freeing the cooperating organization from legal liability.

Some organizations are utilizing the telephone to contact employee references. It is thought that the manner in which a reference responds will confirm or support an interviewer's opinion. Lack of enthusiasm or reluctance in the response may indicate that the reference is unwilling to provide a positive report. Many organizations when contacted in such a manner will refuse to respond unless they are certain of the caller's identity.

Testing

Tests are included in the selection process because they can either furnish information that cannot be obtained any other way or validate information secured by some other method. The tests are not in themselves used as a selection determinant, but rather as a supplementary device utilized as objectively as possible. Consequently, test scores are combined with other factors to help the manager formulate a balanced judgment about a prospective employee.

The possible threat of discrimination suits has forced many organizations to abandon their testing procedures as part of the selection process. This action, however, may not protect an organization from legal scrutiny. Other organizations have moved to validate their test procedures either by in-house or outside specialists. Though there are several methods of test validation, most organizations are utilizing the content validation method. Test experts believe that tests developed under this method are actually valid before they are administered to an applicant. They base their opinion on the fact that the tests include questions and tasks that are truly representative of the job. For example, a systems programmer's position would be analyzed and a test developed that included job tasks, such as the ability to code job control statements and/or troubleshoot an internal problem in an operating system.

The tests, which are principally psychological, are grouped together in the following five categories:

1. General intelligence tests
2. Aptitude tests
3. Proficiency tests
4. Tests relating to occupational interests
5. Personality tests

1. GENERAL INTELLIGENCE TESTS. These are designed to indicate a person's capacity to understand and learn. They cannot be used to indicate his ability to apply his learning and understanding in his work. General intelligence tests measure such traits as verbal and numerical ability, word fluency, abstract and logical reasoning, space perception, judgment, and memory. The results of such a test may be given either as a total score, called a global score, or as separate scores for each element of the test (such as verbal, numerical, or abstract reasoning).

Test instruments included in this category are, California Test of Mental Maturity, and the SRA–Primary Mental Abilities Test.

2. APTITUDE TESTS. These are designed to predict success in an occupation or future assignment by measuring the traits or abilities necessary for success in a specialty. The tests measure logical thinking and reasoning, instruction comprehension, coding ability, numerical ability, memory, verbal ability, and other required traits or abilities.

The Programmers Aptitude Test, and the Revised Programmers Aptitude Test are the most popular in the aptitude test category.

3. PROFICIENCY TESTS. These are constructed to measure either a person's ability to perform a task or his practical knowledge of a specialty. In essence, they measure the mental and physical capability of an applicant. The applicant is required to perform a given task that simulates a real job setting, such as writing a program, drawing a system or program flowchart, wiring a control panel, or keypunching a deck of cards.

The NCR–Electronic Data Processing Test is a good example of a test in this category. However, many organizations are performing job analyses and preparing tests that relate to their own data processing positions.

4. TESTS RELATING TO OCCUPATIONAL INTERESTS. These are designed to measure an applicant's occupational interests through numerous, rather indirect questions concerning his own characteristics. The tests do not provide an indicator of ability or success, but they should reflect the general scope and strength of an individual's interests. In evaluating this type of test, the applicant's likes and dislikes for various activities, persons, and things are compared with those of persons who have become a success in a given field. It must be remembered, though, that the results provide no proof that the applicant himself may be qualified for achievement in the occupational grouping or that his interests will remain unchanged.

The Strong Vocational Interest Blank and the Kuder Preference Tests for Vocational and Personal Interests are the most popular test instruments in this category.

5. PERSONALITY TESTS. These constitute an attempt to determine the general psychological makeup of an individual in terms of traits that cannot readily be determined by direct observation or interviewing. The traits investigated include emotions, confidence, stability, aggressiveness, sociability, extroversion, objectivity, and impulsiveness. Such tests attempt to determine an individual's attitudes toward himself, toward others, and toward various aspects of life, as well as how he thinks others regard him. If he has not been properly trained in testing procedures, the user of this type of testing device should be very cautious in how he interprets the results. However, he does not necessarily have to rely upon himself for qualified interpretation. Many colleges and universities maintain centers for test administration and interpretation. Furthermore, there are psychologists in private practice who also provide such services.

Nevertheless, personality tests are still highly controversial. They have their supporters, of course, but there are also many people who are convinced that the tests should be scrapped and that other means should be used to secure the same information. Without weighing all of the arguments, it may be appropriate to refer here to a colleague of the author's, who strongly advocates the use of this type of test in personnel selection. He supports his argument by stating that in those instances where the organization executives have overridden a negative recommendation by their psychologist, they have subsequently been proven wrong.

Before leaving the subject of personality tests, it may be interesting to briefly discuss a recent and perhaps somewhat unorthodox innovation in personality testing. This is the now-increasing use of handwriting analysis as a tool for personality assessment. Graphologists contend that handwriting is a spontaneous expression of a person's feelings, thoughts, and attitudes.

In most instances, the sample used is the handwritten application or other documents used in the recruitment process. The applicant may also be asked to write a brief statement about his interests, or some other subject, on an 8½" x 11" sheet of unlined paper. A trained graphologist takes the handwriting sample and analyzes it in terms of the strokes, slants, spaces, and signs, as well as the size of the margins. The results of the analysis are then interpreted by the graphologist to arrive at a personality profile of the applicant.

Though this testing technique has been assailed or ridiculed by many people, it does appear to be gaining in industrial acceptance, as indicated by the fact that some of the prestigious "Fortune 500" companies are now using it as part of the selection process. Such users apparently accept the idea that a valid correlation exists between the graphologist's assessments and the applicant's actual characteristics.

One of the major problems with handwriting analysis is the exactness of the method of analysis. The analysis is based on a graphologist's judgment because there are no measurable or ratable scales available for evaluation purposes. Also, empirical studies conducted by testing experts have shown that attempts to relate the handwriting elements to personality traits rarely yield positive results. Physical handicaps (such as a vision defect) may affect the validity of the test results.

The Guilford-Zimmerman Temperament Survey and the Minnesota Multiphasic Personality Inventory are two of the more popular personality tests administered to potential candidates.

Review Questions: Group 3B

1. What personality traits or job skills are desirable in a potential candidate for a data processing position?
2. Why is the personnel selection process such a costly item?
3. What are the sources for potential employees needed in a data processing activity? Discuss briefly the merits of each source.
4. Why is the interview such an important tool in the selection of personnel?
5. What is the purpose of a proficiency test?

TRAINING OF PERSONNEL

Training is a method of teaching theory and application to people in order to increase their operational effectiveness. Because it is essential to have personnel who are able to analyze problems and develop solutions for them, one important objective of any training program should be to encourage the development of the ability to think, rather than the learning of a set of techniques to be applied in accordance with a predefined set of rules.

There are several major advantages accruing to the organization that conducts an efficient personnel training program. Such a program:

1 Increases personnel efficiency because the employees are informed about the organization's policies, practices, and procedures. Also, it reduces the "break in" time, thereby making a person fully productive sooner.

2 Helps to reduce personnel turnover. People who are given training feel that the organization is interested in them and that it is willing to utilize their abilities.

3 Instills a spirit of cooperation and teamwork in the employees. People work better when they feel that they are a part of the organization. Training gives them an opportunity for promotion, acquiring responsibility, and performing new functions or activities.

4 Lowers the operating costs. A person functions more productively when he understands what must be done and what he is expected to do in accomplishing the goal.

5 Eases the manager's work load. A properly trained person accomplishes the assigned tasks with less supervision, thereby enabling the manager to devote more time to other management activities.

Training Methods

There are many methods that can be used, but all of them customarily fall into one or another of two major categories. These categories are formal training and informal training.

The actual choice of training program and method depends on the current and future objectives of the organization. A manager must realistically assess the skills and abilities of his own staff to select the best approach. He must also extend the assessment beyond his own activity to all functional activities within the organization for training of managerial and user personnel. Training for these personnel may well provide future benefits in the form of improved communications and tangible benefits.

FORMAL TRAINING

Formal programs are concerned with specific techniques, such as those involved in management games and programmed learning, as well as seminars conducted by equipment vendors. Formal programs provide intensive training in problems of varying degrees of difficulty that an individual may or may not encounter in an on-the-job situation. The material presented is either generalized or specialized depending upon the training objectives and needs of the organization.

Much of the training utilizes a classroom situation. A typical formal program is generally concentrated into a brief time span—a day, several days, or a week—or it may be extended over a period of weeks or months. Some programs are conducted on the basis of one full day of classes per week. Others represent a type of work-study program, in which employees work in the morning or afternoon for several hours and then attend classes either before or after the work period.

One disadvantage to the formal method is that a person in training is at least partially nonproductive for some period of time. However, training costs are incurred with the anticipation that short-term losses will eventually become long-term gains.

The actual choice of formal training program depends on the current and future objectives of an organization. An organization will train and develop employees, teaching them skills required to perform their tasks, preparing them for acceptance of additional responsibilities or placement in more demanding jobs, and instructing them in the management process.

The most commonly used methods in a formal training program are:

1. Management games
2. College and university courses
3. Programs offered by professional associations
4. Programs offered by management consultants
5. Training supplied by hardware vendors
6. Professional education services

7. Programmed learning

8. Organizational training groups

1. MANAGEMENT GAMES. These constitute a teaching technique designed to develop the decision-making ability of an individual; experience in management functions; and the effective utilization of resources.

Most management games are group-participation activities based on the use of competitive teams. In a typical game, each team is given a set of conditions to apply in order to produce quantitative results. Although the educational value and effectiveness of these games have been questioned by some authorities, management games have proven to be beneficial in providing employees with awareness of how interdependent activities affect both the management process and the steps involved in decision making.

The games customarily considered most relevant to training in the data processing field are general management games and functional games. General management games are most commonly used for training managers. These games utilize abstract models of generalized companies in generalized industries, with emphasis on executive decision-making activities that can be affected by a number of interacting variables. Ordinarily, the playing of these games involves the use of medium- or large-scale computing systems, although some games are handscored instead. Functional games are aimed at developing specific skills or techniques through simulating one element or one aspect of the business structure, such as managing a programming function. The design of a functional game may require the use of competing teams or the interaction of an individual within the parameters and constraints of a game, i.e., holidays, limited budgets, and so on. Most of these games are played in conjunction with a computer.

2. COLLEGE AND UNIVERSITY COURSES. Many colleges and universities are well-equipped with specialized equipment, facilities, and instructors to provide a variety of data processing programs, such as lectures, courses, workshops, institutes, and conferences. Some of these programs are specifically tailored to the needs of a particular organization or industry. Most, however, are general programs intended to provide training in a variety of subjects for many interested persons. In many cases, the educational institutions award credit hours, which may be applied toward degree-granting programs—thus enabling participants to continue their formal education after the training session has been completed.

Anyone desiring information about available courses should contact the registrar's office or the continuing education office at local colleges and universities.

3. PROGRAMS OFFERED BY PROFESSIONAL ASSOCIATIONS. These organizations conduct specialized seminars and development programs for members and nonmembers. The American Management Association, for example, offers a variety of seminars for the development of personnel. And such organizations as the Association for Systems Management, the Data Processing Management Association, and the Association for Computing Machinery offer seminars on a local,

regional, or national basis for interested persons. They also offer self-development programs through participation in study groups, informal discussions with other members, and information made available through newsletters, journals, and other association publications.

4. PROGRAMS OFFERED BY MANAGEMENT CONSULTANTS. Using the programs provided by management consultant firms is becoming a popular way of providing training for an organization's personnel at all levels, so that these firms are now very much involved in the training of personnel. They have developed a variety of general and specialized seminars, which are available in all major U.S. cities. In addition, they also develop, on a contract basis, special seminars and programs designed to fit an organization's own needs and desires. These customized courses may be presented by either the consultant's staff or the organization's own training specialists.

5. TRAINING SUPPLIED BY HARDWARE VENDORS. Hardware vendors are currently the major suppliers of training and media for managerial, user, and data processing personnel. However, the vendors' preeminence is diminishing, for there is now a discernible trend away from them and toward other sources.

One of the most frequently cited reasons for this trend is the increase in costs. Furthermore, the vendors' courses continue to be offered at geographical locations that are not readily and generally convenient for many organizations, so that customers have to pay travel and lodging expenses as well as the service fee.

Another reason—perhaps the most important one—for the move away from vendors' instruction programs is customer dissatisfaction with the subject matter offered. The subject matter is either too general or too positive about the environment created from the use of the vendor's hardware. Customers would prefer a more universal approach to such subjects as data communications, data base management, structured programming, and so forth.

Although vendors maintain a fairly standard range of available courses, their teaching methods have changed since the inception of third-generation hardware and concepts. Therefore, it is useful to consider the overall topic under two separate headings: teaching methods and course offerings.

Teaching methods. The traditional classroom method of teaching and learning now supplements rather than dominates vendor education services. The new approach to vendor-provided training is based on the use—singly or in combination—of such media as programmed instruction materials, student texts, student workbooks, study guides, reference manuals, audio-education packages, video tapes, practical exercises, and systems exercise card decks.

The programmed instruction materials, generally referred to as PI materials, utilize the basic concept of the student reading short, sequential explanations of the material and then answering questions on his reading as he goes. Only after demonstrating his comprehension of one segment of the material does the student advance to the next segment. The student is able to learn at his own pace while on the job. His progress is evaluated through a test administered by the vendor or the organization's training group. The PI materials are used to cover introductory, preliminary, or background data with a follow-up of a day or more in a classroom. This follow-up is sometimes referred to as the workshop session or simply as the wrap-up.

Student texts, workbooks and study guides have also been developed by the vendors to augment the training process. The texts are limited to the presentation of an introductory or single data processing concept. Unlike the reference manuals, the student texts are written in a more descriptive manner, with examples and illustrations to facilitate understanding. This approach bridges the gap between classroom instruction and the use of reference manuals, which are generally written to provide information for people already possessing basic knowledge of the subject matter. The student texts are also very useful for self-teaching and self-development. Most of these texts are available only from vendors; some, however, may be obtained through publishers.

The reference manuals are written to provide either very specific data about a subject or generalized or introductory information. They have traditionally been used as textbooks in the vendor courses, although unlike most textbooks, they include very few teaching-type examples. Manuals currently play a supplementary classroom role, being used to amplify information taught by the instructor, as well as to provide reference aid in the solution of problems.

Audio education is also used by the vendors as a multi-media technique. The typical audio-education package consists of an audio tape and an illustration book or packet. The student concentrates on listening to the tape for the basic subject matter, referring to his illustration book or packet as specifics are noted on the tape. Audio-education packages are used for teaching various generalized and specialized topics. If an adequate number of illustration books or packets are available with an organization, a number of people can participate in one session. However, the vendor audio-education packages are intended primarily for use as individualized learning tools. After a user has completed his learning session, the materials may be passed on to another user in the organization. Depending on the subject matter involved, a test to assess comprehension may be administered by the vendor's organization or the organization's training group. Some audio packages have been established as prerequisites for entry into vendor classroom training sessions.

Video tapes are also used as a multi-media technique. The video tapes may be used for independent study in the same manner as audio tapes. Or they may be used for group training sessions conducted in-house. In either case, the video tapes are supplemented by other instructional media to facilitate student learning.

Systems exercise decks are used primarily for training operating personnel in computer operation. They teach an operator to initialize the processor, load jobs, and respond to interrupts.

Course offerings. The course offerings cover executive orientation, general data processing orientation, professional development, hardware operation, and applications.

The executive orientation courses are designed to familiarize the upper echelon with the components of a computer or unit-record system and with programming languages, systems design, and the role of data processing and its functional organization. Such courses are not intended to make the executive an expert, but rather to enable him to communicate more effectively and to understand his involvement in data processing.

Many of the executive series courses have been tailored for specific industries, e.g., airlines, grocery, hospital, education, government and so forth.

The general data processing orientation courses provide introductory, background, or basic information about the hardware, programming languages, operating systems, etc. Some of these courses, taken by data processing personnel, serve as prerequisites for subsequent professional, applications, and hardware courses. And some courses provide general orientation for users and other people not directly involved in data processing.

Professional development courses, designed for people directly involved in data processing, deal with specifics in systems analysis and design, programming languages, operating systems, data management concepts, and other related subjects. In an attempt to increase the educational effectiveness of these courses, the vendors have recently integrated these offerings with the use of the various teaching media. The use of these media has reduced the amount of time spent away from an organization by employees receiving vendor-supplied training. (There are also other benefits, which are discussed under programmed learning, below.)

Hardware operation courses, which also utilize the various teaching media for instruction, are designed to teach the fundamentals, operation, and wiring of unit-record, computer, and peripheral equipment.

Applications courses are designed to provide students with the fundamental concepts of the subject matter, together with specific information on the application and also on the conversion and operational requirements. At present, most of these courses have the classroom-lecture setting as their mode of instruction; however, there are also a few that have been established as audio-education packages. Applications courses include general-concept courses, industry-oriented courses, and hardware-oriented courses. A typical general-concept offering would be an introduction to material requirements planning or introduction to linear programming. Industry-oriented courses include such topics as demand deposit accounting for financial institutions, computer-assisted instruction languages for educational institutions, or text processing for a publishing firm. There are many hardware-oriented courses. One example is IMS/VS Data Communications Programming for IBM hardware.

6. PROFESSIONAL EDUCATION SERVICES. Within the last few years there has been an increase in the number of companies offering data processing educational services for presentation in major cities throughout the country. These companies have developed seminar packages for managerial and data processing personnel to cover such topics as programming techniques, controls, applications, and fundamental concepts. The subject matter is concentrated, in that

the seminar sessions last only between one and five days, with the average being two or three days.

These company-supplied seminar sessions are considered to be less expensive than the courses offered by vendors. Furthermore, they tend to offer a broader viewpoint and/or more of an in-depth approach to a particular topic. Also, many of the topics covered in the seminars are not normally included in vendor-supplied training programs. One major reason for these last two differences is that the seminar leaders are people who come from diverse backgrounds and who have distinguished themselves in the subject matter.

7. PROGRAMMED LEARNING. Programmed learning techniques are designed and developed to train personnel quickly and more effectively at a lower cost per student. A number of different programmed learning media have evolved since the original concept was developed by Harvard University psychologist B.F. Skinner. However, their advantages are very similar. The principal advantages (which are not mutually exclusive) are:

1. The user may learn at his own pace. He is not required to complete a unit within a given time period.

2. The user actively interacts in the learning process because he is ready to learn and respond.

3. The material is structured to cover large segments of information in a minimal amount of learning time.

4. The student's advancement is based on his achievement; therefore, he is immediately and constantly aware of his progress.

However, there are also disadvantages that need to be understood. The principal ones are:

1. The teaching and test materials are difficult to develop.

2. The development process is very time-consuming. And the costs involved may not be offset by savings in training costs.

3. Failure to design and develop the materials properly results in a user advancing to another segment before mastering the previous segment of information.

4. Some of the subject matter may be affected by obsolescence or changes. Depending on the media form, it may be difficult to respond with a modification or revision.

Initially, programmed instruction materials were made available for the teaching of number systems, data processing concepts, and programming languages. Subsequently, though, the range of materials was expanded by the vendors and publishing companies to include a number of different topics such as structured programming, data communications concepts, and virtual storage concepts.

There are also various specialized forms of programmed learning, among which are computer-assisted instruction materials, single-concept films, video tapes, and audio-education materials.

Computer-assisted instruction (CAI) materials are intended to teach programming languages, the use of conversational time-sharing terminals, and data processing concepts. One disadvantage to the CAI approach is that it requires not only the use of conversational terminals, but also preemption of the computer for educational purposes for a predetermined time period each day. The latter can be a significant problem because only a limited number of courses are available from vendors, professional educational services, and colleges and universities. Also, course materials may not be operable on the organization's equipment configuration. Therefore, the training group will prepare a course package that makes use of the organization's equipment. Furthermore, it can be both difficult and time-consuming to develop CAI materials.

Single-concept films are increasing in popularity as a form of programmed learning. At present they are being prepared by professional educational services, colleges and universities, and in-house training groups. Some of the popularity may be attributed to the fact that these films can be mounted in 8-mm cartridges and used in desk-top viewers by either individuals or groups. The films are used to teach hardware operation, programming languages and techniques, data processing concepts, systems analysis and design techniques, and many other topics. In some cases, the films are supplemented by textual materials that develop the film concepts and provide written problems for the students to solve.

Video tapes are used to teach programming languages, hardware operation, applications, and many other subjects. These tapes have been developed by vendors, consulting firms, and companies involved in education services for use in their seminars and workshops and for in-house training at a customer's facility. A number of such tapes have also been developed by colleges and universities for training of their own students and for client organizations. In-house training organizations have also developed a number of the video tapes for training of their own employees.

Audio education is another popular form of programmed learning. The popularity may be attributed to the practical convenience of the tape cassettes and tape players used with many of the packages. The audio-education tapes are used in conjunction with other instructional materials to teach such topics as terminology, programming fundamentals, systems analysis and design concepts, and applications. Audio-education packages have been developed by vendors, consultants, professional associations, professional educational services, colleges and universities, and in-house training groups.

8. ORGANIZATIONAL TRAINING GROUPS. Many organizations recognize that the operational effectiveness of the data processing organization is dependent upon sound training practices. They also know that costs can be reduced and savings realized if the personnel concerned—managerial, user, and data processing—are all trained effectively. That is why many organizations either

are establishing or already have in-house training groups to develop, implement, and coordinate training programs and resources. Used effectively, these in-house training groups can help remedy what has been a fairly common organizational deficiency—that of being very methodical in providing training for data processing personnel, but being lax about including users and managers. Adequate training for user personnel in particular must be arranged prior to conversion and implementation of a system and/or a program; and the effect of that training must be evaluated following the implementation.

The dynamic and innovative nature of data processing requires that continuing education be developed and implemented to maintain and update the professional skills of data processing personnel. This becomes an essential part of career development, or career pathing as it is referred to in some organizations. The availability of such a training program will help to minimize or eliminate turnover because the personnel will be less fearful of becoming technically obsolescent. Also, the data processing personnel will maintain a greater level of proficiency and this should result in better, more durable, and less costly information processing systems.

INFORMAL TRAINING

Informal training programs are designed to involve the participant in the learning process while in an actual on-the-job setting. This alleviates or eliminates some of the confusion that can occur in moving from the theoretical to the actual environment. There is also the advantage that the person is not only learning but also working to some extent, thereby providing some return on investment almost immediately. The disadvantage is that the training period must be somewhat lengthy to cover an adequate number of situations and experiences.

The most popular forms of informal training are:

1. Job rotation
2. Special assignments

1. JOB ROTATION. Job rotation is probably the most frequently used informal training method, especially for people entering a data processing occupation at the trainee level. This method involves training of personnel either in the various activities of one particular function or within the entire organizational structure. Effective use of this technique requires that the organization's training coordinator or functional manager develop a job rotation plan for each person that is based on both the organization's objectives and the person's skills and abilities. The plan must include the sequence of activities to be followed; the type, extent, and length of training to be given at each activity; and an evaluation technique that will indicate if the trainee is qualified to move to the next phase. To be beneficial to both the trainee and the organization, this method requires a great deal of coordination. The need is apparent when many employees are involved in job rotation.

2. SPECIAL ASSIGNMENTS. The special assignments approach to training is used primarily for employees in managerial or management training positions.

The technique is also used for employees who are not in a formal management training program but who have demonstrated high potential for managerial responsibility. In this method, the trainee is assigned a specific task to perform or goal to attain. He is kept under observation during the performance of his duties in order to determine how well he defines an objective and plans the goal-attainment process. The special assignments should be used to maximize the individual's skills, abilities, and potential, rather than to correct his weaknesses to any large degree. Very often the employee is assigned to a position of supervisory responsibility so that he can be evaluated in terms of his ability to handle such an assignment and to work with others. If this is to be an effective form of training, the results of the assignment must be discussed with the trainee in order that he can learn from his experience. This discussion should be conducted immediately upon conclusion of the assignment. It should not be postponed until the periodic employee appraisal is conducted, for the delay would only defeat the purpose of training and minimize the learning experience.

Career Development

Career development is referred to as career pathing in some organizations. The concept involves the design and development of a formal personnel development for data processing personnel. The purpose of such a plan is to develop personnel with the skills to perform the necessary data processing functions, to upgrade the proficiency skills of the staff for future projects; and to manage the activities of others.

To initiate the career development process, the data processing manager must first perform a job analysis to determine what job skills are needed by the staff. For this step to be effective the manager should review each job description to ensure that it reflects the current requirements of the position. The manager must then either perform a skills inventory or review the organization's existing skills inventory. The data from the job descriptions and the skills inventory will enable the manager to identify the skills needed by the staff and those required by the organization to fulfill the stated objectives.

The manager must compare the skill needs and the skills available to the long-range plan developed for the data processing organization. This analysis will provide the manager with an assessment of current and future needs. Armed with this information, the manager must determine the kinds of training required by the staff, and the schedule for such training.

An important part of this personnel development plan is a career path—a progression path—for the personnel. The path must be graphically illustrated (see Figure 3.2), and the requirements for each position must be identified to enable the personnel to determine what they must "know" in order to advance. The advancement process itself must be monitored through the administration of a proficiency test. These tests must be properly designed and validated to ensure their effectiveness. The test results and the employee performance appraisals can be used to determine personnel growth and needs.

The formal plan will improve employee morale because they will have a clear indication of future growth possibilities. The organization should develop and maintain qualified people and also provide standardized training for all personnel. The end result should mean improved productivity and fewer project overruns.

Review Questions: Group 3C

1. Why should a personnel training program be developed in every organization?
2. Management games are included in many formal training programs. Why?
3. There is a growing trend toward including programmed learning methods in training programs. Why?
4. What steps must be taken by an operations manager to ensure the effectiveness of the job rotation method of informal training?

APPRAISAL OF PERSONNEL PERFORMANCE

The appraisal, or merit-rating, process is implemented during the executory phase of management, when the goal-attainment plan has been initiated and is operative. The bases for judgment are the performance standards previously defined during the pre-executory phase. Primarily, the appraisal process is intended to provide periodic evaluation of an employee's actual and potential performance. Yet, directly and indirectly, much information can also be learned about an organization's policies and problems.

A well-executed personnel appraisal program has the following effects:

It is an indicator of a person's performance and improvement. The manager rates the employee's performance for the appraisal period as unsatisfactory, fair, average, very good, or outstanding. The ratings provide the manager with a relative measure of the employee's performance compared with that of others in the same job. The appraisal also affords the manager an opportunity to recognize and commend employee self-development. Such an action very often provides a motivating stimulus for continued self-development and performance improvement.

It identifies the strengths and weaknesses of an individual. This information enables a manager to conduct an effective counseling session with the employee. Furthermore, it enables the manager to recommend a development plan for improvement and acceleration of growth. This must be a tangible plan to benefit the employee and the organization, for the organization can ill-afford to have a manager expound some vague plan for maximizing the strengths and potential of an employee.

The manager gains a new understanding of his employees, for the appraisal increases his awareness of their current efforts and contributions. Also, it may provide some indication of the type and level of assistance that may be anticipated in the future. In addition, it identifies continuing above-average or outstanding performances, which may subsequently be rewarded by salary increases, new assignments, or promotions.

 It identifies the skills and abilities possessed by an individual. This identification of capabilities provides the manager with an informal skills inventory file. The information is especially useful when the manager wishes to delegate additional responsibility to an employee, make assignments to special projects, or promote personnel.

 It provides an evaluation of the personnel selection and training techniques. The manager can check his decisions on personnel selection with the appraisal results. Also, he can determine whether or not the training programs are adequate.

It can provide data on the adequacy or inadequacy of company policies and/or practices. Very often a manager learns that the lack of compatible or relevant policies or practices hinders an employee's efforts. For example, he may learn that an employee is being required to computerize a payroll application within the same parameters previously applied to the unit-record approach.

The Appraisal Process

Personnel appraisal requires an unbiased rating of an individual's current performance, in a number of preselected traits and characteristics, and his potential performance. The actual performance—for the various traits and characteristics, which may include such items as accuracy or appearance—is gauged in terms of a predefined standard established during the organizing function of the pre-executory phase. The standard must stipulate clearly what has to be accomplished or what is acceptable to meet current operating needs, policies, or practice. And it must cover a range of measurable levels, so as to provide for performance comparisons of employees. The standard then becomes the yardstick for determining whether an employee's actual performance is at, above, or below the planned level.

Actual performance should be determined only after the manager has had an opportunity to observe the employee for a reasonable amount of time. One brief observation is insufficient and can lead to inaccuracy in performance measurement and subsequently in the full appraisal. Repeated observation is also necessary to isolate any weak, unsatisfactory, or barely acceptable performances. When he observes such conditions, the appraiser should make a brief report of the fact, together with a tangible illustration. This information is needed because there is more involved here than simply determining work performance: the manager has to be concerned with correcting the situation. The information provides the basis for an effective counseling session. Furthermore, in addition to being prepared for discussion of the problem, the manager has to be ready to recommend action for improvement or fortification of a trait or characteristic.

He needs to determine the type of training program that should be planned and implemented to expedite the employee's development.

An employee's potential performance has to be rated separately because of the subjective nature of the evaluation. Potential performance is an estimate or projection by the appraiser of an employee's capabilities. It often has little factual substance and tends to be biased. Nevertheless, potential must be rated because it becomes the basis for planning the employee's future course and development. To realize this performance potential, the manager must obviously develop and implement a meaningful training plan.

It is important to add that such a training plan must also be realistic, in that some employees will not rise beyond a certain level of competence or proficiency. In such instances, the manager has to be concerned with having the employee maintain a satisfactory performance level. This does not mean the employee should receive no more training after reaching that point, but that he should be given training appropriate to the maintenance of his level of proficiency.

Actual and potential performance are sometimes confused by the appraiser. For example, one data processing manager was dissatisfied with the "low" output of a programmer whom he had rated as a good "software type." The programmer, however, was not writing any software packages; instead, he was being utilized for performing modifications and maintenance to existing programs. Therefore, he had been rated for what he could possibly do and not for what he had actually been doing. Another manager once rated the output capability of one of his programmers by the man's size and weight. He held the opinion and the expectation that the programmer could "out-produce" anyone else because he was bigger. Eventually, the programmer's failure to produce in direct proportion to his anatomical structure resulted in a lower performance rating.

Although these two examples represent flagrant violations of the very purpose of performance appraisal, they are not isolated cases. Providing for an objective appraisal is easier said than done. It is very difficult to refrain from becoming subjective when evaluating the various traits and characteristics. Deliberately or accidentally, the appraisal process often becomes a reward or punishment mechanism rather than a management tool.

Appraisal Characteristics and Traits

The characteristics and traits most frequently evaluated during the appraisal process are:

1. Quantity and quality of work
2. Economy of time
3. Thoroughness
4. Attitude toward superiors
5. Attitude toward job

6. General knowledge
7. Accuracy
8. Versatility
9. Personal appearance
10. Other characteristics and traits

1. QUANTITY AND QUALITY OF WORK. The quantity and quality to be produced are measured against the performance standard established for each individual position or occupational grouping.

2. ECONOMY OF TIME. This characteristic is concerned with a person's ability to organize and use his time effectively. A person capable of properly organizing his project time will register high productivity. However, the appraiser needs to determine if the desired quality level was also achieved.

3. THOROUGHNESS. The appraiser must determine the degree of completeness that can be attributed to the task or tasks accomplished by the employee. He must also ascertain if the projects have truly been completed, in that some employees "complete" their projects quickly, but are found to be still adding, changing, or correcting something many weeks or months later. But if they are still unfinished after a reasonable time has elapsed, the manager should assign some other staff member the responsibility for satisfactory completion of the project. The manager should then make note of this fact for use in the subsequent appraisal and counseling session.

4. ATTITUDE TOWARD SUPERIORS. This indicates an employee's ability to accept and follow instructions under adverse as well as favorable working conditions. A person with an uncooperative or rebellious attitude will not be very dependable or reliable and certainly cannot be counted upon to accept responsibility.

5. ATTITUDE TOWARD JOB. This depends very much on whether or not the employee is in the right job. He may be unhappy or unsuccessful because he has been placed in the wrong position. It is also possible that the employee is bored with his present position because he has exhausted its challenge or because it may have become a kind of dead-end job with no place to go until someone else dies, retires, or is promoted. A negative attitude may also be evident if the employee is not qualified for a position, if he has been inadequately trained, or if he has apparently misunderstood the duties and responsibilities of his position. Evaluating an employee's attitude toward his job is most difficult unless the manager has had an opportunity to steadily observe the employee and collect adequate data.

6. GENERAL KNOWLEDGE. In appraising this characteristic, the manager evaluates an employee's ability to utilize his knowledge of data processing, a subject-matter specialty, the organizational structure, and the workflow. There may be a tendency on the part of the manager to overestimate what the general requirements for a position should be. The appraisal should be based on the job knowledge criteria stipulated in the job description for that position. The general knowledge requirements for a junior programmer position, for example, will not be comparable to that of a senior programmer. It would be grossly unfair for a

manager to apply the general requirements of the latter's position to all programmer positions in the organization.

7. ACCURACY. This trait may be appraised individually or as part of the thoroughness trait. It is concerned with an employee's ability to perform a task or series of tasks with exactness and precision. This implies that when the project is completed, it satisfies the desired objectives; will be useful in the future; will have relatively low maintenance requirements; and will be easy to change or modify.

8. VERSATILITY. This trait is generally used in appraising upper-level positions in the data processing function, where the personnel are often required to work under adverse conditions or to take on a multiplicity of projects within a normal workday. In determining versatility, the manager evaluates the employee's ability to cope with stress and other environmental conditions. People who are potential managers must have the ability to operate in a dynamic environment that is characterized by ever-changing conditions and requirements.

9. PERSONAL APPEARANCE. This trait is used to evaluate such factors as neatness, grooming, general appearance, dress, and posture. What constitutes acceptable or presentable appearance will depend on existing organizational policy. There is a tendency to emphasize this trait in the appraisal of data processing personnel because a presentable personal appearance can help make the employee and/or his material acceptable to others and can remove some preliminary barriers in face-to-face contact. The reason for applying this emphasis is that many executives believe that the appearance of a person is an excellent indicator of several characteristics, such as ability to organize, resourcefulness, attitude toward job and supervision, cooperation, and initiative. There is, however, no scientific support for such beliefs.

10. OTHER CHARACTERISTICS AND TRAITS. These include health, maturity, problem-solving ability, punctuality, ability to grasp instructions, judgment, and many others. The list can be very long indeed, depending on differences among organizations, occupational groupings, and the level of detail required in characteristic classifications.

Appraisal Techniques/Formats

There are a number of specialized formats available for recording the manager's appraisal of a subordinate. These can be used to provide a historical record for employee development and other decisions. Among the most frequently used appraisal techniques/formats are:

1. Graphic scales
2. Checklists
3. Narratives
4. Critical incidents
5. Man-to-man comparisons
6. Forced choices

NAME_____ DATE_____

Job classification |_____

How long has employee been under your supervision?_____ mos.

How long in present classification? _____ mos.

Quartile Points \\ TRAIT	Unsatisfactory				Fair				Average				Very Good				Outstanding				Score
	1 Q 1	2 Q 2	3 Q 3	4 Q 4	1 Q 5	2 Q 6	3 Q 7	4 Q 8	1 Q 9	2 Q 10	3 Q 11	4 Q 12	1 Q 13	2 Q 14	3 Q 15	4 Q 16	1 Q 17	2 Q 18	3 Q 19	4 Q 20	
Quantity of Work—The amount of efficient and productive output achieved.																					
Quality of Work—The degree of accuracy, dependability, and thoroughness of the output achieved. Consideration should be given to degree of difficulty, but not to quantity.																					
Job Knowledge—The amount of knowledge and skill possessed to perform the tasks assigned.																					
Initiative—The sense of responsibility possessed by an individual to generate action when required, and the perseverance for completing an assigned task.																					
Cooperation—The ability to work with and for others. Considerations should be given to morale, tact, ability to accept criticism, courtesy, and friendliness.																					
Judgment—The ability to analyze situations and available data to arrive at sound conclusions.																					
Adaptability—The ability to be involved successfully in several activities at one time.																					
																				Total score	

Rater _____ Date _____

Date rating discussed with employee _____

Employee reaction to rating _____

_____

_____

Figure 3.4 Graphic scale: sample personnel rating form

PERSONNEL RATING PROFILE

Trait or Characteristic	Employee — Value					Employee — Value					Employee — Value				
	unsat.	fair	avg.	v. good	outstand	unsat.	fair	avg.	v. good	outstand	unsat.	fair	avg.	v. good	outstand
	1 2 3	4 5 6	7 8 9 10 11 12	13 14 15 16 17	18 19 20	1 2 3	4 5 6	7 8 9 10 11 12	13 14 15 16 17	18 19 20	1 2 3	4 5 6	7 8 9 10 11 12	13 14 15 16 17	18 19 20
Quantity of Work															
Quality of Work															
Job Knowledge															
Initiative															
Cooperation															
Judgment															
Adaptability															

INSTRUCTIONS: For each employee shade the center bar over to the equivalent numerical score rating for a given trait or characteristic.

Figure 3.5 Graphic scale: sample personnel rating profile

NUMERICAL RATING COMPARISON									
JOB CLASSIFICATION									
CHARACTERISTIC OR TRAIT	TOTAL POSSIBLE SCORE	EMPLOYEE NAMES							
QUANTITY OF WORK									
QUALITY OF WORK									
JOB KNOWLEDGE									
INITIATIVE.									
COOPERATION									
JUDGMENT									
ADAPTABILITY									

Figure 3.6 Graphic scale: sample numerical rating comparison

1. GRAPHIC SCALES. These scales represent the more popular type of rating form in use today. As illustrated in Figure 3.4, the kind of scale known as the personnel rating form includes a listing of the desired traits or characteristics (plus a brief definition of acceptable performance) on the left side of the form. The rest of the form is usually occupied by a series of blocks for indicating the rating degrees possible for each trait or characteristic, ranging from unsatisfactory to outstanding. There is one block for each rating degree, so that the employee's attainment level for each trait can be clearly indicated.

The results on the rating form can then be plotted in a rating profile, as illustrated in Figure 3.5, and subsequently compared to that of another employee. Alternatively, the rating-form results can be used to develop a numerical rating comparison, as shown in Figure 3.6. In this, each segment of a degree block is assigned a numerical value to provide a final rating score for an employee.

Some graphic-scale forms include a comment block on the front or reverse side to provide additional information on a particular trait. Comments, though, may be somewhat biased. Furthermore, they are sometimes used to defend the rater's position rather than provide meaningful information useful in a planning session to indicate areas for employee improvement.

2. CHECKLIST. This technique is used either by itself or in conjunction with another method. It utilizes an extensive checklist of questions about the employee's behavior and traits. The rater simply marks a "yes" or "no" answer to each question. Some checklists list statements about behavior that are applicable to several positions in the organization. When performing his appraisal, the manager is asked to check only those statements that are applicable to an employee's position. This procedure is not very satisfactory because some confusion may occur over which statements are relevant to a given position.

The checklist technique does not require an evaluation of performance but rather a report of it by the rater. Each trait has a specific weighted value, which goes toward determining the final score. Evaluation of the score is then implemented.

3. NARRATIVES. This format utilizes a subjective evaluation technique to determine an employee's outstanding, above average, satisfactory, and unsatisfactory actions and contributions regarding job performance. The technique implies that the rating will be determined through utilization of predetermined standards for comparison, and that it will be made objectively and factually. Such an evaluation can be used to great advantage in the planning session that follows the appraisal.

4. CRITICAL INCIDENTS. The appraiser observes the employee's behavioral patterns while on the job and records any critical incidents as they occur. The behavioral aspects that constitute critical incidents are predetermined in order to provide for standardization of reporting and appraising. Furthermore, each of the incidents is assigned a weighted value for rating purposes. Then the score values are collected and tallied for purposes of comparison. The following represents the type of report that may be made based on an observation of a critical incident and used in the appraisal: The employee has personally developed the necessary systems and procedures required by the corporation's subsidiaries to implement engineering cost accounting and reporting. The employee indicated an outstanding proficiency in his specialty. In accomplishing his assigned duties he totally disregarded adverse working conditions, long overtime hours, minimal availability of the computer, and the lack of machine operating assistance.

5. MAN-TO-MAN COMPARISONS. In this technique, certain traits are selected for inclusion in the appraisal process. The selected traits are then matched to the employees within the organization. The person who most closely personifies the trait is placed at the top of the scale; the person who least meets the qualification is placed at the bottom; and one person who is considered to be average for the trait is placed in the middle of the scale. Every employee is then rated

against the three men on the scale and is awarded a score for the trait on the basis of the comparison. The evaluation and rating process is repeated for each trait. Then the scores for all traits are tallied to provide the basis for overall comparisons.

6. FORCED CHOICES. This rating technique makes an attempt at removing bias from the appraisal process. This is accomplished by forcing the rater to choose from among predetermined descriptive statements those that are applicable to the employee being appraised. The rater's choices are compared against the list prepared by a specially organized committee of managerial or senior personnel in the functional activity, or by a personnel specialist. The list of applicable statements is developed after a study of the existing manpower resources. Based on the relative importance of each statement in the listing, a numerical score is assigned to each statement. The responses made by the rater are compared and scored to arrive at a total score. The rater is then notified how the employees for a given position compare with each other in a quartile ranking. The forced-choice technique cannot be used for planning, counseling, or follow-up purposes, because the rater is not made aware of the desired behavioral norm or standard established by the committee or personnel specialist. It may also be difficult to compare the results of a previous appraisal period because the norm or standard may have changed.

Communicating the Results

It can be said that the primary purpose of any appraisal program should be personnel development. It can also be said to be almost universally true that people want to know where they stand and that they appreciate a fair and constructive evaluation of their performance. Therefore, when an appraisal has been completed, the results should be communicated to the employee. Furthermore, if the manager handles the communication process correctly and does not dwell on minor weaknesses, the employee will not resent being criticized if the appraisal is based on objective fact and not on biased opinion.

The success of the counseling session that follows the appraisal depends not only on the appraisal itself but also on what happens during the session. This is why it is important for the manager to make careful preparations for the interview. In addition to trying to anticipate at least some of the questions the employee will raise during the session, the manager must be prepared to handle the inevitable employee reaction to the appraisal. A negative reaction badly handled can bring on an argument that can disrupt the session by creating an air of hostility and antagonism. Therefore, the manager must be ready to listen to the objections presented by the employee and to present tangible facts and situations. Lastly, the manager must consider the employee's strengths and weaknesses that he plans to discuss, as well as the corrective action or improvement he will recommend. This type of preplanning helps to make the counseling session beneficial for both parties.

Having completed his planning, the manager is ready to discuss the rating results with the employee. This is a serious matter that should be conducted in a professional manner. Too often this aspect of the appraisal process is conducted in such a poor manner that it produces no tangible benefit for either party. Unfortunately, in these instances, it may produce ill will that can have a long-lasting effect on the organization. The manager, therefore, must try to place the employee at ease as much as possible. He should then proceed to explain the purpose of the interview and the rating plan used. After that, he proceeds to convey the rating results to the employee. It is at this point that the manager can expect some of the reaction or questions, or both, which he had anticipated in the precounseling phase. This is why he should begin by emphasizing the employee's strong points, giving him a clear understanding of what he is doing well. Any praises that are extended should be sincere and not merely platitudes intended to soothe an employee, for insincerity can be readily detected and does more harm than good.

After giving the employee an opportunity to absorb the results relating to his strengths and self-improvement, the manager should advise the individual of his weaknesses or traits that require improvement. In this presentation, the manager should avoid comparative discussion of anyone else—including himself. Above all, the manager should not dwell unendingly upon errors. Nevertheless, he needs to be prepared to cite specific examples or incidents relating to the employee's problem areas. This is also a good time to clear up any misunderstandings about exactly what is expected from the employee. The manager should allow the employee to raise questions and discuss the problems.

It is important that the manager be aware of his own biases and prejudices. Very obviously, there are traits a person favors and others that irritate him, and it is these kinds of likes and dislikes that can so easily lead the manager into a closed-mind attitude. Therefore, such biases and prejudices must be recognized, avoided, minimized, or masked. An open mind on the part of the manager is essential in order for a feeling of mutual confidence to develop between him and the employee.

The discussion should then move on to ways of improvement. Improvement must come in the form of corrective action that will involve some self-improvement plan and/or participation in a formal or informal training program. If there are any desirable traits or characteristics that need to be developed further, then these must also be discussed with the employee, because improvement in this area could lead to a promotion, new responsibilities, or a salary increase.

In the concluding phase of the counseling session, the manager should discuss the effect and meaning of the rating. He should also mention the follow-up appraisal that will be conducted within a reasonable time after this meeting. Each successive appraisal has some effect upon the growth status of an employee, for it shows whether he has progressed, stood still, or regressed. A manager must be willing to accept the fact that some members of his functional activity will be average performers. As such, they will remain at the same level throughout their period of employment. It is obvious that their appraisal ratings will be relatively the same for each appraisal period. However, this does not mean that they should be omitted from the regular appraisal process. It is important that *every* employee clearly understand his status because it may motivate him either to improve or at least to maintain an acceptable performance level.

The follow-up is an essential element of the appraisal and counseling process. Therefore, the manager should continue to exhibit interest in the employee's work and progress after the initial appraisal. Failure to do so and failure to conduct a significant follow-up will destroy any mutual confidence and trust established during the appraisal process.

During the initial counseling session the employee may have disagreed with the results and indicated constructively why his point of view should be supported and the rating changed. If so, the manager must investigate the assertion and communicate his findings to the employee during a meeting after the follow-up has been completed. If the manager decides the rating should be changed, he should make sure it is done promptly, because in many instances the rating form becomes a historical record that is used for a multiplicity of purposes. The follow-up also provides the manager with an opportunity to determine if, as a result of a promise of training made during the previous session, the employee is now involved in a meaningful, utilitarian training program.

Review Questions: Group 3D

1. Why must an organization develop a personnel appraisal program?
2. A manager must evaluate actual and potential performance separately during the appraisal of an employee. Why?
3. What is the most popular rating method in use today? Would you recommend using it or would you prefer to use some other method or methods?
4. Many organizations appraise their personnel, but do not communicate the results to the employees. Is this a good or bad policy? Why?
5. What is the purpose of the follow-up that is conducted after the appraisal and counseling session?

SUMMARY

The "information explosion" has created new employment opportunities in the data processing industry. The growth in the number of installations has increased the need for qualified personnel.

In this chapter, we began by discussing the elements of job analysis and construction of job descriptions. The analyses confirm the requirements that are stipulated in a job description for each position.

Due to the complexity of the manpower requirements, a variety of occupational groupings have evolved. Within each of the major occupational groupings there are a number of related occupational or job titles grouped in a hierarchy according to the three classification levels—specialist, skilled, and trainee.

When the personnel requirements have been defined, the manager must concern himself with the recruitment, selection, training, and appraisal of personnel. Recruitment and selection can be difficult because of the skills required in data processing occupations and the limited supply of qualified persons. Personnel selection may be accomplished through the use of tests and interviews. This is a very costly effort, and an organization must strive to select the best possible candidate for each position. Proper selection may also minimize the rate of employee turnover. A manager should never overlook the possibility of recruitment and selection from within. Utilizing personnel with the proper aptitude, background, and experience, from an internal source, will reduce hiring and job-orientation costs.

The effectiveness of any organization is dependent upon the quality of its personnel. Their quality and effectiveness can be developed and maintained through formal and informal training programs. An employee development program that includes both types of programs is advisable for most occupational groupings and organizations. It must be emphasized that organizations can no longer afford to approach training in a haphazard manner. Failure to provide training programs can result in high employee turnover and a waste of valuable resources.

To determine the effectiveness of any operation it is necessary to periodically appraise the organization's manpower resources. The appraisal process indicates an employee's actual performance, his potential, and—through use of a follow-up procedure—his development. The appraisal process may be conducted in a variety of ways; however, it is ineffectual unless the results are communicated to the employee. It is important that the technique be divorced from any direct or immediate salary increases. The appraisals should be used primarily for employee training and development.

CASE STUDY 3.1

The Winston Wire Works

Charles Willis, the manager of programming and systems for the Winston Wire Works, has just completed the quarterly employee appraisal. The company uses a graphic rating scale to evaluate each trait or characteristic as very good, good, fair, or unacceptable. Each of these rating degrees has a numerical score ranging in descending value from four to one. The traits or characteristics included in the form are: quality of work, appearance, technical ability, creativeness, initiative, and cooperation.

The company has a policy of granting merit increases on the basis of appraisal results. The percentage of increase is left to the discretion of the manager. There is an unwritten policy that an employee will not receive more than two consecutive merit increases in a year, an exception being made when an employee performs in an outstanding manner. Company policy requires that the manager communicate the appraisal results and amount of salary increase, if any, to the employee.

In carrying out the quarterly appraisal, Mr. Willis began by speaking first to the employees with the highest ratings. This decision was based on his belief—widely known by his subordinates—that the people with high ratings need very little counseling because they are professionals and know exactly what is required of them.

William Harris, a senior systems specialist for the company, was called into the office for his counseling session. At the outset, Mr. Willis announced rather apologetically that Mr. Harris would not receive a merit increase for the coming quarter. This was necessary because Mr. Harris had performed at an unsatisfactory level during the previous three months.

Mr. Harris had been somewhat prepared for some unfavorable news because he had not been among the first to be called in for a counseling session. Nevertheless, he was both shocked and angered by the manager's statement. Mr. Harris asked why his rating had dropped two rating degrees, reminding Mr. Willis that in the previous period his performance had been rated as "good." No merit compensation had been granted at that time because he had received increases in the two previous quarters. Mr. Willis replied by stating that the specialist was already the highest paid member of the department.

Mr. Harris then countered by noting that he had been in the department longer than any other person; also, that he had been assigned a disproportionate share of the departmental workload because of his background and experience. What was more, during the past quarter alone, he had completed the development and implementation of a project that netted the organization $100,000 in tangible savings.

The manager acknowledged these facts. Then he severely criticized what he said was Mr. Harris's inability to secure the cooperation of the data processing operations manager during recent parallel tests, a significant inability. Mr. Willis went on to say that this failure alone was serious enough to negate all other favorable aspects of the appraisal. The specialist replied by reminding Mr. Willis that they had previously discussed the matter at length and that, as a result of their conversation, Mr. Willis had determined that it was his own responsibility to discuss the matter with Arthur Carney, the operations manager. Mr. Willis had agreed with Mr. Harris that it was very important to have operations personnel involved in parallel testing.

Mr. Willis now stated that it was the responsibility of the systems analyst on the project to secure the cooperation of all parties concerned. The ability to work with and through others is a very essential trait in a systems analyst. He further added that if Mr. Harris was unable to improve this situation significantly, his performance rating would remain at its present lower level.

Mr. Harris asked about his past experience in dealing with people. Mr. Willis stated in a somewhat harsh tone, "I don't care about the past—it is the future I am concerned with." Mr. Harris replied, "Well, I guess I will have to start shopping around for a new job," and he walked out of the manager's office.

Discussion Questions

1. How would you rate Mr. Willis's conduct of the appraisal?
2. Do you feel that the graphic-scale rating method is appropriate for this organization? Would you suggest that a new or additional form be used? If so, which one?
3. What additional characteristics or traits, if any, would you recommend for inclusion on the appraisal form?
4. How would you evaluate Mr. Willis's conduct of the counseling session following the appraisal?
5. Do you agree or disagree that a single characteristic or trait should affect the entire appraisal result?
6. Do you feel that Mr. Harris exhibited a bad attitude toward the job and his manager? On the basis of his last remark, would you ask for his resignation? Would you discharge him?
7. Did Mr. Willis offer any constructive criticism or tangible solution to the problem?
8. How should the appraisal and counseling session have been conducted?

CHAPTER 4

Management Control Through the Use of Documentation Standards

INTRODUCTION / Standards are an important part of the management process in that they directly affect the optimal utilization of the human, hardware, software, material, time, and budget resources. The standards are developed or established during the planning function for use in managing operations during the pre-executory and executory phases.

Data processing standards may be placed in either of two major classifications: documentation and performance.

Documentation standards provide the guides to be followed in developing and executing an operation. These standards are developed during the planning phase and subsequently applied during the other functions of the management process. Included in this category are the policy manuals, operating procedures, information processing systems documentation, codes, and so forth. This chapter will discuss the documentation standard and the documentation of information processing systems.

Performance standards are the yardsticks or measures that are used to monitor an activity and to establish and/or maintain uniformity in a process or project. Performance standards are an important part of the controlling function in the management process. Chapter 5 is devoted to a discussion of performance standards.

THE DEVELOPMENT, IMPORTANCE, AND DOCUMENTATION OF STANDARDS

Methods of Developing Standards

Some standards are developed by governmental agencies; technical societies; and trade, manufacturers', and industrial associations. However, most standards are developed by each organization for its own use.

There are four basic methods used in the development of standards. They are:

1. Estimating
2. Experience basis
3. Scientific techniques
4. Records basis

1. ESTIMATING. Standards set by estimation are often referred to as guesstimates, because they are simply reasonable approximations of what models should be. As there needs to be an element of flexibility within a standard, guesstimates can be adjusted in line with current needs and operating conditions.

2. EXPERIENCE BASIS. Using experience is a common standards-developing technique. The manager applies his prior training, experience, knowledge, and other factors to determine the requirements and methods to be applied. The danger in utilizing this approach is that the manager may not evaluate all of the necessary elements in an existing situation or setting for inclusion in a standard. However, based on his past experience, an effective manager can produce meaningful standards.

3. SCIENTIFIC TECHNIQUES. These techniques utilize various scientific procedures, such as time study, mathematical models, measuring instruments, and specially designed software. In addition, provision is generally made for personal factors, fatigue, equipment, and delays. The application of some of these techniques may require specialized training or experience. As a result, the manager may need to secure the assistance of in-house or external activities in the development of a standard.

4. RECORDS BASIS. This method utilizes empirical data collected from payroll, accounting, budget, or other types of records. A standard developed from such data is reasonably accurate because it is based on available information about a past performance for personnel, equipment, funds, or materials.

REFORMULATION

In the development of a preliminary standard, the manager may utilize any one of the four methods or a combination of them. After he has formulated the standard, it is implemented and then evaluated to determine its effectiveness. The evaluation must include a feedback procedure aimed at locating problem areas. Subsequently, the manager may find it necessary to reformulate the standard, in which case he has to determine its probable effect on the operation before actuating it. The feedback procedure is reinitiated to ascertain whether the correction or modification provides a satisfactory answer or solution to the problem. The effective standard must then be established as one of the interacting control elements in the management process.

The Importance of Standards

Before a manager develops a standard, he must fully understand its importance to an organization. The same applies to the upper echelon in the hierarchical structure, without whose support no standards program can be effective. It must be readily accepted that standards are an important tool in planning, as well as the means of simplifying the organizing, coordinating, directing, and controlling functions of the management process.

Standards are important because they can:

1. Determine the effectiveness of the organization
2. Be a basis of communications
3. Minimize the impact of personnel changes
4. Ensure compliance with the policies and practices
5. Minimize the effect of changes
6. Be used to establish schedules
7. Be used to determine manpower requirements
8. Be an aid in cost estimating and budgeting

1. THE EFFECTIVENESS OF THE ORGANIZATION. In the dynamic process of management, the manager must constantly monitor output in order to determine his function's progress and effectiveness. This determination is made by comparing the results of the operation plus resource utilization with the level of desired quality and achievement. The specifications must be defined by the manager during planning, in that they become the standards for preparing schedules, determining resource requirements, and balancing resource utilization. For example, a manager who has established personnel performance standards in his programming activity will be able to determine if a programmer is discharging his duties and responsibilities at the desired level of performance. This is because the programmer's effectiveness is measured by his ability to function within or above that standard.

2. A BASIS FOR COMMUNICATIONS. A standard serves as a communications medium between the various functional activities that are directly and indirectly involved in data processing operation. It becomes a documented source of information on such items as design and testing practices for systems and programs, change procedures, acceptable documentation formats, standard charting symbols, authorized codes, and management controls. For example, the standardized charting symbols used in system and program flowcharting can be clearly understood by the systems, programming, operations and audit personnel. Furthermore, standardized documentation of data processing applications enables the internal and external auditors to audit and review the operational systems and programs.

3. THE IMPACT OF PERSONNEL CHANGES. Personnel turnover can be very costly and disruptive to an organization, especially in terms of having to train new employees. To help cope with this problem, standards must be developed and implemented for symbols, labels, abbreviations, charting techniques, input-

output specifications, macros, and other programming, analysis, and documentation techniques. These standards can be readily employed in training new personnel, thereby reducing the break-in period and maintaining the production schedule with only minimal disruption.

4. COMPLIANCE WITH POLICIES AND PRACTICES. Every organization needs to establish policies and practices that will serve as guides for managerial activity. These provide for uniform adaptation and enforcement of duties, responsibilities, and administrative and operating practices in the management process. Also, they relieve the manager of the responsibility for making repetitive decisions for similar problems and situations. Record file retention policies, absence reporting, and supplies requisitioning procedures fall into this general classification. In addition, the availability of standardized practices and policies enables the manager to delegate authority to his subordinates. Each subordinate can avail himself of this standards information to complete any assigned task with a minimal amount of supervision.

5. THE EFFECT OF CHANGES. It is necessary in data processing to establish standards that will simplify the transition from one system into another, as well as from one type of hardware to another. To provide for a more orderly conversion, standardization must be developed for such items as charting symbols and techniques, tables, label conventions, and documentation of applications. Simplifying the conversion process reduces costs and errors, thereby expediting the return on investment in a new system, program, or hardware. Standards are also used effectively in feasibility studies to reduce cost and time expenditures incurred in the conduct of such a project. Through the application and utilization of established standards, much time can be saved in the preparation of cost and savings schedules, the determination of conversion and production schedules, and the initial design of proposed systems.

6. ESTABLISHING SCHEDULES. In both planning and directing, the manager needs performance standards in order to develop realistic project or operation schedules. These standards are applied to the allocation of resources and to the selection and evaluation of personnel and equipment. They effectively indicate the time required to perform an operation or task through application of the necessary resources.

7. MANPOWER REQUIREMENTS. Manpower requirements must be quantified. However, before this can be accomplished, the manager has to develop the measure of personnel performance required for an effective operational system. The established standard is then used to develop a production, conversion, or planning schedule based on projected results. For example, when a manager establishes a keystroke productivity standard for his keypunch personnel, he defines the number of card columns to be punched and the type of data. Then he evaluates the source documents to be processed in order to establish his projected productive capability. After that, the keystroke rate is applied to total production requirements to indicate the number of keypunch personnel necessary for an effective operation.

8. COST ESTIMATING AND BUDGETING. It is essential in any organization to

have standards available for indicating the cost of an operation or modification. Before any decision can be made, it is necessary that cost estimates be available and budget requirements be established. Failure to make a sound financial projection can cause rejection or reduction of an operation or project. Furthermore, it can prove to be a costly venture if the monetary requirements are overestimated or underestimated: underestimating costs may make it necessary to borrow money or reallocate additional funds; overestimating costs can be a wasteful practice in that more funds may have been borrowed or allocated than needed, or some other activities may have been curtailed or postponed to divert funds to this project.

Data processing personnel must constantly provide cost and savings data for existing or proposed projects. It is essential, therefore, that effective standards are developed to ensure that all cost evaluations are conducted on the same basis.

Documentation of Standards

To be effective, a standards program must provide for the recording of all documentation and performance standards used by the organization. The reasons for recording the materials is that it:

1. Provides a permanent record
2. Establishes a basis for audit and review
3. Makes communicable information available

1. A PERMANENT RECORD. A documented standards program provides a permanent record of the policies, practices, procedures, and techniques to be enforced within an organization. These can be distributed in the form of what is called a policy or practices manual in order to ensure uniform application in all situations and problems. Included in such a manual are specific items such as attendance reporting, sick-leave policy, authorization limits on purchase requisitions, grievance procedures, safety guides, and many other topics.

Performance standards for data processing and other functional activities are properly recorded in data processing or industrial engineering standards manuals, which are intended for use in planning, organizing, scheduling, budgeting, and costing activities. The availability of such standardized data ensures that the necessary manpower, material, equipment, and fiscal requirements are ascertained and met. The documented performance standards include all the relevant factors and variables in each calculation; this provides for uniformity of application, saves recalculation time, and reduces or eliminates errors (see chapter 5).

Systems, programming, and operations documentation of procedures and techniques are made available in data processing manuals. Such documentation includes console operating instructions, descriptions of systems, program listings, standardized macros, and numerous other related items.

2. A BASIS FOR AUDIT AND REVIEW. To retain their effectiveness, standards

must be reviewed periodically in terms of their currency, relevancy, clarity, and compatibility. Failure to maintain currency affects the validity of managerial decisions made on the basis of an existing standard. The relevancy must be questioned to determine its contribution to the effectiveness of the existing operation. If a standard has lost its value, it must be deleted or reconstructed to avoid any confusion or problems arising from its continued existence. Clarity is necessary to eliminate misinterpretation, which can result in the misuse of valuable resources. A standard must also be reviewed to determine its compatibility with other existing standards. If there is a conflict with such standards, then some modification or change must be made. This is not a simple task because the manager has to define, limit, analyze, and evaluate the problem. When the problem has been isolated, he determines the best approach and then implements it in the form of a revised standard.

3. AVAILABILITY OF COMMUNICABLE INFORMATION. Documentation facilitates an interchange of information between intra-functional and inter-functional activities, subsidiaries, satellite units, and other organizations. This capability is particularly important when a manager is responsible for a centralized or host data processing organization and must disseminate the information to reporting or distributed units. It is also important in instances where large organizations, such as holding corporations, require an interchange of information between the subsidiary organizations and the corporate offices. The documentation on a unique program, for example, would be submitted to the holding corporation's administrator of data processing, who would arrange for copying and distribution of the documentation. Any subsidiary that could utilize the computer program would have the capability of implementing it, with little or no delay and at a fraction of the original development cost.

Review Questions: Group 4A

1. Name and briefly describe the techniques used to develop a standard.
2. What are some of the tangible benefits that may result from the application of standards to the management process?
3. Why is it important to document standards?

GUIDELINES AND ENFORCEMENT

Guidelines for Documentation

There are guidelines or rules that should be followed in the effective documentation of standards. These guidelines specify that:

1. All documentation must be identified
2. The standard must include a statement of purpose
3. Master set and copies must be given maximum protection
4. Revisions should be in the form of complete pages

5. Specialized symbols should be used to indicate new and/or revised materials
6. Specialized symbols should be used to indicate deletions
7. Effective dates of revision must be indicated

1. IDENTIFICATION OF DOCUMENTATION. A brief but self-explanatory title must be included on the first page of each standard in order to facilitate identification. In addition, the date the standard became effective should be given at the top of each page to indicate the currency status of a standard. Furthermore the manual should be identified, by code number or some other means, at the top of each page. This system of page and content identification simplifies the maintenance and filing procedures. Figure 4.1 shows two examples of identification headings used on documentation. The ones illustrated are for the first page of a standard; subsequent pages would include the same information except for the title.

2. STATEMENT OF PURPOSE. Each directive, policy, practice, or standard must carry a general statement of purpose as its first entry. The statement should be written in layman's terminology so as to make the document's purpose readily identifiable by any member of the organization. In Figure 4.2 are given two sample paragraphs, each of which could be a statement of purpose on a document.

3. PROTECTION FOR MASTER SET AND COPIES. It is best to store the complete and updated master standards in a separate building with fire-resistant rooms, which should have a fire-resistance capacity of not less than two hours and be equipped with an automatic sprinkler system. The materials should be kept in noncombustible containers, such as metal files or cabinets. Safeguarding complete and updated master standards provides protection against loss, fraud, theft, destruction by fire or other disaster, access by unauthorized personnel,

Figure 4.1 Samples of identification of documentation

R. S. COMPUTATIONS, INC.   Data Processing Manual 10.1
                                 September 22, 19__

                  Data Processing Glossary

R. S. COMPUTATIONS, INC.   Data Processing Manual 10.1
November 10, 19__   Part I
                                 Chapter 5
                                 Section 11

                  Data Processing Glossary

1. GENERAL

The purpose of this instruction is to prescribe the documentation format for data processing applications.

1. GENERAL

This instruction prescribes the numbering systems which are to be used to facilitate the identification of computer programs, magnetic tapes, and/or magnetic disk packs.

Figure 4.2 Samples of statement of purpose

and illegal alteration of modification of their contents. (The subject of safeguards is also discussed in chapter 10.)

Similarly, copies of the documentation must be maintained and kept in separate areas for reasons of security and internal audit control.

There is now an increasing trend toward the auditing of data processing procedures and programs by internal and/or external auditors. The auditors' review process includes a comparison of the master documentation with the copies. In addition, it involves detection of possible fraud and includes tests for currency, relevancy, clarity, and compatibility.

4. Complete pages for revisons. Changes in the manuals should be in the form of complete pages. This permits complete withdrawal of the old page and insertion of the new one. The new pages are identified by the effective date and the standard's identification at the top of each page.

Page substitution eliminates the necessity of entering or deleting materials by pen or pencil. Generally, the responsibility for performing these alterations is delegated to a secretarial or clerical employee, who performs the task on a "when-time-is-available" basis. Consequently, changes are either made in an incomplete and inaccurate fashion or are not made at all. This haphazard approach destroys the accuracy, relevancy, and timeliness of a standard. In the experience of this author, the substitution of complete pages has proved to be the more popular and effective method for maintaining documentation.

5. Specialized symbols and new and/or revised materials. Specialized symbols such as a single "*" or "@" should be used to identify the new and/or revised material added or inserted on a page since the last revision. This will readily indicate to the reader where a change has been made. Figure 4.3 illustrates the use of the "@" symbol to identify a revision of a paragraph that has been revised to clarify the instructions, data flow, process, and responsibilities. If the special symbol was not included at the beginning and end of the revised material, the user would have to read both the deleted page and the new page to learn what had been specifically revised in the paragraph.

(*Before Revision*)

4. The payroll clerk will forward the clock cards to the control clerk for posting to the Input Register before being submitted to the Keypunch Section.

(*After Revision*)

@ 4. The payroll clerk will forward the employee clock cards to the data control clerk. The data control clerk will post the batch control information to the Input Register. After the information has been posted, the batched clock cards are submitted to the Keypunch Section for conversion. @

Figure 4.3 Identification of material revisions

6. SPECIALIZED SYMBOLS AND DELETIONS. Specialized symbols such as an "*" or "@" may also be utilized to indicate deletions. However, to clarify the difference between a revision and a deletion, it is recommended that a double "**" or "@@" symbol be used for deletions.

In Figure 4.4, a single asterisk symbol appears at the beginning and end of the revised paragraph. This alerts the user to the fact that a revision has been made. In continuing with the review, the user will note the double asterisk symbols within the paragraph. These symbols may indicate the deletion of one or

Figure 4.4 Identification of sentence deletions

(*Before Revision*)

4. At the end of each month the data processing operations group will prepare a listing of all scrap loss transactions. The data records will be sorted by accounting charge code. All items in charge code 3645 will be listed on 3-part, 10×13 form. Items in charge code 8966 will be listed on a 6-part, 8½×11 form. Other charge codes are listed on 2-part paper.

(*After Revisions*)

* 4. At the end of each month the data processing operations group will prepare a listing of all scrap loss transactions. The data records will be sorted by the accounting charge code, record positions 44–47.** All items in charge code 8966 will be outputted on a 6-part, 8½×11 form. All other charge codes will be outputted on a 2-part, 8½×11 form. *

```
b. As an aid in preparation of the M-98B report.
8. @@
```

Figure 4.5 Identification of paragraph deletions

more sentences at this point within the narrative. In the example given, only one sentence had been deleted. This was the sentence about charge code 3645. In addition, some changes were made in phraseology, as well as in clarification of form size.

Figure 4.5 illustrates the use of the double "@@" symbol to indicate deletion of the final paragraph of a procedure. In this example, it is unnecessary to utilize a single "@" symbol to indicate a revision. The double "@@" symbol following the paragraph number immediately signals the deletion of the previous material.

The "@" and "*" symbols can also be used, in their appropriate single or double forms, to indicate that a major portion of the material has been added, revised, or deleted on a page. These should be positioned in the upper-left and lower-right corners of a page for prompt identification. Figure 4.6 illustrates the use of a single "*" symbol at the top and bottom of a page from a unit-record-oriented procedure. In examining the before and after segments, it can be seen that changes have been made to the control levels, card columns, and file disposition. Consequently, each part of machine operation #5 has been affected. This is why it is more practical to simply begin and end the page with a special symbol rather than individually mark each change on the page.

7. EFFECTIVE DATES OF REVISION. To maintain and ensure currency, it is necessary to include the revision date at the top of each page. This indicates the effective date of the addition, deletion, or modification to the standard. In addition, the date of previous issue for a given page should also be included at the top of each revised page.

Figure 4.7 illustrates a suggested date block to be included at the top of each page. The inclusion of the date simplifies filing of changes and auditing of the manual.

When revisions are received by a manager, he reviews them to determine their effect on his functional activity. Following the review, he communicates the revisions to the affected subordinates. If any clarification or orientation is required, the manager is in a position to take immediate action. Prompt action will eliminate or minimize any subsequent problems.

D. P. Operations Manual 10.2   October 15, 19＿
Part I   Job Number RS-103
Chapter 5
Section 10

Machine Operation #5
Merge and Sequence Check

A. Select the previously reproduced property accounting summary cards, which are in sequence (Intermediate) property class (card columns 1–5) and (Minor) line number (card columns 6–7), and place these in the primary feed of the collator. Select the consolidated property accounting cards, which are also in sequence by property class and line number, from file cabinet 2-E and place these in the secondary feed of the collator. Wire the control panel to merge as follows:

Control Level	*Field Identification*	*Card Columns*
Minor	Line Number	6–7
Intermediate	Property Class	1–5

B. Sequence check the merged file using the same controls as indicated in step A.
   1. Hold the file for Operation #7, Step B.

Page 15

(Bottom of Page)

Figure 4.6 Identification of major revisions on a page

Enforcement of Standards

Behind each standard there must be some enforcement provision that has the backing of the executive committee. Every standard is in danger of falling victim to indifference and casualness if the upper echelon does not clearly state that it expects them to be followed as prescribed unless modified or deleted.

Figure 4.7 Identification of revision date

R. S. COMPUTATIONS, INC.   Data Processing Manual 10.1
       Reissue *May 31, 19＿*
       Replaces issue of *Dec. 1, 19＿*

Data Processing Glossary

(Top of Page)

* D. P. Operations Manual 10.2   December 1, 19 __
Part I   Job Number RS-103
Chapter 5
Section 10

Machine Operation #5
Merge and Sequence Check

A. Select the previously reproduced property accounting summary cards, which are in sequence (Major) ledger code (card column 37), (Intermediate) property class (card columns 2–6), and (Minor) line number (card columns 7–8), and place these in the primary feed of the collator. Select the consolidated property accounting cards, which are also in sequence by ledger code, property class, and line number, from file cabinet 2-E and place these in the secondary feed of the collator. Merge the files, controlling as follows:

Control Level	Field Identification	Card Columns
Minor	Line Number	7–8
Intermediate	Property Class	2–6
Major	Ledger Code	37

B. Sequence check the merged file, using the same controls as indicated in Step A.

   1. Hold the sequence checked file for Operation #6, Step A.

Page 15*

(Bottom of Page)

Failure of the executive committee to assume this responsibility may result in subordinates assuming authority for policy making and direction that has not been delegated to them. Lack of adherence to standards may result in problems, bottlenecks, implementation of faulty corrective procedures, unnecessary fiscal expenditures, and interruptions in the production schedule.

Enforcement is not only concerned with adherence. It also involves:

1. Audits and reviews
2. Temporary standards
3. Modification and revision
4. Distribution and follow-up

1. AUDITS AND REVIEWS. Standards have to be audited and reviewed periodically to maintain their effectiveness. Otherwise, they may fall into a state of disregard and misuse. Some persons will completely avoid using them due to a lack of confidence; others will apply them only selectively, for their own advantage. It is clear, therefore, that an outdated or obsolete standard can become the source of problems and result in ineffective decisions. It is also clear that every

effort must be made to uncover any deficiencies and to correct them accurately and promptly. This can best be accomplished through regularly scheduled audits and reviews of existing standards. If the task is too massive, then the most frequently used standards should be examined regularly, with all others being reviewed on a sampling basis to ease the workload. However, an adequate number must be covered during each review to ensure that every standard receives at least one audit per year in terms of its currency, relevance, clarity, and compatibility.

2. TEMPORARY STANDARDS. Enforcement is also concerned with the temporary modification and/or revision of standards. One of the major problems is the unwarranted and illegal change or modification of a standard, which can affect the standard's accuracy, compatibility, and relevance. In some instances, such as satellite operations, it may be necessary to deviate from an established standard. However, such departures must be approved by the controlling standards group. This procedure involves submitting a written request containing a complete explanation for any deviation. Because of its ultimate effect upon the overall organization, a deviation must be evaluated by the control group in terms of relevancy to a given standard and compatibility with others. Subsequently, the group will either grant its approval or reject the request. Approval, though, should be limited to a specified time period. Upon expiration of the dated approval, the original request must be reviewed before any extension is granted or revocation made. This procedure provides a form of management control to prevent a proliferation of deviations.

Many organizations facilitate identification of authorized deviations by printing them on nonwhite paper and filing them in front of the affected pages in the appropriate standards manual. The deviations are also identified by the words, TEMPORARY STANDARD, and placement of the effective duration period at the top of the first page. Figure 4.8 illustrates a page heading as it may appear on a temporary standard.

When a temporary standard is extended, a cover page with the new effective period indicated must be issued. This removes the necessity of any pen or pencil alterations, as well as any doubts or confusion regarding the effectiveness of the standard. When audits and reviews are made, the outdated standards must be removed from the manuals if this has not been done already.

Figure 4.8 Sample page heading for a temporary standard

TEMPORARY STANDARD

R. S. COMPUTATIONS, INC.   Data Processing Manual 10.1
                                            Effective Period:
                                            Sept. 15, 19__ to
                                            Oct. 15, 19__

```
┌─────────────────────────────────────────────────────────────────┐
│                    TEMPORARY STANDARD                             │
│  R. S. COMPUTATIONS, INC.              Data Processing Manual 10.1 │
│                                        Effective Period:          │
│                                        Sept. 15, 19__ to          │
│                                        Oct. 15, 19__              │
│  N.B. Temporary Standard for the Alexander Street Office Only.    │
└─────────────────────────────────────────────────────────────────┘
```

Figure 4.9 Example of a temporary standard for a selected group

If a standards deviation is authorized for only a selected group or function, this must be clearly indicated at the top of the first page. This point is illustrated in Figure 4.9.

3. MODIFICATION AND REVISION. Every organization needs to establish a procedure for the proper modification or revision of a standard. This activity can be performed only by the standards group, with the proper approval of the executive committee. If formulating a change, the standards group should consult the affected personnel and give them an opportunity to review the drafts and make suggestions. Occasionally one of the parties affected may become uncooperative or resentful and may provide some distorted information or deliberately omit some facts. This problem can be overcome by verifying the data through direct observation or by checking with an alternate source. Despite these hazards, the personal contact will help to "sell" the standard because people are generally averse to unexpected and impersonally presented changes.

The modified standard should then be prepared for approval by the chief administrative officer in the organization. He should be a member of the executive committee and be at least two levels above the manager of the standards group. When the executive committee has approved the standard, it is then published.

4. DISTRIBUTION AND FOLLOW-UP. Following publication, the standard is distributed to all functional activities that maintain standards manuals. The master copy should be placed in the appropriate master manual and filed in a protective facility. A reference copy should also be maintained in the standards group for use by standards personnel and other members of the organization not having immediate access to the manuals.

The distribution pattern for all changes and/or additions is stipulated in the distributions paragraph of the foreword to each manual. A sample distributions paragraph is included in Figure 4.10. Following initial distribution of the manual, each subsequent distribution pattern is shown on a change sheet. A sample of a change sheet is illustrated in Figure 4.11. The change sheet is a multi-purpose document. Its primary purpose is to alert the user that his function's copy of the relevant manual must be updated and to identify the pages affected in the attachment paragraph. The change sheet also provides limited instructions for updating the manual in paragraph 1. The second paragraph provides a historical

Data Processing Manual 10.1   R. S. COMPUTATIONS, INC.
Part II   November 10, 19__

FOREWORD

1. *PURPOSE.* This part of DP Manual 10.1 contains the electronic data processing procedures necessary to the implementation and operation of the Inventory Control functional area.

2. *FORMAT.* This part of the manual is divided into sections; each section represents a specific report and/or output to be derived from the computerized process.

3. *CHANGES AND SUPPLEMENTS.* Changes and supplements to this manual will be distributed in the form of complete pages or sections. This will permit withdrawal of the old page and insertion of the new page. New pages will be distinguished from old pages by the date at the top of the page.

New and/or revised material that has been added to a page since the last revision will be indicated by a single "@" symbol preceding and following the material added. When a portion of the text has been deleted, double "@@" symbols will be inserted to denote the deleted material. In the event that a majority of the text on a page has been changed, a single "@" symbol will appear in the upper-left and lower-right corners of the page.

Recommended changes to this manual should be brought to the attention of the Corporate Standards Group.

4. *DISTRIBUTION.* Changes or supplements will be forwarded from the Corporate Standards Group direct to the functional activities concerned through normal channels, unless otherwise specified. However, to ensure that staff and operating activities maintaining basic manuals receive all changes, the user should advise the publications distribution section of the proper routing for all changes and/or additions to the manual.

Figure 4.10 Sample foreword to standards manual

record of the previous page changes made to this standards manual. The change sheet also explains the use of the special symbols and identifies the distribution pattern for the standard.

The distributed copies are inserted in the appropriate manuals by the secretarial staff in the various receiving groups. To ensure proper updating by the users, the standards group conducts periodic audits to determine content currency and validity.

A follow-up should be conducted on each reissued standard within a reasonable period of time to determine its effectiveness. The determination is made by comparing the standard's functional effectiveness with planned objectives. If it fails to meet the desired objectives, the standards group must then continue with the application of the feedback concept (discussed in chapter 1) to resolve the problem.

```
┌─────────────────────────────────────────────────────────────────────┐
│  CHANGE 3                            R. S. COMPUTATIONS, INC.         │
│  Data Processing Manual 10.1         December 8, 19__                 │
│  Part II                                                              │
│                                                                       │
│  TO BE FILED IN FRONT OF PART II, DP MANUAL 10.1, JANUARY 2, 19__     │
│                                                                       │
│      1. Changes to this manual are made on a page basis. Upon receipt of each │
│  change, the user will insert the change into its respective place in the manual. │
│  The numbered change sheet will be filed as directed for reference purposes. │
│      2. Previously published changes are as follows:                  │
│          Change 1, April 9, 19__, Sections 1 and 14                   │
│          Change 2, May 12, 19__, Section 22                           │
│      3. The symbols "@" and "@@" are used throughout to indicate additions, │
│  deletions, and revisions.                                            │
│                                             E. A. Szweda              │
│                                             Vice-President            │
│                                             Administrative Services   │
│  Attachment:                                                          │
│      Change 3—Insert pages where indicated                            │
│      Section 9 (13.1, 13.6)                                           │
│  Distribution:                                                        │
│      To all holders of Part II, DP Manual 10.1                        │
│                                                                       │
└─────────────────────────────────────────────────────────────────────┘
```

Figure 4.11 Sample change sheet

Review Questions: Group 4B

1. In the documentation of standards, certain guidelines must be established. What are these?
2. Why are special symbols used in the documentation of standards?
3. Behind each standard there must be some enforcement provision. Why?
4. How should temporary deviations to a standard be handled?

DOCUMENTATION STANDARD FOR AN INFORMATION PROCESSING SYSTEM

The documentation standard for an information processing system outlines the content and format for each document that describes the system from its preliminary design to implementation. Each document in the standard serves a particular purpose, such as identifying the data processing policies, practices, procedures, requirements, and preparatory actions for others to follow.

The documentation of an information processing system provides or may provide the following benefits:

A content and format guide for documentation of all data processing procedures, policies, practices, and requirements.

A complete record of an information processing system, from analysis to implementation and subsequent maintenance.

A method for the generation, maintenance, and dissemination of technical and support data for a particular program, system, or project.

Instructions for the preparation of input and interpretation of the reports and/or output.

Data for simplifying and facilitating either conversion to new or upgraded hardware and/or software or adoption of a new approach.

Data on system and performance requirements, codes, schedules, resources, budgets, and other related elements for use in hardware, software, and system feasibility studies.

Data for efficient scheduling of operations and equipment.

Data for development of budgets and cost/savings estimates.

A communications medium for the transfer of information.

A basis for audit and review procedures and updating that is required as a result of a modification or change.

Data for the development of long-range and contingency plans.

MANAGERIAL RESPONSIBILITY

Many data processing managers do not wish to become involved in documentation of systems because they consider it threatening to their own indispensability. Or, they dismiss it on the grounds that it is too time-consuming and that it detracts from performance of normal daily activities and development of new systems and programs. The programming managers and software systems personnel will frequently promote the argument that documentation standards limit their creativity and force them to program less efficiently. Based on the programmer turnover rates experienced by some shops, it would behoove the programming manager to enforce the documentation standard by assuming the stance that no program is finished until the documentation has also been completed. Some managers often regard the expenditure of funds to be inadvisable for such a relatively nonessential item as documentation. This form of negative or ill-advised thinking either floats down generally from the upper echelons or results specifically from the executive committee's lack of awareness about the importance or significance of documentation.

Despite any absence of encouragement from above, a manager should assume a positive approach to documentation; the most economical and efficient way to do anything is to execute it correctly *the first time*. Prevention of problems is less costly in terms of both manpower and money.

Some managers prefer to excuse themselves from responsibility by using the timeworn phrase, "We are too busy at the moment; we will complete the documentation when things ease up." In the experience of this author, though, a data processing group never realistically reaches a point where "things ease up."

The dynamic nature of data processing calls repeatedly for the development of new applications and for the maintenance and improvement of old ones. So the things-ease-up argument clearly indicates that a manager has failed to schedule time in the overall project for the documentation task. Nevertheless, no system is complete until it has been thoroughly documented. Therefore, a manager should realistically expect to allocate between 5 and 25 percent of project time for the generation and maintenance of documentation. The actual allocation of time may depend on the size and complexity of the information processing system, amount of programming involved, number of interfaces with user personnel and other interrelated activities, and the types of hardware involved.

ELEMENTS OF AN INFORMATION PROCESSING STANDARD

The documentation standard for an information processing system consists of a number of descriptive elements. The principal elements and their components are:

1. The system abstract
2. The system flowchart
3. The program abstract
4. The program logic description
5. Layout specifications
6. User instructions
7. Operating instructions
8. Program listings
9. Glossary
10. Test plan

For each system, the applicable descriptive elements on the above list are grouped together and incorporated into the system description manual and the appropriate software and user manuals to provide the details needed in order to understand, develop, activate, operate, and maintain a system.

1. THE SYSTEM ABSTRACT. The system abstract is a general description of the total system—a summary of the various interacting elements. It describes the data manipulation and computational phases; the conditions and/or parameters required; the interfaces between input, output, and data base files; and information about the hardware and software. The abstract is written in layman's terminology, which facilitates understanding by managers, auditors, and other interested personnel.

A typical system abstract (as illustrated by the form shown in Figure 4.12) may contain the following information:

A descriptive title that aptly identifies the system for the user.

The functional area in which the system is operative. This may require the development of a functional-areas listing, such as Payroll, Accounting, Indus-

SYSTEM ABSTRACT	APPLICATION NO.	EFFECTIVE DATE ___ / ___ / ___	PAGE ___ OF ___

SYSTEM TITLE

SYSTEM DESCRIPTION

EQUIPMENT CONFIGURATION	RELATED SYSTEMS
STORAGE REQUIREMENTS (PRI. & AUX.)	PROGRAMMING LANGUAGE(S)
INPUT DESCRIPTION	OUTPUT DESCRIPTION
APPROVED BY	APPROVAL DATE

Figure 4.12 System abstract form

trial Engineering, Production Control, etc. Some organizations prefer to use a numerical code for identification purposes. (The code may be inserted in the Application No. block shown in the illustration. Some organizations prefer to use a more elaborate scheme for identification and control purposes.) This can prove to be a disadvantage unless all the users have a working knowledge of the coding scheme.

The effective data showing when the system was operative after testing and debugging. When a change or modification to the system is made, the revision date must be shown on the abstract. In some organizations, an "R" is appended to the date to provide a revision reference. In addition, some organizations include a copy of the previous abstract, along with correspondence and other relevant data, in the reference section of the system description manual.

A clear and concise description of the system, written in layman's terminology. This description states the objectives of the system, required functions, performance parameters, interfaces between the various files, and the interrelationship of the various functional elements of the organization affected by the system. This segment is used by audit personnel to provide for verification of actual performance in terms of stated goals.

Equipment configuration—that is, the type of data processing equipment used, including the peripheral equipment and special features, to achieve the objective. However, this segment should not include information about equipment or features that are part of the basic hardware complement but that are not utilized in the system being described.

The systems that are interrelated to the system described in the abstract must also be identified. This is particularly important because any changes to the described system must also be analyzed to determine their impact on the related systems.

The maximum primary and auxiliary memory storage requirements needed to perform the computer-related operations. For the sake of clarity, each type must be identified separately.

The programming language or languages used in the computer-related operations such as BASIC, COBOL, PL/1, ALGOL, FORTRAN, RPG, AUTOCODER, etc. The language of the primary program or module and the language or languages of the subprograms or modules.

A description of the input, output, and data base files, given in layman's terminology. This should include form names and numbers, as well as assigned file names. (If an organization utilizes data base files, the input and/or output blocks could be subdivided to facilitate separate identification.)

The date of approval by the manager of the systems group.

The actual form layout adopted by a data processing organization depends on its goals and needs. An alternative to the kind of form shown in Figure 4.12 is a

R. S. COMPUTATIONS, INC.

Part II

Data Processing
Manual 10.1
May 17, 19__

Abstract of Hourly Payroll Program

Purpose: This system is designed to process the hourly rated employees payroll. It provides for computation of gross pay; social security, federal, state, and city taxes; and the application of deductions for determination of net amount. The system utilizes a single program written in Report Program Generator on an IBM 370/135 computer.

The basic employee information and computations are printed on the Statement of Payroll Account issued to each employee. The program provides for punching of calculated current earnings cards for use in the Labor Distribution System; a year-to-date taxes and earnings record for use in various management reports; and a draft card used in printing the employee payroll draft.

In addition, the program utilizes several subroutines. These provide for: processing of cash advances and adjustments; processing of garnishments and other types of levies; determination of taxable earnings and limits under the social security law; determination of deductions that cannot be applied against the current payroll; and the accumulation of total earnings, taxes, and deductions for preparation of departmental controls.

Method: Sets of cards (one set per employee, with cards grouped by card code) are read into the computer in employee number sequence. For each employee there is a basic employee information and rate card; a second basic employee information and rate card if an employee carries a dual rate; current earnings cards; cash advances or adjustments; the year-to-date taxes and earnings record; priority deductions (deductions not applied in previous payroll processing), garnishments, or levies; and current payroll deductions.

Restrictions: The following represent processing restrictions within the computer program:

1. The cards must be within employee number sequence
2. The card set for each employee must be in a controlled order sequence, based on card code in card columns 79–80
3. Each employee card set must contain a tax and earnings card, card code 48 in card columns 79–80

Storage Requirements: 4,000 positions of primary core storage.

Equipment Specifications: IBM 370/135 computer equipped with a Disk Operating System.

Figure 4.13 Alternative system abstract

very simple form on which can be stated the purpose, method of processing, restrictions, and storage and equipment requirements. A completed example of this type of form appears in Figure 4.13.

The original copy of the abstract should be maintained with the entire documentation package for a given system in a separate fire-resistant room. Reproduced copies should be placed in each documentation folder distributed to the systems, programming, operations, and user groups.

2. The system flowchart. Included in every documentation folder must be a complete system flowchart. Such a chart is the basis for the development of an entire system. It provides an overall picture, which can be used to:

Indicate the origination, flow, and disposition of data elements

Indicate major operations and users

Indicate the type and extent of management controls

Implement forms, and reports control studies

Give management an understanding of a system

Identify any bottlenecks and duplications of effort

Serve as a basis for audit and review

Effect or investigate changes in an existing system

Identify the entry, use of forms, and disposition of forms in a forms control study

Identify the work flow in a reports control study

The system flowchart (see Figure 4.14) is used by the software personnel to identify the data flow and identify the programming requirements. The flowchart is also utilized by the user and audit personnel to describe the general system logic and its capabilities.

The symbols drawn on the flowchart should be the standard developed by the American National Standards Institute (ANSI).

3. Program abstract. The program abstract is a detailed description of the processing logic and requirements for a given program. (A separate abstract is prepared for each program used in the system.) The logic segment is described in the program description block. In this part of the form, we identify the program's initialization or housekeeping procedures, condition checking, computational requirements, editing, subprogram, subroutine, and/or module references, breakpoints, and data linkages. The processing requirements segment of the abstract is used to identify the related programs; the hardware configuration required to execute the given program; the special hardware features required by the program; the program's primary language and the language of the subprogram, subroutine and/or modules; the storage requirements for execution of the program; and a description of the program's inputs and outputs in terms of file numbers, form numbers, file names, etc.

The program abstract (see Figure 4.15) may be prepared initially by the systems analyst or a programmer and is used as a communications tool to describe in general terms the program's requirements, computational and data handling procedures. The finalized abstract is included in the documentation manuals for the systems, programming, operations, and user manuals.

4. Program logic descriptions. Program logic descriptions may be illustrated in the form of a program flowchart, program narrative, decision table, or

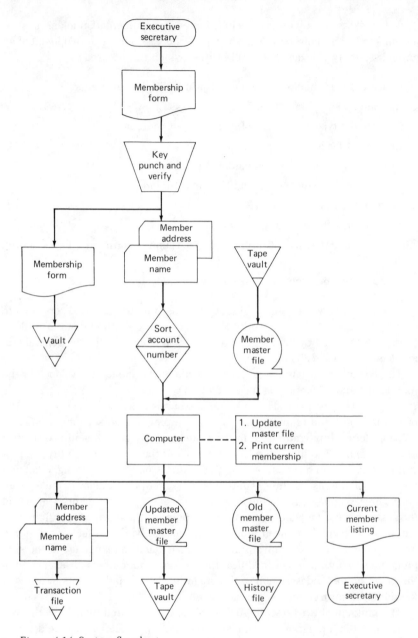

Figure 4.14 System flowchart

PROGRAM ABSTRACT	APPLICATION NO.	EFFECTIVE DATE ___ / ___ / ___	PAGE —OF—

PROGRAM NAME	PROGRAM NO.

PROGRAM DESCRIPTION

RELATED PROGRAMS

CONFIGURATION REQUIRED	SPECIAL FEATURES UTILIZED

LANGUAGE (S)	STORAGE REQUIREMENTS (PRI. & AUX.)

INPUT DESCRIPTION	OUTPUT DESCRIPTION

PROGRAMMER	APPROVED BY	APPROVAL DATE

Figure 4.15 Program abstract form

HIPO structure. Any of the previously mentioned techniques may be used to describe a problem's logic in a symbolic format—an essential tool in the design, development, implementation, and maintenance of a computer program. Carefully prepared logic will help to ensure that a program is meeting its stated objectives; to facilitate desk checking; to facilitate the preparation of "artificial test data" and the test plan; and to furnish an effective communications medium for data processing personnel.

a) Program flowcharts. There are two basic types of program flowchart. They are the (1) macro-diagram and the (2) micro-diagram.

(1) The Macro-Diagram. The macro-diagram illustrates the overall logic for each computer program; that is, it indicates the major decisions and alternate paths, the operations, and the linkage to subroutines and subprograms. These generalized operations have to be translated into detailed steps on a micro-diagram before any program coding can be initiated.

A macro-diagram should be machine- and software-independent, but applica-

Figure 4.16 Simple macro-diagram

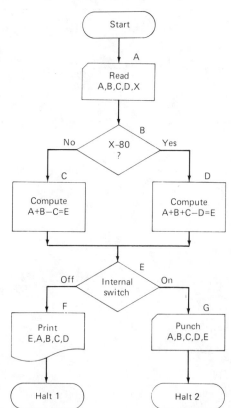

ble to any hardware configuration or programming language. It must be clear and complete, but brief so as not to duplicate the charting performed on the micro-diagram.

Figure 4.16 illustrates a simple macro-diagram. The logic indicates only the major operations and does not attempt to specify the many detailed steps required to accomplish each major task. For example, the card input operation identified as "A" calls for the inputting of a record, its storage, and definition of the data elements contained therein. This relationship is further illustrated in Figure 4.17, in which step "D" of the macro-diagram is translated into the required number of steps on the micro-diagram.

Figure 4.17 Comparison of macro-diagram and micro-diagram steps

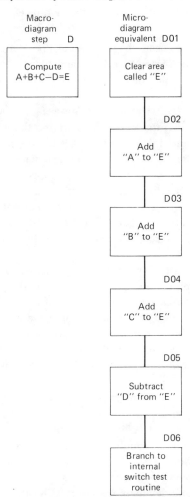

There are certain rules for the preparation of macro-diagrams that must be implemented in order to establish an effective documentation standard. These rules specify that:

The symbols used should be the standard ones developed by the ANSI.

The macro-diagrams should be drawn on paper that can be readily reproduced so as to simplify distribution of copies. In some organizations, the diagrams are drawn on 8 ½" x 11" white bond paper, which can be quickly reproduced on most copying machines. Organizations with more sophisticated copying machines can use paper of larger sizes, as well as flowcharting worksheets.

Copies of the diagrams should be replaced in the various documentation folders.

Each diagram should contain an identification block for providing the necessary identification data.

Each symbol on the macro-diagram should be identified by an alphabetic character in sequence from A to Z. If more than 26 symbols are required, a double-letter identification mode can be used; that is, from AA to ZZ.

(2) The Micro-Diagram. The micro-diagram is a detailed translation of the logic operations shown on the macro-diagram and the input, output, data base and storage requirements included in the layout specifications. It illustrates in logical sequence the data transfer, decision, calculation, exception, input, and output steps. Depending on the policies and practices of the data processing organization, the micro-diagrams may be generalized or detailed. In the latter form, each symbol drawn on the diagram is the equivalent of one source program language statement. In a generalized version of a micro-diagram the programmer depends on his memory and/or notes to code all of the necessary source program steps.

In many installations the systems group prepares the macro-diagrams and, after a review of the requirements, submits them to the programming group for preparation of the micro-diagrams and coding of the computer instructions. In some installations, the micro-diagrams are prepared by the systems personnel, who will then submit them to the programming group for coding. In still other installations, the programming staff prepares its own macro- and micro-diagrams based on information obtained from the system abstract and from the systems personnel.

b) *Program narrative.* The program logic narrative form illustrated in Figure 4.18 is a detailed expansion of a program abstract. The programmer writes a concise description of each labeled routine (procedure segment). Initially, the logic narrative represents a "rough" description of the steps to be executed in each segment or module. After the information has been desk checked, it is then coded into computer instructions. A test plan and test data must be prepared for the testing and debugging sessions. After the program has been com-

MAINLINE ROUTINE:

This routine reads the Master Group Life Insurance File and the transactions (Insurance Authorization Cards, Payroll Change Cards, and Cancellation Cards). These are compared by employee number. On a low comparison, due to a new authorization, a branch is made to AUTHINS. When employee numbers are equal, a code check is made. The code 7 cancellation causes a branch to the CANCINS routine. The change cards cause a branch to UPDATE. A high condition on the reading of a transaction card will cause a branch to WRITETAP.

AUTHINS:

This routine creates a new insurance record for writing on tape. It also calculates the annual insurance premium and punches a deduction authorization card for payroll purposes. A branch is back to the Mainline Routine.

CANCINS:

This routine is used to delete a record from the Master Life Insurance File. The record is written on the Inactive Master Insurance File. Also, a deduction cancellation card is punched for the payroll program. A branch is back to the Mainline Routine.

UPDATE:

This routine is used to generate changes to the Master Life Insurance File for an existing record. If a change affects the rate, the annual premium will be recalculated and a new payroll deduction card is punched. A branch is back to the Mainline Routine.

WRITETAP:

This routine copies the Master Group Life Insurance tape. A branch is back to the Mainline Routine.

Figure 4.18 Program logic narrative form: example A

pletely tested, debugged, and accepted for implementation, the program narrative must be finalized and inserted into the appropriate documentation manuals.

In some organizations, the programmer will first prepare a program flowchart and then convert the information into a program narrative.

c) Decision tables. Decision tables (see Figure 4.19) provide a structured procedure that identifies the conditions to be tested for and the actions to be taken in a given problem. The decision tables are becoming a popular analysis and design tool for systems analysts, but they also have been used for software projects for a number of years. A decision table can be given to a programmer by a systems analyst or a senior programmer for coding a program. Or, the com-

SYSTEM ___ Registration ___

Page ___ 1 ___ of ___ 1 ___

Analyst ___ R. Szweda ___

Date ___ 4/3/19 ___

Student Registration Procedure	1	2	3	4
A	If First Year Student	y	y	n	n
B	If Second Year Student	–	–	y	y
C	If First Semester	y	n	y	n
D	If Second Semester	–	y	–	y
E	Enroll in D.P. Concepts	x	–	–	–
F	Enroll in BASIC	x	–	–	–
G	Enroll in Intro. COBOL	–	x	–	–
H	Enroll in FORTRAN IV	–	x	–	–
I	Enroll in Intro. Assembler	–	–	x	–
J	Enroll in PL/1	–	–	–	x
K	Enroll in Intro. Systems	–	–	x	–
L	Print Student's Schedule	x	x	x	x

Remarks Area

Figure 4.19 Example of a decision table procedure

pleted table data can be translated into a program flowchart which is then manually coded into a source program. An organization that is equipped with decision table software can convert the decision table data [into a set] of descriptive statements that will ultimately be a computer program.

d) HIPO structure. The HIPO structure is an IBM technique to illustrate the "top-down" approach to program design and maintenance. The concept is not limited to programs and program systems because it is also very useful for systems analysis and design.

Using the HIPO technique, a systems analyst or programmer divides a planned program into component parts. The initial approach is to define the high-level blocks that may serve as the control module and perform input/output functions and other dummy operations. The high-level block is then subdefined into a second-level block that may be further subdefined into lower levels until the function is broken down into the smallest detail necessary to understand the job.

Contrary to the belief of many, the HIPO technique is meant to complement the traditional documentation methods, not replace them. The HIPO technique provides for cross-references to routines, labels, layouts, documents, and flowcharts so as to tell a complete logical story of the program and/or system.

One of the primary advantages of this technique is its emphasis on functions. The user has a very clear understanding of the processes that support each function and the interfaces required.

Figure 4.20 provides a simple illustration of a payroll program that may initially be subdefined into a control module and then component modules at the second level to perform various required payroll operations. Each module will be coded individually with proper linkages to form a functional program.

Figure 4.20 Top-down structure for an hourly rated payroll program (programming modules to be developed)

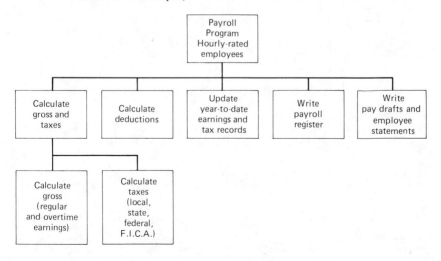

5. LAYOUT SPECIFICATIONS. The documentation must include complete layout specifications because they affect each project. The principal items included in the specifications are:

a) Card input/output
b) Printer output
c) Optical scanning and/or MICR document input and output
d) Magnetic and/or paper tape input and output
e) Data base element index
f) Random access layouts
g) Primary and auxiliary memory layouts
h) Console typewriter/keyboard input and output
i) Visual data displays

a) *Card input/output.* The input and output formats for punch cards must be clearly specified. A very important part of the systems analysis and design activity is to develop and establish these formats to facilitate detailed programming and/or wiring.

The general rules for card layout standards are:

Each card format used must be illustrated on a card layout form; to reduce the number of pages in a folder, a multiple-card layout form can be used (see Figure 4.21)

Figure 4.21 Sample card layout form

Vertical lines should be drawn separating each field in order to identify field definitions

Horizontal lines should be drawn over each field in order to identify field names

Each layout form should be identified with the name of the application or system, the program name and number, and the effective date.

Sample copies of the card forms used should be included in the appropriate documentation manual. Provision should also be made for inclusion of a reference relationship to the application, the program names and numbers utilizing the cards, and effective dates. Generally, this type of information is found on the back of the cards included in a manual. When this approach is undesirable or not feasible, the card may be attached to a sheet of bond paper and the relevant information listed below the card in the space remaining.

Some organizations prefer to use a record format, a form for which is illustrated in Figure 4.22. In addition to stipulating the physical location of the data elements, the form provides for entry of assigned program mnemonics, count, and data-type specification. These provisions enhance the value of the documentation for an organization. Preference for the record format is based on the fact that the format simplifies the replication process and ensures uniformity in layout form utilization.

b) Printer output. The printer output specifications (see Figure 4.23) must be developed and illustrated on a printer spacing chart before any detailed programming or wiring is initiated. When the chart format is approved by the user, the chart becomes the basis of vendor form ordering and approval specifications. Under no circumstances should the data processing organization release its only copy of a printer spacing chart, which is to be produced as a preprinted form, to the vendor. This may well lead to misunderstandings, delays in shipment, and the need to redraw the layout form to verify the accuracy of a vendor's form proof. An error or omission in preparing a new printer spacing chart for the vendor could prove very time-consuming and costly to the organization. The original copy must be photocopied to produce at least one copy of the printer spacing chart. The photocopy is used as a basis of verifying the accuracy of the vendor-produced report form. Also, the copy is included in the system description manual as part of the system's documentation.

Following the development and implementation of the desired output format, the printer spacing chart becomes the basis of all subsequent report evaluations, modifications, and maintenance.

The physical specifications for a form vary for the different printer devices and vendors. They are included in the equipment manuals and should be checked before any detailed planning and design is initiated.

A completed printed sample of the output should be included in the appropriate documentation manual. It will be used by the auditor for comparison purposes and by the executive committee as a source of information. A reproduction, or carbon copy, of this form should also be included in the user's manual (if applicable) and in the operator's manual.

Each planning chart and sample form should be identified with the application or system name, report title, program name and number, and effective date.

A record format form (see Figure 4.22) may be used to supplement the plan-

Figure 4.22 Sample record format form

RECORD FORMAT FORM					
FILE MNEMONIC _____ DATE ___ / ___ / ___					
RECORD MNEMONIC _____					
RECORD POSITION		FIELD LABEL	PROGRAM MNEMONIC	LENGTH	DATA CHARACTERISTICS
FIRST	LAST				

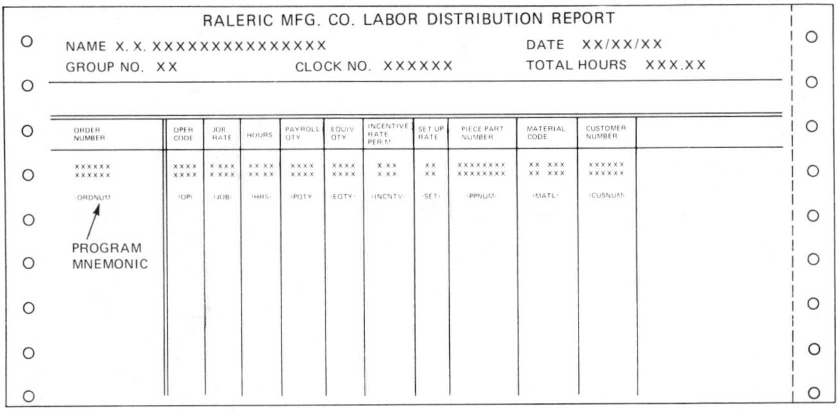

Figure 4.23 Printer spacing chart

ning chart. This form provides for inclusion of the output record program mnemonics in the documentation.

c) *Optical scanning and/or* MICR *documents.* Samples of the optical scanning documents used for input and output purposes and the magnetic ink character documents (MICR) used for input, together with the document planning forms, must also be included in the documentation package. Each planning form and sample document should include the same identification specifications as previously indicated.

The design specifications for OCR, OMR, and MICR documents are given in the vendors' equipment manuals. A sample of a planning layout for an OMR document is illustrated in Figure 4.24.

Copies of the actual form samples should be included in the appropriate documentation manuals.

d) *Magnetic and/or paper tape input and output.* The format of magnetic and paper tape records used for input and/or output must be clearly specified. On each tape layout form (see Figure 4.25), there must be a reference linkage to the application or system; program name(s) and number(s); assigned name for a tape; and input or output specification. Owing to the length of a tape record, there may be need for several record layouts in the manual.

The general rules for tape layout standards are as follows:

Vertical lines should be drawn to identify each field

Field names should be printed over the horizontal lines in a given field

All special characters used for tape processing, such as record, block, end-of-tape, or end of transmission marks, should be illustrated

The blocking factor for each magnetic tape should be specified, namely, fixed-fixed, fixed-variable, etc.

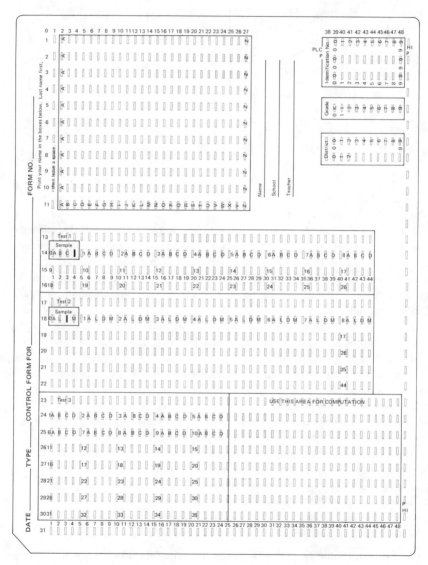

Figure 4.24 Sample planning layout for OMR document

140

FILE MNEMONIC ____________ RECORD MNEMONIC ____________

SECURITY CLASSIFICATION ____ LENGTH ____ BLOCK FACTOR ____ BLOCK SIZE ____

DATE ________

MNEMONICS
DATA CHARACTERISTICS
MNEMONICS
DATA CHARACTERISTICS
MNEMONICS
DATA CHARACTERISTICS
MNEMONICS
DATA CHARACTERISTICS
MNEMONICS
DATA CHARACTERISTICS
REMARKS

Figure 4.25 Tape layout form

If no blocking factors are used, the specification should be included to indicate the length of a record—fixed or variable.

An organization may prefer to utilize a record format form as previously illustrated in Figure 4.22. When coupled with a file specification (see form illustrated in Figure 4.26), the record format provides additional relevant planning, implementation, and documentation data not available on the tape layout form illustrated in Figure 4.25.

e) Data base element index. The data base element index form is used as a data collection instrument during the problem definition and analysis phase and subsequently for the design and development of a system/program. The primary purpose of this form is to identify all the sources of the data elements and how they are used within a system or group of systems. In addition, the form is used to collect other meaningful data such as, length of the field, data name and labels, type characteristics, and field justification. A suggested format for a data base element index form is illustrated in Figure 4.27.

A brief explanation of the illustrated form is as follows:

Column A is a sequential number used for document control purposes and also to identify the sequence of the items in a file or form.

FILE SPECIFICATION	APPLICATION NO.	PROGRAM NO.	PAGE ___ OF ___
FILE MNEMONIC			
STORAGE MEDIUM		STORAGE MODE	
HEADER LABEL DATA			
TRAILER LABEL DATA			
RECORD TYPE		MAXIMUM LENGTH	
BLOCK FACTOR		MAXIMUM SIZE	
RECORD SEQUENCE			
FILE SECURITY CLASSIFICATION		RETENTION PERIOD	
FILE DESCRIPTION			
APPROVED BY		DATE	

Figure 4.26 File specification form

DATA BASE ELEMENT INDEX

Application _____

Analyst/Programmer _____

Page _____ of _____

Date _____ / _____ / _____

NO.	DATA NAME	DATA LABEL	PROGRAM ID.	LENGTH	MEANING	CODING	SOURCE	TYPE	FIELD JUST	FORMAT TYPE	FILES	CODES	DISPLAY	OTHER
A	B	C	D	E	F	G	H	I	J	K	L	M	N	O

Figure 4.27 Example of a data base element index form

143

Column B identifies a data field name utilized by the users in referring to a field and/or label/title/heading appearing on an input/output document or display.

Column C is the data label/mnemonic used in a computer program to identify the element.

Column D is the program identification number in which the label/mnemonic appears.

Column E is the length of the data element.

Column F is optional and may be used for some annotative data. The item may be used to provide a meaning if the data field name in column B is not self-explanatory.

Column G provides one or several illustrations of coding for the data element. This is particularly useful in identifying the display format on an output or report and for program design and coding.

Column H identifies the source of the data element. The source may be a document, in which case it is necessary to identify the form and form number. Or the source may be a computerized output, and this file and application must be identified.

Column I indicates whether the field is alphabetic, numeric, or alphameric.

Column J is the field justification—left, right, or full field.

Column K is the length format—fixed or variable.

Figure 4.28 Record layout worksheet. Courtesy IBM Corporation

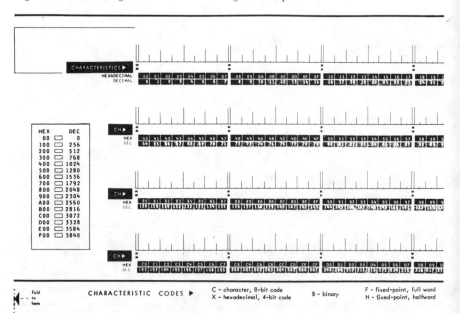

Column L identifies the specific files in which the data element may be found.

Column M is the coding structure used to identify the data elements. For example a "1" would identify a male and a "2" a female in a sex code field. The use of this column can be effective only if there are a few entries. Where more than five or six entries must be shown, it is recommended that the form's user indicate the specific part of the documentation manual in which the code listing may be found.

Column N identifies how the output/report is displayed and the devices, forms and/or files are used.

Column O can be used as a miscellaneous field for providing additional information about the data elements. For example, a data element used in a FORTRAN program may be identified by type specification—integer or real.

The form may be modified to meet the needs of the organization. The data base element index will be included in the documentation manuals for the systems and programming functions.

f) Random access layouts. The specifications for random access devices are very similar to those of tape devices, with the exception that the former include a record of assigned and unassigned memory locations, wherever applicable.

In the interest of file security, the unrelated storage assignments should be identified solely as reserved areas without any detailed data specifications. This information is generally shown on a record layout worksheet (see Figure 4.28).

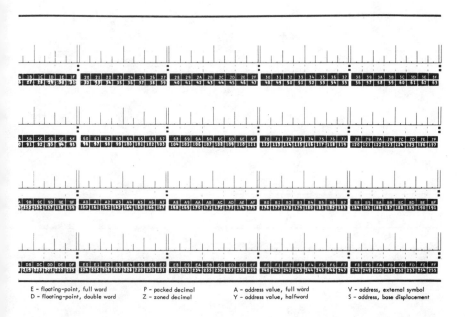

| E – floating-point, full word | P – packed decimal | A – address value, full word | V – address, external symbol |
| D – floating-point, double word | Z – zoned decimal | Y – address value, halfword | S – address, base displacement |

CONSOLE INSTRUCTION SHEET	APPLICATION NO.	EFFECTIVE DATE ___/___/___	PAGE __ OF __

PROGRAM NAME	PROGRAM NO.

CONSOLE OUTPUT	EXPLANATION AND OPERATOR ACTION

SPECIAL INSTRUCTIONS

PROGRAMMER	APPROVED

Figure 4.29 Console instruction sheet

The user may prefer to utilize record format and file specification forms instead of the vendor-recommended forms for a given storage medium.

g) Primary and auxiliary memory layouts. Occasionally a program requires the allocation of special internal-storage areas for tables or record construction. These may be specified on a record layout worksheet (Figure 4.28) or a record format form (Figure 4.22).

Allocations on an auxiliary memory device, such as disk, drum, card random access or data cell, may also be specified on these forms, which are used to effectively indicate the assigned locations and their data characteristics.

h) Console typewriter/keyboard input and output. The console typewriter/ keyboard can be used very effectively for such items as input data entry; specification of output medium and/or mode; definition of parameters; presentation of error messages; initiation of checkpoint, restart, and recovery procedures; and establishment of management controls. The information is documented on a console instruction sheet (see Figure 4.29). The console instruction sheet describes to the systems analyst, programmer, console operator, user, and auditor how to use the computer program. The documented functional data for this form must be developed by the systems and programming personnel.

i) Visual data displays. Despite the increased use of such devices as the cathode-ray tube display, many organizations fail to include a replication of the output in their documentation. Though most of the peripherals are installed at the same location as the main computer, a copy of the output should be included in the system description, user's manual, and operator's manual. The documented terminal display illustrates the output format as it should appear in response to a desired action. The terminal output format is supplemented by the operating instructions developed for the user and for the operations personnel.

Figure 4.30 illustrates a bed census display generated on a display station for

Figure 4.30 Visual data display format

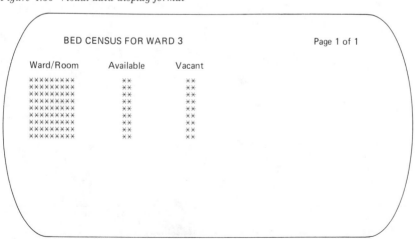

use in a hospital information system. The user-requested data will be displayed below the program-generated columnar descriptors.

6. USER INSTRUCTIONS. These provide the clerical and control procedures describing *who* does *what* and *when*. They describe input preparation and submission, interrelationships between data elements, priority designations, clerical

Figure 4.31 Sample user instructions: standard procedure

RALERIC CREDIT UNION	DATA PROCESSING MANUAL 10.1 November 21, 19___	
STANDARD PROCEDURE		
Subject: 　　REQUEST FOR MAILING LABELS		Application No.
Performed by	Action	
User department Data processing	1. Complete the "Request for Labels" form (CU-123). Indicate the sequence of account numbers for which output is desired. Forward the form to Data Processing. 2. Keypunch and key verify the "request" cards (CU-010). 3. Sort "request" cards on account number, card columns 5-1. 4. Process the "request" cards on the computer using program 02-02-087. 5. Forward the output to User Department. 6. File the "Request for Labels" forms in File Drawer 23A.	
Prepared by	Approved by	Approval date

processing, data element descriptions, authorizations required, accuracy and procedural controls, coding structures, and distribution patterns by functional title. This information is developed and implemented in a user's manual; it is also included in the system description manual. The user instructions should be established in two modes: the (*a*) normal mode and the (*b*) alternate mode.

a) *The normal mode.* The normal mode specifies the procedures to be followed in the regular operation of a given system. These procedures, sometimes referred to as job-preparation procedures, generally deal with the input, output, and update segments of a system.

The input segment specifies the input sources, purpose and functions served, contents, element descriptions, references required, editing instructions, samples, and document identification. The output segment specifications include the medium and mode, element descriptions, formats, query responses and requirements, validity checks, and samples. The update segment provides a complete description of all expected inputs to be entered or processed against existing files; it identifies the inputs, formats, sources, volumes, and retention, frequency, and error-correction procedures affecting the updating process.

An extract from a user's manual is illustrated in Figure 4.31. A code listing that may be part of the user instructions is illustrated in Figure 4.32.

b) *The alternate mode.* The alternate mode consists of a set of procedures— sometimes called contingency procedures—that facilitates processing of a system under other than normal conditions. "Other than normal conditions" may

Figure 4.32 Sample user instructions: code listing

R. S. COMPUTATIONS, INC.	DATA PROCESSING MANUAL 10.1
November 10, 19__	Part II

TRANSACTION CODES

Internal Transactions

Type of Transaction	Code to Change Balance Forward Record
1. Establish Due Out for all types of Back Orders	111
2. Increase Due Out for all types of Back Orders	211
3. Decrease Due Out for all types of Back Orders	311
4. Establish Due In	113
5. Increase Due In	213
6. Decrease Due In	313
7. Raise Stock Level	511
8. Decrease Stock Level	531
9. Change Unit of Issue Code	009
10. Physical Inventory Overage	651
11. Physical Inventory Shortage	671

describe such situations as those resulting from fire, flooding, vandalism, hardware failure, power failure, or serious human error. An alternate mode procedure is developed only after the manager has carefully analyzed the effect and cost of a processing delay upon the overall organization. Processing of critical systems may require the development and testing of one or several alternate-mode operating procedures. Depending upon the level of importance, the manager may establish alternate procedures to facilitate processing under a revised operating schedule, reduced or limited scope of operations, or a revised processing mode. Or the alternate procedures may allow for processing at a back-up facility on a limited or relatively normal operating schedule.

The alternate procedures are generally maintained in a binder and indexed with tabs designating the condition covered—Destruction of Data File, Loss of Power, etc.

Some organizations prefer not to include the alternate-mode user instructions in their standard documentation package. Instead, they limit access to key individuals. Nevertheless, it does not in any way reduce an organization's security if the fact that alternate processing procedures are available is made known in the systems description, user's manual, and operator's manual. For it is essential that key operating personnel and key user personnel must have some form of access to the alternate procedures.

Limited-access provisions do not always work as well in practice as originally planned in theory. For example, an analyst taped a codified listing of alternate procedures to the slide tray of a desk. When he left the organization, his successor found the listing, but he disposed of it because he did not understand the codified jargon. Subsequently, when a question arose about a back-up procedure, a file-cabinet search had to be made in order to determine procedural availability. Another organization was even less fortunate in its handling of alternate procedures. A listing of the available alternate procedures was taped to the side of a bookcase; the procedures themselves were maintained in an unmarked binder in the bookcase. One day, the painters came along and removed the contents of the bookcase and stacked the material on the floor. They removed the listing and placed it with the temporarily displaced materials. After the paint had dried, a young secretary was asked to replace the materials in the bookcase. She refiled all of the materials except for the unmarked binder. That she simply laid on top of the bookcase until its proper placement could be ascertained. Then the secretary became involved in other responsibilities and forgot about the binder. During the clean-up process, the listing was never replaced. Subsequently, the procedural binder was also misplaced. As fate would have it, the organization had no back-up for the back-up.

7. OPERATING INSTRUCTIONS. The operating instructions are the complete specifications for data processing activities and those external activities involved in the preparation and processing of data on unit-record, peripheral, or computer equipment. They describe the equipment configuration requirements; instructions for setup and teardown; instructions for translation or conversion of

inputs and/or source documents; checkpoint, recovery, and restart procedures; all error messages and correction procedures; and console messages and responses. In addition, wiring diagrams should also be given for unit-record operations that require the use of complex control panels.

Figure 4.33 Form for card punching and/or verifying instructions

CARD PUNCHING AND/OR VERIFYING INSTRUCTIONS					
APPLICATION NAME			APPLICATION NUMBER	EFFECTIVE DATE	
SOURCE DOCUMENTS USED	DATA FIELD	COLUMNS FIRST	LAST	FUNCTION	COMMENTS
CARD FORM NO.					
PROGRAM CARD NO.					
SWITCH SETTINGS					
ON OFF SWITCH					
☐ ☐ PROGRAM UNIT					
☐ ☐ AUTO FEED					
☐ ☐ AUTO SKIP AUTO DUP.					
☐ ☐ PRINT					
☐ ☐ SELF-CHECKING NO.					
SPECIAL FEATURES USED					
☐ ALTERNATE PROGRAM					
☐ AUXILIARY DUPLICATE					
☐ HI-SPEED SKIP					
☐ SELF-CHECKING NO.					
FUNCTION CODES					
PUNCH	P				
VERIFY	V				
PUNCH & VERIFY	PV				
DUPLICATE	D				
SKIP	S				
SELF-CHECKING NO.	NCK				
RIGHT JUSTIFY	RJ				
LEFT JUSTIFY	LJ				
ZERO FILL	ZF				
ZERO FILL & RIGHT JUSTIFY	ZFRJ				
ZERO FILL & LEFT JUSTIFY	ZFLJ				

The operating instructions may be grouped in four general categories:

a) Setup instructions
b) Instructive output
c) Alternate mode
d) Emergency operations

Figure 4.34 Machine setup form

MACHINE SET-UP FORM				PAGE_____						

APPLICATION NUMBER_____ STEP_____ DATE_____

INPUT DATA CARDS		OUTPUT DATA CARDS	
STACKER NO.	DESCRIPTION	STACKER NO.	DESCRIPTION

DATA NAME NUMBER	I/O	RING IN	OUT	DESCRIPTION	DISPOSITION

DATA NAME NUMBER	I/O	VOLUME SERIAL NO.	DESCRIPTION	DISPOSITION

PRINTER FORM NAME	FORM NO.	NO. OF PARTS	WIDE	NARROW	CARRIAGE CONTROL TAPE	6 L.P.I.	8 L.P.I.	ALPHA	NUMERIC

OTHER:

a) *Setup instructions.* This group of instructions specifies the operational order of the programs, hardware devices utilized, parameter and/or job control entries, and input and output requirements.

Figures 4.33, 4.34, and 4.35 illustrate three types of forms included in the setup segment of the operating instructions. Figure 4.33 shows a form for card punching and/or verifying instructions. The form may be modified for other types of key entry devices. Figure 4.34 shows a form for the setup of computer hardware. Figure 4.35 shows a form that may be used for parameter and/or job control entries.

b) *Instructive output.* The instructive output segment contains information on the special instructions or signals emitted on the hardware to direct the equipment operator during processing. For computerized operations, the operator is provided with programmed error messages; processing diagnostics indicated by the operating system; checkpoint, recovery, and restart procedures; and query responses and requirements. For unit-record operations, the signals and messages result from machine operations controlled by a wired control panel and a series of edit checks. The console instruction sheet (see Figure 4.29) may be used for documentation of instructive output.

c) *Alternate mode.* The alternate-mode procedures provide the operations personnel with the detailed contingency plans for functioning under abnormal conditions. The contingency plans are developed only for those systems that have been evaluated and classified as critical.

Figure 4.35 Sample format for parameter card

PARAMETER CARD FORMAT

APPLICATION NAME	APPLICATION NUMBER	EFFECTIVE DATE
Columns	Data Description	

The actual plans may not be included as part of the system description manual or operator's manual. However, they must be readily available when the conditions for implementation are evident. As had been previously suggested, some notation or evidence of existence must be included in the appropriate manuals. Such precautions do not compromise a company's security or back-up capability.

Each plan must be properly identified for the specific function it is to serve. Following its development, the plan should be tested and debugged. It should also be subjected to periodic audits to determine its operational effectiveness.

d) Emergency operations. These procedures delineate the action to be taken by an operator in the event of a disruptive event, such as fire, flooding or water damage, vandalism, power failure, or personal accident or illness. The emergency operating procedures are concerned with such factors as the powering down of the hardware, notification of key personnel, demounting and storage of essential records, location of firefighting equipment and fire exits, evacuation of personnel, and storage of programs.

Planning for such contingencies is very important because they can seriously affect both personnel and property. Being prepared can prevent loss of life and property, thereby bringing about considerable monetary savings. Nevertheless, for reasons unknown, many installations fail to include this category of procedures in their standard operating procedures.

These emergency operating procedures are not normally part of the operator's manual, but rather are kept separately in what is called the emergency procedures manual. It is maintained on the manager's desk or at the console of the computer. The operations personnel should be trained in the execution of these procedures. Scheduled drills or training sessions should be held periodically to maintain an "emergency readiness" level.

8. PROGRAM LISTING. The program listing segment of the documentation is actually divided into three segments: source program listing, object program listing, and job control listing.

The source program listing must be a complete program from which the operational object program has been assembled or compiled. The source program coding must also match up with the program logic description used in the documentation package for the given system.

The object program listing must be a complete listing that includes all software displays, such as division maps and the job control statements. This listing is the output generated when the operational program was fully tested and debugged. All documentation that is relevant to the given program must match up with the object program listing.

The job control listing can be an 80–80 listing of the job control language used in the given program. But, it would be more meaningful to include an explanation of the job control language and logic.

Each listing must be properly identified with the system and program numbers, and the compilation date. The listings are included in the documentation package for any subsequent planning, modification, maintenance, or audit. In most organizations, the source and object program listings will be included in the documentation maintained for systems and programming personnel only. The job control listing will be included in the documentation for the systems, programming, and operations personnel.

When an organization utilizes a library of subroutines, subprograms, or modules, it should make sure that the applicable listings are included in the appropriate documentation manuals. Each such listing should be attached to the applicable main program or control module. The value of the documentation increases if the listing includes a brief narrative of the purpose and specifies the required implementation procedures.

In some organizations, the internal auditors require that a memory dump of each operational program be included with the object program listings. The dumps can provide an audit trail for periodic audits of the documentation. However, the value of including a memory dump is questionable. To be effective, persons working with the dump must be familiar with the object code of the particular hardware and format of the dump.

9. GLOSSARY. A glossary is a vital link in the communications process between data processing personnel and non-data processing personnel in the organization. The semantics problem resulting from the use of specialized terms necessitates the standardization of the vocabulary. Consequently, there are three major vocabulary groups, or glossaries, that systems personnel must develop, maintain, and learn. These glossaries are categorized as:

a) Data processing terms
b) Specialized terms and abbreviations
c) Mnemonic labels

a) *Data processing terms.* The systems group must establish a glossary of the terms most frequently used within the data processing function. It is not necessary to define each of the terms because such definitions may be extracted from the many glossaries available from the various professional societies and vendors.

b) *Specialized terms and abbreviations.* Each organization and/or industry has its own set of particular terms or jargon, which affect data processing personnel and non-data processing personnel. Many of the terms are acronyms or abbreviations not readily found in any dictionary or technical text. To facilitate understanding of these terms, a glossary of specialized terms should be published as a standard. A sampling of such terms is included in Figure 4.36.

c) *Mnemonic labels.* Many organizations use standardized mnemonic labels in an effort to facilitate the training of personnel and employee understanding of documentation and programs. Such labels are meaningful because they relate more directly to an operation being performed or a referenced field; for example, the label PRINT may be used to identify a series of instructions that are executed to output a line of printed data. The use of such terms also simplifies the maintenance of programs, as well as their conversion, modification, and audit.

Word/Term	Abbreviation
Abrasive	ABRSV
Backplate	BKPLT
Capstan	CPSTN
Daily	DLY
Elastic	ELAS
Fabric	FAB
Gauge	GA
Handbook	HNDBK

Figure 4.36 Sample glossary of specialized terms used in a manufacturing organization

Figure 4.37 illustrates some suggested mnemonics. It is important to note that the selected mnemonics must have universal understanding—their length is affected by program syntax.

Review Questions: Group 4C

1. What is a system abstract? What information does it contain?
2. Why would a manager consider the development of alternate-mode procedures?
3. What is the purpose of an emergency procedures manual? What type of information should it contain?
4. Why are glossaries an important part of a documented data processing system?

Figure 4.37 Suggested glossary of mnemonic labels used by a financial institution

Data Names (User Field Names)	Standardized Program Mnemonic
Account Number	ACCT
Completion Date	COMPDAT
Due Date	DUEDAT
Fee	FEE
Interest	INT
Last Name	LASNAM
Month	MO
Partial Payment	PARPAY
Suffix	SFX
Year	YR

(Operation Name)	
Move Input Record	MVINPT
Clear Page	CLRPAG
Delimeter Test	DLMTST
End Table Look-up	ENDTLU
Clear Entry	CLRENT

10. TEST PLAN. This segment of the documentation is actually comprised of three parts: test plan, test data listing, and test results.

The test plan delineates the specific tests which the system and/or program must satisfy before they may be implemented for productive use. The test plan begins with an identification of the purpose or the objectives to be accomplished. For a systems test, the test plan must identify the document, data, hardware, software, and personnel support required. For a program test, a lower level of support would be required, but would include many of the previously mentioned support factors. In addition, the test plan must identify what specific conditions must be met, and the test operation setup and termination for the operations personnel.

The test data listing identifies the "artificial" and "live" test data used to determine if the specific criteria have been met. This same test data should exist in its original form, on cards, tape or disk for subsequent use in maintenance and audit runs. The "artificial" test data listing should identify which rules, test conditions, checks and/or edits are being evaluated by the test data.

The test results segment will be the actual results achieved during the test operation. The test output must be properly annotated to identify the error checks, editing procedure results, management controls, and tolerance checks that were made. The test results will subsequently be used for comparison with outputs from subsequent audit and maintenance runs.

DOCUMENTATION PACKAGE DISTRIBUTION

All of the items that are included in the documentation standard are not included in each of the documentation manuals established for the systems, programming, operations, and user personnel. The distribution may be effected as follows:

SYSTEMS GROUP

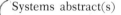

Systems abstract(s)

Systems flowchart(s)

Program abstract(s)

Program logic description(s)

Layout specifications

User instructions

Operating instructions

Program listings

Glossaries

Test plan

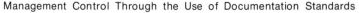

Systems abstract(s)

Systems flowchart(s)

Program abstract(s)

Program logic description(s)

Layout specifications

Relevant user instructions

Relevant operating instructions

Relevant glossaries

Program listings

Test plan

USER PERSONNEL

System flowchart(s)

User instructions

Relevant glossaries

OPERATIONS GROUP

Systems flowchart(s)

Program abstract(s)

Relevant user instructions

Operating instructions

Relevant program listings

Relevant glossaries

DOCUMENTATION CONTROL AND RECORD MANAGEMENT

Control of Documentation

To realize the benefits of documentation, the executive committee must develop a control standard. The control is necessary to ensure the accuracy, completeness, and efficiency of the documentation. Failure to attain this documentation status will minimize the effectiveness of the resources employed in the management process.

The effective control of documentation is contingent upon the following:

1. Security
2. Content
3. Communication of revisions

1. SECURITY. The documentation must be maintained in a fire-resistant vault or cabinet outside of the data processing function. Access should be limited to the systems manager and his assistant. Whenever documentation is withdrawn from the file cabinet or vault, a strict signout control must be maintained in order to deny access to unauthorized personnel and to prevent possible loss, destruction, or accidental or deliberate alteration of the material.

The organization should give serious consideration to the feasibility of maintaining an off-premises facility for safeguarding and storing the documentation. (Additional information on the control of documentation is given in chapter 10, under the subject of peripheral controls.)

2. CONTENT. The documentation must contain the complete informational record on any system, application, or program that is currently operational. Because of its vital effect on the operation of a data processing activity, the documentation should be audited at least once each year by the internal or external audit staff. The audit should be concerned with verifying the accuracy, relevancy, and completeness of the documentation. (Additional information on audits is given in chapter 10.)

The level of completeness is affected by the contents of the documentation. Therefore, a content standard must be established and maintained. The following stipulations represent the minimum standard necessary to achieve the required completeness:

All documentation should be maintained in a permanent cover or folder. The maintenance of documentation on a reel of magnetic tape or a disk pack does not negate the need for a hard-copy reference.

All documentation folders should be clearly identified to simplify location and retrieval. Identification should be on the outside of the folder, preferably on the spine and front of the folder or cover.

All folders should contain a numeric identification system as part of the label. To facilitate storage and retrieval, the folders should be filed in that sequence.

Each change or modification to a folder should include a revision page.

The first page of each documentation folder should be a table of contents.

3. COMMUNICATION OF REVISIONS. The distribution of revisions affects all organizational elements that are directly or indirectly involved in the system. Therefore, to ensure a smooth flow of resources, it is necessary for the systems group to communicate the extent of involvement to each affected functional activity by means of conferences and/or discussions. The revisions should be detailed in a clear and concise manner.

When making a presentation to the user department personnel (including management), the systems personnel must avoid the use of data processing terminology. The jargon tends only to build—or raise higher—a communications barrier.

Communicating the information is particularly important with regard to employees who have been performing their tasks repetitively for such a long period of time that they now perform largely by rote. To avoid confusion, waste, and reruns, it is also necessary to make sure that these persons really do understand the changes.

In addition, the communications process indicates if any additional orientation and/or training of personnel is necessary. And it also indicates whether the documentation is adequate, the stated goals have been met, and any problems remain to be resolved.

SUMMARY

Developing effective standards and documentation is a very important part of the management process. They are necessary in the successful execution of the pre-executory and executory phases. Standards and documentation are essential for the determination and maintainance of the overall effectiveness of an operation or organization.

The standards discussed in this chapter are the guides, policies, practices and procedures that must be followed in any organization to ensure compliance with management decisions. These help to maintain a smooth flow of productive resources in accordance with the plan established by the upper echelon. The documentation provides a formal record of the upper echelon's operating decisions.

Standards and documentation have become a communications medium for managers, auditors, users, and data processing personnel. For the manager, this means having a vehicle for defining his specific needs. For the data processor, it means having to design, develop, and implement more relevant and meaningful systems, applications, or programs. For the auditor, it means having the mechanism for ensuring compliance. For the user, it means being given the necessary materials to actuate an operationally effective process.

Each organization must realistically determine how much documentation and standardization is adequate and how best to maintain an effective level. The issues must not be clouded over by the cries of the alarmists who speak of high costs, disruption in employee morale, loss of creativity and efficiency. A quick cost determination may be made by evaluating the impact of personnel changes and loss of services. How much does it cost to train a new employee? Or, what is the cost in delayed processing to an organization?

CASE STUDY 4.1

The Sevierville Electric Company

The Sevierville Electric Company is a large electric utility serving approximately one million customers in a medium-sized metropolitan area. The company is equipped with second-generation computing and some unit-record equipment.

The primary data processing application is calculation of electric- and steam-power utilization and customer billing on a cycle basis. Meter installation and maintenance is also a major application, this being primarily a file update type of processing that occurs almost daily. The next major user is the payroll department; it utilizes the equipment for processing of six different payrolls—hourly, weekly, semimonthly, executive, incentive, and sales commissions. The advertising department makes daily requests for printing of mailing labels and envelopes.

An error in a number of customer bills was discovered by an auditor for the State Public Service Commission. To locate the source of the error, the programming manager was called upon to check the computer programs involved. In attempting to check the first program, he found only a source deck listing. The object deck was in condensed form, thereby preventing the printing of a "quick and dirty" object code listing. Finally, a suitable listing was made available by reassembling the autocoder source deck.

The mainline processing appeared to be logical and correct. Some questions arose over the manner in which a multiplication subroutine was written. However, the logic was assumed to be correct though the technique was not considered to be the best.

The manager then moved to verifying a second program used for calculation of the actual customer bill. Again the mainline processing was assumed to be logical and correct. The same multiplication subroutine was used in the second program.

The decision was then made to keypunch some test cards and run a test on the computer. The test data was also calculated on an adding machine to arrive at a planned result. The output from the two computer tests did not match the planned results. The multiplication subroutine was immediately suspect. A check of the programming staff revealed that the person responsible for writing the subroutine was no longer in the employ of the organization.

The programming manager decided to telephone the former employee at his new place of employment. The programmer indicated that he had made a change to the subroutine but could not remember the nature of the change. After gaining some information about the programmer's technique of writing subroutines, the programming manager decided to compare the two subroutines.

In his inspection, he found that the subroutine in the first program had one less instruction statement than that of the second program. The missing card was duplicated and inserted into the first program. The source deck was subsequently reassembled and retested. However, no improvement over the test was evident.

The programming manager then decided to check each step of the subroutine. In the process, he found that half-adjust positional alignment was incorrect; this had resulted in a significant error in favor of the company. Upon completing his inspection, he then proceeded to reassemble and retest the first program. This time the outputted result matched the planned result. A change was made to the second program; then it too was reassembled and retested. The actual output matched the expected result.

The programming manager placed the new program listings in his desk. He instructed the secretary to type a new listing of the multiplication subroutine and insert it into the binder containing the various subroutines available to the programmers.

Discussion Questions

1. From your reading of the case study, what major problems, if any, would you say existed in this organization?
2. What solutions would you have applied to the problems detected?
3. Did you agree with the testing procedure? Could it be improved? If so, how? If not, why not?
4. In your opinion, do you feel that the programming manager was correct or incorrect in telephoning the former employee? Why?
5. Would your answer to the previous question be any different if the programming manager had waited until the evening to contact the programmer at home?
6. Would you fault the former employee for failing to remember the change he had actuated? If so, why? If not, why not?
7. Do you agree with the actions taken by the programming manager after he rectified the error condition?
8. What suggestions or recommendations, if any, would you make to the information systems director regarding this aspect of his function?

Management Control

Through the Use of

Performance Standards

INTRODUCTION / The succesful management of a data processing activity is dependent upon the availability of performance standards for scheduling and project planning. Schedules must be developed for and within the various functional activities to reduce and/or eliminate the setting of arbitrary deadline times and dates, as well as to provide a more realistic measure of actual and expected progress. In many organizations, the term "scheduling" is synonymous with "machine loading." Machine loading, however, is but one part of the operations activity and does not encompass the work of the software, systems, training, or systems planning groups.

Scheduling involves the allocation of human, material, software, and hardware resources to the performance of a task, operation, application or development, and implementation. The schedule must be both reasonable and realistic, so as to allow for achievement of the desired objective or flow of work; it must also be flexible enough to permit modifications when required.

The concept of project planning is entirely dependent upon the early development of a realistic schedule. The existence of a schedule enables the manager to coordinate, direct, and control the activities and events generated by the executive committee, users, and data processing personnel. A delay of any activity or event may be considered as a deviation from the schedule. The manager must evaluate the effect of the delay on the overall schedule and the project. Based on his analysis, he may then find it necessary to alter the schedule or select and implement an alternative course of action.

The constant flux within an environment or situation requires that the manager apply the principles of dynamic management to his activities; that is, the principles founded on the concept of dynamic management as a constant monitoring of the productive process and its results. This realistic approach must be applied to every plan and schedule developed and implemented in the management process.

SCHEDULING AND PERFORMANCE FACTORS

The scheduling factors vary for each functional group—software, systems, operations, etc.—in data processing. Consequently, each group must develop its own schedule after having carefully considered the internal and external influences directly and indirectly affecting it. For instance, the operations activity is affected by those factors that influence the manipulation and collection of data and the production of information and outputs. The schedule of the software group is affected by a different set of factors, which are inherent in the planning, development, testing, and implementation of a program. The systems group is influenced by those variables concerned with systems analysis, design, development, and implementation. The training group's schedule depends primarily upon the type and level of training to be provided. The planning group's schedule is affected by the types of projects with which they are concerned.

In the development and implementation of a new system, personnel from the data processing functions may be integrated into a project team to accomplish a given task or objective (see chapter 2). The integrated approach requires only a minor alteration to the scheduling technique. Rather than viewing each activity as mono-functional, the project manager must allow for the interaction of the scheduling variables of the groups in preparation of what should be a multi-functional plan.

To understand scheduling factors and their effects more fully, it is useful to undertake an analysis of the various scheduling factors that must be considered. This is best done by following the basic system of divisionalization in dealing with the five groups in the data processing function (see chapter 2). These are the operations, software, systems, training, and planning groups.

THE OPERATIONS GROUP

Scheduling Factors

The operations group is primarily responsible for the transcription of data and its classification and manipulation to produce outputs and information necessary for operation and management of the overall organization.

The production schedule for this group is generally established on a weekly basis, with provision for daily requirements. It includes the continuous production needs, special and one-time requests, and reruns. Schedules for computer operations must, in addition, allocate time for preventative and emergency maintenance, program assembly and compiling, program testing, and training needs. The basic production schedule is primarily affected by:

1. Priorities
2. Volumes
3. Operations required
4. Input availability
5. Output requirements
6. Reporting frequency
7. Personnel skills
8. Documentation availability

1. PRIORITIES. With a few minor exceptions, priorities in an organization do not remain fixed for any long period of time. This is not an unfavorable condition because it may indicate that new and more important systems are being processed. It may also denote that, based on available utilization statistics, a more effective allocation of resources is attainable by reshuffling the priorities in the production schedule. A priority status should be allocated to a system only after an assessment of its relative importance to the overall organization has been made. The decision should not be arbitrary but based on fact. Nor should a priority assignment be made on the basis of internal political or social relationships. One criterion to be applied is cost of delay. Systems that may be significantly delayed without affecting the normal operational activities of an organization should be granted a lower priority status. However, applications such as payroll, accounts payable, and accounts receivable are generally exempt from any priority status evaluation. These are regarded as critical or vital to the normal operation of the organization.

When a delay occurs due to a hardware malfunction, loss of power, operator error, or other emergency condition, the manager must determine the delay's effect on the day's schedule. Depending on the length of delay, the priorities may be dispensed with until normal operations are resumed. The cost of delay would again be used as one of the major criteria in determining which systems will be processed and when.

2. VOLUMES. Before any time estimates can be developed for each operation, the operations manager must know the work load. Volume statistics must be gathered on the source documents received, cards or records transcribed and processed, and outputs produced. Collecting source documents counts may be a simple or complex problem. If the operations group has developed a document control system, then this will in most cases be a matter of tabulating item, batch, or transmittal counts. For example, volume statistics such as document, line, item, and record counts may be gathered from a transmittal document (see chapter 10).

When such documents are unavailable, the manager must gather data by sampling or physical counts. Sometimes quantitative data may be derived by determining the number of cards punched per document and dividing this into total card volume, as illustrated in Figure 5.1.

Whichever technique is applied, it is important that the manager secure quantitative data based on good representative periods. Whenever possible, the

METHOD:	No. of Source Documents Processed	=	Estimated Card Volume
			Estimated Average No. of Cards Punched per Source Document

$$\text{METHOD:} \quad \text{No. of Source Documents Processed} = \frac{\text{Estimated Card Volume}}{\text{Estimated Average No. of Cards Punched per Source Document}}$$

$$\text{APPLICATION:} \quad \text{No. of Source Documents Processed} = \frac{62{,}500}{25}$$

$$\text{RESULT:} \quad \text{No. of Source Documents Processed} = 2{,}500$$

Figure 5.1 Example of method for estimating document volume

minimum and maximum actual or anticipated volumes must be determined to offset work load fluctuations. Failure to analyze volume data may lead to unexpected work loads that could possibly destroy the operational effectiveness of a schedule. Figure 5.2 illustrates use of a chart on which volume stability can be plotted and evaluated.

Statistical data on cards and records must be collected to determine their effect on the input preparation and processing segments of the schedule. As cards are a popular form of input, they will affect all types of unit-record and computing equipment, as well as many manual operations. The statistics may be collected by counting the actual number of cards either as they pass through a sorting device equipped with a counter or by using a tabulator or computer. Counts may also be derived by analyzing document control records maintained by the control clerk, summary total lines on reports, transmittal or batch control records or actual production data.

Figure 5.2 Sample chart for plotting volume trends

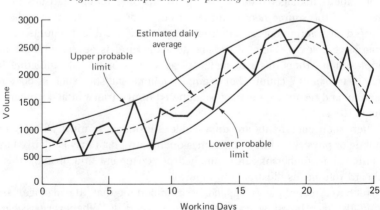

Output statistics are also very significant in schedule development. The output may be a complete report, a calculated result, one element of an application, cards, magnetic tape, or other media. The output requirements significantly affect machine loading. Most of the output is currently generated on tabulators in unit-record operations, and printers in computerized activities. The volumes may be collected by actual count, although this may not be very practical when physically counting printed pages. On some reports, a page number is printed by the equipment at the top or bottom of the form. On some forms, though, consecutive numbers are preprinted by the vendors. These counts may be gathered by the equipment operator, control clerk, or operations manager and posted on a data control form. The statistics may then be tallied to develop quantitative data on output production. Statistics on drafts, checks, or invoices may be secured from the accounting or treasury departments, or by checking beginning and ending control numbers. Where budget figures are available for chargebacks, these may possibly be used to develop output statistics. If statistics are unavailable, then the manager must apply some sampling techniques to determine the tabulator, printer, and other needs.

Having collected the statistics, the manager evaluates and analyzes the interaction between source document, card, record, and output volumes for each application in the basic production plan. The analyses may be displayed in the form of individual and composite graphs.

3. OPERATIONS REQUIRED. The operations manager must analyze the applica-

Figure 5.3 Example of chart for indicating estimated production requirements

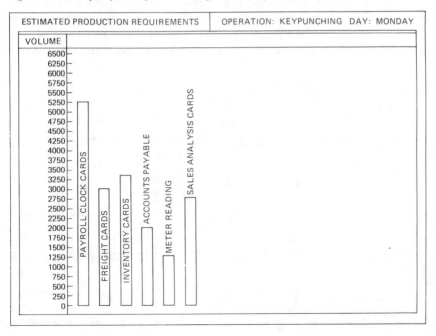

tions documentation to determine the operations and steps required to achieve the desired objectives. This necessitates a detailed breakdown of the manual, semiautomated, and automated operations in the work flow. The automated operations must specify each unit of equipment utilized, as well as the number of passes or runs to be processed on each device. Ultimately, this information should be coupled with the volume data and machine processing speeds to develop the production schedule. Graphs or charts (see Figure 5.3) may again be used to indicate the machine and manual loads.

4. INPUT AVAILABILITY. This element is concerned with the rate of flow and type of input. The rate must be analyzed to determine the peaks and valleys occurring during the day, week, and month. The peaks if not anticipated or expected can generate many problems for the operations manager. Analysis may reveal the need for some alternative action on the rate of flow before a schedule is developed. Input type affects both speed and accuracy. Source documents that are to be transcribed efficiently to card, tape, disk, or drum record formats must be legible, as well as properly designed and colored. Legibility layout and code construction are particularly important in key punching and data recording operations. Ideally, the data to be transcribed should appear on the source document in large, legible, well-spaced characters set on one line reading from left to right in the sequence of the record format. If the documents are unacceptable for transcription purposes, the information will have to be encoded on transcription forms or alignment sheets or in a rubber stamp block imprinted on a source document (see Figure 5.4). Or, an apron may be attached to the form on which the desired information is arranged in transcription sequence, as illustrated in Figure 5.5. The transcription speed is also influenced by the number of card columns or positions to be keyed, duplicated, and skipped per record. Therefore, in order to expedite the input preparation and verification process, repetitive data that can be duplicated should be positioned on the left side of the source docu-

Figure 5.4 Rubber stamp imprint

DATA PROCESSING	INVOICE SECTION	PURCHASING	
VENDOR NUMBER	DATE RECEIVED / /	PRICE APPROVAL	
DUE DATE / /	TERMS	TERMS APPROVAL	
TAXABLE AMOUNT	INVOICE CLERK	F.O.B. APPROVAL	
NET AMOUNT	STANDARD COST PER C	GOVT. CODE	COMMERCIAL CODE
DISCOUNT AMOUNT	ACCOUNTING CLASS	APPLY ON CODE	

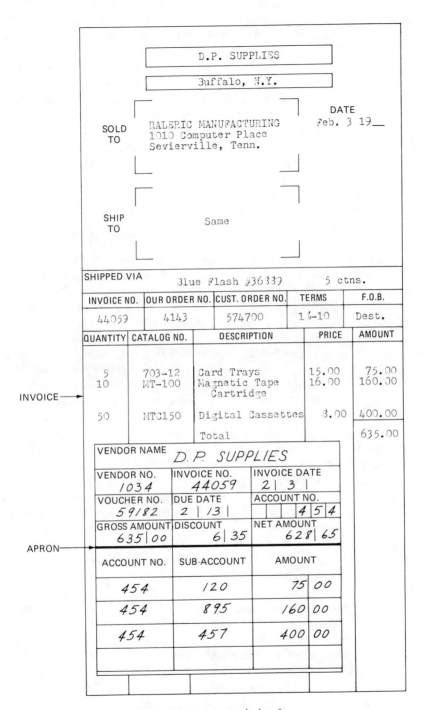

INVOICE ⟶

APRON ⟶

		D.P. SUPPLIES			
		Buffalo, N.Y.			

SOLD TO
RALERIC MANUFACTURING
1010 Computer Place
Sevierville, Tenn.

DATE
Feb. 3 19__

SHIP TO
Same

SHIPPED VIA	Blue Flash #36339		5 ctns.	

INVOICE NO.	OUR ORDER NO.	CUST. ORDER NO.	TERMS	F.O.B.
44059	4143	574700	1 %-10	Dest.

QUANTITY	CATALOG NO.	DESCRIPTION	PRICE	AMOUNT
5	703-12	Card Trays	15.00	75.00
10	MT-100	Magnetic Tape Cartridge	16.00	160.00
50	MTC150	Digital Cassettes	8.00	400.00
		Total		635.00

VENDOR NAME   *D. P. SUPPLIES*

VENDOR NO.	INVOICE NO.	INVOICE DATE
1034	44059	2 | 3 |

VOUCHER NO.	DUE DATE	ACCOUNT NO.
59182	2 | 13 |	4 5 4

GROSS AMOUNT	DISCOUNT	NET AMOUNT
635 | 00	6 | 35	628 | 65

ACCOUNT NO.	SUB-ACCOUNT	AMOUNT	
454	120	75	00
454	895	160	00
454	457	400	00

Figure 5.5 Apron attached to form

ment and transcription format. Also, the fields to be recorded should be grouped to eliminate or minimize skipping, in that skipping reduces productivity through interruptions in the keying process. In addition, the operations manager must determine the amount of numeric, alphabetic, or alphameric data to be transcribed. Due to keyboard design on the input recording devices, numeric data can be entered more rapidly than alphabetic or alphameric data. The operations manager must also be concerned about the transcription error rate. Experience has shown that an increase in alphabetic and alphameric content on a source document tends to increase the error rate.

5. OUTPUT REQUIREMENTS. To determine output requirements, the operations manager must review and evaluate the documentation, data gathered on required operations, and the printing formats. An analysis of the printer spacing charts will enable the operations manager to determine data type, spacing, and skipping requirements affecting printer and tabulator productivity. In computer printer operations, large volumes of output may be expedited through the use of interchangeable numeric print chains or bars and preferred character features. For example, a printer equipped with a numeric print feature and interchangeable cartridge is capable of achieving a rate of 1,285 lines per minute for numeric output. The same printer without the optional items can achieve a rate of only 600 lines per minute. Actual speeds in both cases depend on the operation. Spacing and skipping must be evaluated in conjunction with lines and pages of print to estimate processing time requirements when volumes are known. The other output media, such as cards, magnetic tape, microfilm, and so forth, would also have to be evaluated. It is conceivable that if the operations manager found his computer processing capability to be output-bound, he could utilize offline peripheral equipment for output functions.

6. REPORTING FREQUENCY. The reporting cycle must be analyzed to indicate the peaks and valleys in the overall work load. The cycle is graphically plotted for each workday of the month to indicate heavy, normal, and light days, as well as the expected demand upon resources. If the peaks appear to be too radical, the operations manager may initiate a reports audit to determine if priorities may be reassigned or if scheduled due dates or times may be readjusted to correct the imbalance.

7. PERSONNEL SKILLS. The effectiveness of the schedule is very dependent upon personnel availability and proficiency. The two factors are not independent of each other. The operation must be adequately staffed with personnel possessing a reasonable degree of training and experience. Inexperienced and/or poorly trained personnel limit an operations manager's ability to function effectively within the schedule. Therefore, the operations manager must initially assess the capabilities of his personnel. The skills inventory, coupled with knowledge of the work flow, enable him to determine the individuals to whom specific functions may be assigned. This assessment is also useful in determining assignments for processing in an alternate or emergency mode of operations. As a result, an intensive orientation and training program may have to be conducted to improve the productive capabilities and proficiency levels of the

REPT. NO.		OPERATOR NO.		DATE		SHIFT			BATCH NO.
		KP	VERIFY				KP	VERIFY	
						1			
						2			
						3			

MACH. TYPE	MACH. TIME	S	CLERICAL	OTHER CODE	OTHER TIME	CARD VOL.	CARD COL S.	FORM NO.
								ERRORS

Figure 5.6 Unit-record production control record form

personnel. The productivity and proficiency may be monitored through the use of a production control record as illustrated in Figure 5.6 (this particular form is appropriate for monitoring unit-record operations).

8. DOCUMENTATION AVAILABILITY. An efficient operation depends heavily on the availability of good documentation. The documentation for each system should be the normal and alternate mode procedures contained in the operator's manual (see chapter 4). The lack of documentation precludes the operations manager from detailing the tasks and developing a preliminary schedule. It also prevents him from determining the training and orientation needs of his personnel. In addition, it hampers his ability to develop the necessary control procedures to ensure uniformity and accuracy of processing.

Preliminary documentation should be made available to the operations manager when program, systems, and parallel tests are conducted. This will enable him to evaluate each manual and machine operation to be performed and to estimate or compute the required processing time. This data must be compared against the existing schedule to identify overlapping operations, bottlenecks, and problem areas that may cause delays in processing. Very often this evaluation is not made and everyone is optimistic that if any problems occur these may be readily resolved. This is wishful thinking and a most unrealistic attitude. The purpose of scheduling is to ensure concurrency of operations. Failure to achieve this goal increases the operating costs through a misuse of resources.

In computerized operations, it is very important that checkpoint, restart, and recovery procedures be included in the operator's manual. This will help to reduce rerun time scheduling and manipulation of the existing schedule when problems occur.

Integrating these factors into an effective production schedule will require the development and implementation of performance standards for the manpower and machines before time estimates or computations can be made. The end result will be a plan covering all of the operational details contributing to goal attainment. The operations group's schedule must be flexible enough to allow for reruns resulting from contingencies and machine or human errors, and to allow for the processing of special or one-time reports—reports such as payroll data on selected job classifications during contract negotiations. If the basic production schedule is heavy, there will be little time for special or one-time reports, which may then be either processed on an overtime basis or submitted to a service bureau.

Performance Factors

The factors are the performance standards for the operations group. In some organizations, the standards are called the production or equipment utilization standards. They may be described as such because of their effect on time allocations for the hardware, personnel, and production.

The performance measures for the operations group bear directly and indirectly on productivity. Although some of them do reduce time available for production, they are necessary to sustain that capability. The performance standards may be arranged according to the following major classifications:

1. Machine measures
2. Testing standards
3. Training standards

1. MACHINE MEASURES. The measures within this classification affect the ability of the operations group to produce a desired report and/or output. These standards must be developed before any production schedule can be formulated. They are the basis for allocating and controlling the available hardware, software, human, and material resources.

Owing to the number of interacting variables, the machine measures may be subdefined into standards for the following seven categories:

a) Unit-record production
b) Computer production
c) Preventative maintenance
d) Emergency maintenance
e) Rerun time
f) Idle time
g) Special requests

a) *Unit-record production.* The unit-record production standards may also be referred to as either punched card standards or EAM equipment standards. Within this category, separate production standards are developed for such devices as keypunches, key verifiers, interpreters, reproducers, etc., in that there are no applicable universal standards for each subcategory of equipment. In the sorter category, for example, an organization may utilize one or several different types. It may be equipped with an IBM 082, 083, and/or 084 sorter, with operating speeds of 650, 1,000, and 2,000 cards per minute respectively. Therefore, one common standard for the sorting equipment may not be entirely practical. However, the manager must establish a standard for each sorter type.

Consider the following example. A manager must determine the scheduling requirements for sorting 15,000 cards on five columns on an 083 sorter. To determine the production time requirements, he may utilize any one of the following approaches. First, he may use a precalculated graph, such as the one illustrated in Figure 5.7. This graph has been plotted to provide a machine time requirement (lower line) and machine time plus handling time (upper line). As a result of examining the graph, the manager may estimate that 19 minutes will be required to sort each column. This figure must then be multiplied by five—the number of columns to be sorted. Therefore, approximately 95 minutes will be required for the sorting operation. However, some setup time must be added. So the manager estimates that five minutes will be required for setup. Therefore, an estimated 100 minutes will be required in the schedule for this sorting operation.

Figure 5.7 Example of precalculated sorting graph

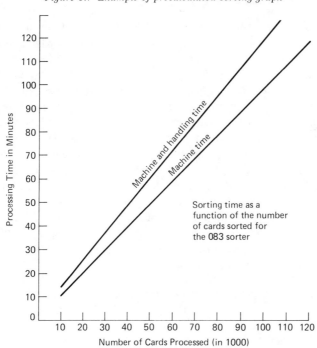

A second approach may be to utilize the following formula:

$$\text{Machine Time} = \frac{\text{Number of cards} \times \text{number of columns}}{\text{Sorter Speed (cards per minute)}}$$

$$\text{Machine Time} = \frac{15,000 \times 5}{1000}$$

$$\text{Machine Time} = \frac{75,000}{1000}$$

$$\text{Machine Time} = 75 \text{ minutes}$$

At this point in the calculation, 75 minutes represents an optimal requirement and does not include handling time. Therefore, the manager must continue with the calculation process. For this example, handling time will be calculated as a percentage of total time, using an operational effectiveness factor.

$$\text{Total Time} = \frac{\text{Machine Time}}{\text{Operational Effectiveness}}$$

$$\text{Total Time} = \frac{75}{.70}$$

$$\text{Total Time} = 107 \text{ minutes}$$

This result is incomplete because, realistically, setup time must be added. Initially, a manager may project approximately 5 minutes, which would cover the transporting of the materials to the machine area; the positioning of supporting equipment, such as a portable rack; and the checking of the operating procedure. Therefore, the total machine time plus setup would equal about 112 minutes. This represents a variance of approximately 12 minutes from the data gained by utilizing a precalculated graph. Although the calculations are not as exact, it must be remembered that both schedule values are approximations that are subject to modification as the utilization statistics become available.

To shorten the second approach, a manager may establish an effective machine speed. This speed is an average that will apply to all sorting operations for a given type of device. It is based on the utilization statistics available to the manager and includes a handling factor of approximately 20 to 30 percent. The machine speed average is sometimes referred to as net speed. Utilizing the same basic statistics as previously shown and a net speed of 750 cards per minute, the calculation may be executed as follows:

$$\text{Sorting Time} = \frac{\text{Number of cards} \times \text{number of columns}}{\text{Net Speed}}$$

$$\text{Sorting Time} = \frac{1,500 \times 5}{750}$$

$$\text{Sorting Time} = \frac{75,000}{750}$$

Sorting Time = 100 minutes

Sorting Time	100 minutes
Est. Setup Time	+ 5 minutes
Est. Sorting Requirements	105 minutes

For large-volume operations, an average net speed may not be satisfactory. In that case, the manager need only modify the sorter speed by the handling factor and use the reduced operating speed as the divisor.

Similar calculations using relevant formulas can be made for scheduling operations on the keypunch, key verifier, reproducer, collator, calculator, tabulator (accounting machine), interpreter, and punch machines.

b) Computer production. The computing production standards may be difficult to establish. Program running or elapsed time may be determined by calculating the amount of time required to perform each function in a program. The functional times are then added together to determine total processing time. These timings generally include the input/output media, blocking factors, record sizes, volumes, arm movement, rotational delay, container position, etc. However, they do not include lengthy or excessive operator intervention, or programmer inefficiency. The timings may further be affected by the type and level of operating system and by multi-tasking. For most managers, it would be simpler to closely monitor the processing of selected data during the parallel test and extrapolate. Or, the manager may use simulation to predict the timings. The simulation may be performed manually or with a computer. Basic data about the program—data such as processing flow, data files, priority, etc.—is inserted into a mathematical model that represents a hardware configuration. As a result of the simulation, all timings and utilization figures will be outputted in a report format for scheduling purposes.

These figures are preliminary and should be used only for planning the initial schedule requirements. However, as utilization figures become available, the values may be modified upward or downward. In a multi-tasking environment, an average figure may have to be developed because elapsed time will vary each time a program is processed. For more accurate information, a manager may acquire a computer performance monitor to measure actual utilization of the hardware and software.

c) Preventative maintenance. The standard for preventative maintenance is established on the basis of information supplied by the equipment manufacturer in his proposal. The proposal states only the time requirement and does not indicate the day or shift for performance of the maintenance. The day and shift are negotiable because of the constraints within which the vendor and the organization must function.

The standard must be included in the schedule and closely monitored because it limits hardware availability for production. Monitoring is also necessary to ensure proper equipment maintenance. If actual maintenance time is significantly below the standard, then either the stated requirement was incorrect or maintenance service may be incomplete. When time requirements exceed the standard, the original specifications may have been understated; or the engineers performing the maintenance may be slow or improperly trained. Also, it may be that either the age of the hardware or heavy utilization requires additional preventative maintenance. If so, then the standard must be modified to reflect this condition.

Very often, early production models require the on-site installation of numerous engineering changes. The maintenance engineer may install some of the devices during the preventative maintenance period. Consequently, he may exceed the scheduled time allocation, thereby incorrectly reflecting a variance in the standard. Before any revision of the standard is made, the situation should be discussed with the vendor's sales and/or maintenance representative. Very often, managers persuade the maintenance engineer to perform only the most important functions and postpone others until the next scheduled period. This enables the manager to return the hardware to production status sooner. Some managers habitually cancel maintenance sessions to retain the computer for productive services. Some may cancel the maintenance session because their production may be lagging. Nevertheless this can be a shortsighted attitude that can subsequently lead to a frequent need for unscheduled maintenance.

d) Emergency maintenance. Emergency maintenance—sometimes referred to as downtime, or unscheduled, maintenance—requires development of a standard to cover that unit or element of time when the hardware is disabled due to some malfunction. Initially, this type of standard is difficult to establish because of the limited information available to the manager in terms of downtime frequency.

A preliminary standard may be established from the estimated downtime value provided by the vendor. A portion of this value is based on the Mean Time Between Failures (MTBF) statistics resulting from the vendor's equipment-testing program. This provides a failure frequency standard. If the number of failures consistently exceeds the standard, then the manager must make some investigative assessment of the quality of preventative maintenance.

The MTBF provides a failure frequency rate but does not indicate the estimated downtime allocation for scheduling purposes. A preliminary value is again supplied by the vendor. This is included as a part of the estimated downtime in the vendor's hardware proposal. It represents the result of downtime statistics collected by the vendors for similar hardware.

To collect data and to determine variances, a log of service calls, elapsed response time, and maintenance time must be kept. This data may subsequently be used for the upward or downward revision of the standard. As the equipment ages and/or utilization increases, emergency maintenance needs may grow. This may necessitate an upward revision of the emergency maintenance standard.

When an organization acquires older equipment, it will be necessary to ascertain the hardware's history, together with the actual or average failure rate. Also, it may be advantageous to learn why the equipment was released by the previous user. This data will enable a manager to establish a more realistic downtime standard for that hardware.

e) Rerun time. This is a contingency allocation built into the schedule to provide for the reprocessing of a report, output, or operation. The contingency covers the human, machine, program, or data errors occurring in the productive process. Initially it will be very difficult to project the time loss attributable to these conditions. However, as operational statistics become available, they may be used to develop an effective rerun time standard. Also, from this data, a percentage for each error category may be established by utilizing the following formula:

$$\text{Percentage of (Type of) Error} = \frac{\text{Time Lost Due to (Type of) Error}}{\text{Total Productive Time}}$$

Errors reduce operational effectiveness and cause a loss of confidence in the data processing department. Therefore, every effort must be made to eliminate, minimize, and control their occurrence. The data errors may be controlled through the use of management controls (see chapter 10). The machine errors may be due to malfunctions resulting from improper preventative maintenance, component failure, or age of the hardware. To deal with these errors, a manager may find it necessary to implement a series of management controls and/or to closely monitor the hardware failure frequency and preventative maintenance. Operator errors may be reduced or eliminated by providing for more effective direction and control of the personnel, good documentation, and intensive training for operations and user personnel. Errors caused by faulty programs may be resolved through detailed desk checking, preparation of good test plans, construction of complete test data, intensive testing of the object program, and complete verification of test output.

f) Idle time. An idle-time standard provides a buffer in the schedule for unexpected events. This element is sometimes referred to as slack time—built into the schedule to cover such events as excessive reruns, unscheduled maintenance, special report requests, etc. There is the danger that in maintaining a contingency buffer, a manager may restrict the implementation of a valuable decision-making report simply because time is not available. The operations manager must assess the cost of delay, the value of each report, and its impact on the idle-time standard. The effect of an idle-time standard may be more significant on an organization functioning on a one-shift basis. The organization may have to develop alternate operating procedures. On the other hand, an organization functioning on a two- or three-shift basis in the operations activity has more flexibility because of its ability to overlap production backlog from one shift to another.

g) Special requests. Specials are one-time or short-term reports or outputs designed for a specific decision-making purpose. Included in this category are such reports as wage and salary data for labor contract negotiations. Often, these requests can be readily absorbed into the normal operating schedule. However, in some organizations, the number of requests for special reports or outputs is high. Therefore, the operations manager must examine his production schedule to establish an average time availability for specials. In some organizations, requests for special reports occur on a cyclical basis, such as before, during, and after labor-contract negotiations. From an analysis of the production records, the operations manager will be able to develop an average time requirement. When no data or experience is available, the manager may initially project a one percent time requirement in the schedule for special requests.

The number of requests for special reports can become unwieldy if not controlled. Therefore, it becomes necessary that an administrative procedure be developed and implemented requiring practical and economic justification of such requests.

2. TESTING STANDARDS. Testing standards must be developed and included in the schedule to maintain the operational effectiveness of an organization. The standard is developed to meet the functional needs of the programming, systems, operations, planning and development, and audit personnel. The types of standards within this category are:

a) Program assembly and compile
b) Program testing
c) Magnetic tape
d) Forms testing

a) *Program assembly and compile.* The projected time standard for assemblies and compiles is affected by the hardware, operating system, language processor, program development, and maintenance requirements. In developing an overall time requirement, the operations manager or programming manager initially determines the estimated program translation time. This can be done by dividing the language processor speed into the estimated number of source program statements or instructions. Or, the operations manager or programming manager may gather data on program sizes to establish an average program size; he then divides this average by the language processor speed to calculate an average translate time.

The number of compiles or assemblies required in a schedule period will depend on the type and number of new programs being developed, and/or existing programs modified. The time standard may be determined by multiplying the average translation speed by the average number of programs requiring translation.

b) *Program testing.* A program-testing standard provides for the testing and debugging of new and modified programs. Testing may require from 5 to 25 percent of the available schedule time. As recommended earlier, a minimum of 20 minutes test time should be allocated for each programmer. Failure to provide adequate test time causes slippage in implementation schedules and results in a waste of valuable resources.

c) *Magnetic tape.* An organization may choose to develop a norm for testing the quality and condition of its magnetic tape. The test is made by passing each reel through the tape transports twice. The first pass performs a writing function and the second reads back the written data. As a result, it is possible to determine if the tape is worn, stretched, scratched, or damaged.

The testing process may be conducted when a new shipment of magnetic tape is received, to select a source of supply, or to establish a purchasing specification standard. More frequently, the standard is the basis of a tape maintenance and rehabilitation program. The average time for testing a 2,400-foot-long reel is approximately five minutes. This value, however, is affected by the number of channels available on the computer and by the manner in which the test program was written. Average time may be increased if the program does not overlap tape rewinding; it may be decreased if more than one channel is available.

It is difficult to establish a norm for magnetic disk pack testing. However, this may be accomplished by developing a load-dump program, which would test reading and writing on the disk. This is a time-consuming process and should be performed only when damage may be suspected. However, some organizations use this technique to test new shipments.

d) *Forms testing.* The standard for forms testing is eatablished to evaluate the quality and effectiveness of a form. When a new form is designed, the vendor is asked to submit a paper and/or carbon dummy. The dummies are then processed on the equipment to determine if form objectives are realized. Similar testing may be conducted for the MICR, OCR, and OMR types of forms.

This standard is generally established only in medium- or large-sized data processing organizations. However, many organizations in search of cost-reduction cases will frequently have their systems and/or advanced planning personnel evaluating forms construction. As a result, new specifications may be developed that may reduce the form's cost. Forms testing may also be conducted to verify a vendor's compliance with contractual obligations. In this case, an average time standard should be established on the basis of the type of testing to be conducted.

3. TRAINING STANDARDS. To maintain or increase operational effectiveness, training must be provided. Generally, it is limited to systems analysts, programmers, and console operators. However, organizations equipped with online input, output, data communications, and/or data collection terminals must also provide training for users.

The actual schedule requirements depend on the level and extent of training to be provided. As the training plan is evolved, the time requirements for each element or phase should be closely monitored and recorded for subsequent scheduling purposes.

Also, demonstrations may be included in this standard. It is difficult to establish a true time standard because the number of demonstrations conducted will vary. However, the length of such demonstrations can be controlled by providing a standardized routine. Some organizations, in order to minimize

Schedule Factor	Percentage	Time Factor
Nonproduction Requirements		
Maintenance Standards		
Preventative Maintenance	10.0	4:00 hrs.
Emergency Maintenance	.5	12 mins.
Reruns		
Machine Error	.5	12 mins.
Program Error	.5	12 mins.
Operator Error	.5	12 mins.
Data Error	.5	12 mins.
Idle Time	1.0	24 mins.
Program Development and Maintenance	12.5	5:00 hrs.
Setup Time	2.0	48 mins.
	28.0%	11 hrs. 12 mins.
Machine Time Available	40:00 hrs.	
Nonproduction Requirements	−11:12 hrs.	
Production Time Available	28:48 hrs.	

Figure 5.8 Example of projection of production time availability

disruptions in the productive level, allow demonstrations to be performed only on a fixed schedule basis.

Initially, the data processing manager must project the time available for productive purposes. The approach begins with specifying the base time available and applying the operations standards against this value. Figure 5.8 illustrates the constraints and their effect on a one-shift schedule for a data processing organization. The organization is supported by three programmers. Twenty-eight percent of the schedule is required for application of the various standards. This will consume 11 hours and 20 minutes of the base shift. However, 28 hours and 48 minutes remain, which may be presented as an average of 5 hours and 46 minutes a day.

Review Questions: Group 5A

1. What is meant by the term "scheduling"?
2. Why must volume statistics be evaluated when preparing an operation's group schedule?
3. How is setup and handling time included in the production schedule?
4. What is the purpose of establishing an idle-time standard?

THE SOFTWARE SYSTEMS GROUP

Scheduling Factors

The software systems (programming) group is responsible for the preparation of new programs; the writing of utility, conversion, and modular programs; maintenance of existing operational software; designing general-purpose systems programs such as compilers, operating systems, data base management systems, microcode, and telecommunications software; and developing software processors to optimize the utilization of storage space and/or running time. In performing these tasks, the software personnel may analyze system flowcharts; develop decision tables, program outlines, and/or top-down structures; code instructions; devise data structures, desk-check coding and logic; devise test plans and test data; compile or assemble source programs; test and debug programs; and prepare documentation. Each of these activities affects the development of a schedule for the software systems group.

The scheduling factors are qualified by such variables as type of operating system, programming language, program size, input/output, complexity, language, programmer efficiency, and testing. The size variable relates to the number of statements, instructions, or storage requirements in a program. Most frequently, program size is expressed as storage requirements or instructions; for example, 32K, 32,000 positions, or 150 instructions. Sometimes, though, program size is simply expressed in number of pages; for example, "12 pages of coding." Input/output refers to the number and types of devices controlled by the program. Certain devices, such as graphic and audio terminals, require more programming interface than a card reader or card punch. (A related factor is that, as additional devices are included in a program, the program's size increases because additional memory positions are required for a work area and controls.) Often the devices are listed in order of interface difficulty from simple to complex. Obviously, more development and test time will be required for more sophisticated input/output devices. Complexity varies according to the length of the program, number of tasks to be performed, and the number of input/output devices used. It may be expressed in levels from simple to very difficult. The language variable refers, obviously, to the programming language in which the problem is to be coded. If several programming languages are generally used in an organization, these must be scaled by levels of difficulty from the absolute to procedure-oriented. Programmer efficiency is a subjective evaluation of a programmer's productivity. Generally, an efficiency factor is assigned on the basis of position and classification level within the programmer's occupational grouping. Consequently, time allocations for senior personnel will be significantly less than those allowed to trainees or juniors. Testing is concerned with testing requirements and the ability of programming personnel to secure adequate machine time to debug a program. Very often a schedule slips considerably because of a lack of adequate machine time for testing and debugging.

In the development of a schedule it is necessary to divide the programming function into the performance categories of (1) new program development and (2) maintenance of existing programs.

New Program Development

In the development of a new program and/or software, the software systems personnel execute a series of tasks that must begin with an analysis of the problem and/or software requirements and terminates with the implementation of a desired solution. This detailed process involves the following activities:

1. Analysis of requirements
2. Design of a solution
3. Development of the solution
4. Testing and debugging
5. Implementation of the software system and/or program

1. ANALYSIS OF REQUIREMENTS. The first step in the software development process begins with an identification of a problem and/or software requirements. It is essential that the software personnel understand what is to be done, the reasons behind the need, and the boundaries for the project. This information is partially gathered from memos and other documentation and through interviews with user, systems, managerial, operations, and other software personnel.

For the applications programmers, this process of analysis begins with interviews with the user and systems personnel in order to identify actual need, scope of the project, software requirements, and the data flows. In addition to the interviews, the applications programmer must analyze the job specifications (systems flowcharts, systems abstracts, decision tables), data specifications, required computational and data handling procedures, and exception processing requirements.

The systems programmers, too, must determine the requirements for a desired software package or the problems in an existing software system. If a problem is involved, the systems programmer may find it necessary to write some software routines that may detect and identify the cause of the software failure. In addition, the programmer may have to analyze the costs or advantages of utilizing other compilers, data structures, modifying an operating system, or evaluating a software package for possible use by the organization.

The scientific/technical programmer must also become involved in analysis even though his problems and/or requirements may require the use of mathematical solutions. The programmer must consider the formula or formulae involved and the available mathematical software, in addition to the job and data specifications.

In each case, the programmer after having analyzed the problem and/or requirements must make recommendations to the programming manager regarding the feasibility of continuing the project. The programming manager must then make a go/no go decision based on the findings and review of the user's objectives.

2. DESIGN OF A SOLUTION. The design of a solution or an alternative approach is not initiated until the software personnel have received formal approval. In some organizations, this approval may come directly from the steering committee, whereas, in other organizations it may depend on user acceptance of your proposal. The design process may include such tasks as describing the software logic using program flowcharts, decision tables, program narratives or outlines, and/or top-down structures; performing trade-offs on input/output, storage requirements, and run times to produce an optimal solution; building in the necessary management controls, design compilers, operating systems, and telecommunications software.

Here again the programmer must prepare formal documentation for presentation to the programming manager and users. The information will again be used to determine if it is feasible to proceed further with the project—another go/no go determination.

3. DEVELOPMENT OF THE SOLUTION. The development process deals with producing the component parts of the suggested alternative program and/or software system. Included in this segment are such tasks as program coding; preparing recovery procedures; preparing interfaces with other programs and/or software systems; preparing memory maps; devising algorithms; coding and debugging modifications to operating systems, compilers, executives, etc.; writing manuals to assist the applications programmers; preparing instructions for user and operations personnel; developing "artificial" and "live" test data; devising test plans; and preparing a conversion plan to a new program, software system, compiler or operating system.

This segment of the software development process is very difficult to quantify in terms of a performance standard; yet, such a standard must be prepared in order to plan, organize, coordinate, direct, and control a data processing operation. A great deal of coordination is required between systems, operations, software, training, and planning personnel during this phase of a project.

4. TESTING AND DEBUGGING. The testing and debugging segment is very important to the development of a new program and/or software system. Yet very frequently, this phase of the project is done very poorly. The test data and test plan that had been devised earlier are now applied to the testing and debugging process. The testing must be performed in such a manner as to completely test a program or software package. The testing process must ensure that the programs will accept a full range of allowable input, detect all faulty inputs, test all interfaces, perform the necessary condition and code checking, test various input combinations, and determine that every instruction in the program has been executed.

The results of the test process must be compared to the expected results prepared in the test plan and coordinated with user personnel. When "live" data is used the coordination requirements are greater because of the volume of data that is tested and must be checked. It will also be necessary to provide the operations manager with a time estimate for computer and peripheral equipment utilization requirements.

The test process may also require the development of patches and fixes that will enable a faulty applications program to run or to utilize a compiler, executive, operating system, data base management software, and telecommunications software. These temporary patches and fixes must be subsequently improved or recorded and incorporated into the appropriate software and/or program.

A performance standard for testing must also include some provision for assembly and/or compilation of programs.

5. PROGRAM AND/OR SOFTWARE SYSTEM IMPLEMENTATION. After the software has undergone complete testing, has been fully debugged, and has been accepted by the users, the process of implementation must begin. A major part of this process is to coordinate with all parties concerned to determine when the software will be utilized for productive processing. It also requires the training of user and operations personnel in the utilization of the software. Documentation for operation of the software, recovery procedures, file security, and exception handling must also be finalized and distributed. The software items must also be fully documented and included in the appropriate documentation manuals.

The implementation process may also include a monitoring system to provide feedback on the operation of the software. The monitoring process should be established for software packages, operating systems, compilers, and other systems software items, as well as applications programs. For example, installing release changes to the operating system is a responsibility of the systems programmers in most organizations. The release change must be tested to some extent to ensure its operational effectiveness, but it is very often difficult, if not impossible, to test the effect of the change on applications programs. When an applications program is being processed, an error or problem may occur that had not been previously detected. The error may be due to the change in the operating system or because the operating system and the applications program do not interface correctly for some reason. The systems software programmer may then be called on to make an emergency fix or patch to permit running of the applications program.

Maintenance of Existing Programs

One of the responsibilities of the software function is to maintain the existing applications programs, software packages, compilers, executives, operating system, data base management software, and telecommunications software; generate the updates (releases) to the operating system and/or software package and microcode. The need for change may result from changes in organizational objectives, new contractual requirements, new legal requirements, and/or poor program or software performance.

Initially, the maintenance programmer must evaluate the impact of any changes or proposed corrections to the existing software. Part of the process involves a review and examination of the documentation that is in existence for a program and/or software package. Quite frequently, the maintenance programmer loses time because he must generate documentation to perform an impact evaluation. The programmer must also review the files and data structures to evaluate the impact on inputs, outputs and storage. There is also a need to evaluate the impact of the change on related information systems and/or software. In many organizations, the maintenance programmer is required to report on the results of his investigation to the programming manager for a determination on the feasibility of continuing with the maintenance project.

When a maintenance project is approved, the maintenance programmer will be involved with designing and developing the necessary changes and/or modifications; testing and debugging the changes, testing the operational effectiveness of the complete program and/or software system, and revising the documentation to reflect the changes that have been made to the system.

Performance Standards

There are a number of available methods for estimating the software systems effort, some of which are very sophisticated, others very general. Each programming manager must evaluate his own staff and determine whether a particular method is acceptable as is, needs to be modified, or needs to be abandoned in favor of developing a new method. In developing a new method, the performance standard for the software systems group is affected by such factors as program size, program complexity (simple, complex, very complex), required processing functions, available personnel skills, and knowledge of the task (functional area, operating system, software, etc.). Each of these factors has to be applied and then quantified in order to arrive at an estimate of time needed for software analysis, design, development, testing, implementation, and maintenance.

The component parts of an estimating method may include the following factors:

1. Input/output requirements
2. Required processing functions
3. Knowledge of the task
4. Available personnel skills
5. Delays and other factors

1. INPUT/OUTPUT REQUIREMENTS. The performance standard must consider the number and types of input/output devices that must be used in the required program solution. A program that requires card input from a single file and outputs the information on a printer will be less complex than one requiring inputs from several internal/external sources and/or distribution of outputs to several sources.

2. REQUIRED PROCESSING FUNCTIONS. The required processing functions include such factors as data handling, computational, linkage to other programs and/or modules, and exception processing. The data handling procedures would

include such items as combining, editing, checking, rearranging, accessing, retrieving, and searching for data elements. The greater the number of manipulations required within a program, the more complex is the process. The computational procedures may involve the use of simple arithmetic functions to the inclusion of vendor-supplied or in-house written statistical packages and other mathematical algorithms. Coding the formula or formulae may not be as difficult as understanding the user's requirements.

3. KNOWLEDGE OF TASK. Knowledge of tasks is concerned with the degree of knowledge required to analyze, design, develop, test, implement, and maintain the software. The knowledge is a composite of the programmer's understanding of the functional area, operating system, compiler, and so forth, and the requirements for a given problem. Some projects require an in-depth knowledge, whereas other projects require only some or very limited familiarity with the subject matter to successfully execute the project. The knowledge requirements will help to determine the degree of complexity that is assigned to a programming and/or software project.

4. AVAILABLE PERSONNEL SKILLS. The programming manager must be able to match the skills of his personnel with the job tasks in the software project. Personal expertise is a composite of personality, job, and experiential skills. The personality skills include such factors as analytical ability, creativity, communications ability, and objectivity. A maintenance programmer must possess analytical ability to facilitate problem definition. The job skills include such factors as flowcharting ability, good coding skills, speed, accuracy, testing and debugging skills, and documentation skills. A programmer that exhibits great attention to detail may be particularly skillful at program coding, developing test data, and debugging software. The experiential skills may result from on-the-job experience and/or training and education acquired in such areas as programming languages; operating systems; hardware; program organization and structure; file and data structures; file access techniques; data base management; telecommunications software; statistical techniques; and microcoding. The availability or nonavailability of such skills may affect programmer performance on a software project. To improve on the skills of the software personnel, many organizations perform a skills inventory and use the data gathered to develop training programs for the software personnel (see chapter 3).

In some organizations, the assignments are made on the basis of job titles. For example, a senior programmer would be given more complex software tasks to perform, although he may also be given simpler tasks to perform but allocated a shorter time-frame for project completion. With the advent of modular programming, it will be necessary for a programming manager to evaluate the skills of the software personnel more carefully in order to maximize their capabilities.

5. DELAYS AND OTHER FACTORS. Most project plans do not allow for delays and interruptions in the schedule. The delays may result from an inability to gain adequate computer time to perform the necessary testing and debugging or the inability to have the users coordinate and verify test results as originally

scheduled. Other factors that may affect the schedule are such items as absenteeism, vacations, holidays, and special assignments. Many organizations place a loading factor of 5 to 10 percent on the project time estimates to compensate for delays and interruptions. Some organizations place a loading factor of at least 20 percent and as high as 25 percent for the interferences. The actual loading factor should be determined by the organization after a review of its own policies and practices.

Another factor that must be built into the schedule and/or standard is documentation time. A manager must expect to allocate a minimum of 5 to 10 percent in the overall project schedule for documentation. New programs that are not properly documented will be difficult to maintain and may lose their utility within a very short time period. If a maintenance programmer must work on a project that has little or no documentation, it will be necessary to establish some documentation before he can assess the impact of a change or trace the flow through a program. Failure of a systems programmer to document changes and limitations to operating systems, compilers, executives, etc., may also lead to a waste of valuable resources.

The schedule and standard may be monitored through the use of a Programming Activity Report form as illustrated in Figure 5.9. The schedule itself may be displayed using a GANTT chart to show the status of a programming project (see Figure 5.10).

Figure 5.9 Example of programming activity report form

PROGRAMMING ACTIVITY REPORT	NAME		ENO.		WK. ENDING

PROJECT NUMBER	PROGRAM NUMBER	DESCRIPTION	ACTIVE CODE	REG. DAYS*	O.T. DAYS*	EST. CMPLT. DATE	PERCENT COMPLETE*

ACTIVITY CODES: FOR MAINTENANCE ACTIVITY, PREFIX CODE WITH "M"

PROBLEM DEFINITION	10	TEST AND DEBUG	40	INSTRUCTOR	70
FLOWCHARTING	20	PREPARE TEST PLAN	45	ATTEND TRAINING SESSION	80
CODING	25	EVALUATE TEST RESULTS	49		
DESK CHECKING	30	DOCUMENTATION	50		
TEST DATA PREPARATION	35	MEETINGS	60		

*SHOW TENTHS

PROJECT NUMBER _____ NAME_____

EST. START DATE _____ EST. COMPLETION DATE _____ DATE_____

PROGRAM PLAN

MONTH	JAN					FEB				MAR				APR					MAY				JUNE				JULY					AUG			
WEEK	1	2	3	4	5	1	2	3	4	1	2	3	4	1	2	3	4	5	1	2	3	4	1	2	3	4	1	2	3	4	5	1	2	3	4
PROBLEM DEFINITION																																			
FLOWCHARTING																																			
CODING																																			
DESK CHECKING																																			
TEST DATA PREP.																																			
TEST PLAN PREP.																																			
TEST AND DEBUG																																			
EVALUATE TEST																																			
DOCUMENTATION																																			
CUTOVER																																			
	PROGRESS		SCHEDULE																																

Figure 5.10 *Example of bar chart used to show status of programming activity*

Review Questions: Group 5B

1. What variables affect the programming schedule?
2. What is the purpose of a test plan?
3. Why must the programming manager and/or project manager allocate a loss or delay factor to be included in the software project time estimates?

THE SYSTEMS GROUP

Scheduling Factors

The systems group has the responsibility for analysis, design, development, implementation, and maintenance of manual, unit-record, and computer-based information systems. The activities of the systems group are influenced by the interests of the upper echelon and users. The organization's information systems must be designed so as to provide inputs into the organization's decision-making process. This approach requires that more consideration be given to how the information is to be used and not simply processing data to produce information that may have little or no value.

The principal factors affecting the systems group's schedule are:

1. Definition of the objective
2. Systems analysis

3. Systems design
4. Systems development
5. Systems implementation
6. Systems evaluation

1. DEFINITION OF THE OBJECTIVE. The definition process is initiated by a request from a user, directive from the steering committee or the upper echelon, or an initiative undertaken by the data processing organization. The request must be investigated to determine if it has merit for additional consideration or to determine if it is included in the organization's long-range plan for future development. The investigatory process may be simpler if the organization maintains a well-documented survey (see chapter 8). To be effective, it is necessary that the same criteria be applied to each request considered by the systems personnel. The results of the investigation may be presented to the systems manager and/or the steering committee to determine if the project merits additional consideration.

2. SYSTEMS ANALYSIS. This is the first stage of a feasibility study (see chapter 8). During this stage the systems personnel work in conjunction with the user departments to gather information about the existing procedure (system) to determine whether a new application should or must be developed. Gathering information about the existing system will involve conducting interviews with managerial and user personnel, observing the processes currently conducted, and, in some instances, developing and using questionnaires for data collection. The data gathered during this part of analysis will help to identify attitudes that may be predictors of future success, data on volumes and processing times, information on the processing cycle that will identify the peaks and valleys, quality control data, and response time requirements. In addition, the analyst must review the documentation on the existing system such as system flowcharts, system abstracts, decision tables, input, output and storage specifications, user instructions, and documentation on software used in the system.

With the aid of various checklists, the information is gathered and subsequently analyzed to evaluate the operational effectiveness of the current approach and the need for an alternative approach. The analyst will use the data to prepare recommendations regarding the feasibility of considering an alternative approach. The systems manager by himself or in conjunction with the steering committee will review the recommendations and determine if the analyst should proceed with the next phase of the project. A review of the long-range plan may reveal that a particular application is scheduled for revision within the near future and any changes at this point in time would be of a temporary nature and could prove to be costly to effect.

3. SYSTEMS DESIGN. The analyst must consider the problems that must be solved or the requirements that must be met and generate a new design. From the various options that are available to him the analyst must select the one option that will best meet the needs of the organization. In this determination, the analyst must consider such factors as hardware, input/output alternatives, file

structures, response time requirements, exception processing requirements, manual procedures, and forms.

Much of the emphasis will be on data flows and processing of data with little regard for decision making—a very common mistake committed by systems personnel. If a system is to be meaningful and contribute to the operational effectiveness of the overall organization, then it must provide the kinds of information that can be used in the decision-making process. Another problem during the design phase is one of failure to include users in the design process. Many analysts will disagree with that comment because they feel that the specifications are presented to the users for their agreement and approval with the "sign-off" procedure. Unfortunately, many users do not understand the specifications presented to them or are able to review the materials only superficially because they do not understand the technical specifications. Decision tables can be better understood by users than the traditional system flowchart. If the analyst were to review the specifications with the users, that would assist them in better understanding the design and determining if it meets their needs.

The design must be documented and, along with some estimated cost-benefit, run-time, and volume estimates, should be presented to the systems manager for review. In some organizations, the steering committee (see chapter 2), will again become involved in the decision-making process. The decision will either be to proceed with the project, delay the project until a more suitable time in the future, cancel any further consideration of the project, or proceed with certain modifications.

4. Systems development. The approved design for a given system must now be generated. This requires that the component parts of the system must be developed and then integrated into a controlled procedure that will produce the desired end results. If the design phase was properly done, then much of the groundwork for the development has already been accomplished.

In some organizations, IBM's TAG approach is used for automating the design and development process. Others use the Hosykyns system to aid in the process. Researchers at the University of Michigan are experimenting with an approach labeled as ISDOS for describing a system's requirements and producing some of the detailed work needed. These approaches are helpful in reducing the amount of time required to design and develop a system, but they cannot complete the process by themselves. Much work still remains to be done.

There is still a need for the traditional approaches to systems work. Systems flowcharts and decision tables must be described; input, output and file specifications must be developed; necessary management controls must be identified, exception processing routines must be developed, user instructions must be written, installation and conversion plans must be developed, training requirements must be outlined; test plans for systems and parallel testing must be developed; and a project schedule and plan must be developed.

5. Systems implementation. The implementation phase is concerned with converting from the existing system to the proposed system. An important part of this process will involve the conversion of various data and files from one for-

mat to another. Data and file conversion will require the development of procedures for execution of the process and controls to ensure accuracy and completeness of conversion. This phase will also be concerned with training of users, managerial, and data processing personnel in the operation of the new procedures. Coordination with all parties to ensure a smooth cut-over from one approach to another will be very time-consuming but necessary. There must also be a procedure developed to handle all in-process transactions. These are items that are caught in the middle of the old and new approaches and must be included in the new system.

6. SYSTEMS EVALUATION. This phase of the systems cycle involves a review and evaluation of the progress being achieved under the new system. This follow-up is conducted to determine if the new system is performing as had been planned; if the savings stated in the feasibility study had been achieved; if the costs had been minimized, stabilized, eliminated, or increased or if new costs had been incurred; if the training and documentation was adequate; and so forth.

A system evaluation may also be performed as a system audit. System audits may be performed to evaluate existing systems, data entry procedures, management controls, user procedures, data structures, available hardware and/or software, and documentation and performance standards.

Performance Standards

Many people argue that it is difficult to develop performance standards for the systems group because the tasks and activities performed within the systems group are not as clearly defined as in other functional activities. The statement is not valid because it is possible to quantify the various tasks and activities as they occur in each phase of the systems cycle. The systems cycle is generally defined as the analysis, design, development, implementation, and follow-up phases.

The analysis phase is a data gathering and data evaluation phase. Therefore, the systems manager must allocate a time estimate for such activities as interviews with managerial and user personnel; observation of user personnel; collection of sample documents, policies, and organization charts; preparation and collection of questionnaires; preparation or review of flowcharts, decision tables, systems abstracts and other relevant documentation; evaluation of required management controls; and evaluation of input, output, and file specifications. Some of these tasks require only a limited amount of time to perform, whereas others may require several man-days of effort. Interviews with user personnel may require only fifteen to twenty minutes if the interviewer has prepared for the session. Analysis of inputs, outputs, and files may require from two to four man-days of effort depending on the complexity of the system. The time may be reduced if well-prepared checklists are used for the data gathering and data evaluation process (see Figure 5.11).

The design phase is the second part of the feasibility study. During this

1. What is the purpose of the form?
   a) Does the form correlate with that purpose?
   b) Does the form correlate with the system's objectives?
2. Utilization volume?
3. Cost? (Last contract price.)
4. What is the functional relationship of this form to other forms in this and other systems?
5. Is the form temporary or permanent?
6. Is the title descriptive and meaningful?
7. What information is entered at time of origination?
8. What information is added subsequent to origination?
9. Have all the necessary information elements been included on the form?
10. Are there any unnecessary information elements on the form that may be deleted?
11. What use is made of each element of information on the form?
12. What is the volume and significance of errors in origination and processing?
13. What approval signatures are required?
14. What information is transferred to other forms, reports, or records?
15. What is the disposition of each copy?
    a) Does each copy serve a necessary purpose?
    b) Is the distribution adequate?
16. Are there any written procedures governing the preparation and use of the form?

Figure 5.11 Sample checklist for form appraisal

phase, the systems personnel are concerned with designing a user-oriented system that will contribute to the decision-making process in the organization. This phase is concerned with the charting of the alternative approach using system flowcharts, decision tables, program flowcharts, logic narratives, and top-down structures for the proposed systems and software in the project; design of input, output, and file specifications; design of new forms; and the preparation of documentation that will help the user to fully understand the proposed approach. The use of checklists is again advisable to help reduce the time requirements and to ensure uniformity in the design process.

The development phase is involved with the generation of the necessary system components. The phase includes such activities as the design of detailed system flowcharts; preparation of more detailed program logic descriptions; coordination of program testing and debugging; preparation of test data and test plan for the systems and acceptance tests; preparation of training outlines and materials for the training of user, operations, and other data processing personnel; preparation of the project schedule and plan; and preparation of user instructions and systems documentation.

The implementation phase involves the transition from the present approach to the new approach. The factors that must be quantified in this segment are conversion of data and files from the old to the new approach; preparation of conversion procedures and controls; training of personnel systems and parallel testing; documentation; and coordination of cut-over. The time estimates for many of these factors will be very lengthy and developing the standard for each will require intense consideration. The one factor that is usually underestimated is the documentation factor. Many organizations fail to include any time for the task, whereas others include only a nominal time. A manager can expect to spend from 20 to 25 percent of project time for the documentation task.

Figure 5.12 Systems analyst activity report form

SYSTEM ANALYST ACTIVITY REPORT	NAME		ENO.	WK. ENDING
	F M LAST			MO. DAY YR.

PROJECT NO.	PROJECT TITLE

START DATE	ESTIMATED COMPLETION DATE	PERCENT COMPLETE

ACTIVITY CODE	REG. DAYS*	O.T. DAYS*	ACTIVITY CODE	REG. DAYS*	O.T. DAYS*	ACTIVITY CODE	REG. DAYS*	O.T. DAYS*	ACTIVITY CODE	REG. DAYS*	O.T. DAYS*	ACTIVITY CODE	REG. DAYS*	O.T. DAYS*

ACTIVITY CODE	REG. DAYS*	O.T. DAYS*	ACTIVITY CODE	REG. DAYS*	O.T. DAYS*	ACTIVITY CODE	REG. DAYS*	O.T. DAYS*	ACTIVITY CODE	REG. DAYS*	O.T. DAYS*	ACTIVITY CODE	REG. DAYS*	O.T. DAYS*

ACTIVITY CODES: FOR MAINTENANCE ACTIVITY, PREFIX CODE NUMBER WITH "M"

PROBLEM DEFINITION	10	INTERVIEWING	20	SYSTEM FLOWCHARTING	30	PROGRAM FLOWCHARTING 35
PREPARE TEST PLAN	40	SURVEY	50	FEASIBILITY STUDY	55	SYSTEMS AUDIT 57
SYSTEM TEST	60	PARALLEL TEST	62	PROGRAM TEST	65	FOLLOW-UP 67
DESIGN SYSTEM	70	FORMS DESIGN	72	VENDOR SPECIFICATIONS	75	VENDOR PROPOSALS 77
DOCUMENTATION	80	USER TRAINING	90	ATTENDING TRAINING	95	
* SHOW TENTHS						

ACCOMPLISHMENTS:

PROBLEMS:

PLANS FOR TOMORROW:

The follow-up phase is sometimes referred to as the post-operational phase because it is concerned with a review and evaluation of the newly implemented system. The systems manager should have a standardized checklist of the items that he wishes to have checked during the review process. Some of the problems encountered during the follow-up phase are the result of user misunderstanding. Quite frequently, the training and coordination effort has not been done as well as it should have; as a result, the users do not have a firm grasp of the process. This may be corrected by providing some additional training for the users. The documentation may also be a problem because it may be inadequate or too technical. This, too, may be easily corrected, but it requires additional time and effort.

Some managers allow from 5 to 10 percent of project time for corrections and modifications. This factor may be significantly reduced if the project is closely monitored and consideration is given to coordination and training throughout the life of the systems cycle.

The data for developing and monitoring a performance standard for the systems group will come from a Systems Analyst Activity Report Form (see Figure 5.12).

Review Questions: Group 5C

1. Some managers argue that it is difficult to quantify the activities of the systems personnel; therefore, no attempt should be made to develop a schedule for the systems function. Do you agree or disagree with the statement? Explain your answer.
2. Of what value are checklists in the development of a new system?

SCHEDULE DEVELOPMENT AND EVALUATION

Development of a Schedule

With the performance standards established, the data processing manager can develop a project or operation schedule. The primary purpose of the schedule is to achieve a desired objective or to produce a number of outputs within a given time-frame that effectively utilize the available resources. Development and availability of a schedule will enable a manager to:

Determine and provide for adequate resource requirements

Establish realistic due-out times for each output

Reduce machine conflicts resulting from the need for processing of two different outputs or reports simultaneously

Determine the due-in time for source documents and data elements

Scheduling is a difficult task, but a most important one. Its complexity varies with the size of the installation and/or project. As the size of a project or installation increases, the number of internal and external influences, and their interaction, increase correspondingly. This forces the data processing manager to customize a schedule for each functional activity. He must apply his knowledge, standards, and records to develop a schedule that will fit his needs and desires. The value of an operationally effective schedule will exceed the cost of preparation.

The construction of a schedule begins with identification and analysis of the tasks to be performed. This information is available from procedural documentation, interviews, or activity specification sheets (see Figure 5.13). It must be

Figure 5.13 *Example of activity specification sheet*

ACTIVITY SPECIFICATION SHEET

PROJECT NO. _____

PROJECT TITLE _____ DATE |__|__|__|__|__|__|
Mo. Day Yr.

EVENT _____

_____

_____

_____

_____

_____

_____

_____

_____

_____

_____

_____

PRECEDING EVENT _____

_____

SUCCEEDING EVENT _____

ESTIMATED TIME
REQUIREMENTS _____ _____
Man-Days Man-Hours

ESTIMATED
COMPLETION DATE |__|__|__|__|__|__|
Mo. Day Yr.

augmented by due-out and due-in times or dates, as well as by actual or estimated processing time for the required activities.

The schedule that is developed must be flexible in order to provide for some manipulation should problems or delays occur. If buffer or idle time is available, then the difficulties are minimized. However, where no slack exists, the data processing manager will have to adjust the planned schedule.

A number of different schedule formats can be designed and developed, in accordance with individual needs and desires. The documentation is necessary because no data processing manager can hope to retain a schedule in his memory and expect to direct and control effectively. The schedule indicates when his equipment and personnel are busy or idle; what they are being used for; and whether or not he has the capacity to assume new functions.

The tasks or activities, their interrelationships, and the time requirements in a schedule may be illustrated in one of the following ways:

1. Operational flowchart
2. Machine-load schedule
3. GANTT chart
4. PERT network

1. OPERATIONAL FLOWCHART. On an operational flowchart, each system or subsystem is broken down into the required clerical and equipment steps and operations. To each step or operation is affixed an estimated or standardized time element. The manager may then total the machine and clerical time requirements in order to determine project needs, as illustrated in Figure 5.14. The time elements are also summarized for each type of hardware device. Subsequently, the totals are consolidated to produce a daily and weekly machine-load schedule.

An operational flowchart can be used very effectively in analyzing and determining the resource requirements in a unit-record operation. For totally computerized operations, this type of flowchart is of limited value, for only the auxiliary or offline operations and clerical operations may be specified. The processing within the central processing unit cannot be readily estimated or standardized. It is possible to calculate the processing time requirements by utilizing the instruction, together with input/output timings found in the hardware and programmer reference manuals. But this is not a very simple task and most time-consuming. If the micro-flowchart is sufficiently detailed, the time requirements for each instruction can be calculated to produce an elapsed processing time. In a multi-programming environment, the manually calculated elapsed time figures may be very inaccurate. Under this type of software arrangement, the elapsed time is affected by such factors as program priority; input/output, channel, and controller delays; the amount of multi-tasking; and operator efficiency. Processing time is also affected by equipment features, software capability, input/output volumes, and data set organization.

2. MACHINE-LOAD SCHEDULE. For scheduling of equipment operations, a machine-load schedule may be prepared. However, an individual schedule for

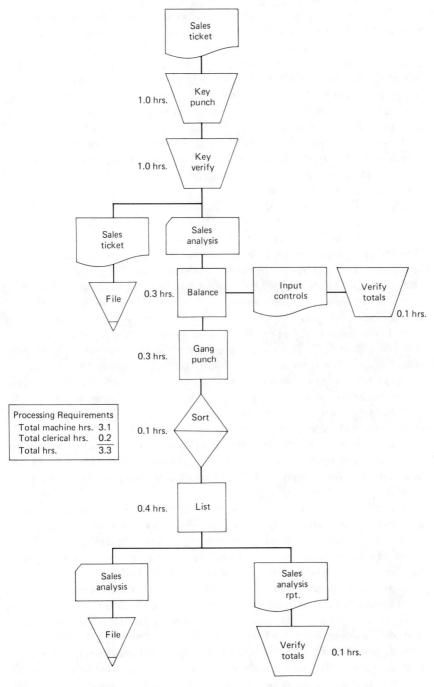

Figure 5.14 Operational flowchart: sales analysis application sample

each category of equipment must be developed. These schedules identify the machine requirements for a given day and can be expanded to cover a week.

In developing a machine-loading schedule, the data processing manager allocates to each machine the required production activities on the basis of priority and of due-in and due-out requirements. As the allocation is made, the data processing manager becomes aware of any machine conflicts, thus enabling himself to reschedule operations with a lower priority. An example of a machine-load worksheet is illustrated in Figure 5.15.

3. GANTT CHARTS. GANTT charts may also be used to graphically illustrate a schedule. Of the types of documentation formats discussed here, the GANTT charts enjoy universal application. They may be easily applied to machine loading and to project scheduling.

Each of the steps or operations is drawn on the graph in its operational sequence for a given time-frame. The chart is arranged in selected time units and each step, operation, project, or application is plotted in a horizontal line showing the start and stop parameters for each. Figure 5.16 illustrates the use of a GANTT chart to identify the production load for an IBM 026 keypunch machine. This chart is established for an eight-hour period and subdivided into ten-minute time elements. Machine 01 has been scheduled for keypunching of payroll clock card data. This will utilize approximately seven hours of machine time. The use of a modified GANTT chart for a sales analysis application is illustrated in Figure 5.17. This chart indicates the required machine operations in their sequence of activity and given time-frame. In this example, the keypunching and verification functions overlap. However, the succeeding operations cannot be overlapped because of their sequential dependence upon each other. The GANTT chart shown in Figure 5.18 illustrates the overlapping of functions in a project to install a computer.

Though the GANTT chart identifies the tasks and their duration, it does not show their interrelationships. Nor does it show the effect of a delay on the overall project. Also, it may be difficult to work with on a large project involving many tasks.

4. PERT NETWORK. The use of a PERT network in scheduling requires the detailing of activities and allocation of time elements for each activity. This technique requires considerable preparation and planning time and its value for development of a machine-load schedule is questionable. However, it is an excellent tool for development and implementation schedules.

Figure 5.19 illustrates the use of a PERT network for the planning of a computer installation project. This may be compared with the GANTT chart illustrated in Figure 5.18. In the PERT network it can be seen that the relationships of the individual work efforts to each other and the overall project are clearly visible. This definition of work efforts and relationships demands more detailed planning than any of the other scheduling formats. It demands consideration of the resource allocations, unnecessary work efforts, conflicts, waste, and deficiencies. This, however, enables the data processing manager to divide the overall problem into manageable portions. Nevertheless, this approach to planning may

MACHINE-LOAD SCHEDULE WORKSHEET

APPLICATION NUMBER	OPERATION	OPER. NO.	MACH. FUNCTION	VOLUME	ESTIMATED PROCESSING TIME	DUE IN		DUE OUT		PRIORITY
						DAY	TIME	DAY	TIME	

Figure 5.15 Machine-load schedule worksheet

Figure 5.16 Sample use of a Gantt chart

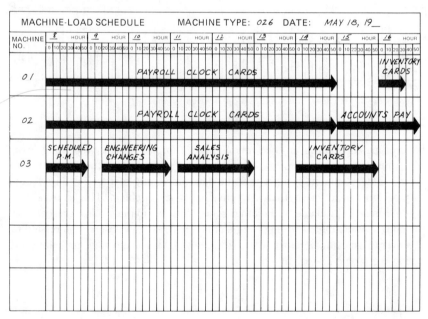

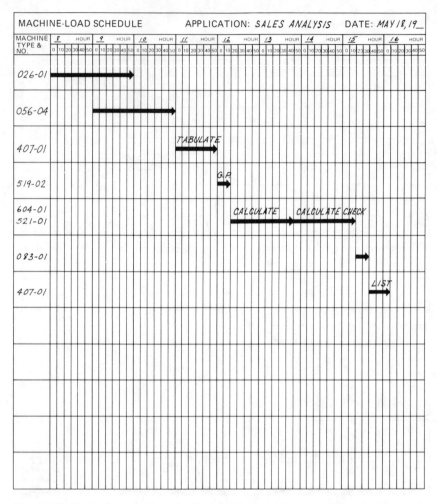

MACHINE-LOAD SCHEDULE   APPLICATION: *SALES ANALYSIS*   DATE: *MAY 18, 19__*

MACHINE TYPE & NO.	*8* HOUR	*9* HOUR	*10* HOUR	*11* HOUR	*12* HOUR	*13* HOUR	*14* HOUR	*15* HOUR	*16* HOUR
026-01									
056-04									
407-01				TABULATE					
519-02					G.P.				
604-01 521-01					CALCULATE		CALCULATE CHECK		
083-01									
407-01								LIST	

Figure 5.17 Gantt chart: sales analysis application sample

be too time-consuming, in that, among other things, the data processing manager must not spend more time on the PERT network than on the project itself.

In the development of a network the data processing manager will undoubtedly become aware of alternative approaches to the problem. This is an advantage not readily available in the other scheduling techniques. Also, the network
provides a quick means of reporting status, changes, and progress as related to
the overall goal. As a result, the PERT network is a useful tool in helping to
define the problem areas in a project.

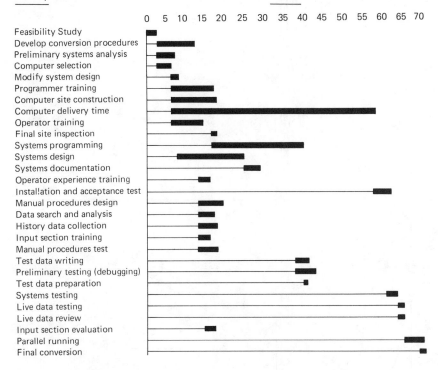

Activity	Weeks

Feasibility Study
Develop conversion procedures
Preliminary systems analysis
Computer selection
Modify system design
Programmer training
Computer site construction
Computer delivery time
Operator training
Final site inspection
Systems programming
Systems design
Systems documentation
Operator experience training
Installation and acceptance test
Manual procedures design
Data search and analysis
History data collection
Input section training
Manual procedures test
Test data writing
Preliminary testing (debugging)
Test data preparation
Systems testing
Live data testing
Live data review
Input section evaluation
Parallel running
Final conversion

Figure 5.18 Gantt chart showing overlapping of functions in computer installation project

Schedule Evaluation

The effectiveness of a manager's schedule is determined by the available feedback. As stated earlier, the need for a feedback reporting mechanism is an integral part of the goal-attainment process. Feedback is particularly important for data processing functions. Once a system is implemented, its activities or the influences affecting it do not remain static—objectives can change; current objectives may not be met; priorities or requirements change; work loads increase. The effects of these changes or conditions must be quickly detected, identified, and analyzed before any appropriate action can be taken.

The feedback available to the manager may take the form of statistical, oral, or written reports. Most of the feedback on the activities within the systems, programming, advanced planning and development, and training groups may be derived from daily or weekly activity reports. However, in evaluating machine loading, the feedback may be more elaborate. It may be generated from such items as a system measurement instrument, system utilization monitor, computer performance analyzer, or computer performance monitors. The actual

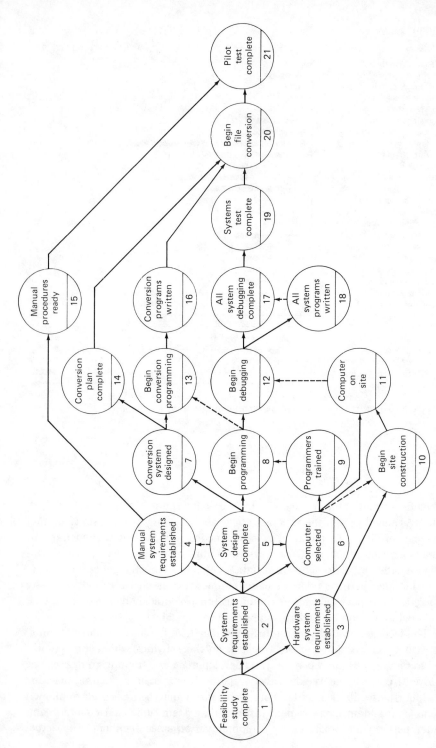

Figure 5.19 PERT network as used in planning computer installation project

names for the devices or packages used in collecting the data may be more exotic. However, their basic function is to monitor or measure personnel and hardware performance and utilization.

The feedback should provide a quick means of reporting status, changes, and progress. A well-designed reporting system can provide a data processing administrator or manager with the following types of information:

Overall hardware utilization

The activities accounting for the utilization

Cost accounting data for chargebacks

Partition utilization statistics in a multi-tasking environment

Program efficiency

Programmer efficiency in testing

Operator efficiency

Rerun statistics

Shift productivity

This type of information may be developed from the data gathered through one of the following methods:

1. Manual recording
2. Automatic recording utilizing an internal clock
3. Hardware performance monitoring
4. System utilization software

1. MANUAL RECORDING. This technique involves the use of a wall clock or punching clock for data collection. When using a wall clock, the operator manually logs the start and stop times for an operation based on his clock reading. When a punching clock is used, the start and stop time recording is made on a prescribed form inserted in the device; this form of recording may provide a reading in hours and minutes or in hours and hundredths of hours. In both methods, the operator must enter the application name or number, together with the estimated or actual input/output volume, on the utilization record. The data on the logs or records must subsequently be translated to produce a machine-sensible record. The machine records are then manipulated and summarized to produce the desired management reports. However, owing to the limited amount of feedback collected from this method, only generalized reports may be prepared. For example, although the feedback provides the elapsed processing time for a report or output, it does not actually indicate the status of the CPU, input/output devices, or other hardware features.

2. AUTOMATED RECORDING UTILIZING AN INTERNAL CLOCK. An internal clock may be a hardware or software feature in the form of subroutine or subprogram. The timer can be reset every 24 hours and may be used to output clock and elapsed time on card, tape, disk, or printer media. This recording technique is more accurate and not dependent upon the operator to record hardware utiliza-

tion. Volumes and job identification data may also be outputted automatically if incorporated into the software. The output may then be manipulated and summarized to prepare a variety of utilization reports and statistics.

3. HARDWARE PERFORMANCE MONITORING. The hardware performance monitors are portable devices used to measure and record computer activity or utilization. Electrical probes are connected to the wiring to detect and record status signals. These signals study the activity of the central processing unit in relation to data channel and input/output component usage. The signal impulses are connected to counters located in the monitor device. These record the duration of an event or activity or the number of times it occurs. For example, in monitoring the CPU, the device may be wired to collect data on the total available time, supervisor time, wait time, and/or busy time. On the other hand, if connected to a disk drive, it may collect data on seek times and seek counts.

The data from the counters is generally recorded on magnetic tape, which is part of the monitor device. Subsequently, tabular reports, summary reports, and graphs may be prepared from the tape in order to indicate system and device utilization. This information may be used by the planning, systems, and software personnel to evaluate the effectiveness of the existing configuration, operating system, program coding, and file structures. It may also be used in the survey and feasibility studies to provide quantitative work load data. The availability of this information will enable the systems analyst to determine if and when the hardware can absorb another report. Also, when conducting a feasibility study for hardware acquisition, the systems analyst will have valuable information about the present configuration available.

There is no interference with the operation of the computer because the monitor is connected only to critical wiring points in the computer circuitry. Also, the device can be connected to the computer within a relatively short period of time.

Though the monitors are capable of determining the time and type of activity during a computer run, they do not specifically check the program. Therefore, they are not capable of indicating undesirable conditions occurring in a program. Also, the purchase price of a monitor is very high. However, some monitors may be leased on a short-term basis.

4. SYSTEM UTILIZATION SOFTWARE. Computer system utilization may also be monitored through the use of specially designed software packages. These are installed as part of the operating system software to collect data about the applications in the job stream. The job control card activates the system utilization software and indicates the category of reporting information to be collected. Information on each job is recorded on a tape or disk drive. Subsequently, the information is extracted from the medium by a report generator program. This will permit the processing of management reports on productivity, testing, reruns, billing, cost control, compilation, and/or assembly.

The software requires a minimum amount of core storage and is less costly than a hardware monitor. It requires no operator intervention because the necessary data gathering is activated through the job control cards preceding each job. The software package is also capable of performing a dynamic trace on an instruction being executed. This feature permits the identification of sections of inefficient coding in a program. The collected data may be subsequently processed to indicate activity and utilization. The output must then be carefully analyzed to identify the problem areas and determine the appropriate corrective action.

There is some degradation of the system because the software monitor must make use of the hardware's input/output and processor time for checking utilization and activity. Also, the software package must be tailored to the computer's operating system. If an organization upgrades its software to a new operating system, investment in a new monitor package may be required. However, some vendors provide a trade-in allowance to minimize the loss of investment.

The choice of monitoring technique is dependent upon the data processing manager's needs and objectives—what does he wish to monitor or measure? Cost also becomes a major consideration. A manager must evaluate the start-up, maintenance, machine, and analysis costs. An organization with a small-scale computer or minicomputer may not have very much need for a hardware or software monitor. However, whatever measurement technique is selected, the manager must evaluate the feedback carefully to maintain an effective operation.

Review Questions: Group 5D

1. Why should a manager develop a schedule for his functional activity?
2. Can simulation be effectively applied to the development of a schedule?
3. Why would someone describe a software monitor as an inefficient way to seek efficiency?
4. How would you defend your decision to acquire a hardware performance monitor for your computer equipment?

SUMMARY

Before a manager can begin to direct and control an activity, he must have a plan and/or schedule to achieve a desired goal. In formulating his plan or schedule, the manager must consider the function's duties and responsibilities, because these have to be converted into events, steps, and operations. Each of them must then be allocated an estimated or standardized time element, each of which may have to be adjusted or modified because of a limited time-frame.

The duties and responsibilities must be converted to performance standards, which become the basis of scheduling and controlling. The performance standards are then available for the detection, identification, and correction of problems resulting from the application of manpower, machine, and material resources.

PERFORMANCE STANDARDS

Keypunching

    Keystroke Requirement Formula:

    Total Keystrokes Required = No. of Cards × Average No. of Columns
                                             per Card

Performance Standards

Type of Keypunching	Potential Hourly Key Stroke Rate
Numeric	10,000
Numeric with Some Alphabetic	8,000
Mixed Alphabetic and Numeric	5,000
Alphabetic	4,000

Key Verification

    Standards and formula same as for key verification. However, a factor of 3 percent must be added to allow for stoppages due to error detection.

Sorting

    083 Sorter Speed: 1,000 c.p.m.

        Sorting Time Requirement Formula:

$$\text{Sorting Time} = \frac{\text{No. of Cards} \times \text{No. of Card Columns}}{\text{Sorter Speed}}$$

Graphically, the time elements may be illustrated on a GANTT chart, operational flowchart, or a PERT network. For illustrating machine loads, the GANTT charts are adequate. However, for indicating interrelationships and overlapping activities, a GANTT chart or a PERT network is more satisfactory. The GANTT chart and the PERT network are also more suitable for scheduling the activities of the systems, software, training, and planning groups.

When a schedule is implemented, the manager must collect data on the progress or status and compare the feedback with the planned performances. The inclusion of the feedback concept provides the manager with a very important tool for detecting and solving problems—one that enables him to evaluate both personnel and equipment performance. Moreover, it enables him to evaluate the procedures, training, manning requirements, and work load. And it also gives him the opportunity to determine if additional responsibilities or more complex tasks can be assigned to personnel who are performing above-standard. Also, with the schedule and utilization records or activity reports on hand, the manager will be capable of developing a budget control approach, as well as a basis for personnel appraisal and evaluation.

As a result of the many interacting elements in the productive process, the manager may experience some difficulty in establishing a schedule. However, without a schedule he will find it very difficult to optimize the utilization of his manpower, material, machine, and money resources. Through the use of a schedule, the manager may be able to apply 20–20 hindsight as foresight—based on standards and utilization experience.

CASE STUDY 5.1

Ruth's Creations

The systems personnel are in the process of parallel testing a new inventory-control application. As the manager of the operations group, you are concerned with the effect of this application on your activity. You are particularly concerned about the key punching, verifying, and sorting effort. There will be approximately 1,000 transaction cards to be keypunched and verified at the end of each day. These are punched according to the information given in the accompanying transaction card format. The cards are to be sorted on the stock number before they are written on tape for subsequent processing. See performance standards on page 206.

TRANSACTION CARD FORMAT

Field Description	Cards Columns	Type of Information *
Accounting Class Code	1–4	A/N
Stock Number	5–19	N
Description	20–28	A/N
Status Code	29–30	A/N
Unit of Issue	31–32	A/N
Transaction Code	33	N
Procurement Type	34	A
Quantity	35–40	N

* A/N = alphameric
  A = alphabetic
  N = numeric

Discussion Questions

1. Given the accompanying information on performance standards, how much time will be required for keypunching?
2. How much time will be required for the verification effort?
3. How much time will be required for the sorting effort?
4. Two of the keypunching machines are not fully loaded. One of the machines is available for four hours and the second for two hours. Can this be of any benefit to you?
5. Develop an argument to justify a different approach to sorting.
6. What graphic method would you use to illustrate the schedule? Explain your answer.
7. What type of monitoring technique would be most effective in this situation? Explain why.

CHAPTER 6

The Budget Process

INTRODUCTION / The budget is an essential element of financial control for the data processing manager. The budget for a project or a functional activity is an outgrowth of the manager's short-term and long-term plan(s). Its purpose is to quantify the human resource, software, hardware, supplies, contractual services, maintenance, and physical plant needs in a given plan or group of plans. Though a budget is generated from the needs of a plan, frequently the merit of a project or a course of action is affected by the size of the budget and not the overall feasibility of a plan. This form of rationalization is contrary to sound management practice.

The estimated and/or actual expenditures to support the productive and developmental activities of the data processing function are presented in a budget. Therefore, all "needs" must be costed realistically and "padding" eliminated. Overstatements of costs may occur in anticipation of cutbacks resulting from an expected negotiation process with users or other managers, or an attempt on the part of the data processing manager and/or his subordinates to complete a project or an activity within a project under the budgeted estimate. Upper echelon and/or steering committee involvement in the activities of the data processing function will quickly identify any unscrupulous budgeting practices.

Included in the budget may be a category for recording income generated from the sale of hardware time, consulting, programming and/or other services. This segment of the budget may be very difficult to estimate due to the uncertainty of such sales and fluctuations in demand.

For purpose of discussion, we will address ourselves to the cost of a project and the cost of the data processing department as separate entities. Some overlapping may occur due to similarities in the costing process, but there are some unique problems related to each situation.

DATA PROCESSING COSTS

The costs included in the budget may be categorized into the following major areas: human resources, hardware and software, supplies, physical plant, and services. The human resource costs are primarily based on employee salaries and fringe benefits for such items as Social Security payments, contributions to retirement programs, paid vacations and holidays, professional society dues, and insurance programs. Training costs for users, managerial personnel, and data processing personnel may also be charged to this category. In some organizations, the costs of retraining, severance pay, and labor negotiations, resulting from the displacement of non-data processing employees due to the installation of data processing hardware and/or systems may be charged to this segment of the budget. The hardware and software costs will include such items as rental, leasing, purchase price (if on cash basis) or the amortized portion of the purchase price (if on an accrual basis); maintenance; purchase of spare parts; transportation costs; taxes; and the cost of documentation. Frequently, costs incurred as a result of attendance for training and orientation on new hardware and/or software at a vendor's site will be included in this budget category. The category may also include the costs related to supporting equipment such as binders, bursters, decollators, and testing equipment. The budget for supplies will include such items as disk packs, diskettes, microforms, magnetic tape, paper tape, continuous printing forms, optical scanning forms, card forms, programming sheets, and adhesive-backed products for preparation of charts and/or documentation. Physical plant costs include such items as power lines, wall and floor outlets, air conditioning and humidification, raised flooring, glass walls, floor space allocation charges, space rental or leasing charges, utilities, and draperies. Custodial and security services may be included in this budget category but, in other organizations, these costs are included in the services category. The services category will include expenditures for such items as attorney fees, facilities management contracts; artists, typing, and reproduction service fees; employment agency fees; time-sharing services; books, periodicals, and advisory services; communications, systems and programming consultants; data transcription and verification services; and messengers. The category may also include charges for architect's fees, engineering and inspection fees for site evaluation, and custodial and security services. The two latter items may also be included in the physical plant category in some organizations.

The proper categorization of costs must be done by the data processing manager to ensure that the costs will be applied uniformly for each given project and/or activity. The manager may require the assistance of an accountant to facilitate the initial classification of costs.

The costs that are incurred prior to the implementation of a system or application or the installation of hardware or software are referred to as one-time, conversion, start-up, initialization, or preinstallation costs. Costs that represent an expenditure of funds to maintain utility and operation of a system, application, hardware, or software are referred to as continuing or recurring costs.

PROJECT CONTROL

Project Costs

As cited earlier, the manager must use the budget for control purposes. On a project basis, the manager must make an effort to minimize and/or eliminate the possibility of a cost overrun. For example, a new student registration system has been budgeted for $250,000, but the project is only 75 percent complete and the current expenditures are exceeding the total estimated cost. The overrun may be the result of using faulty personnel costs and/or invalid time estimates for the various tasks in the project.

Most managers fail to recognize that the personnel are productive only 75 percent to 80 percent of the time, not 100 percent. The loss in productivity is due to such nonproductive factors as vacation time; holidays; illness; staff meetings; training sessions for data processing personnel; travel and attendance at professional society and/or vendor seminars; administrative tasks and other assigned responsibilities. It is possible that an average of 520 hours per year or as much as 10 hours per week may be applied to nonproductive effort for each employee. Based on an annual work schedule of 2,080 hours (40 hours per week x 52 weeks) the actual number of hours may be only 1,560 hours (2,080–520). The manager must evaluate his own organizational setting to determine the actual or average number of hours that must be allocated to nonproductive effort. The manager who uses calendar time instead of the available productive hours will actually be using an unrealistic time value that could cause project-time overrun.

The project overrun problem is further complicated by managers who do not realistically reflect personnel costs. Some managers divide the annual salary figure of 2,080 hours (40 hours per week x 52 weeks), to calculate an hourly cost rate. Unfortunately, that calculated rate does not include the overhead cost for such items as fringe benefits, payroll taxes, employment agency fees, training, etc. The overhead costs must be added to the annual salary figure to help calculate the "true" average hourly cost rate for each data processor involved in a given project. The calculated figure must be reviewed periodically and revised to reflect increases or decreases in costs and salaries.

Project Budget

The project budget is prepared when the data processing manager and/or his subordinate is given approval to initiate the project.

In most organizations, any preliminary costs associated with the project are not charged to the project but to an overhead account in the systems function. The project costs are allocated by the activity items, such as systems analysis, program testing, and so forth. Each activity must reflect the adjusted personnel cost (salary plus overhead) for the item. Also, a small percentage of the total budget must be set aside as a contingency fund for possible emergencies dealing with unforeseen circumstances that arise during the life of the project. The project budget must also include funds for project administration. Project administration will include such items as secretarial services, artists for any special graphics, communications services, or outside printing.

A form that may be used for budget preparation and control purposes is illustrated in Figure 6.1. Initially, the form may be used to prepare budget estimates

Figure 6.1 Example of budget control form

Item	Category (Direct, Indirect)	Start M/D/Y	Complete to date				Notes
			M/D/Y	Actual cost	Est. cost to compl.	%	
TOTALS							

BUDGET AND CONTROL FORM   Review Date ___ / ___ / ___

Project Number _____   Authorization Date ___ / ___ / ___

Project Name _____

_____

Projected Completion Date ___ / ___ / ___

Actual Completion Date ___ / ___ / ___

Project Leader _____

User(s) _____

Type of Project _____

and targeted completion dates for each activity in the project. The initial time and cost estimates may be subject to change following review by the data processing manager, executive committee and/or steering committee.

Once the budget is approved and it becomes operational, the manager uses the budget form to post feedback data and monitor actual expenditures, completion percentages, and the anticipated completion dates. The manager must carefully monitor the budget to prevent potential time and/or cost overrun. Problems may arise from poor performance in a given activity, poor estimates of costs, and/or invalid time estimates for the various required tasks. The manager must also be cautious of dealing with inaccurate feedback on actual progress. Some subordinates may accidentally or deliberately overstate their performances and this may subsequently result in a project time and/or cost overrun. There is also the danger that an inaccurate picture may result from clerical errors in reporting and/or posting. For example $2,500 has been allocated for forms design, but only $200 has been recorded as expended and the activity is reportedly 98 percent complete. There may be an error in the expenditures and/or completion figures, or the initial budget estimate was grossly overstated. In any event, the situation requires immediate investigation by the manager and a correction or adjustment should be made, if necessary.

Project Feedback

The manager must periodically (daily, weekly, or monthly) evaluate the project's budget and time schedule to identify:

Activities that are past scheduled completion date.

Activities for which there has been no significant progress during the evaluation period.

Activities that are in danger of falling behind schedule.

Activity costs that are in danger of exceeding the budgeted estimate.

Activities that have exceeded budget and are not yet completed.

The evaluation enables the manager to determine which activities require his attention and those progressing as planned. For those activities requiring immediate attention, the manager must determine if additional personnel and/or specialized personnel are needed to put the project back on schedule or to eliminate any potential problems. Also, the manager may find it necessary to allocate part of the contingency fund to one of the activities or reallocate some of the funds allocated to other items that are no longer needed.

The manager must also determine if this project is interacting properly with other projects scheduled by the organization. The manager must eliminate and/or minimize any potential conflicts that may arise from contention for available resources due to potential or actual overruns.

Review Questions: Group 6A

1. What is the purpose of a budget in a data processing organization? *monitoring & control financially activities*
2. A project manager has calculated that a particular programming project will require five weeks of effort. The manager then proceeded to "block-in" five weeks on the calendar. Was this action correct or incorrect? Why or why not?
3. Why must a manager gather feedback on the progress of a project?

DEPARTMENTAL CONTROL

Departmental Costs

One of the major difficulties encountered by the data processing manager is the proper identification and allocation of costs. The costs are the expenditures supporting the department's developmental and production facilities. For control purposes, the costs must be allocated to the appropriate expense items in cost centers established within the departmental framework. The manager will find it very convenient to establish the functional activities, such as systems, programming, operations, etc., as individual or multiple cost centers. The operations function may be subdefined into three cost centers: data control, data entry, and computer operations. The latter may be further subdefined into additional cost centers, if the computer is operated in a multi-tasking environment, with one for each partition. The allocated costs are used to calculate an hourly project or production cost for each cost center.

The costs are allocated as direct or indirect. Direct costs are those that are clearly attributable to a particular account, whereas indirect costs are not. The salaries of systems, programming, data entry, and other data processing personnel involved in the development of a specific project and/or production of a given application are direct costs. (Salaries will be the largest direct cost in a project or department.) However, such items as holiday pay, sick leave pay, vacations, and other fringe benefits are classified as indirect costs. Also included as direct costs may be such items as subcontractors (systems, programming, and temporary help, and others performing specific work on a project); travel and lodging; machine rentals or usage charges; and supplies. The indirect costs will include such items as administrative costs; payroll taxes; utility, communications, and space charges; insurance; interest charges; asset depreciation; and so forth. The manager should solicit the aid of the accounting department to determine proper allocations and specific charges or percentages attributable for a cost category. The latter situation is particularly applicable for direct costs, e.g., rate of depreciation for supporting equipment.

Departmental Budgeting

The budget for the department is a composite of repetitive operating costs for current systems and applications and developmental costs for prospective systems and/or programs. Some managers simply add a percentage factor of 6 percent to 25 percent to the continuing costs for the current budget to allow for increased costs and growth in each category. The danger in this rationalization is that the manager may get badly "stung" if the wrong percentage figure is chosen. Monies allocated for developmental purposes may have to be applied to the production cost categories, due to poor estimating. There is also the danger that the manager may not have a "good handle" on anticipated developmental costs. The manager with intermediate and long-range plans for the organization will have a much better grasp of the projects to be undertaken during the coming fiscal year. Also, the manager must have a good estimate of the number of anticipated preliminary investigations and probable maintenance requirements for currently operational systems and programs. Some of the systems/program changes will result from external requirements, such as changes to the Social Security tax rate. Information on other changes may be less known and the manager will have to make an estimate based on his intermediate and long-range plans and the personnel utilization data from the previous year.

In preparing the initial budget, the manager must identify the cost centers to be used within the department. The manager must then determine the administrative costs for each department and proportionately apply this overhead to each of the cost centers. In many organizations, preliminary investigations for systems and/or programming effort are considered as overhead and would be applied as such to the systems and programming cost centers. The manager is now in a position to deal with the individual cost centers. Initially, the manager must identify the salary costs for the center's manager(s), secretarial and data processing personnel, and the indirect costs for fringe benefits and related salary items. The direct and indirect costs may be shown as individual line items or totaled as Salaries and Fringe Benefits. The manager must also provide for possible salary increases resulting from labor negotiations, merit reviews, cost-of-living increases, and/or bonuses that may be applicable within the budget year.

The costs include those for training of data processing personnel; supplies; consulting; subcontractors; travel and lodging; space; communications; utilities; insurance; professional society memberships; subscriptions to magazines and newspapers; advisory services; employment agency fees; recruitment, selection and testing of personnel; documentation; depreciation on furniture and supporting equipment; legal, architect, and/or engineering fees; messenger and/or other distribution charges; construction and/or reconstruction charges; use of time-sharing and/or service bureaus; software and/or hardware maintenance; relocation expenses; and so forth. In some organizations, costs related to hardware and software, such as utilities, maintenance, and so forth, may be allocated to prime-shift and off-shift categories.

Having listed the costs, the manager must determine the available hours of productivity, expected utilization percentage and the expected production hours for each cost center. The budgeted cost data is divided by the expected production hours to calculate the hourly cost rate for each center.

To illustrate the point, consider a programming function as one of the cost centers within the data processing department. The function is manned by a manager with an annual salary of $20,000, a secretary with an annual salary of $10,000, and seven applications programmers with annual salaries of $14,400 each. The fringe benefits and other related salary items are identified as 34 percent of base salary. The work week for all personnel is 40 hours.

For the operations and related cost centers, the manager must evaluate the estimated percentage of increase or decrease for each system/application. Data for performing an evaluation of growth patterns must come from the equipment utilization statistics maintained by the operations manager. Supplies utilization data may also be helpful in performing in a growth analysis. The available information must be supplemented by the data processing manager's own intermediate and long-range plans. The analysis will determine the department's resource needs and the ability of the existing resources to cope with the possible changes.

COST CENTER—PROGRAMMING

Cost Item	Cost
Allocated for Data Processing Administration	$ 7,500
Manager of Programming	20,000
Secretary	10,000
Programmers (7)	100,800
Fringe Benefits and Related Costs	44,472
Supplies	2,000
Training	5,000
Travel and Lodging	2,500
Consulting and Subcontractor Fees	4,400
Professional Memberships	300
Subscriptions and Advisory Services	665
Employment Agency Fees	1,800
Rent	7,200
Utilities	600
Hardware Depreciation	163
Furniture Depreciation	1,640
Total Cost	$209,040
Available Production Hours	14,560
Expected Utilization Percentage	75
Expected Available Production Hours	10,920
Hourly Cost Rate for the Center	$ 19.14

The manager must also project the resource requirements for developmental and conversion work for new systems and/or programs. If the in-house resources are not available or are inadequate, the manager may then find it necessary to provide monies in the budget that will enable the organization to have the necessary work performed by a subcontractor and/or service bureau.

Having developed a realistic budget the manager will have a tool that will enable him to:

Reduce or eliminate pockets of inefficiency that affect profitability.

Reduce and/or control the costs of data processing.

Provide for more realistic cost estimates and billing charges.

BILLING METHODS

Methods

Billing methods may represent a realistic approach to controlling the efficient use of data processing services, or they may be a reaction to the mounting costs of data processing. (Data processing costs are reportedly increasing at an annual rate of 25%.) The decision to charge for data processing services must be made on a positive note. The method selected must help to control costs and provide for an optimal rate of return on investment (ROI).

The three approaches most commonly used are: no billing, full billing, and partial billing. In some organizations, the term billing may be replaced by chargeout or chargeback. Statistically it is very difficult to determine which of the three methods is most frequently used by the data processing organizations.

NO BILLING

Under a "no billing" approach, the data processing services are provided to users at no cost. The executive committee considers data processing to be a necessary overhead item for the entire organization. The primary advantage to this method is that it enables the data processing department to service a user whose application initially provides only a marginal rate of return on investment. But on a long-term basis the economies are very evident and these will substantially affect the profitability of the overall organization. There are, however, some significant disadvantages to this billing method. Other departments are most willing to have data processing absorb some of their work because it reduces their own departmental operating budgets and the applications have little or no cost-benefit justification. There may also be a tendency on the part of the data processing manager to accept nonessential jobs in order to develop a departmental workload. Data processing managers are often willing to assume these jobs in order to demonstrate their own department's capabilities. This form of "artificial loading" may backfire for a manager, especially when the demand for data processing services increases sharply. The manager may find himself in a position of "keeping out" a critical or essential job that may affect an organization's profit picture because the hardware is fully loaded or resources are not available. Attempts to "bump" nonessential users out of the service queue are generally unsuccessful or not achieved without a great deal of screaming by the users.

An organization that elects to use the no billing approach must carefully monitor the kinds of systems/applications that are to be automated. Proper use of feasibility studies (see chapter 8) and involvement by the executive committee and/or steering committee (see chapter 2) will help to ensure that only beneficial systems/applications are automated.

FULL BILLING

This form of billing arrangement means that the data processing department is operated as a cost center and it is the intention of the executive committee to break even or show a profit on the operation. The data processing department is reimbursed for services performed for user departments. To properly effect this form of billing, the manager must have a realistic hourly rate structure for estimating and billing purposes. Also, the manager must closely monitor his budget to adjust the rates whenever necessary to reflect increased costs and/or utilization.

One of the major difficulties with this approach are the wide fluctuations in the hourly billing rates. If the machine loading is light, then the rates for computer services will be high. If the machine loading is heavy, then the rates for services will be somewhat lower. Another problem is with maintaining adequate resources to meet the fluctuating service levels demanded by the users. An organization may be forced to maintain nominal resource levels and subcontract for additional resources to meet increased user demands. Subcontracting may present some communications and control problems for the data processing manager, but this may be the best alternative. It may be difficult and costly to acquire additional staff and/or hardware to meet the increased demand on short notice.

In some organizations, the problem is complicated by policies that permit users to solicit bids for services from external organizations. Such practices place the in-house data processing department in a competitive position and it ultimately may not be able to survive the competition.

If an organization elects to use the full billing approach, then it must be willing to use a stable hourly rate for all developmental and productive billings. This may be unacceptable for the data processing manager, but most necessary to minimize the impact of billing on an annual basis. It may be possible to charge a lower average rate based on overall use of services rather than a singular use.

PARTIAL BILLING

Under this approach the users are billed for services based on a predetermined utilization formula. The formula may consider such factors as job priority, hardware utilization, number of transactions processed, turnaround time requirements, response time requirements and so forth. The formulation is designed to have the larger and more demanding users pay for a greater portion of the data processing development and production costs based on their needs. The smaller user with fewer demands on the data processing organization will pay proportionately less for the services requested and received.

The effectiveness of this billing approach is based on reliable utilization statistics. For production billings, an organization must use a hardware monitor or the utilization statistics available from some of the operating system software. The statistics gained from these tools may also be used effectively for scheduling purposes, evaluation of efficiency levels, and in determining the actual machine loading when decisions regarding hardware/software upgrading, downgrading, or elimination are made.

The partial billing approach receives greater acceptance from users because they are not forced to cope with fluctuating rates, and/or the billing rates are more reasonable. The executive committee may also find that this approach may help to stem the mounting costs and provide better justification for service demands by users.

Review Questions: Group 6B

1. What is the purpose of a cost center?
2. What effect does the "future" have on a departmental budget? Be brief in your response.
3. Select one of the billing methods and briefly discuss its advantages and disadvantages.

SUMMARY

Budgets are a means of monitoring and financially controlling the activities of the data processing department. The budget must be regarded as a dynamic tool in the management process and not a static one. The manager cannot prepare the annual budget to satisfy the executive committee and then set the document aside until the next year.

The use of a dynamic budget requires an effective cost accounting system that will identify the utilization of all resources (hardware, software, human, materials, time, and money). In this manner, it will provide the data processing manager with a tool that will enable him to make the data processing department a more efficient function, avoid the political problems that are inherent in attempting to keep all users happy, and to help justify to the executive committee the need for any additional resources.

Though many organizations establish budgets for projects, they ignore the actual data because it is felt that the "bucks" are moved internally only on paper and the overruns don't really mean anything. Also, many data processing managers subscribe to the fatalistic theory that budget overruns, particularly on projects, are inevitable and that no amount of preplanning will avert or correct the situation. Another favorite ploy has been to tell users that they cannot be serviced due to a lack of funds and/or resources. The users will "scream" to the executive committee and they in turn will provide data processing with additional resources. All of these techniques have been used and are used by data processing managers. Unfortunately, the rationalization only tends to hurt rather than help the data processing manager.

CASE STUDY 6.1

The Raleric Toy Company

The data processing manager for the Raleric Toy Company has prepared a budget for a new Customer Billing and Information System that is to be implemented within three months from the start date. The printed budget for the project is as follows:

Item	Cost	
Preliminary		
Preliminary Analysis	$ 5,000.	
Proposal Preparation	2,500.	
Total Preliminary		$ 7,500.
Detailed		
Systems Analysis Tasks	$10,000.	
Systems Design Tasks	17,000.	
Programming Tasks	10,000.	
Documentation Tasks	2,000.	
Implementation Tasks	5,000.	
Total Detailed		$44,000.
Post-Implementation		
Follow-up	$ 1,500.	
Total Post-Implementation		$ 1,500.
Total Project Costs		$53,000.

Discussion Questions

1. What is the amount budgeted for project administration?
2. Given that the work week is 36.5 hours and that a senior systems analyst will be used at half-time on the project, what is the hourly cost for the senior systems analyst?
3. Given that the project will require the use of a senior systems analyst (half-time) and a systems analyst (full-time), what are the number of hours of systems effort required on the project?
4. In terms of time control, can the manager or the reader of the budget effectively identify the completion dates for each activity or tasks required?
5. Can this budget be improved on? If yes, how specifically? If no, why not?

CHAPTER 7

The Design and

Layout of

Data Processing Facilities

INTRODUCTION / One of the most important aspects of a data processing operation is the orderly integration of the manpower, equipment, materials, and supporting services to maximize productive capability and output. The effective interaction of these resources is affected by the availability of a favorable working environment—one that will satisfy the functional needs of the personnel and help maintain a high morale level. Optimizing this relationship is not a simple task, because the layout is influenced by the functional activities served by data processing, as well as by factors not under the direct control of either the manager or the organization—factors such as local building codes and geographical location.

The data processing manager becomes involved in the design and development of a facilities layout whenever:

A new data processing function is established

Converting to a new equipment configuration

Expansion occurs resulting from the addition of personnel and/or equipment

The primary external supporting service or input facility is relocated

Data communications, data collection, teleprocessing, or time-sharing systems are considered and/or installed

Flexibility for expansion had not been included in the original design

Environmental security must be established or improved

Corporate acquisitions are made

Organizational consolidations are planned and/or made

An intensive management information system is being investigated and/or planned

THE OBJECTIVES OF LAYOUT PLANNING

The primary goals in planning a data processing installation layout are to provide for optimal utilization of resources within minimal space requirements at the lowest possible cost. These generalized aims must include the following specific objectives:

1. Efficient utilization of space
2. Minimization of materials handling
3. Elimination or minimization of health hazards
4. Maintenance of high employee morale
5. Efficient utilization of manpower
6. Provision for flexibility needed for changes or expansion
7. Provision for the movement and quality of air
8. Provision for proper color schemes
9. Provision for proper illumination
10. Provision for a safe working environment

Utilization of Space

A good layout represents a fixed expense, so that every effort must be made to maximize the rate of return for each square foot of space being paid for. Due to the emphasis on cost, organizations frequently load an area without considering the actual space requirements for equipment, maintenance, safety, and personnel. This type of attitude can be a major factor in personnel problems and high employee turnover.

The specified space needs for hardware must be secured from the vendor. These specifications indicate precisely the amount of space needed for each unit—in terms of height, length, width, and maintenance areas. Figure 7.1 is an extract from planning specifications furnished by a vendor.

Consideration must also be given to space for worktables, workbenches, desks, chairs, file and parts cabinets, storage cabinets, temperature and humidity control units, and other supporting equipment. The needs will vary according to the hardware configuration and the objectives of the functional activity.

The width of the aisles must be adequate to permit the flow of materials, machines, and manpower without danger of injury or damage. It is desirable that five-foot and four-foot widths be maintained for traffic and work aisles respectively. Minimum acceptable tolerances for each type is four and three feet.

Very often, organizations fail to provide adequate space between units. This causes traffic and clearance problems, or else interference with operation of other units when preventative or emergency maintenance is being performed. In planning his facility, the manager of the data processing operations function must also provide space for operator mobility at and between the machines. These space requirements may or may not be included as part of vendor-supplied specifications included in Figure 7.1. The manager must allow at least

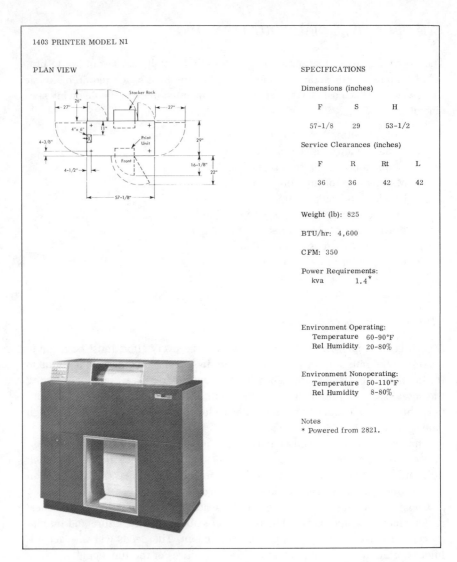

PLAN VIEW

SPECIFICATIONS

Dimensions (inches)

F	S	H
57-1/8	29	53-1/2

Service Clearances (inches)

F	R	Rt	L
36	36	42	42

Weight (lb): 825

BTU/hr: 4,600

CFM: 350

Power Requirements:
kva   1.4[*]

Environment Operating:
Temperature   60-90°F
Rel Humidity   20-80%

Environment Nonoperating:
Temperature   50-110°F
Rel Humidity   8-80%

Notes
* Powered from 2821.

Figure 7.1 Sample extract of planning specification. Courtesy IBM Corporation

three feet behind the printer for the forms rack and forms changes. Depending on the type and size of equipment, four to five feet must be allowed between machines; this figure will also vary due to cabling and maintenance requirements.

In the keypunching, verifying, and data recording areas, at least three feet should be left clear between units to allow for operator movement.

Minimizing Materials Handling

The flow of materials can consume a large percentage of available production time if not properly controlled. Every effort must be made to provide for a smooth flow of materials from input to output. This may be somewhat difficult because it is not always possible to provide an ideal productive balance. However, an imbalance may be minimized by positioning supporting equipment, such as control panel racks, near their respective machines: magnetic disk packs, cartridges, cassettes, and tapes should be near the drives in the computing area; printer output forms should be near printers, and storage racks for punched card stock should be near the key punch machines and punching devices.

Avoiding Health Hazards

The manager must eliminate or minimize all existing and potential health hazards to be in compliance with the Occupational Safety and Health Act (OSHA). Failure to deal effectively with such dangers can result in high absenteeism, payment of fines levied by the Employee Safety and Health Administration, liability suits, and even loss of life—problems that could be very costly and disruptive to the productive process.

One of the more significant health hazards is noise. Noise is an interference or an undesirable sound resulting from human speech, equipment operations, echoes, and vibration, or from any combination thereof. Prolonged exposure to high auditory levels becomes annoying to employees. What is more, it can reduce their productivity and may also result in injury to their hearing. The level of noise is measured in terms of decibels. It used to be reported by experts that exposure to a level of 100 decibels for a prolonged period of time would reduce productivity and be harmful to employees. However, studies conducted by Corliss and Berendt at the National Bureau of Standards have indicated that the exposure level for a full working day should not exceed 85 decibels.

To minimize environmental noise hazards, organizations are now using such sound-absorbing materials as acoustical tile, draperies, carpeting, partitions, and acoustical enclosures.

Acoustical tile on hard walls, ceilings, and floors help to reduce interference caused by the operating equipment, transmission of noise to other areas, vibration, and echoes. The sound-absorbing effectiveness of acoustical tile decreases somewhat as the size of the room increases. But room size can be partially offset by installing a dropped ceiling, as well as acoustical tile.

Drapery materials are used for sound absorption in a number of facilities. However, they are reported to be costly and only partially effective. There is also concern about the potential danger from the static electricity levels of fibers used in drapery materials, for the antistatic sprays applied to such fabrics have been only temporarily effective.

Carpeting is also used in many installations. However, careful consideration must be given to selecting a yarn or fiber that will maintain a static electricity level below 2,000 static volts, which is the maximum allowable level for the operation of most computer equipment. (The human threshold level is somewhat higher, ranging from 2,500 to 3,500 volts.) Static electricity affects magnetic recordings and may cause random or intermittant errors in the equipment. The effect on humans is primarily one of petty annoyance, however, because it could be the cause of an accident that would affect the group's productivity. It is important to note that the static voltage levels in fibers, fabrics, and yarns may increase because of improper humidification of the work area.

Often it is possible to isolate or reduce the noise level by setting up a partial wall between the source of the noise and the employees. Or, it may be necessary to totally enclose the source of the interference and install sound-absorbent materials on the inner walls and ceiling; this is more practical than partial walling because it significantly reduces the reverberations.

In open office areas, it is advisable to use acoustical covers on the equipment. Such covers can reduce operating noise levels by as much as 50 percent. Also, some of the covers are useful in reducing the operating temperature of the equipment.

Another health hazard in many installations is dust. It may be introduced into the environment through windows, doors, machine operation, materials handling, and the air-conditioning system. For all practical purposes, windows should be opened only in cases of extreme emergency. However, it is best to make alternative arrangements so that the windows can be kept shut, even in an emergency.

Doors in an installation must be properly sealed so as to limit the amount of dust entering the work area. Well-sealed doors also help reduce the transmission of noise to other areas.

For security or other reasons, some installations do not allow their housekeeping maintenance staff in the equipment area. Consequently, the areas go uncleaned unless a manager or some of the personnel clean superficially with a dry mop or broom. Nevertheless, it is essential that routine maintenance be performed regularly in order to remove the loose dirt or dust particles.

Improperly installed air-conditioning units can also be responsible for introducing dust, foreign materials, and even corrosive elements into the working environment from either inside or outside the building. Therefore, caution must be exercised by the planners to eliminate the possibility of dust and other contaminants entering through the fresh-air intakes. Without regular inspections and systematic filter changes in the air-conditioned and data processing units, operations can be stopped and personnel and input/output media affected by faulty air-conditioning.

Maintaining High Employee Morale

A favorable work environment can do much to maintain employee morale—an important determinant in high quantitative and qualitative productivity. The manager must provide an adequate work area for each individual, avoiding the establishment of isolation pockets and heavy traffic aisles, which can disrupt the productive process. Visitor chairs should be furnished at those desks where frequent callers stop. Desks and work stations should be positioned so as to avoid having employees working in their own shadows. There should also be an adequate number of telephones and a limit on the number of people sharing one extension line. This is particularly important where incoming and/or outgoing telephone traffic is heavy.

Conference rooms, where provided, should be planned so as to allow about thirty square feet of floor space per person for groups of ten or less. For larger groups, approximately twenty square feet per person should be allocated. Coat storage must also be provided for employees. One six-foot-long coat closet meets the needs of about twenty-four people, though it would be more desirable to provide individual lockers for everyone.

Efficient Utilization of Manpower

The manager must design the layout for the most efficient utilization of manpower. By positioning the equipment to avoid and/or remove bottlenecks and by minimizing materials handling, the manager can reduce setup and handling time, as well as personnel idleness—both forced and voluntary.

Despite the fact that a manager has followed the recommended planning practices, he may find it necessary to make some adjustments. To minimize the need for such changes, a manager should solicit the views of his subordinates after he has prepared a preliminary layout design.

In one computer installation observed by this author, the front of the printer was positioned toward the wall. This was done to prevent visitors from viewing any sensitive output on the device. However, this placement also interfered with the operator's normal view of the printer. Consequently, he was forced to make numerous visual checks on the printer to ensure that it was functioning correctly. Obviously, this approach fails to consider the proper utilization of the manpower resource. It can also encourage operator dependence upon the console lights for printer problem indication.

Another consideration in optimizing manpower utilization is to place the group leader's or manager's office in a centralized location conveniently accessible to the subordinates. This eliminates the necessity to walk distances whenever a question or problem arises.

Flexibility for Changes or Expansion

A planner must have 20–20 hindsight disguised as foresight when designing the layout. The arrangement must be flexible enough to allow for some future modification or expansion without a a major redesign. Providing for the future is just as important as taking care of current needs. The problem is to determine the proper balance. Determining flexibility needs may be projected on the basis of the future objectives of the organization. The manager should consult the organization's long-range plan for data processing to determine what the future growth requirements may be.

The Movement and Quality of Air

The movement and quality of air in an environment is another important consideration. The air already present must be recirculated and fresh air must be introduced. The freshness of the air affects the heat load, relative humidity, filtration, and capacity of the atmosphere inside the building. Therefore, there must be a proper balance between fresh and recirculated air, which in turn, means that the inflow of fresh air must be carefully regulated. The existing air supply should be kept moving to eliminate or reduce stagnancy and odors. It should be filtered to remove dust particles, which affect personnel, equipment, and materials. The quantity and quality of air are best controlled through an air-conditioning system. This process regulates temperature and humidity levels within predefined ranges under a variety of external climatic conditions.

The temperature is measured in terms of degrees Fahrenheit. When the temperature level exceeds 90°, it will induce fatigue in the personnel and utlimately reduce their productivity. Higher temperatures may also adversely alter the materials used in the productive process. For example, some types of magnetic tape have been known to stretch slightly due to increased temperature levels. The electromechanical and electronic equipment may also be affected by high temperature, causing components to act erratically. The vendors have indicated broad temperature limits for the hardware. For example, one vendor recommends a range of 60° to 90°, whereas another specifies limits from 60° to 80°. Such parameters are somewhat deceiving and unrealistic because they fail to consider human comfort. It is much more appropriate to pick a range such as 70° to 72°, which would provide for both computer reliability and personnel comfort. In any event, an organization should pick an optimal temperature point and closely regulate that limit.

The amount of moisture in the air—measured as percentiles of relative humidity—must also be controlled, because it affects the mental alertness of the personnel, the operating efficiency of the equipment, and the texture of such materials as card and forms stock. Furthermore, it increases the heat load in an area as a result of condensation, thus causing a rise in static electricity voltage. Punched card stock, to select one example of moisture effects, is very difficult to process under excessive humidity conditions. The fibers begin to break down, causing jams and misfeeds in the equipment.

The permissible humidity ranges are very broad. The humidity level must be set at a realistic point to prevent condensation on the walls and windows, as well as to reduce the static electricity levels. Most organizations set the humidity level at 50 percent and attempt to control it within a 3 percent range.

There are several different types of air-conditioning systems that can be utilized to control the temperature and humidity ranges. The most popular of these is the underfloor system. This system utilizes the space between the regular building floor and the raised floor. The raised floor, which may also be described as a floating, elevated, or pedestal floor, is an excellent way of supplying air directly to the computer or the room. Also, it reduces the cost of duct work.

It is also necessary to install temperature and humidity recording instruments. These provide a continuous record of the conditions in the environment. Whenever possible, the instruments should be equipped with visual and/or audible alarms to alert the personnel to possible deviations or problems. The manager should also consider if the use of portable instrumentation is necessary to provide for a better balance of control.

The actual kind and type of equipment selected for an installation varies according to the processing equipment configuration, its usage, and the environment. Due to the complexity of the interactive factors, the author strongly recommends the use of an experienced air-conditioning design engineeer, who will be familiar with the distribution systems and mechanical equipment, as well as with the building codes affecting their use.

Proper Color Schemes

Color schemes have a significant psychological effect on personnel and personnel performance. Colors evoke varied reactions from almost all people, so that their effective use can help to establish a satisfying work environment. In addition to providing a stimulus and maintaining employee morale, colors are also used for safety purposes.

Colors can be categorized, in terms of the responses they evoke, as restful, cool, depressing, and warm.

Restful colors, such as beige and light green, are easy on the eyes and reflect light very well, thereby improving the level of illumination in an area. Other colors in pastel shades also offer good reflecting surfaces. Blues and greens have a tendency to induce a cool feeling; yet, when applied judiciously, they can be used for psychological comfort in an environment where heat dissipation may be high. Blacks and grays are depressing colors. Although most of the new data processing equipment now is painted in light shades of gray or green, some older units in black or gray may still be present in an installation. If the equipment is owned, rather than leased, by the organization, it can be painted in a more relaxing color scheme. In contrast to these depressing colors are red, yellow, and orange, which generate a feeling of warmth and excitement. Although such colors can cause fatigue when used monochromatically on large areas, they can be effectively applied to smaller areas, where, for example, they can effectively offset the effect of cool air flowing from the air-conditioning ducts.

File cabinets, desks, and other accessories are available in a variety of colors. Carefully chosen colors can make these items helpful in improving the environment through use of a coordinated color scheme. Furthermore, the supporting equipment currently available within an organization can be repainted in accordance with the general principles and goals of such a scheme.

Color coding is a most useful element of layout design when used to help improve personnel safety. Tops and bottoms of stairways should be painted yellow. Low-clearance areas should be marked with yellow stripes. And all emergency facilities should be painted red. This applies to fire call boxes, fire extinguishers, emergency telephones, and, in some cases, also to first-aid kits.

Proper Illumination

Poor illumination can be either a principal or supplementary cause of mental errors, accidents, and fatigue. The dimmer the illumination, the greater tends to be the number of errors, etc. On the other hand, very bright lighting can also have negative effects. Aside from its direct effect on the eyes, a high level of illumination can raise the heat load in a work area. In addition, it can cause glare when the light is reflected from walls, ceilings, and lighting fixtures.

The illumination requirements are determined by the availability of natural light from nearby windows and skylights, the amount of detail work to be performed, and the different levels of illumination needed at different areas within the environment.

Providing proper illumination can also mean providing an emergency lighting system, for there is a trend today toward designing and building windowless environments in order to simplify the air-conditioning and security requirements. The emergency system has to be equipped to automatically turn on battery-operated lights when a power failure occurs. It is equally important that the installation have a sufficient number of these lights and that they are installed and positioned so as to provide suitable emergency lighting.

Illumination for a data processing activity is provided by an incandescent or a fluorescent lighting system. Each system offers significant advantages and disadvantages, which must be evaluated in terms of tangible cost. Figure 7.2 summarizes the comparative merits of the two systems. The comparison shows that the installation cost of fluorescent fixtures in an existing environment would be higher than that of incandescent fixtures. However, this would be offset by lower operating and maintenance costs. In a totally new environment, though, the incandescent system would lose its advantage of lower installation cost in another way: because of the system's 60 percent heat load (almost double that of the fluorescent system), a more powerful air-conditioning unit would be needed, thereby increasing the overall costs.

Over-illumination can occur with either system, although glaring tends to occur more frequently with the incandescent system. That can be turned to good advantage, though, in instances where a demand for highlighting can be met by using this system's direct-light capability. The fluorescent system, which gives off a more diffused light, is much less effective for highlighting but correspondingly produces much less glare.

Under-illumination is also a problem with either system, but it can be more easily corrected in the fluorescent system, partly because there is less danger of glare. Furthermore, the use of brightly colored paints with a good reflecting sur-

	Incandescent	Fluorescent
Installation Cost	Lower	Higher
Operation Cost	Higher	Lower
Maintenance Cost	Higher	Lower
Additional Heat Load Generated	60%	35%
Direction of Light	Downward	Upward and Downward
Highlighting Effectiveness	Good	Poor

Figure 7.2 Comparison of incandescent and fluorescent lighting systems

face on walls and ceilings, combined with the fluorescent system's excellent indirect-light capability, can produce an increased level of glareless illumination.

It is recommended by processing equipment vendors that an average minimum illumination of 40 footcandles be maintained throughout the equipment operation area. The amount of light required in the other areas is difficult to determine exactly because of the variety of tasks being performed. Footcandle recommendations for the specific tasks may be obtained by consulting the lighting handbook published by the Illuminating Engineering Society.

Proper illumination can also be used to provide an element of safety in the working environment, particularly in the areas in front of and behind the equipment. In some instances, for example, there is insufficient illumination in the rear area, where the field engineers maintaining the equipment must work. Also, the storage areas for data, card, and form stock are deliberately kept dimly lit because they are not used much; this, though, is a false sense of economy. For reasons of safety, as well as efficiency, morale, etc., it is essential that the entire working environment be properly lit.

Another safety factor relating to illumination is the need for the lighting system to be arranged so as to place traffic aisles on separate circuitry from the general working areas. This makes it possible to turn off the lights in various parts of the environment without creating a safety hazard.

A Safe Working Environment

Safety represents both a layout factor and a human attitude. These must be given careful attention in the planning of any facility or operation. But safety does not end with the planning process; rather, it should be a habit planned by the manager and then maintained and enforced by him. Failure to apply safety attitudes and practices continually and effectively will be reflected in employee carelessness, which, in turn, can create serious problems.

The planner must first determine the existing safety codes established and enforced by federal (OSHA), state, and local governmental agencies, together with those developed by the organization's own safety engineer. These codes have a significant effect on actual design and construction of a data processing facility.

Safety in an environment is concerned with:

1. Emergency aisles and exits
2. Smoking practices
3. Emergency operating procedures
4. Fire detection and prevention
5. Electrical power requirements
6. Good housekeeping

1. EMERGENCY AISLES AND EXITS. Though there are usually company restrictions affecting the use of emergency aisles and exits, many managers fail to observe them. The author personally observed one instance in which an emergency aisle was used for the storage of supplies, thereby reducing the passageway width to only 30 inches. When this was called to the attention of the manager, he was quick to reply that no one used the passageway, ignoring the fact that this represented an emergency route in the event of fire or other disaster. This happens in many organizations. In fact, even emergency exit doors are allowed to become temporarily blocked. And landings on stairways are used as temporary storage facilities. The manager must enforce practices against the illegal and unwise use of such areas and facilities. He must also ensure that emergency passageways are properly illuminated and that exits are clearly marked.

2. SMOKING PRACTICES. These represent a potential hazard. The chief cause of fire is carelessly discarded cigarettes in storeroom areas or trash containers. What is more, the common and offensive habit of placing lighted cigarettes on the edges of tables, desks, and machines is always a threat to the well-being of both people and property.

To eliminate carelessness with cigarettes, the manager must make sure there are enough ash trays and must prohibit placement of lighted cigarettes on various surfaces or in unauthorized containers. However, it is even safer to ban all smoking in the operations and storage areas. This will greatly reduce the likelihood of fire damaging the equipment, injuring employees, and destroying vital data.

3. EMERGENCY OPERATING PROCEDURES. Every person in the data processing activity must be trained in the implementation of emergency operating procedures. This requires their familiarity with the emergency operating procedures, which should be kept in a binder on the manager's desk and/or the console operator's desk.

4. FIRE DETECTION AND PREVENTION. Devices to detect and prevent fire represent a critical element in the design and operation of a facility. Fire-detection devices are designed to discover a fire at its incipient stages and provide an early warning. In most instances, the types of fire-detection devices to be installed will be stipulated by the organization's insurance company. However, if none are specified, the planner should select a device that offers maximum detection ca-

pability and that provides for emergency shutoff of the electrical power to the data processing equipment and the air-conditioning plant. A less sophisticated device that may be used is an automatic smoke detector equipped with an audible and/or visual alarm.

Because so many facilities used by the data processing operations group are equipped with sprinkler systems, data processing managers are equipping installations with waterproof equipment covers. The availability of the covers in the installation may help eliminate or minimize water damage. This type of system helps to reduce the water damage somewhat. Many organizations are now equipping their data processing installations with waterproof equipment covers to reduce water damage.

The prevention of fire cannot always be achieved because of employee carelessness, combustion of stored materials, equipment failure, vandalism, accidents, sabotage, or an act of God. Safety regulations and building codes require that fire-retardant construction materials be used as a preventative safety measure. They also require installation of fire-fighting equipment.

Portable fire extinguishers should be conspicuously and conveniently placed throughout the installation, preferably on wall hangers. They must be recharged and/or examined at least once each year, with some provision for servicing only a few units at a time or obtaining loaners so that the installation is never without protection in the event of emergency.

The employees all need to know how to operate the fire extinguishers. They also need to know which kinds of extinguishers to use in case of an emergency, for using the wrong one can do much more harm than good. Class C fires (fires in live electrical equipment) require the use of carbon-dioxide or dry-chemical extinguishers. Class A fires (fires involving paper, wood, or cloth) should be tackled with extinguishers using soda-acid, foam, water, or antifreeze agent.

5. ELECTRICAL POWER REQUIREMENTS. Electrical power can be an enemy as well as a friend. It is important, therefore, that the personnel know the location of the circuit box and how to turn off the power supply serving the data processing equipment and the air-conditioning unit. It is also useful to arrange for having additional turn-off switches placed near the exits for use in emergency.

Personnel must be warned to turn off the mainline switches on the equipment when they are correcting jams so as to avoid the possibility of electrical shock or of injury caused by moving parts. The manager must periodically spot-check such situations to ensure compliance with such safety rules. One of the severest hazards involves electrical cords and outlets. In some instances where planners fail to provide an adequate number of wall or floor outlets, the employees use extension cords to connect several machines with one outlet. These cords stretched across the floor create a serious tripping hazard. One solution is simply to disconnect equipment when it is not in use. Although this approach may be acceptable in slow productive periods, it is impractical during peak periods. In addition, it endangers the life and serviceability of the electrical cords and plugs. The cords may become worn and frayed, thereby exposing the live wires. Also, when the plugs are disconnected from the outlets, they are left on the floor where they may be stepped on. This can break the contact points or the wire connection to them, thus ultimately endangering the user.

Another problem occurs when floor outlets are left in position after equipment has been moved. In one installation this author observed, the manager simply inverted a large green basket over an outlet in the middle of a traffic aisle until a work order for disconnecting the outlet could be prepared. He rationalized his action by stating that no one would trip over a *green* basket. Another tripping hazard is created by the power and signal cables used to connect the various units. This may be partially overcome by building a bridge over the cables, but a more effective method is to install raised flooring to conceal the cabling beneath the work surface.

6. GOOD HOUSEKEEPING. A clean shop is said to be a safe shop. So the manager should establish and enforce rules for maintaining a clean work environment. Good housekeeping requires that each person cooperate and share the responsibility of maintaining a satisfactory environment.

A primary problem is to have files, cartons, and other items returned to their proper storage locations. Frequently, control panels are placed behind or propped up against the machines rather than being returned to the storage racks. Misplaced panels represent a potential slipping and tripping hazard. Placing panels on top of storage or file cabinets is also a very bad practice. Cases and cartons of card stock are frequently left standing in front of a card punch machine or in the keypunch area. Only the necessary card stock should be placed near the device; others should be returned to the storeroom or placed in a storage rack. The same problem affects the use of printer forms. Empty cartons must not be left lying on the floor or on top of cabinets, for they constitute both a safety and fire hazard. In installations where cards are retained for scrap salvage, caution must be exercised to reduce the fire hazard potential. Precautions must also be taken in stacking the cartons or cases to prevent them from toppling. Generally, the cartons or cases are not packed tightly, so they are unable to sustain the weight of other cases or cartons. Consequently, a stack may resemble the Leaning Tower of Pisa.

Another frequent housekeeping problem is trash. Card chips strewn about the floor represent a potential slipping hazard, especially on a waxed surface. Trash from the card punches, reproducers, and printers should be placed in large containers. These should be located near the equipment to permit prompt disposal. Small containers should be placed in the keypunch area near each machine to collect all scrap and chips. The floors must be cleaned and containers emptied each day to remove all debris from the working area.

Whenever a field engineer completes either preventative or necessary maintenance on the equipment, the area should be checked for any parts that may be left on the floor or on the equipment. Also, any spilled oil or cleaning fluid must be wiped up. When oil continues to drip or leak, the vendor should be notified immediately in order to correct the situation and to eliminate the potential hazard.

Rolling carts can be used very effectively to reduce or eliminate personal injuries caused by lifting or carrying materials. Caution must be exercised not to overload the carts. Sorting racks must be provided where a high volume of card sorting is performed. The racks eliminate the hazardous practice of stacking file trays on the floor around the machine or on top of a worktable.

Proper knives and/or staple-removing devices should be available for opening paper cartons. These implements enable employees to avoid painful paper cuts. In addition, it is important that materials are stacked within safe reaching heights. Where cards and records are stacked on high storage racks, ladders must be furnished to eliminate climbing on the racks.

Review Questions: Group 7A

1. What are some of the conditions or reasons why a data processing manager would have to prepare an installation layout?
2. What are some of the factors that a manager must take into consideration when evaluating his space needs on a layout?
3. Name and discuss some of the health hazards that should be considered in the design of a layout.
4. What would your reaction be if someone suggested painting a large wall surface, faced by the keypunch operators, in red?
5. Would it be technically and operationally feasible to maintain the temperature of the computer environment at 66°? Why or why not?
6. A computer room has been equipped with an automatic sprinkler system. However, to minimize water damage, the lines over the equipment have been disconnected. Does this system provide the type of fire protection required in the environment?

SITE EVALUATION AND DETAILED PLANNING

Site Evaluation

The most difficult part of selecting a site is having to choose an optimal location for the operation's function. The selection process is difficult because the operations group is intensely affected by organizational objectives, the human element, external and internal influences, environmental control, and the work flow. These factors are less critical in selecting facilities for such functional activities as systems and programming; the planning for these groups is primarily concerned with work-space allocation and involves little or no productive equipment. (The process of designing the facilities for systems and programming is given later in this chapter.)

Before a new site may be considered or an existing facility evaluated, the manager must be aware of the overall space, structural, power, and air-conditioning needs. These are but guesstimates and will have to be modified when detailed planning is begun. The figures must be reasonable because they are an important part of the preliminary survey. In addition to the generalized space and environmental requirements, the manager must also evaluate the site in terms of efficiency, flexibility, comfort, security, and safety.

The site evaluation or selection is generally limited to choosing from among the following:

An area within the organization's existing facilities

An area or building available for lease, rental, or purchase

A building or area specifically constructed for the purpose

A special facility such as a mobile trailer or van.

In evaluating each of these possibilities, the primary consideration is space availability. This availability must be compared with the estimated current, proposed, and future needs, which are based on data from the vendors, on survey and/or feasibility studies, and on projections resulting from an analysis of the short-term and long-term goals set by the manager and executive committee. Following the determination of space adequacy, the manager must give consideration to environmental factors, location, communications capability, zoning restrictions, objectives, and costs. These considerations may be grouped within the following categories:

1. Location
2. Floor loading capacity
3. Temperature and moisture control
4. Power

1. LOCATION. Location is an important factor in reducing or eliminating various internal or external hazards within an environment. It is also an important factor in the complicated process of optimizing productivity.

Ideally, the operations facility is housed in a fire-resistant room or building isolated from high temperatures, corrosive substances, water and/or utility pipes, outside walls, windows, and unauthorized personnel.

Most installations are located in an area near or relatively near to the chief supporting activity, or they are centralized for the benefit of all activities in the organization. The practice of locating the data processing operations group near its primary supporting activity was established when unit-record equipment had to be located near the payroll activity. Centralization, on the other hand, occurs when the executive committee believes that this will strengthen the overall effectiveness of the organization. However, neither of these two basic arrangements offers any guarantee of the best security, efficiency, flexibility, safety, or comfort.

In many organizations, the data processing operations activity becomes a public showcase. This decision generally overrides all efficiency, safety, cost, and security considerations. Such an installation is generally glass-enclosed and often placed in the front window. The location leaves the activity vulnerable to vandals, rioters, storms, or even such occurrences as out-of-control motor vehicles. The glass is usually the nonsafety type, which can cause lacerating injuries. However, building codes in some areas now require the use of tempered, laminated, or wired glass in modern construction. The glass also poses a blow-out possibility during a fire, but this can be minimized by installing an external sprinkler system to provide a blanket of water.

The glass also creates some air-conditioning and humidification problems due to condensation. The moisture caused by condensation, for example, will produce structural damage if not controlled.

Accessibility for delivery of equipment and supplies is another consideration involved in selecting a location. It may be impossible to move equipment into an area without reconstructing a series of doorways, passageways, windows, or outside walls; or without utilizing a crane to lift the equipment to an upper floor or the roof because the freight elevator is inadequate or unavailable. Thus, making an installation accessible can prove to be extremely costly.

The communications capability of each site must be surveyed, particularly if data collection, teleprocessing, or data transmission systems are currently in use, on order, or represent a possible future acquisition. Limitations imposed on signal cable length could affect the location of a facility dependent upon the use of these media for input, and/or output.

Land, construction, and insurance costs are significant factors affecting the selection of any site. The cost of constructing a new facility or remodeling an existing site can result in the modification of the original construction plans or selection of an alternate location. Insurance costs may force selection of an alternate site due to high premiums for fire and liability coverage. Zoning regulations may affect selection because the area may not be available for industrial or business development. Or, there may be construction limitations or requirements stipulated in building codes that will affect the layout design.

Location may also present some security problems for a manager. The major problem for most organizations is to limit access to the operations area. In many instances, direct access through a public hallway or an outside door is possible. Access may be limited by stationing a security guard to inspect all employee identification; by installing badge readers or other access control devices on the doors; by limiting entry to key holders; or by installing heavy-gauge, closely woven metal screens on the windows and doors (see chapter 10). It may be much simpler to locate the activity in an interior area on an upper floor, in that security problems have also arisen where outside air-intake facilities for air-conditioning have been located at ground level.

It may not be entirely practical to locate a facility below ground level or in an area through which heat, gas, and water pipes pass. Below-ground sites may be exposed to the danger of flooding caused by water-main breaks, storms, or sewer backup. Furthermore, service piping is often concealed by the suspended ceiling or raised floor. The potential danger to personnel, equipment, and materials in this type of environment is quite high.

There is also a sociological consideration in selecting the proper location. If a facility is located in a high crime area, it may be difficult to recruit personnel of both sexes for other than normal day-shift schedules. Consequently, some organizations even provide taxi and/or charter bus service for their personnel on the off shifts.

The sites considered should be evaluated in terms of cost and in terms of the advantages and disadvantages of each location. The costs must be allocated between capital and operating expenditures. Capital expenditures, which may be amortized over a period of years, include the cost of construction and the purchase of fixed equipment. Operating expenditures, the recurring expenditures necessary to keep a facility operative, include the costs of utility services, replacing filters in the air-conditioning system, and other necessary items.

2. FLOOR LOADING CAPACITY. After having selected sites that meet the basic space requirements and provide flexibility for expansion and a potentially optimal location, the planner must investigate the floor loading capacity. Rated floor loadings should be available from the organization's engineering department or the building's manager. If none are available, it may be necessary to arrange for a consulting engineer to make the necessary determinations. The floor must be able to sustain the weight of the data processing and auxiliary equipment, the furniture, and personnel, and still have some allowance for safety. The requirements should be checked with local building-code provisions to ensure compliance. The overall weight must not place any stress on the walls or the structure that would require reinforcement-type construction, for that would increase installation preparation cost.

One of the major problems in evaluating flooring construction is to determine its ability to sustain a concentrated floor load. A concentrated floor load is one that is applied to a very small area within the entire environment. This condition generally exists where medium- or large-scale computing systems are positioned in a small area to gain optimal productive effectiveness. Rated floor loadings specify the maximum uniform load that may be distributed, but they generally do not indicate a floor's ability to support a single or several concentrated loads in a given area. For most data processing operations, uniform distribution is not feasible if there is also to be an optimal productive flow or balance of operations. Therefore, if objectives are to be achieved, it may be necessary to reinforce the permanent flooring.

Most types of flooring construction, with the exception of tile-arch, do have the capacity to support data processing equipment without reinforcement. Tile-arch, which is generally found in older buildings, requires reinforcement. Materials such as prestressed slab, reinforced concrete, and wood are more desirable, although these too may require structural reinforcement or some load redistribution.

In newer installations, it has become a practice to install raised flooring. This type of flooring is constructed over a permanent base in order to provide an area for power cables, signal cables, air-conditioning ducts, and recessed electrical outlets. In addition, raised floor can be used to redistribute the effect of a concentrated load on a permanent floor, although the raised flooring installed in such a manner must be capable of supporting the maximum weight. Support for the raised flooring is provided either by fire-resistant frame or by stringers that rest on pedestals. The flooring surface is wood or tile that is installed in sections, which can be easily removed to make the space accessible.

A floor rating of 150 pounds per square foot is desirable but is not commonly found except in warehouses, basements, or first-floor levels of office buildings. An acceptable minimum may be a rated capacity of 100 pounds per square foot.

3. TEMPERATURE AND MOISTURE CONTROL. The movement and quality of air are very significant factors in site evaluation. Earlier in this chapter, we generalized about the effects of air-conditioning on personnel and equipment in the environment. Here we will provide additional information.

Air-conditioning requirements for each site vary according to the physical characteristics of the room or structure, the personnel, the kind and type of processing equipment, the amount and type of illumination, the level of relative humidity, and the supply of fresh air entering the environment. Humidity and temperature requirements vary among vendors, so where an equipment mix of several vendors is used, the parameters will be more difficult to calculate. The heat generated by the hardware is the single most significant factor in determining the heat load imposed on the air-conditioning system. Added to this calculation are the values for the sun's influence, for body heat produced by the employees, for heat from lighting fixtures, and for heat generated in another area but transmitted through the walls or ceilings surrounding the operations activity.

After considering the heat-generating factors, the planner must consider the environment's fresh-air intake. The inputted air may or may not add to the heat load, depending upon the outside temperature and relative humidity. Warm air may have to be cooled and excess moisture removed to maintain a desired humidity level. In the cooler months, larger quantities of fresh air are introduced into the air-conditioning system to assist in the cooling process.

A number of different air-conditioning systems are available and each must be evaluated for a specific application. An organization should not rely upon a building's central air-conditioning system to accommodate the needs of a data processing operation's activity. The air-handling units may be window units or free-standing units, which are successfully used in small- or medium-sized installations. Or, they may be built-in units, which have the greater cooling capacity needed to provide satisfactory service for large installations.

The effectiveness of any air-handling unit depends upon the control and recording techniques utilized. It is desirable that the air-conditioning system be equipped with a recording device providing a written record of the environmental conditions for historical and reference purposes. Some of the instrumentation can either electrically or pneumatically activate the control mechanisms in the air-handling units to correct deviations from established environmental standards. Control units of this type are costlier but more effective than maintaining separate unit controls for the humidifier and air-conditioner. Separate controls utilize a separate dry bulb temperature gauge and relative humidity indicator for recording. Consequently, they require manual adjustments that tend to reduce the effectiveness of the air-handling units and to generate personnel problems as a result of the fluctuations in the temperature, humidity, and air flow.

Penetration and condensation of moisture are two problem-causing conditions for a data processing operation. Moisture comes through walls, floors, and ceilings that are made of such porous materials as cinderblocks or concrete. In most instances, this can be corrected by applying waterproofing or vapor-sealing materials to the affected surfaces. Where the condition persists it will be necessary to construct a wall within a wall. The inner surface of the inside wall is then vapor-sealed or waterproofed and provision is made to drain off the moisture penetrating the outer wall.

Condensation usually occurs around window areas and causes water accumulations. It is generally corrected by installing a double window or by constructing a wall across the window. The double-window method is much less costly except where thermo-pane or heated glass panels are used. However, this technique is not always satisfactory because there is a tendency for some condensation to form on the metal frames, thereby enabling moisture to collect and cause safety and structural deterioration problems. The wall-across-window method is more desirable because it helps to reduce the heat load. This method is becoming more popular and is the basis of the windowless installations. The most significant disadvantage to this type of construction can be having personnel affected by claustrophobia. It is difficult to screen the data processing personnel for this type of psychological condition. Therefore, the offsetting solution may be to construct false windows in the environment. This is accomplished by placing several panes of translucent plastic or glass in front of warm-light fluorescent fixtures, thereby giving the illusion of daylight coming through a window. Some of the ersatz windows are framed with drapes to create a more authentic illusion and to remove the feeling of a closed-in room.

Condensation that forms on air-conditioning ducts and pipes can be overcome by insulating the surfaces.

4. POWER SUPPLY. The availability and the quality of power at a site must be evaluated for current and future needs. The overall requirements must include the needs of the lighting system, air-conditioning units, and the data processing equipment.

Current transmitted by the utilities or produced by an organization's own power plant should present no power problems because the equipment vendors are able to offer or modify units to operate on the available current supply. To offset voltage fluctuations due to dips and surges, some engineers have recommended the installation of voltage regulators on feeder lines leading into the circuit panels.

The power supply is channeled into the building through the power service entrance from overhead or underground lines. From the distribution panel, the power is relayed to one or more branch circuit panels located in the installation.

The panels are equipped with circuit breakers or fuses to take care of any overloads in the current. Circuit breakers—which are more convenient and more commonly used—serve for normal current overloads, whereas fuses are better for protection in severe overload conditions because they have a higher current-interrupting capacity than circuit breakers and will respond much more rapidly to a severe overload condition. After a circuit breaker trips due to an overload condition, it can be quickly reset. Under similar circumstances, fuses are damaged and must be replaced. Another consideration is that the feeder circuit switch must be turned off to deal with a fuse, thereby neutralizing all devices on that branch circuit—which does not occur on branch circuits controlled by circuit breakers. There is a danger that if all power is immediately neutralized, there may be a loss of data or damage to the equipment and its components. In an emergency, power may be turned off selectively for any unit by tripping the assigned breaker. Further, individual breakers provide for an orderly shutdown and greater flexibility in preserving important files being operated.

The circuits for the data processing equipment must be kept independent of those for the air-conditioning units, lighting system, and auxiliary equipment. The branch circuit panels should be divided to separate each element so that an overload in one will not affect or cause a malfunction in any of the others. The circuits in the panels must be properly identified to indicate the facilities controlled by each, for in an emergency there is no time for guesswork. As part of the emergency operating procedure, personnel in the organization must be familiar with safe operation of the control panel.

The availability of electrical power for equipment operating in an online, real-time, or time-sharing environment can be critical or costly. In such situations, provision for standby power to eliminate or limit the interruption to a very brief period of time must be made. Even in less critical environments, it may be necessary to provide auxiliary power where frequent power interruptions or outages occur. The auxiliary power may be supplied by a generator or by a feeder line connected to an alternate substation. However, where auxiliary power service is established, it is necessary to ensure the quality of the power—that is, voltage fluctuations should be controlled. Voltage fluctuations may affect the speeds and accuracy of the equipment; in some instances, they can cause malfunctions.

HOW LAYOUTS ARE MADE

When consideration has been given to all of the interacting factors, the manager is then ready to optimize the layout. This involves using a layout diagram and simulating the manpower, materials, and machine resources in actual production.

The layout diagram is produced by arranging templates, illustrations, or models on grid paper or hardboard to provide a scaled version of an optimal operating facility. The layout development process is concerned with three basic elements:

1. Planning tools
2. Space allocation
3. Optimal equipment placement

Planning Tools

The available planning tools enable a manager to manipulate and hypothesize the physical arrangement of his processing and supporting equipment into an optimal productive layout. The manager is thereby able to evaluate each arrangement before a final architectural drawing is made.

The equipment may be represented on the planning layout by templates, illustrations, and/or models.

Templates are used to illustrate computers, data communications devices, unit-record equipment, desks, tables, chairs, files, furniture, and supporting equipment. They provide two-dimensional outlines of the equipment, specifying the height, depth, width, operating area, and maintenance requirements (see Figure 7.3). The height, depth, and width dimensions are particularly useful in determining the proper setting and angle for battery-operated emergency lights, as well as in evaluating space needs in terms of space availability. For equipment requring a power supply, the template indicates the location of the power exit. This enables the manager to determine the necessary placement of a device near an existing or proposed power supply. Templates may be replicated on a copying machine to produce a number of desired units. The copies are then cut up to enable the planner to use each object on the template individually.

The cutouts may be manipulated until the layout has been optimized, at which time they may be affixed to the grid paper or hardboard with paste, glue, or cellophane tape. The layout may then be reproduced on a copying machine, photographed, or prepared as an architectural drawing. Templates are very useful, although some planners criticize them for failing to give the illusion of perspective.

Illustrations are frequently used in the layout planning process. They are generally of two types—the artist's sketch of an object that may be readily reproduced and the adhesive-backed block. The sketch-type illustrations provide some realism, which may be lacking in the block-type illustrations. Both types can be reproduced or photographed when the layout has been completed. When utilizing illustrations, the planner must indicate the overall space requirements for each object on the grid paper or hardboard. Also, he must make provision for such items as control panel clearances, work area, maintenance requirements, equipment dimensions, and power cable exits. The use of illustrations in layout development tends to increase planning time and effort.

Three-dimensional models (see Figure 7.4), constructed of wood, plastic, or paper, also may be used for physical planning. Paper models are generally

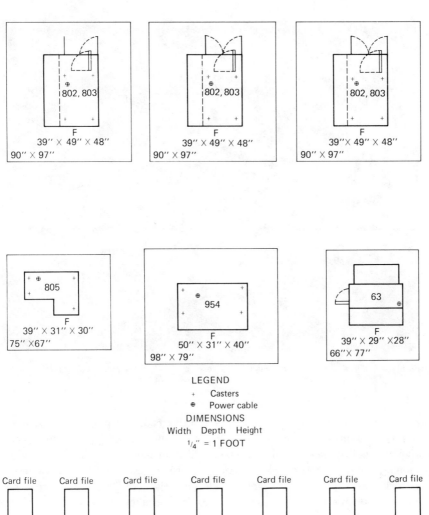

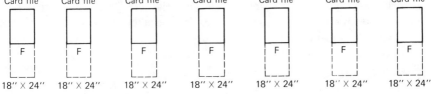

Figure 7.3 Physical planning template. Courtesy IBM Corporation

flimsy, whereas plastic and wood ones are sturdy. The models are positioned and repositioned on the grid paper or hardboard until a layout plan has been developed. To facilitate reproduction of the layout, the planner must outline the external surfaces of the objects on the grid paper or hardboard, which is a time-consuming chore. Like the illustrations, some models make no provision for location of the power cable exits, clearances for maintenance and control panel

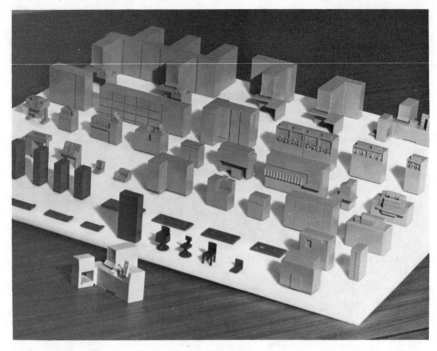

Figure 7.4 Three-dimensional models. Courtesy "Visual" Industrial Products, Inc.

housings, or work station requirements. But the models do provide a sense of realism and afford a better perspective than two-dimensional or illustrated objects.

The types of planning tools selected will ultimately depend upon individual preferences. Their use enables a planner to visualize several alternatives and to rework these until he has reached a desirable layout. Though this process is time-consuming, it is less costly than preparing architectural drawings for each possible arrangement.

Space Allocation

The manager begins the space allocation segment of physical planning by outlining the external area for the facility on the grid paper or hardboard. After identifying the external parameters, he must specify the internal limiting factors, such as stairwells, elevators, windows, permanent partitions, doors, emergency exits, and columns affecting the room. The air-conditioning unit, radiators, ductwork, and piping or conduit must also be illustrated. Next, the planner must indicate electrical power outlet locations and their respective voltage capacities.

The layout diagram at this point primarily identifies the available floor space and major constraints regarding the machines, materials, and manpower.

Optimal Equipment Placement

Utilizing the data collected on the work flow the manager can begin to position his productive equipment. Their placement will be affected by the availability of electrical power outlets, signal cable lengths, and floor loading capacity. If load redistribution is necessary, then the manager must develop alternative arrangements to design an operationally effective environment.

An analysis of the process flow also enables the manager to determine optimal placement for both the portable and stationary materials handling equipment. Portable equipment offers greater placement flexibility in the layout, yet it too must be optimally positioned to achieve maximum utilization and effectiveness. In addition, the placement of stationary equipment may be affected by the floor loading capacity. For example, cabinets for punched card storage may have to be placed against the walls, away from the center areas. This arrangement can increase materials handling, so it may be necessary to position the card cabinets in a sequence that will reduce the walking distances to heavily utilized files. Tables, desks, chairs, and other furniture used in the operation must also be positioned on the diagram at this time.

Next, the manager must give careful consideration to the placement of supervisory stations. A significant factor is their accessibility to the operating personnel in order to allow immediate contact when the need arises. In addition, this will discourage the assumption of nondelegated authority by the subordinates when a decision has to be made and no one in authority is readily available. If an enclosed area is to be constructed for managerial personnel, the space allocation for one such person may range from 100 to 125 square feet.

Having positioned the productive equipment, supervisory stations, and supporting facilities, the manager must then reevaluate his minimal space allocations. He has to consider spaces between machines, in traffic and work aisles, at working stations, and for equipment maintenance. One frequently overlooked factor at this stage is the effect of file cabinets on aisles. Files are repeatedly opened, so that failure to allow adequate clearance in the aisles when the drawers are fully extended, disrupts productivity. Furthermore, people working on the files may have to temporarily stop in order to permit the passage of people and/or materials through the aisles.

Cramped work stations are seldom an inducement for efficiency. In an effort to reduce materials handling and distances, there is a tendency to position tables and other handling equipment too close to the operation, thereby reducing the available work space. Furthermore, the placement of portable handling equipment in the area frequently adds to the congestion. Reserving space between these machines and others for placement and movement of portable equipment can significantly alleviate this type of congestion.

Having completed his assessment of the space allocations for working stations, work and traffic aisles, and maintenance, the manager turns his attention to environmental safety. He must, for example, verify that his layout has not blocked any emergency exits or limited the size of any emergency passageways.

In addition, he should reconsider the placement of fire extinguishers and emergency telephones, for these pieces of equipment *must* be kept accessible. In windowless installations, the manager must reevaluate the placement of battery-operated emergency lights. To prevent interference with the light beams, it will be necessary to ensure that no materials handling or processing equipment gets in the way. The manager must further determine that he has an adequate number of these lights in the installation.

Having completed this preliminary phase, the manager must sample the effectiveness of his design. The process is conducted by simulating the flow of several benchmark applications through the layout to help identify any potential problem or bottlenecks. Modifications can then be made to the layout before it is finalized.

Review Questions: Group 7B

1. Name and describe briefly the tools used in layout planning.
2. What are some of the internal limiting factors a manager must consider in the layout of an operations facility?
3. What is the purpose of simulating the work flow of a benchmark application through the layout design?

LAYOUT OF OFFICE FACILITIES

The office facilities in a data processing organization are used by the personnel involved in programming, systems analysis and design, advanced planning, and training activities. The objectives are concerned primarily with maintaining a flow of communications and with the movement of paper work by the shortest and most direct route. Unlike the operations work area, an office facility is less concerned with productive balance and materials handling. However, environmental considerations such as floor loading, illumination, noise, color, safety, and air-conditioning are relevant for both, although the parameters may be different. Office planning involves the same basic tools and the initial space allocation steps as in the layout of the operations facility. Then the windows, doors, permanent partitions, stairways, columns, ductwork, and any permanent fixtures limiting the available floor space must be marked. The manager then must decide whether the available area will be subdivided into private offices and/or cubicles or left as an open area with only a few office areas for key personnel. If a decision is made to subdivide, more overall space will be required. However, subdivision does afford some degree of privacy and helps reduce or eliminate environmental noise and interference. The space allocation for each employee will be allocated in proportion to the level of importance within the hierarchical structure. A minimum of 70 to 75 square feet should be allocated for each employee. In organizations where an open office area is maintained, the minimum space allocation for a desk and chair combination is, with only minor exceptions, 50 square feet.

There is perhaps a need to give more consideration to traffic aisles and work stations in an open office area. Particular attention must be given to the area behind the desks. The failure to provide adequate space will generally interfere with the smooth flow of employees to and from their work stations. Consequently, this will have a disruptive physical and psychological effect on the other employees in the area. Work stations located near major traffic aisles and elevators must be screened off to reduce and/or eliminate noise and other distractions. The screening may be achieved by installing removable partitions constructed from acoustical materials.

Where file cabinets and desks face each other across an aisle, a minimum of seven feet should be reserved for the combination work and traffic aisle. This allocation of space should provide for both a smooth flow of traffic and minimal distraction to the personnel in the area. This is a consideration most frequently overlooked in the design process.

For both open and enclosed office areas, the minimal space allocations for a traffic aisle width should be five feet for major aisles and between three and four feet for minor or connecting aisles.

Many organizations now include a conference room in an office area. This provides space for meetings with people from other functional activities; enables project leaders to meet with their teams to discuss systems, plans, programs, problems, or progress; facilitates conduct of "sounding" or "brainstorming" sessions; and, to a limited extent, provides a classroom for orientation and training purposes. Organizations that are using egoless programming teams (see chapter 2) must definitely provide such a facility for the required group interaction. The conference room should afford visual and acoustical privacy. The size of a conference room is often determined by the size of the table to be set in the room. For example, a 4' × 8' table seating from six to ten persons (depending upon the type of chairs used) may be placed in a 12' × 18' room. Ideally the chairs in the conference room should be of a pivotal type, with one-foot separations between them. This will permit the audience to face several speakers and to avoid feeling like sardines. A permanent blackboard should also be installed on one of the wall surfaces for use in "chalk-talks" and presentations.

Another special area may be set aside in the office layout for the stenographic pool, plus copying and duplicating equipment. The overall size of this area depends upon the number of personnel to be situated there and the type and number of special devices to be used. However, a minimum allocation of 36 square feet should be included for each secretary. In some organizations, fireproof vaults or cabinets are added for storage of the original copies of documentation and programs. Their sizes vary, so that the specifications should be secured from vendor catalogs.

There is less difficulty in preparing an office layout than an operations one because there will be very little, if any, grouping of major or minor activities due to the variations in the functional activities. The personnel may be grouped by types of activity, such as programming, systems, or training. Or, instead, the systems, planning, and programming personnel may be grouped into teams of major application areas or projects. The work-flow patterns vary with each application, project, or task.

Review Questions: Group 7C

1. Are there any differences in the planning of an office area as compared with an operations room? If so, what are they?
2. Why should a manager consider the use of cubicle enclosure for his programming and systems personnel?

SUMMARY

In this chapter we have been concerned primarily with the layout of the productive facilities in the data processing function. The primary emphasis was placed on the operations activity, where developing the optimal mix of the manpower, machine, and materials resources is essential. Ideally, it would be more advantageous to prepare a layout and construct a building around the design, but the ideal is usually impractical because most facilities must be located within an existing structure. If given the opportunity to select a site, a manager must choose one that will best fit his immediate and future needs. The planner must coordinate the physical and human factors involved into a composite layout that meets both physical and psychological needs. Having given consideration to these factors, he must then prepare the actual layout. With the aid of grid paper or hardboard, plus templates, illustrations, and/or models, the manager develops the layout. To assess the layout, he should simulate the work flow of some representative applications in order to identify the potential problems and bottlenecks. When satisfied that the layout will be operationally effective, the manager must then proceed with the construction details, which will be handled by an architect, contractor, or engineer.

After the site has been prepared, it may be necessary to make some changes or modifications, which may be done with little difficulty if flexibility has been included in the original design.

CASE STUDY 7.1

The Eric Andrea Cosmetics Company

The Eric Andrea Cosmetics Company has recently completed a feasibility study. As a result of the study, the executive committee has decided to upgrade its existing unit-record equipment to an IBM 370/135 computer configuration with a disk operating system. The organization would like to use the existing area for the data processing operation activity.

The operations room is located in the northwest corner of the building. The two corner walls of the building are filled with large ordinary glass windows. The internal side wall has smaller windows between the two single doors on the wall. The room is not equipped with any air-conditioning or humidification control. On warm days, the back windows are opened to cool the room. The side windows are not opened because they are on the wall most affected by the wind, dust, and dirt—these windows are adjacent to the parking lot and in line with the foundry across the road. The room is equipped with an automatic sprinkler system and two soda-acid fire extinguishers for fire protection.

Tahitian sunset (reddish orange) has been applied to the back-window wall. This color was applied to offset the psychological coldness of the room. Shades of vanilla (greenish yellow) and chocolate (light brown) have been applied to the other wall surfaces.

Illumination is provided by an incandescent lighting system. The footcandle capacity is adequate for current needs. Electrical power for the existing hardware configuration is also adequate. The freestanding electrical outlets are located near the respective equipment.

The desks of the control clerk and the manager and his assistant are located in an open area near the side-window wall. These three people share the one telephone line and extension in the room.

The room is 60 feet long and 25 feet wide. The ceilings are 18 feet high and painted in a shade of vanilla. The floor loading capacity of the room is rated at 100 pounds per square foot.

Discussion Questions

1. After reading this case, what initial observations would you make about the acceptability of the existing physical facility?
2. Does the fact that the area is currently located in the northwest corner of the building have any effect upon the site selection? Why or why not?
3. What effect, if any, do the windows have upon the site?
4. Should any recommendations be made to improve the effectiveness of the fire protection in the existing facility? What are they, if any?
5. What comments or suggestions, if any, do you have about the existing color scheme?
6. Without any knowledge of the dimensional requirements of the proposed equipment, what graphic planning can be done at this time?
7. Would you feel it necessary to convert from an incandescent to a fluorescent lighting system? Why or why not?
8. Do you feel that all personnel needs are currently being satisfied? If not, explain why.
9. Are there any safety considerations that should be included in the future plans of the organization?

CHAPTER 8

The Survey and

Feasibility Studies

INTRODUCTION / Because he is constantly involved in some form of decision-making, the manager must have access to accurate, relevant, and timely information. Much of the decision-making data is gathered and/or evaluated during the pre-executory phase, through a review of the long-range plan for the data processing organization, reviewing or gathering survey data, and conducting feasibility studies. These tools help the manager to define an objective; evaluate the organizational setting; consider possible courses of action; select an optimal course of action; and determine operational effectiveness.

The documented survey provides preliminary and general information about the overall organization; its data processing function; the data processing equipment, applications and software; and, possibly, additional information about any interacting satellite activities. The survey information, therefore, provides a basic orientation about the environment in which a goal or series of goals is to be attained.

The feasibility studies evaluate the technical, economic, and operational feasibility of existing or proposed information and/or software systems, resource allocations, schedules, hardware, or performance standards.

THE SURVEY

Before any plan can be formulated, the manager must understand the environmental setting in which the plan is to be developed and implemented. The process requires a firm understanding of the influences and constraints imposed by the organization on the objectives, plans, and activities of the data processing function. In addition, the manager must understand the extent and value of contributions made by users. Performing these evaluations requires information about the overall organization and its data processing attitudes, needs, and capabilities. This type of information is available to the data processing manager and his staff by gathering and documenting the data, or reviewing and evaluating the documented survey data.

The concept of the documented survey is subject to many pros and cons. This author recommends that an in-depth survey be performed by a data processing manager, on a one-time basis, to gather data about the organization and the role of information processing within that organization. It is not intended that the survey data be gathered on a when-needed basis, because this generally means that such a procedure is limited in scope, depth, and time. This, in turn, can mean that the information gathered may be incomplete and/or inaccurate.

Figure 8.1 Suggested standard for processing requests for data processing services Raleric, Inc.

Data Processing Manual 10.1
February 3, 19—
Justification for Data Processing Services

1. General

1.1 This instruction prescribes the procedures for handling of requests for the services of the data processing organization.
1.2 Form R-2264, "Request For Data Processing Services," shall be issued when the services of the systems, software, or operations group is required.

2. Requesting Organization

2.1 The organization requesting data processing services shall:
  (a) issue Form R-2264 in duplicate, retaining one copy and forwarding the original to the data processing administrator.
  (b) provide concise, accurate details, and an analysis of costs to manually produce the required data.

3. Data Processing Organization

3.1 The data processing organization shall:
  (a) immediately acknowledge receipt of Form R-2264.
  (b) determine the scope and objectives of the request.
  (c) review the available information and determine if the request is unacceptable, requires additional investigation, or is acceptable.
    (1) If unacceptable, an immediate response must be made to the requesting organization.
    (2) If additional investigation is required, the requesting organization must be notified to supply additional details.
    (3) If acceptable, a case number will be assigned to the request and the data processing administrator will schedule and allocate the necessary resources to the project.

The survey data must be documented to form a data base or catalog of information. This documentation will enable the data processing manager or administrator to answer queries raised by the executive committee regarding the information processing function. Also, it can be used to help evaluate the validity of requests for information processing services (see Figure 8.1) and to provide comparative data for cost-benefit analysis in feasibility studies. In addition, it is extremely useful in planning the approach for a feasibility study and/or systems analysis and formulating the questions to be raised by an interviewer in either of those fact-gathering techniques.

In the context defined by this author, then, the survey is not a substitute for a feasibility study, for a feasibility study culminates in a recommendation to the executive committee calling for the expenditure of funds and allocation of resources. Nor is the survey intended to be used as an analysis of an existing system to give managers a list of areas requiring improvement. Also, the survey is not to be used as a systems audit or reports control study designed to evaluate the effectiveness and documentation of existing operational systems. But much rather, it is an updated document providing selective background information about the organization. Much of the information contained in the documented survey can be used to explain current needs and attitudes and, to a limited degree, future trends. The survey data may also help to identify the source of any problems or significant constraints. For data processing personnel, the documented survey provides information that will help them to better understand the overall organization and the functional activities affected by a systems and/or software project.

The major categories of information gathered for inclusion in the survey are:

1. General organization information
2. Data processing hardware and software currently used
3. The data processing organization
4. Satellite organization interaction
5. Information processing systems
6. Data processing hardware/software on order/replacement

General Organization Information

To gain an understanding about an organization it may be necessary to study its:

1. History
2. Size
3. Structure
4. Type
5. Product or service

1. HISTORY. Historical data is gathered or analyzed in order to provide an understanding about the organization's evolvement. The history may explain the executive committee's involvement in information processing functions and ac-

tivities; executive committee preference for certain projects; the organization's policies, practices, and philosophies; the constraints affecting the organization; organizational strengths and weaknessess; and the source of problems. Some of the historical information may be gathered from materials provided to new employees. However, to achieve a fuller background, it may be necessary to research the annual reports, organizational publications, industry reports, a stock prospectus, stock analyst reports, etc.

2. SIZE. The size provides some preliminary information, which is used in conjunction with data or equipment and systems. This information enables the manager to determine the type of hardware and software an organization is capable of supporting, as well as to arrive at a judgment about the sophistication of the currently operational systems and those under development or proposed.

Figure 8.2 Example of overall organization chart

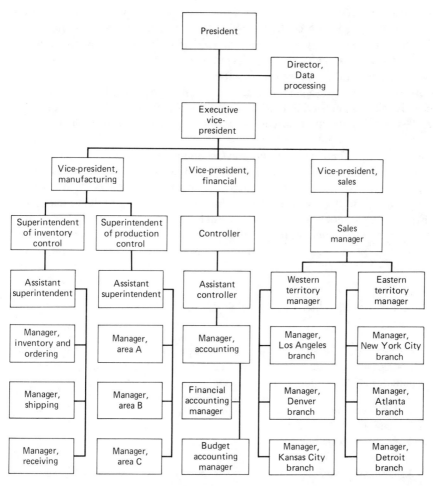

3. STRUCTURE. The structure delineates the responsibilities and lines of authority within the organization. Information on the structure is generally secured from the organization chart (see Figure 8.2), job descriptions, and functional activity managers. This information is particularly useful when determining the functional activities affected in the analysis, design, development, implementation, maintenance, and audit of a system. Also, it provides relevant and necessary data for the formulation of questions to be used in the interviewing of personnel. The structural information can also be very useful in estimating the time requirements for interviews, flowcharting, data analyses, etc., in a project schedule.

4. TYPE. Type identifies the primary activity of an organization. It indicates if an organization is involved in manufacturing, business, medical, commercial, educational, research, governmental, religious, utility, or service activities. Organization type will significantly affect the type of data processing hardware and software selected and the information systems developed and implemented. For example, in a manufacturing organization, the primary emphasis may be on inventory and production control systems. In a hospital, on the other hand, the emphasis may be placed on the medical record or accounts receivable systems.

5. PRODUCT OR SERVICE. The product line or services offered by an organization may also affect hardware and software selection and information systems development. For example, an organization engaged primarily in scientific research will be interested in hardware with fast internal computational capability and slower input/output speeds. The applications in this example would be mathematically oriented.

The organizational information provides the manager with some preliminary information about the environmental setting. However, this information must be supplemented with other interacting data contained in the survey. In some organizations, the history, size, product line or service, organization charts, and listing of managerial personnel are maintained in a policy standards manual. Very often, information on the structure and manning can be secured from the internal telephone directory. The manual and directory may be used very effectively in a survey which has to be done with minimal research time and effort.

Data Processing Hardware and Software Currently Used

This segment of the survey provides a detailed census of the existing information processing capability in the central organization. The following types of information may be gathered in this segment:

1. Unit-record equipment
2. Computing equipment
3. Software availability
4. Peripheral equipment
5. Utilization statistics

1. UNIT-RECORD EQUIPMENT. The manager must determine the number and types of devices available for input preparation and processing, as well as their rated processing speeds. This list should also include information on the special features installed on a given device. For example, a keypunch machine may be equipped with an alternate program control. The listing should also indicate the costs of the devices, whether they are being rented, leased, or purchased. The cost data should include a separate category for maintenance charges for each device.

This information will enable a manager to evaluate the unit-record processing capability of the organization. The cost data would be available for any comparative cost analysis.

2. COMPUTING EQUIPMENT. The inventory of computing equipment is more detailed because of the number of features and supporting devices required in a configuration. Figure 8.3 illustrates an inventory listing for an IBM 370/145 processing unit.

As for unit-record equipment, the rental, lease, or purchase costs and maintenance charges should be included. In addition, information about real-time and time-sharing capability should be included as part of the inventory.

Additional technical data for such items as densities, transfer rates, storage capacities, etc., should be included as part of the computing equipment census. The technical data is not always readily available or known in an organization. Frequently, the vendor's representative must be contacted to secure information regarding a particular device. Therefore, the technical information should be a part of the basic equipment survey.

3. SOFTWARE AVAILABILITY. This segment of the survey should identify the capabilities of the operating system and programming languages and include narrative descriptions of the special software packages, such as cash-flow analysis. Programming languages provide an indicator of the types of applications processed and their level of sophistication. It may also provide some measure of

Figure 8.3 IBM 370/145 Processing Unit Inventory

Type	Model	Description	Quantity
3145	I02	Processing Unit *(512K)	1
	4660	ISC - 3330's	
	6982	2nd Selector Channel	
	6983	3rd Selector Channel	
	7855	3215 Adapter	
	8810	Word Buffer	
3047	01	Power Unit	1
3215	01	Console Printer	1

*Includes 256K of Intel Memory

programming capability in an organization. However, one must be careful to identify subsets of higher level languages in use. The subset is generally less powerful than the complete language. It lacks certain processing capabilities associated with larger primary storage needs. In addition, it may require additional coding to effect the same result.

4. PERIPHERAL EQUIPMENT. An inventory of the supporting peripheral equipment must also be made to provide a more complete picture of productive potential. The availability of such devices as point-of-sale or data communications equipment may indicate somewhat more sophisticated applications and the need for additional management controls. The full impact of these devices cannot be asessed until the currently operational systems are evaluated.

5. UTILIZATION STATISTICS. The utilization statistics are an important part of the survey because they indicate whether or not the hardware is being used to its fullest capacity. A powerful computer that is only partially utilized leaves time available for the development of additional systems. The utilization statistics may be extracted from the job accounting records or output from hardware or software performance monitors. Wherever possible, fluctuations in the processing cycle should also be noted, e.g., conversion to a new data base for all of the corporation's manufactured items. This information would help to explain any unusual increase in hardware utilization required by the massive conversion to the new data structures, etc.

The information collected identifies the available productive capacity of an organization. Some of the data for this segment of the survey may be extracted from an equipment status report detailing all of the equipment currently installed and related costs.

The Data Processing Organization

Though the manager has familiarized himself with the general organizational setting and the productive power of the hardware and software, he must also study the data processing function that is responsible for maintaining that capability. To gather data for this segment of the survey requires an evaluation of (1) organization and manning and (2) standards.

1. ORGANIZATION AND MANNING. The survey of this element begins with an analysis and documentation of the organization chart. In addition to delineating the lines of authority and responsibility, the chart should indicate the manning strength for each position. This data provides the manager with an assessment of the manpower resource capability.

A job description for each position must also be included in the documentation to support the organization and manning data. This data provides the data processing manager with an assessment of the manpower resource capability. As indicated in chapter 3, the manager still has the problem of matching personnel skills with the tasks to be executed.

Some organizations maintain confidential or semiconfidential personnel authorization and manning reports, which classify the positions within data processing by functional activity. These reports may include the person's salary or salary range for that position, plus a job description. Many of the organizations provide a copy of the overall organization and manning report to the data processing administrator for use by the systems, software, and information systems planning managers. The reports can be useful for feasibility study and project planning purposes.

2. STANDARDS. In this section, the manager is concerned with determining the documentation and performance standards (see chapters 4 and 5) used by the data processing organization. If a good documentation standard has been implemented and is enforced, the analysis of existing and proposed systems will be more effective.

The performance standards are used primarily for planning, scheduling and budgetary purposes. If the performance standards are realistic, they will also serve as an excellent indicator of personnel experience and know-how.

If the organization has a career planning or job progression path chart, then that information too should be included in this section of the survey. This information will provide the manager with some insight into the personnel development plan that has been established for the data processing personnel.

Satellite Organization Interaction

The hardware installed at a satellite function will vary from an input/output terminal to a minicomputer or medium-sized or, in some groups, a large-scale computing system. The software utilized at each of the organizations will also vary. The available productive capacity must be evaluated because of its actual or potential influence on the operational effectiveness of the centralized data processing organization. It must also be determined if the satellite organization is part of a network that shares the resources or the data base. The former may be a time-sharing system or a remote job entry facility. The latter may be a distributed system that permits computers to communicate with each other, providing different resources and services.

The data processing manager must understand the interaction of the satellite facility with his own facility. Often the outputs from the centralized data processing activity are transmitted to the satellite facility for production of a final report or desired output. For example, the payroll data may be processed at the central location and a portion of the output is transmitted to the satellite for preparation of the payroll drafts and statements. Or, a retail establishment may use a data collection device and then transmit inventory data via a telephone line to the central facility for updating of the centralized inventory file and to process stock replenishment for the branch store.

The data processing manager must be aware of the hardware, software, and information processing systems that are operational at the satellite. In some instances, the satellite operations may be part of a contingency plan.

The manager must also be aware of the organization and manning at each satellite facility. In some organizations, the central organization may sometimes use systems and software personnel from a satellite for a project or team.

Information Processing Systems

Gathering data for this segment of the survey may be very time-consuming if adequate documentation of existing and proposed systems is not available. The collected data may be grouped into two classifications: (1) system narratives and (2) quantitative data.

1. SYSTEM NARRATIVES. The desired information must indicate the primary inputs/outputs and the processing performed. This data is available from a system abstract form (see chapter 4). In addition to listing the currently operative applications, the manager must also include those proposed for immediate conversion and future development. Some of this data should be available in the form of preliminary documentation for those applications scheduled for immediate conversion or currently under development. Data on future conversion should be available from the applicable feasibility studies. The manager must also consider those applications related to the activities of the satellite organization.

2. QUANTITATIVE DATA. In an analysis of the current systems, the manager needs to secure input and output volume statistics and actual or estimated processing times. For those systems in the process of conversion, under development, or proposed for future development, the manager should secure estimated processing time. The schedule data will enable the manager to determine the amount of productive time available and required for current and future purposes. Separate statistics should be collected on the involvement of the satellite group in the total process.

Data Processing Hardware/Software on Order/Replacement

This segment of the survey provides an inventory of hardware and software to be installed or upgraded in the future, and the hardware or software that is scheduled for replacement. The listing should include the hardware and software that is under contract and that for which a letter of intent has been executed. Though the latter category is subject to change, it does represent a potential acquisition for planning purposes.

The status of the hardware and software has a direct bearing on the planning, organizing, and coordinating functions; therefore, the manager must secure the specific details of what is scheduled for delivery or release. The information may be grouped into the following categories:

1. Peripheral devices
2. Unit-record equipment

3. Computing equipment

4. Software

1. PERIPHERAL DEVICES. The equipment in this category is designed to support the existing or proposed operational capability. The inventory must indicate the type and quantity on order, proposed application, expected delivery date, special features, maintenance provisions, and costs. The description should be as complete as possible in order to indicate the device capability. For example, the description of a data communications device would include: operating speed, transmission mode, error detection, error correction, transmission code, input/output media, and devices transmitted or received from.

2. UNIT-RECORD EQUIPMENT. The inventory for unit-record equipment is similar to that for peripheral equipment. It may be somewhat simpler because fewer types of devices are involved. The inventory must list the model numbers, quantities on order, special features, proposed use, expected delivery date, maintenance provisions, and costs.

3. COMPUTING EQUIPMENT. Of the three equipment categories this one is perhaps the most complicated, because the hardware descriptions are very detailed. It is suggested that the inventory be presented by component. For example, the central processing unit, input, output, etc., would each be described individually.

4. SOFTWARE. The software listing must identify the operating system, programming languages, and special application packages to be acquired. Included in the listing must be the expected delivery date, brief explanation of the scope, hardware requirements, responsibility for updates, training available, and the applications area to be serviced.

It may be possible to secure some of this information from the equipment status report.

VALUE OF THE SURVEY

The survey in this context provides the data processing manager with meaningful decision-making data. The data gathered should be studied by the data processing manager and his personnel prior to initiating any new development or modification project. This information will help them to define and understand the stated objectives; to establish the checklists used in information gathering; and to help develop the necessary questions and establish the basic rapport when conducting interviews during feasibility studies and systems and software projects. Also, it eliminates the redundant effort in the collection of basic information. Much of this same information is gathered by systems personnel when preparing for interviews, analyzing or modifying an existing information and/or software system, or developing a new system and its associated software requirements.

The data is used to help determine whether the objectives are being accomplished or whether the optimal approach is to be developed within an existing or projected environment.

The value of a survey may be quickly lost, however, if an organization is unwilling to update the information to maintain its currency, relevancy, and accuracy. Maintaining its operational effectiveness will enhance its value in formulating relevant and meaningful approaches and the effective allocation of resources.

Consulting services and management advisory services will generally perform a survey prior to submitting a proposal or after acceptance of a contract. This survey is a preliminary review to familiarize the consultant with the client's organization. These surveys generally focus on the setting of the information processing activity within the overall organization, and its interaction with other functional activities. Depending upon the nature of the proposal or contract, detailed studies of the existing or proposed systems may subsequently be performed.

Review Questions: Group 8A

1. What is the purpose of a survey?
2. Why is it important to gather general information about the organization during the survey process?
3. It has been suggested that, in order to facilitate data gathering, you should extract the organization charts from an employee publication printed last year. What would be your reaction to this suggestion?
4. The equipment status report lists on a single-line entry an IBM 370/138 computer, under the heading of computing equipment. Would this information be adequate for your needs in a survey? Why or why not?
5. What is the value of a system narrative?
6. Why should it be necessary to maintain an inventory of data processing equipment which is on order?

FEASIBILITY STUDIES

A feasibility study can be described as a logical, systematic, and well-documented approach to solving a problem or analyzing a proposal. More aptly, it may be defined as a critical investigation conducted to establish the practical or economic justification, or both, of an idea, standard, technique, software, or hardware. The concept is not new; it has been applied to different problems in varying degrees for many years. Properly executed it becomes a critical examination for determining an organization's needs. The proposal and the existing approach are examined in detail to determine the real justification of a particular approach. The feasibility study also involves an examination of the functional activities that are affected by the proposal and current approach. This provides an insight into the many facets that are often overlooked in preliminary evaluations. For example, what is the effect of the proposal on other functional activities and other systems? A change to one system or software package may have unforeseen consequences on another, if the impact is not reviewed and evaluated. A well-done feasibility study will also involve users beyond the extent of "What would you like?" and "This will solve your problems." The study must encourage the participation and contribution of user personnel directly and indirectly affected by the system. As a result of this critical examination, the analyst will be able to submit to the manager a recommendation that shows the proper cost-benefit relationships of the existing and proposed approaches. This information will enable the steering committee and/or the executive committee to evaluate the effectiveness of the proposal and its impact on the needs and future growth of the overall organization. In some organizations, a feasibility study is referred to as a justification study.

The feasibility study can be used to answer the following types of questions and considerations for an organization:

Whether or not the organization really needs an automated data processing capability

Is an approach technically and/or operationally feasible?

What functions can be automated effectively?

How much and what level of automation can be applied?

What type of hardware to acquire?

What would be the most economical method of acquiring hardware?

Should information processing be performed in-house or at a service bureau?

Should an organization acquire proprietary software products?

What is the most advantageous method of acquiring proprietary software?

How long can an existing hardware configuration continue to meet the needs of an organization?

In analyzing these and many other situations, the feasibility study is basically concerned with an evaluation of the present and future objectives, current operations, and any actual or hypothetical conditions or problems.

To better understand the concept of feasibility studies, it is useful to examine the following categories:

1. Who conducts the study?
2. Objectives of the study
3. The study phases

Who Conducts the Study?

A feasibility study may be conducted by:

1. Management consultants
2. Data processing personnel
3. Study team

1. MANAGEMENT CONSULTANTS. Management consultants may be used to augment an organization's own staff. Or, they may provide the expertise to do a job within a narrow time-frame.

Management consultants will generally provide an impartial, objective study because they are not connected with a particular equipment vendor. A disadvantage may be expense. Consultant rates may range from 2.5 to 3.5 times as much as that paid to an organization's own information processing personnel. However, the consultants provide personnel with the necessary expertise for the limited time required. This is less costly than realigning an organization's own staff to perform the study. Some organizations are fearful of utilizing consultants for specialized projects because they do not wish to have any sensitive data divulged to their competitors. In such situations, it is recommended that the organization prepare and execute a nondisclosure agreement with the consultants.

2. DATA PROCESSING PERSONNEL. An organization may utilize its own information processing specialists to conduct the study. Generally, the organization will attempt to assign personnel to the project who are familiar with the functional area under consideration. This approach may require a realignment of the staff for the term of the project. Some organizations utilize the information systems planning personnel to conduct the necessary studies. In some medium- and large-sized organizations, it is possible to temporarily borrow personnel from a satellite function to participate in the feasibility study.

An organization's own personnel are familiar with the organization and its policies and practices, personnel, and systems. As a result, many of the preliminaries for information gathering may be unnecessary. That information would be gained by reviewing the available survey and systems and software documentation. However, the in-house staff may lack the necessary expertise to perform a successful evaluation of a problem or approach. For example, a staff that is oriented toward batch processing may not be capable of analyzing on-line, interactive applications or hardware.

3. STUDY TEAM. The study team approach brings together a group with varied skills and knowledge, as well as interest in the organization. The team is sometimes referred to as a task force.

The functional area representatives on the study team serve as liaison between the information processing specialists and the activity under consideration. This approach will help to significantly reduce development and implementation costs, and ensure achievement of desired objectives. It will also minimize and/or eliminate user acceptance problems because the users will feel that they are a part of the process and any proposed solution is not being imposed on them. Unfortunately, many systems are designed for the convenience of the hardware and software and not the user. The end result from such a design may lead to poor utilization of a given system, lack of user acceptance, excessive maintenance, and/or chaos. For major systems and software projects, the user representative should be assigned to the project on a full-time basis.

The effectiveness of the study-team approach depends entirely on the use of key personnel to conduct the feasibility study. Subsequently, these same people are utilized in the design, development, and implementation of the recommended approach. Ultimately, the key personnel are reassigned to their functional areas to direct and control the new or modified approach.

There are certain characteristics or qualities desirable for team members participating in a feasibility study:

They should be familiar with the philosophies and objectives of the organization.

The group must have knowledge of accounting and operating methods, as well as legal and audit requirements.

The personnel should be willing to work with details.

They should be imaginative, creative, objective thinkers.

They must consider only the overall needs of the organization.

Obviously, it will be difficult to locate personnel who will meet all of the desired traits or characteristics. However, the executive committee must select persons for this task who will make objective recommendations. The executive committee should also recognize that there may be some need to train the personnel within the study group. This may be necessary because of their lack of familiarity with feasibility study techniques and with the design and operation of data systems.

The composition of the study group and the approach selected will obviously depend upon the scope and objectives of the study; the time available; the type of personnel available; and the budget allocation. An outside source may very often be more objective than an in-house group. However, sometimes these persons too may be pressured into reaching certain conclusions.

Objectives of the Study

The scope and objectives of the feasibility study are generally conveyed to the data processing administrator or manager by letter or memorandum. These objectives provide both a sense of direction for conducting the study and a basis for reviewing progress. As in all management planning, the general objectives must be defined into specific goals. When the definition process has been completed, the specific objectives should be discussed with the executive committee to ensure that the desired goals are being considered. As a result of this discussion the objectives may have to be altered or modified before the actual study is initiated. Sometimes during the study itself it becomes evident that the objectives must be realigned, altered, or modified. This information must be conveyed to the executive committee, along with the practical importance for changing the objectives. A manager should never allow himself to become bound by the objectives when it is evident that some change is necessary. Nevertheless, he needs to be in a position to offer a constructive suggestion when recommending a change. Failure to apply the proper direction in the feasibility study may produce an end result which may be ineffective or of limited value. Among the more typical general objectives may be to:

Reduce clerical cost through reduction of clerical work force

Permit more timely decisions by managers

Reduce high clerical costs by improving the methods of data acquisition and processing

Reduce or eliminate repetitive operations

Evaluate the effectiveness of existing manual and mechanized operations

Reduce or eliminate processing backlogs

Provide new approaches to complex or repetitive computational problems

Review and improve schedules

Measure the performance of a system

Evaluate a software package acquisition

Evaluate the alternatives for acquiring hardware

Develop a data base for all manufactured items

Consider the implementation of computer communications network to expedite inputs from the branch offices

The list by no means exhausts the realm of possibilities. The general objectives must be defined in order to answer the what, why, how, who, when, and where (see chapter 1). These answers must be further broken down into the tasks and operations needed to form the structural framework for the feasibility study.

For example, a memorandum is sent from the executive committee to the data processing manager instructing him to, "Develop and implement an interactive billing and collection system." To define the scope of this objective, the data processing manager must raise the following questions:

Why is this request being made?

Is this a new development or modification of an existing system?

Is this system a subsystem?

What is the expected life of the system?

What functional areas are to be affected?

What are the performance requirements?

What is the required user reponse time?

What resource limitations have been placed on the system?

What time-frame has been allocated for the project?

The responses to these questions will enable the manager to establish the structural framework for the collection of data in the study. The structural framework will specify the tasks and operations for such activities as:

Identifying the necessary functions to be carried out

Description and analysis of the existing system

Determination of required inputs, outputs, and files

Evaluation of alternative approaches

These tasks and operations are not generalized headings because during the definition process the manager will have made certain relevant determinations. For example, in the billing and collection system, some of the required functions may include the following:

An accounting for the charges, allowances, credits, and adjustments

The capability of preparing a follow-up on overdue accounts

The ability to retrieve open accounts

The ability to prepare various management reports, such as a daily trial balance, aging of accounts by stated periods, etc.

This represents but a partial listing of the required functions in a simple billing and collection system. However, as a result of these predeterminations, the study personnel have an awareness of the objectives, scope, and purpose of the study. The information will also enable the study team leader to formulate an approach to the study and a schedule and to identify the resource requirements for the required fact gathering and evaluations. In many organizations, the results of these findings are coordinated with the user function managers, the data processing manager, the steering committee and/or the executive committee. The coordination is necessary to ensure that the necessary budgetary funds are allocated to the study and that an appropriate priority is assigned to the project.

The Study Phases

When the specific objectives have been defined and detailed the feasibility study may be initiated. A basic feasibility study may be composed of six phases:

1. Analysis of existing system or approach
2. Determination of current costs
3. Development of an alternative approach
4. Determination of the proposed costs
5. Advantages and disadvantages
6. Report of findings and recommendations

ANALYSIS OF EXISTING SYSTEM OR APPROACH

The foundation of the feasibility study is an analysis of the present system or approach to a given problem. This phase can be termed as the fact finding or fact gathering phase. It is during this initial phase that the personnel study the current objectives, organizational structure, policies, practices, documentation, schedules, machine utilization, quality of outputs, files, volumes, qualitative controls, work flow, performance requirements, system constraints, internal and external influences, and procedures. The information gathered becomes the basis of comparison for subsequent phases in the feasibility study.

In analyzing the existing system, the analyst and/or study team must determine in detail what is being performed, when it is being done, who performs the work, the complexity of the process, and why the work is being performed. This process results in an in-depth analysis of each function and a determination of its relationship to the total system. In addition to analyzing the operations, the analyst and/or study team also gathers data on volumes, frequencies, and manhour requirements. Also, the management controls employed in the system must be identified and evaluated.

The information is collected by interviewing the managers and the personnel of the affected functional activities. However, prior to initiating the necessary interviews, the analyst must review the available survey data. This will provide the interviewer with background information for defining the problem and planning the interview approach and questions. This information helps the analyst and/or study team establish a basic rapport for the interview because he/they will have a preliminary understanding of the functional area being evaluated.

The information in the interviews should be gathered through the use of standardized checklists (see Figure 8.4), developed for such items as inputs, outputs, data sets, etc. The collected information must then be documented in detail for a subsequent evaluation in this phase. This information enables the analyst and/or study team to determine input, output, performance and reporting requirements, the external and internal influences and constraints affecting the system, current operating costs, and what is currently being accomplished.

The documented data must be collated and correlated to provide the basis for analyses and decisions in this and succeeding phases of the feasibility study. In concluding this phase the analyst and/or study team will be in a position to answer several important questions about the existing operation. These are:

Are current needs and objectives achieved?

Should new or modified objectives be developed?

What types and volumes of input, output, and reference data are being used?

What is the effect of the current system on the user and operating personnel?

What is the efficiency of the existing system or approach?

1. What data files are currently in existence?
2. What is the purpose of each data file?
3. What media forms are used for the existing files?
4. What is the record arrangement in each file?
5. What information is recorded in each file?
6. What is the sequence of each file?
7. What data validation methods are required?
8. What file or data conversion is required?
9. What data is redundant in each file?
10. Do the files interface with any other files?
11. What are the file maintenance requirements?
12. Who is responsible for the file maintenance?
13. What is the frequency of file updating?
14. What is the volume of transactions in the update?
15. Where are the data files located?
16. Is there any back-up provision or security requirement for the existing data files?
17. What management controls are used in the file update process?
18. What is the frequency of references or inquiries to each data file?
19. What reports or outputs are prepared from the data files?
20. What systems utilize these data files?
21. What programs utilize these data files?
22. What is the file retention period?
23. What header and trailer labels are used in each file?
24. What is the file mnemonic?
25. What are the record mnemonics?

Figure 8.4 Standardized checklist for data gathering files

What is the processing sequence of the applications and their input/output requirements?

What is the adequacy and timeliness of user and operating instructions?

What is the productivity for each application?

What is the quality of the user reports?

What is the competence level of the user and operating personnel?

What is the output distribution?

What control procedures are used and what is their effectiveness?

What is the effectiveness of the system's testing and maintenance procedures?

What are the areas of difficulty, if any?

Must the system be totally automatic?

Is there too much manual intervention or not enough?

Can an additional workload be imposed on the existing system?

Can additional hardware be accommodated?

A critical evaluation of the system may disclose that it is no longer responsive to the user's needs. Therefore, new or modified objectives may have to be developed. Or, the existing system will have to be modified or redesigned. The redesign, however, may not necessarily require an automated system.

Information on input, and reference data types and volumes will enable the analyst and/or study team to calculate the costs for phase two, as well as potential applications or approach in phase three of the study. In subsequent phases, it may be necessary to translate these requirements into hardware and/or software specifications. At this point, the analyst and/or study team must also evaluate the impact of the present system or approach on the user and operating personnel. The operating personnel are responsible for the functional effectiveness of the system and, therefore, it is necessary to determine its ease of operation and flexibility. The effect on the users must be analyzed to determine if the system discourages or deters their use of information processing techniques. Or, are there possibilities for future development or expansion of the system?

DETERMINATION OF CURRENT COSTS

In evaluating any system, it is necessary to ascertain the present operating costs. Subsequently, these will be compared with those in the proposed system to determine which are reduced, eliminated, or increased. The amount of cost data required may vary from one organization to another; therefore, this specification should be made by the executive committee prior to the start of the feasibility study. The cost data should reflect not only the operating costs of data processing but also those of the functions or activities affected by the system. In addition, the amortized one-time costs must be included. A complete cost picture will provide a realistic comparative cost base against any proposed system. There is little justification for applying new or additional resources to a system if only marginal benefits are to be achieved.

Accurate data must be gathered by the analyst and/or study team. This data may be secured from available accounting records or from average cost rates for each element in the system. The average cost method is frequently used for comparative cost data. Figure 8.5 illustrates how composite average rates may be developed for the key punch operator and peripheral equipment operator job classifications. The average does not include any allowance for overtime—a figure that is dependent upon organizational policies regarding overtime pay. Therefore, if utilization of personnel on an overtime basis is required, the values must be reflected in the system's costs.

In addition this phase must include relevant equipment costs, including special features; supplies; amortized one-time costs; operation and maintenance costs for processing, electrical power, and air-conditioning equipment; insurance; space costs; and supporting equipment, such as files, desks, etc.

The current costs will be compared with those in phase four of the study. Also, the costs are a necessary part of the benefit and recommendation data included in phases five and six.

Department	Job Classification	Grade	Number	Base	@ 121.3%	Total	Average Rate
				HOURLY RATE			
105	Keypunch	205	1	3.50	4.25	4.25	
	Operator	203	6	3.06	3.71	22.26	
			7			26.51	3.7871
105	Peripheral	209	2	4.29	5.20	10.40	
	Equipment	207	3	3.92	4.75	14.25	
	Operator	205	2	3.50	4.25	8.50	
			7			33.15	4.7357
105	Control Clerk	206	1	3.73	4.52	4.52	
			1			4.52	4.5200
110	Keypunch	205	1	3.50	4.25	4.25	
	Operator	203	4	3.06	3.71	14.84	
			5			19.09	3.8180
110	Peripheral	207	1	3.92	4.75	4.75	
	Equipment	204	1	3.28	3.98	3.98	
	Operator		2			8.73	4.3650

@ Includes Loading Rate for Overhead Costs

Figure 8.5 Examples of composite average rates of hourly wages for specific job classifications

DEVELOPMENT OF AN ALTERNATIVE APPROACH

The development of an alternative approach may be a complex and time-consuming process because it is concerned with planning for the future. The alternative identifies with considerable clarity the approach to be followed. One method of developing an alternative approach may be through the use of simulation techniques. These techniques facilitate the study of an operation or process without direct analysis of the activity. The analysis is performed by constructing a mathematical model to study a real-life situation. The known factors, the characteristics of the unknown factors, and their relationships are processed through the model to produce some probable outcomes and alternatives. These outputs do not provide a solution in themselves but will help the manager in selecting an optimal approach. The simulation outputs generally take the form of plotted graphs, a listing of numerical values, or narrative descriptions. These differ from the detailed descriptions of a system as described in chapter 4. For data processing purposes, it is possible to simulate the management and operational processes, resource requirements, and schedules within the parameters for a given environment. The technique is frequently used when evaluating the need and placement of data communications facilities.

Or, it may be possible to utilize one of the automated approaches to systems design, such as IBM's TAG or the Hoskyns approach. If simulation or one of the automated approaches is not used, then the analyst and/or study team may describe the system utilizing the traditional manual techniques (see chapter 4).

Many alternative recommendations do not require the use of the simulation or automated design techniques. These recommendations may be for systems or software that require the compilation of data, file maintenance, recordkeeping, or some computations. They must be described in sufficient detail to enable the executive committee and other information processing personnel to understand the proposal. The proposal must identify the objectives; impact upon the existing organization; content and format of all records, files, and outputs; estimates of equipment utilization; and preliminary time estimates for development and implementation.

A suggested outline of the data to be included is as follows:

A broad narrative of the scope of the system and the primary reason or reasons for its development and implementation

A system flowchart illustrating the flow of information through the proposed system

System flowcharts of the subsystems, and macro- and micro-flowcharts for programming solutions

A system abstract (see chapter 4) for the system and each subsystem to identify, in layman's terminology, their aims, functions, and equipment requirements

The inputs, outputs, data elements, records, and files should be described in detail. This segment should also include specimen forms and/or illustrations

In addition, the media types, their source and distribution, and actual or estimated volumes must be specified. For long-term applications, the volume projections should be based on three to five years in advance

The suggested management controls and their importance should also be specified

The estimated development, implementation, equipment utilization, and productivity statistics should also be included; this data will subsequently be used to evaluate the system's impact on the schedule, personnel resources, and costs

The security and back-up requirements for the system should also be specified

Conversion needs and problems should also be specified

A program abstract (see chapter 4) for each program in the system. For an existing program, the form will actually record only its current description. However, for a proposed program it will be a generalization of the software requirements. Subsequently, this information must be completed to reflect actual status of the program

Estimated useful life of the system and/or software based on current and projected needs

Test data and plan requirements and the test time needs

Ease of expansion for future growth needs and changes

Any other constraints or requirements such as training needs, special installation arrangements, or compatibility with existing systems should be identified

Some of the information included may have to be modified or revised prior to or during the development and implementation of the system. However, at this point of the study this information serves to indicate "what" is, and "why" it is necessary. Subsequently, it will be used to identify the relative advantages or disadvantages, or both, of the existing and proposed systems. Also, the information may be used to develop the necessary hardware and/or software requirements.

To increase the usefulness of this phase, the systems and/or software should be listed and identified as initial, new, or future development. Systems and/or software in the initial category are developed and implemented first because they are the simplest, provide the fastest rate of return on investment, or are the ones most important to the organization. In the new category are those systems and/or software projects that may not have been previously developed and implemented due to cost; marginal benefit; lack of resources; or the lack of readiness or the inability of the user organization to effectively utilize the outputs and/or reports. Future systems and/or software are those desired or needed, but not currently as important, or dependent on the development and implementation of another system and/or other software.

Due to a lack of necessary expertise, time, or adequate staff, it may be most beneficial to utilize a consultant for this phase of the feasibility study. For an organization initially entering into automated information processing or substantially enlarging that capability, it may be very beneficial to utilize an outside source for this phase. This may help to ensure that only cost justified systems and/or software are recommended.

DETERMINATION OF THE PROPOSED COSTS

Upon completion of phase three, the analyst must define the new, reduced, increased, or eliminated costs under the proposed alternative. This may be difficult because the analyst may not have access to all of the necessary cost data. Costs for such items as site preparation, special equipment, transportation charges, or hardware may not be immediately available. However, it is possible to obtain a fairly accurate and detailed cost analysis through the following methods:

By visiting the facilities of other organizations—particularly those with similar systems, problems, software, or hardware—information can be gained through discussions with the user, operations and executive committee personnel

By conducting preliminary discussions with representatives of various equipment and software vendors.

By attending demonstrations sponsored by the equipment and software vendors.

By visiting the public or organization library and researching handbooks prepared by one of the advisory services.

By conducting preliminary discussions with a consulting construction engineer or contractor.

The costs in this phase of the feasibility study may be classified as (1) Preinstallation costs or (2) Continuing costs.

1. PREINSTALLATION COSTS. Those costs incurred prior to the implementation of a system, application, software, or installation of hardware are included in this category. Sometimes these costs are called conversion, start-up, one-time costs, nonrecurring costs, or initialization expenses. The major costs in this category are:

  a) Site preparation
  b) Special equipment
  c) Transportation charges
  d) Personnel
  e) Training
  f) Travel
  g) Program, file, and data conversion
  h) Initial supplies
  i) Equipment installation

a) *Site preparation.* These costs are concerned with readying a facility or modifying an existing site. Included are such items as electrical power supply and all wiring; air-conditioning and humidity control; sound conditioning; painting; carpeting; draperies; false flooring; environmental security provisions; fire, water, and smoke detection and control; and emergency lighting.

b) *Special equipment.* This category includes any special equipment needed to support the data processing equipment. Included are such items as electrical power generators and voltage regulators.

c) *Transportation charges.* The cost of delivering equipment to a site must also be listed. Included are any insurance expenses involved in transporting the equipment to the site.

d) *Personnel.* These costs are incurred as a result of employing additional and temporary personnel for systems analysis and development, programming, operations, and training. A significant cost is recruitment and selection—an expensive process (see chapter 3). In addition, the cost of conducting the feasibility study should be included in this segment.

e) *Training.* This can be a major cost item if a massive systems and programming effort is underway or if a totally new information processing concept is being introduced into the organization. Included may be the cost of a training instructor. However, some organizations prefer to include this expense under the personnel cost category.

If training is not provided on-site, this cost category should include the fees, lodging expenses, and personnel transportation costs.

f) *Travel.* This category includes costs incurred in traveling to system- and program-testing sessions, hardware or software demonstrations, or visits to other installations. If specific accountability of all costs is required, it may be necessary to include travel costs for off-site training sessions.

g) *Program, file, and data conversion.* This segment includes costs incurred in converting or modifying the existing programs, and the data and files from one medium to another. An organization may utilize software vendors, a service bureau, or another data processing facility to perform the conversions and modifications. Extensive coding and translation of files may also be necessary, which may require the employment of some temporary clerical personnel and data entry machine operators.

In addition to the machine and personnel requirements, control procedures must be developed and tested to ensure conversion accuracy. This includes input audit programs to check the data elements and record formats. The control costs must be included in this cost category.

The costs of parallel or dual operations should also be included. The overlapping of operations may result in additional equipment, personnel, and supplies costs for the required period of time. In converting to online, or online real-time systems, this item could represent a substantial expenditure.

h) *Initial supplies.* This category includes the purchase of furniture, magnetic tapes, magnetic disks, storage cabinets, punch cards, forms supplies, and other materials necessary to effect implementation of a system or installation of hardware.

i) *Equipment installation.* These are costs that may be incurred in the installation of equipment. Included are such items as utilizing a crane to lift a computer or vault to an upper building location and the removal of windows to facilitate entry of the hardware. This cost category is often overlooked in the determination of proposed costs.

2. CONTINUING COSTS. Continuing costs are often called recurring or supporting costs because they represent a repetitive expenditure of funds to maintain utility and operation of the system, application, software, or hardware. The costs may be classified as:

a) Equipment costs
b) Equipment maintenance
c) Software costs
d) Software maintenance
e) Personnel
f) Supplies
g) Utilities

h) Space

i) Insurance

j) Transportation

a) *Equipment costs.* This category includes the expenses incurred in acquiring and utilizing the unit-record, computing, online and offline peripheral, and auxiliary equipment. These costs may have to be identified and listed by projected installation dates. For example, on a long-term project certain pieces of hardware are initially installed. Subsequently, additional components or devices are added as the necessary systems or programs are ready. Therefore, only the actual equipment cost for each phase of the project should be shown.

b) *Equipment Maintenance.* This cost item includes the service charges for preventative and emergency maintenance performed on the information processing and special equipment used to support the operations function. The costs in this category are the fixed annual contract prices negotiated to provide maintenance for leased and purchased equipment.

c) *Software costs.* The costs of acquiring operating systems, programming languages, utilities, and applications software are included in this segment. The expenses are itemized by the type of software to be acquired.

d) *Software maintenance.* The expenses incurred in maintaining the acquired software are shown in this segment. Included would be the costs of related documentation.

e) *Personnel.* These are the salary and fringe benefit costs for the managers, systems analysts, programmers, and operations personnel required to provide continued support for the system, software, and hardware. Where personnel outside of the data processing function are required to support an information processing and/or software system, they too should be included in this expense category.

For example, a data entry clerk may be employed by a hospital in each ward or floor wing to ensure greater input accuracy at a data entry terminal. Though this clerk assists the medical personnel, her primary function is to ensure accurate recordkeeping. Her salary and fringe benefits must be included as a system cost.

f) *Supplies.* The supplies in this category are those required to maintain the operating efficiency of a system, software, or hardware. They include such items as printer forms, punch cards, magnetic tape, magnetic disks, microfilm, and magnetic cards. The supply needs may be calculated from the input, output, and reference data volumes shown in the study.

g) *Utilities.* When the utility expenses can be identified, these should be included to present a more realistic cost-benefit picture. The cost of telephone, telegraph, coaxial cable, leased wire, microwave, or satellite service in a data communications or time-sharing system should be included in this category.

h) *Space.* The determination of a floor or area space cost may be more relevant to the installation of hardware than a system. However, if the implementation of a system requires the specific allocation or acquisition of space, this cost should be reflected here.

When an organization establishes off-site record storage facilities on a lease or rental basis, the cost should be included in this category. If a facility is specially constructed or acquired for that function, the cost may be shown as a one-time cost under site preparation or a more specific category.

i) Insurance. The expenses incurred to provide such insurance protection as fidelity bonds, and equipment or records policies, must be included in this segment. However, it should not include equipment transportation insurance.

j) Transportation. Transportation expenditures may result from the implementation of a system or installation of hardware. Expenses may be incurred for such essential activities as transporting records and documentation to an off-site storage area; transporting inputs and outputs to and from a processing center such as a service bureau; transporting personnel, inputs, outputs, and supplies to and from an off-premises processing facility; to expedite the disposition of outputs and reports to a user; or to expedite inputs for processing.

ADVANTAGES AND DISADVANTAGES

At this point, the analyst must objectively identify the relative advantages and/or disadvantages of the present approach and those expected from the proposed approach. He should detail specifically how the advantages provide for an effective goal-attainment process. The impact of the disadvantages must also be made clear.

The following represents an extract from the advantages listed in an actual feasibility study:

The proposed production control system will improve the competitive position of the organization by:

Reducing clerical effort.

Reducing the number and frequency of errors generated by manual processing.

Significantly reducing the work force.

Maintaining a realistic economic inventory level.

Increasing stock status reliability.

Effecting more efficient manufacturing operations.

Enabling management to obtain reports on a regular and timely basis.

The advantages listed imply a great many accomplishments. However, they do not specify how these advantages will contribute to the more effective accomplishment of the production control objectives. For example, it fails to indicate how more efficient manufacturing operations will occur. In this particular organization, more efficient and economical operations may result from reducing the number of machine setups which will ultimately reduce scrap losses. Improved stock status reliability and economical ordering depend on computerized determination of raw material requirements, automated preparation of purchase requisitions, and more frequent updating of inventory records.

The study listed no advantages for the present system and no disadvantages for the proposed. The following, however, were listed as disadvantages of the existing system:

"A large clerical work force is required.

Sophisticated inventory control methods are lacking.

System is a production reporting system."

The disadvantages do not include any specifics to identify the problems. The large clerical work force is the result of the system's excessive paper handling requirements. The statement regarding the lack of sophistication in inventory control is unclear. The present system utilizes economical ordering (EOQ) models in the inventory control procedures except for a bill of materials explosion. This, however, is due to the lack of a larger computing configuration.

The comparative advantages of a proposed system must adequately justify the application of new or additional resources. The benefits must significantly exceed the costs involved. The actual commitment of resources is a decision by the executive committee. However, the information processing specialists will be responsible for identifying the impact on the organization; applications or systems suitable for immediate or future development; optimal equipment; adequacy of available resources; expected economies; and probable procedures.

REPORT OF FINDINGS AND RECOMMENDATIONS

Basically, the report is a written proposal, based on conclusions reached by the study participants. This proposal should be clear and accurate so that the executive committee can effectively evaluate current and future operations and objectives. The final report should be factual, concise, and direct, including adequate supporting documentation. It should emphasize the strengths and weaknesses of the proposed system or approach to allow adequate consideration by the steering committee and/or executive committee. The report should also include the signatures of those persons who conducted the feasibility study, together with a comment that the group has been impartial.

The report should contain the following information:

1. Definition of task
2. Objectives
3. Summary of current system
4. Description of proposed system
5. Estimated work load
6. Equipment configuration and specifications
7. Costs and benefits
8. Personnel
9. Timetable
10. Summary of findings

1. DEFINITION OF TASK. This is a broad narrative description of the task. It is a general statement indicating the extent of the study, the approach, and the

functional activities affected. The following, for example, represents an extract from a feasibility study:

> "The purpose of this study was to analyze the existing billing and collection system; correct the associated problems; and evaluate the need for electronic data processing support. The first step involved an in-depth analysis of the system, its associated functions, tasks, and methods. The collected information was analyzed to locate the problem areas. Subsequently, the problems were identified as to their nature and effect on the total system. The use of electronic data processing was also evaluated as an alternative approach.
>
> Affected by the study were the Bookkeeping, Billing, Credit, Legal, and Audit Departments."

2. OBJECTIVES. A description of the general scope and specific objectives of the feasibility study should follow the introduction. This identifies the basis from which the study was initiated and the direction of development for a proposed system or approach. The definition of the objectives should agree with that originally stated by the executive committee. To facilitate understanding, the general and specific objectives are listed separately.

3. SUMMARY OF CURRENT SYSTEM. A summary of the current system or approach and its objectives is also necessary. A critical evaluation of the existing system or approach may reveal that it is no longer responsive to the user's current or projected needs. The specific deficiencies and their impact on the organization must be identified. This information will enable the analyst and/or study team to recommend a modification of objectives and/or the system or a total redesign of the existing system or approach. The recommendation for redesign or modification of the system or approach does not necessarily require an automated technique. This information can be used by the steering committee and/or executive committee to determine whether an alternate approach will improve or correct a condition with limited or no expenditure of funds required for new equipment or systems design.

4. DESCRIPTION OF PROPOSED SYSTEM. Also to be included is a detailed description of the proposed system or approach indicating how it will correct or supplant present or future deficiencies. The description should indicate what would be done, when would it be done, who would do the work, how would the work be done, where would it be done, and why would it be done. This detail is necessary to provide the executive committee with an understanding of the proposal. Also, the details are necessary for the complete development of a system when project approval is granted by the steering committee and/or executive committee.

The description should be fully documented (see chapter 4). These documents may subsequently be used for determination of equipment specifications.

5. ESTIMATED WORK LOAD. An estimate of the work load for each system, application, or approach must be included. The estimates should include proposed man-hour and schedule requirements and volume data. The estimated work load should be projected on a three- to five-year basis to reflect a more realistic assessment.

6. Equipment configuration and specifications. A description of the equipment configuration and specifications required should also be included. However, unless an equipment vendor or consultant has been involved in the feasibility study, this segment may be a very rough generalization. The proposed configuration is determined on the basis of input and output types, storage requirements, processing sequences, and work load volume. A processing estimate may be made for each system by utilizing estimated computer speeds. Rerun, handling, and setup time must also be added to the processing time estimates.

Generally these time estimates tend to underestimate the actual requirements because of inadequate speed formulae and incomplete system development. However, the estimates provide fairly accurate data on the operation's personnel requirements, equipment costs, projected total work load, and adequacy of the proposed equipment configuration.

This segment should also identify why the particular hardware is needed. If a recommendation is made for a particular device and/or vendor, the reasons for the choice must be included.

The software requirements (operating system, languages, utilities and applications packages) are also included in this segment. The requirements must be detailed to ensure that the vendor will fully understand your needs, e.g., not merely stating COBOL but ANSI COBOL, if that is what has been requested.

7. Costs and benefits. A comparative cost-benefit chart of the present and proposed system is an essential element of the final report. The chart should identify the current costs; those to be eliminated, reduced, or increased; and new costs generated by the proposed system. The chart should include the costs and benefits of the data processing activity and those of the function affected by the system.

The chart should show specifics, not broad statements. The dollar value attributed to the costs must be reasonable and valid. The same rule should apply to the benefits indicated. There generally is no problem with tangible benefits because a dollar value may be attributed to them. Often the tangible benefits are subdefined into direct and indirect benefits. The former represent the savings derived from such items as the elimination of manpower, reduction of equipment costs, or a decrease in supplies expenses. The indirect benefits are generally more difficult to identify. However, diverting the use of office or warehouse space or furniture for other needs may be described as an indirect benefit.

Most organizations require that a pay-back period be projected. The pay-back may be calculated by dividing the sum of the nonrecurring costs by the estimated annual savings. The result will be the number of months or years required to recover the initial cost.

The intangible benefits are those that should be subjected to the most scrutiny. The benefits are often listed in the cost-benefit charts as improvements in the management of a function or organization. However, the listings make no attempt to apply a quantitative value to these improvements or an estimated probability of attainment. This lack of quantification is unrealistic because the intangible benefits have some effect upon the organization. For example, it is frequently stated that increased costs will be avoided through the installation of information processing equipment. This statement is much too broad and has very little merit. The analyst must identify what costs would increase and the value of the cost avoidance.

After evaluating the comparative data, the executive committee should be able to determine if the benefits to be derived outweigh the costs and disadvantages.

8. PERSONNEL. The personnel segment of the final report is often very closely scrutinized by the executive committee. Primarily, the group is concerned with the impact of the proposal upon the organization. The steering committee and/or executive committee will be concerned with knowing:

If there are any proposed changes to the basic organization structure

If the changes require a realignment of functional responsibilities

If there will be any displacement of personnel

If the displaced personnel can be retrained and/or reassigned to other positions

If additional information processing specialists must be recruited

If additional training must be provided for the existing information processing and user personnel

If the user is willing and ready to interact in the system or approach

With this information, the steering committee and/or executive committee will be able to determine what plans or actions are necessary to minimize any adverse reactions and to ensure the success of the proposal.

A summary of the personnel requirements under the proposed system or approach and brief job descriptions should be included. Salary structures for each position and recruitment, selection, and training costs should also be indicated in order to facilitate cost analyses.

9. TIMETABLE. A proposed timetable indicating when a system, application, or approach will be operational should be enclosed. This schedule should indicate the approximate dates for complete development of a system, application, or approach; installation of equipment; and implementation of the proposal. The schedule should be graphically illustrated by utilizing a GANTT chart, PERT network, or a listing of tasks and events. In addition, the time requirements for file and data conversion, parallel operations, and site preparation should be included.

If a modular approach is recommended, the time-frame and the reasons for choosing this approach must be included.

10. SUMMARY OF FINDINGS. The summary represents the recommendations to the executive committee by the study participants. It should represent the best method for accomplishing a desired objective, not just an alternative merely for the sake of change.

In preparing this segment, the analyst and/or study team must indicate if their proposal represents a feasible approach and one that will support the decision-making needs of the organization.

The feasibility or justification study is an in-depth analysis and evaluation of an existing or proposed approach. The data is collected through interviews, observations, and study of existing documentation, policies, and practices. The data collected will provide information on the scope and objectives of the approach, performance requirements, the internal and external influences, constraints, required interfaces, and current method. When the information has been assembled, the study participants must evaluate it to identify and locate any operational problems. Subsequently, the study participants must determine if it will be necessary to develop and evaluate an alternative concept. In the process, they will also develop comparative cost and benefit data. Ultimately, the study participants will make recommendations to the executive committee for the committee's evaluation and approval. The recommendations do not contain the detailed design or implementation procedures. After approval is granted, the detailed development, design, and implementation of the approved concept must be performed.

Review Questions: Group 8B

1. Define the term "feasibility study."
2. Why must feasibility-study participants be creative and objective thinkers?
3. Why is the study of the present system such an important part of the feasibility study?
4. What information should the final report of a feasibility study contain?

EXECUTIVE DECISION AND RECOMMENDATION DEVELOPMENT

Executive Committee Decision

When the feasibility study has been completed and presented to the executive committee, a decision must be made by the committee to accept, modify, or reject the recommendations. Despite the recommendations made, the ultimate decision must be made by the executive committee. It is only this group that can direct the allocation and application of resources based on need and priorities. Very little justification exists for applying new or additional resources to a system or approach that is functioning satisfactorily, unless a significant cost-benefit advantage can be achieved.

The decision may be based on the following considerations:

1. Equipment utilization
2. Software utilization
3. Expansion potential
4. Personnel requirements

5. Systems or applications

6. Overall cost or benefit

1. EQUIPMENT UTILIZATION. If hardware is recommended, the two prime considerations are need and capacity. The executive committee must determine why the equipment is necessary and if such an acquisition is in the best interests of the organization.

Where there is no prior experience with equipment the evaluation will be more difficult. The committe must determine if the functions to be automated require the size, type, and cost of equipment proposed. A careful analysis of the proposed information processing systems must be made.

Where additional equipment acquisition or replacement is recommended, the evaluation may be somewhat less difficult but no less important. The committee must determine if the proposal is due to the presence of "fill jobs." Very often these filler systems are not cost-justified, or they have not been approved by the executive committee. The fill jobs tend to find their way to the hardware because of the pressure to show high equipment utilization and justify the budget. Also, systems with marginal cost or benefit justification are automated because the information processing personnel are interested in cultivating new users. They regard these as minor investments with the optimistic view that they will get the big jobs later. However, these fill jobs may also consume productive time in the operating schedule. Consequently, they inhibit implementation of more important systems due to a lack of available machine time.

The proposed size, type, and capacity must also be carefully scrutinized to determine if this hardware will adequately support the needs of the organization. The judgment may be difficult to make because the proposed configuration is subject to change. However, the preliminary design information included in the feasibility study will provide a reasonable approximation of basic hardware needs.

The committee should question the adequacy of storage and processing capacity. These items may affect the data handling and output capability of the hardware. Very often, study participants will recommend unrealistically smaller or less powerful equipment to gain approval. This argument represents very often shortsighted thinking in that subsequent upgrading to a more desirable level may generate unnecessary costs and problems. For example, in an organization viewed by this author, the study participants recommended a card-oriented computer rather than the tape-oriented configuration that was both necessary and justified. Consequently, all of the information processing systems were less effective than desired because of the resultant lack of storage and processing capability. After two years of ineffective operation, the organization added the tape processing capability to their existing configuration. Virtually all of the programs had to be rewritten to take advantage of the tape concepts. If the tape-oriented computer had been recommended and approved initially, expenditures for programming, system design, documentation, training, etc., could have been minimized.

2. SOFTWARE UTILIZATION. If software is to be acquired, the two primary considerations are cost and reliability. The organization is interested in acquiring software that will perform the necessary tasks, require nominal maintenance and be available at a reasonable cost. In performing the evaluation, the executive committee must determine what functions the software will perform and what areas of the organization will be serviced. In addition, the hardware requirements must be considered and evaluated. If additional hardware is required, the acquisition may reduce the anticipated benefits. The executive committee must also determine what human and budget resources will be required to implement and subsequently support the software.

Another factor to be considered is the amount of training that will be provided by the vendor and required internally to implement, use, and maintain the software. Internal training will be a "must" in order to give the software personnel an opportunity to utilize the software immediately. There is an additional problem for the executive committee and the data processing manager. Software personnel may feel threatened by the acquisition of software from a vendor. The manager must convince the personnel that the acquisition of vendor software will enable the staff to perform other tasks at a higher creative level.

The feasibility study will undoubtedly contain a comparison of costs for the executive committee, showing the anticipated costs and benefits of having a vendor develop the software rather than using in-house personnel or using in-house personnel and having some of the tasks performed by a subcontractor.

3. EXPANSION POTENTIAL. The executive committee must resolve whether the new system or approach will adequately meet present and future needs. This is not a simple task. The system or approach selected must provide for growth in the organization of tomorrow. This growth may be the result of organizational expansion, or increases in the services or product lines offered. The most direct and immediate impact of such an occurrence may be an increase in the volume of work. The organization's growth may also require the development of additional subsystems or more sophistication in the systems and hardware currently used. The executive committee is in the best position to determine flexibility needs because they have an overall view of the organization, its needs and objectives.

If a proposed solution is found to have limited expansion potential, then the executive committee must determine its durability. How long will the proposed concept support the needs of an organization? If the value justifies the cost of implementation, an interim system or approach may be acceptable. The same critical evaluation must be applied when appraising a proposed hardware configuration. How long will it support the needs of the organization? The same critical evaluation must be applied when appraising proposed hardware.

4. PERSONNEL REQUIREMENTS. The personnel requirements for the proposed alternative must also be analyzed. The analysis must consider the cost-benefit factors and impact upon the organization. Both of these considerations are interrelated. Any changes to the organization will affect the cost-benefit picture. The costs may result from structural changes to the organization, realignment

of responsibilities, recruitment and selection, training and retraining, and displacement of personnel. The impact of these changes may be very pronounced upon an organization. Displacement and/or reassignment of personnel, for example, are potential problems. Therefore, the executive committee must consider what measures are necessary to minimize or limit the negative or adverse effects of any changes.

The staffing requirements may change as a result of the completed design. However, the executive committee cannot afford to wait until such time before considering or developing plans to anticipate any contingencies which may arise.

Very often, only the cost-benefit picture is evaluated. Furthermore, this evaluation is limited to the ratio's effect on the data processing activity. However, this is but one part of the report and it fails to provide a complete cost-benefit or impact analysis.

5. SYSTEMS OR APPLICATIONS. The executive group must carefully study the system, application, or approach involved. Initially, the evaluation is concerned with a study of the system documentation or approach narrative. This documentation will indicate such data as:

A layman's description of the system or approach

Identification of the inputs, outputs, their sources and destinations

Identification of the management control, software, and equipment requirements

The flowchart should also be analyzed to evaluate the work flow, media utilized, processing activity, and control points. The graphics will provide for a faster understanding of the proposal. This understanding is reinforced by the abstracts.

Where a number of systems or approaches are involved, the executive committee must evaluate the proposed items. Are those which affect current, immediate, and future needs included? Are the proposals properly classified? Which are most urgent? Which have been problems in the past?

The information on the system or approach will be used to help evaluate the proposed equipment, software, and the expansion potential.

6. OVERALL COST OR BENEFIT. All of the factors previously discussed affect the overall cost-benefit evaluation. The executive committee must determine if a satisfactory cost-benefit relationship will result from adoption of a recommended proposal. The costs associated with the system or approach must not exceed the benefits to be derived. The benefits, in most instances, are actually negative costs—reductions in hardware rentals, personnel salaries, and supplies. In most organizations, the emphasis is on tangible or actual costs and savings. This is not an unrealistic position. Too frequently, new systems are developed or hardware acquired on the basis of intangible savings—savings or benefits that, for the most part, are generalizations but not quantified. The costs and benefits must be quantified in order to facilitate effective decision making. However, the

values attributed to these factors must be valid and reasonable. The costs of the feasibility study, and those of the design, development, and implementation of the approach or system, must be offset by the benefits or annual savings. The executive committee needs to determine if the cost of the proposal can be absorbed from operating revenues within a reasonable period of time. The committee will not be willing to dip into the capital surplus to support a proposal.

Following an analysis of the feasibility study, the executive committee must either reject, modify, or approve the proposal. If it votes for rejection, then either the project is terminated, only to be discarded, or held in abeyance for subsequent approval. Should the committee elect to modify the proposal, then parts of it may not be accepted or the committee will recommend a different timetable and implementation approach; this will frequently happen when a proposal involves a massive system, such as a management information system. The modifications may be required because the proposal does not blend with the long-term objectives; new performance requirements or constraints are introduced; or limited monetary resources are available. To facilitate development and implementation, the modified proposal may be divided into phases.

If the proposal is approved, then the planning for development and implementation of the system, or approach must be initiated. If hardware/software acquisition is part of the approved proposal, the development of specifications for the vendors must then be undertaken. Ultimately, the vendor proposals must be investigated by the systems personnel and/or advanced planning and development personnel before a contract for equipment acquisition is executed.

Developing the Approved Recommendation

Following the recommendations of the executive committee, the requirements of their proposal must be finalized. The finalization of requirements is not to be misconstrued as an applications analysis. The form of the new system or approach has already been determined during the third phase of the feasibility study—development of an alternative approach. During that phase, the required goals, functions, performance requirements, constraints, interfaces, processing modes, and input/outputs for a new system or modified approach had been determined. The development and evaluation of an alternative concept must be accomplished at that time in order to prepare a realistic cost-benefit picture for the committee. After the proposal has been approved, these design requirements are briefly verified before any final design is initiated. This process is often described as completion of system analysis or completion of system requirements. The verification step or process is necessary because of the length of time required to conduct a feasibility study and secure a decision from the executive committee. During this time lag, changes may occur within the environment that may impose new requirements or constraints upon the proposed system or approach. The verification also enables the analyst to secure a sign-off on the project requirements for a functional activity. The sign-off is necessary to ensure that the requirements remain static and not fluid. Too frequently, project schedules are overrun because the requirements remain in a constant state of flux. The verification process also helps to maintain a channel of communications between the information processing personnel and functional activity. Very often after interviews are completed, the functional activity is unaware of the status of the project until system testing or conversion is initiated.

After the final requirements have been established, the project development and implementation schedule will also be finalized. This schedule will facilitate the completion of the design specifications; establishment of the user procedures; development of conversion procedures; preparation of vendor specifications; preparation of the necessary computer programs; training of personnel; system testing; data and file conversion; parallel testing; and project implementation.

(Implementation planning and preparation, plus the preparation of vendor specifications, are discussed in chapter 9. Additional data on systems, programming, and training tasks; time requirements; budgets; and documentation are given in chapters 3, 4, 5, 6, and 10. Site planning is covered in chapter 7.)

Review Questions: Group 8C

1. What factors are utilized by the executive committee to evaluate a final report and feasibility study?
2. Why must special consideration be given to the personnel impact on the organization?
3. What is the value of providing documented data for the executive committee concerning a proposed system?

SUMMARY

This chapter has been devoted to suggesting how an organization should determine whether, to what extent, and how or how not to utilize a proposed system, application, software, hardware device, idea, or standard. There are many considerations that must be resolved before any decision is made. Therefore, a uniform method for investigation and documentation of each proposal should be followed.

The survey described in this chapter is not synonymous with the feasibility study. The survey is an updated document intended to provide preliminary information about the organization and its setting. It is the source of background information for fact-gathering interviews conducted during a feasibility study and systems analysis. This data enables the analyst to better understand the functional activity affected and to develop the topics or questions for the interviews.

A feasibility study is a logical, systematic, and well-documented approach to solving a problem or analyzing a proposal. Properly executed, it becomes a critical examination for determining an organization's needs, and the cost-benefit relationships of existing and proposed approaches.

The feasibility study begins with an analysis of what is currently being done.

This indicates what type of information is being processed; where it comes from; where it goes; who uses it; why the processing is done; and how the information is processed. This process is then evaluated to determine its responsiveness to current and future needs and objectives. If any deficiencies are found, these must be identified and evaluated to determine if a correction or new design must be developed and implemented.

If an alternative approach is necessary, it should be detailed for proper review and development. The detailed documentation should include flowcharts, abstracts, record layouts, and work-load statistics.

The analysis needs to include a cost-benefit comparison. It must be determined if the benefits to be derived from the proposal surpass the costs involved. Ultimately, the advantages and/or disadvantages of the present and proposed systems have to be objectively identified. The advantages of the proposed system must indicate how they will improve the present goal-attainment process.

The culmination of the study is a recommendation to the executive committee. This group then evaluates how well the proposal suits the needs and objectives of the organization. The committee's task will then be to approve, reject, or modify the recommendation. Approval will mean the preparation of equipment specifications and/or the development and implementation of the completed design.

CASE STUDY 8.1

Raleric Wire Products

The following is a feasibility study conducted for the company by a project team composed of an information processing specialist, a member of the production control department, and a senior merchandise control specialist.

PROPOSAL FOR DEVELOPMENT OF A COMPUTERIZED PRODUCTION AND MERCHANDISE CONTROL SYSTEM

1. Introduction

We believe that progress, which resulted in computers, is a direct result of computer utilization.

We believe that the vast amount of potential savings available can be tapped only through computer utilization.

We have developed our feasibility study based on two applications interacting as one system.

2. Current System

The present system was developed and implemented early in 1962. It utilizes a large clerical work force to handle the clerical needs of the system. To meet the customer requirements, a four-week inventory is maintained. This approach is not very economical.

The current production control system produces weekly reports to indicate the outputs for the current week. However, the cutoff for inputs into the system is Friday A.M. Therefore, there is a slight time lag in reporting actual weekly productive status.

3. Management Information System

Our concept is to be designed as a management information system. This simply means that all information related to the system is contained in the computer for service inquiries and operating decisions. All orders, changes, etc., become inputs to the computer for editing and analysis.

If no errors or exceptions are found, the computer will check the stock levels for the requested item. If available, a select and pack document will be issued. If the item is out of stock, a production request will be issued. When the order is selected and shipped, the information is fed back into the computer. If no shipping notification is received, an exception report is issued.

The information is then available for a variety of analysis reports.

4. Savings

We have estimated the following annual savings to offset the cost of development and to pay for future operation of the system:

Personnel Reduction	$195,000
Office Supplies Reduction	1,500
Scrap Loss Reduction	100,000
Reduction of Inventory Charges	8,000
	$304,500

5. Analysis of Costs and Savings

Data Processing Operating Costs	
Present	$213,700
Proposed	−315,000
Additional Costs	$101,300
Estimated Savings New System	
Estimated Savings	$304,500
Less Additional Operating Costs	−101,300
Estimated Annual Savings	$203,200

6. Proposed Future Applications

The following represent applications to be developed upon completion of the proposed system:

General Ledger
Movement of Personnel
Quality Control Statistics
Industrial Engineering Layouts

7. Implementation Timetable

We anticipate that the system would be operational two years from initiation of the project.

8. Recommendations

—That the proposed system be approved in its entirety. We do *not* recommend partial development because of potential planning, programming, and coordination problems.

—That a computer be placed on order immediately to ensure delivery.

Discussion Questions

1. What are the objectives of the proposed system?
2. What are the advantages and disadvantages of the present.system?
3. What information is available about the proposed application? Is it complete or incomplete? If incomplete, what else is necessary?
4. How effective is the comparative cost analysis in sections four and five?
5. What is the impact of the proposed system on the organization?
6. What is the effect of the proposed future applications on the production and merchandise control system, and on the organization?
7. What is the estimated equipment utilization?
8. In your opinion, how will the executive committee evaluate this study?
9. On the basis of this study, would you recommend approval of the project? Why or why not?
10. Could this feasibility study be improved upon? If so, how? If not, why not?

CHAPTER 9

Hardware/Software
Specifications and
Selection

INTRODUCTION / Following approval of the feasibility study recommendations, the executive committee must determine the best source of acquisition, supply, or development. This is not a simple task. For example,
there are many manufacturers of data processing equipment that produce hardware suitable for most organizations. Each manufacturer offers
a variety of models, and each model has a variety of units. The problem
may be even more complex when an organization has to choose the
source of supply for a desired data processing service (consultants, software, training, facilities management, etc.). Consequently, the number of
interacting variables and suppliers may increase significantly.

The complexity of the selection process requires that the customer,
not the vendor or manufacturer, establish the basis of comparison. The
basis of comparison is written specifications submitted to the vendors
and manufacturers by the customer's organization.

SELECTING VENDORS

Prior to solicitation of vendor proposals, the manager must make certain that
equal opportunity and appropriate consideration is given to all qualified vendors
and manufacturers. It is not in an organization's best interest to forgo the solicitation of proposals. Frequently, a manager will favor a certain vendor or manufacturer because of personal friendship or because of possible personal gain,
previous business exposure, lack of personal expertise, or a belief in the vendor's
or manufacturer's technical ability. Consequently, the manager will never know
whether the feasibility study recommendations can be achieved more economically or efficiently, or both.

The selection process begins with the manager evaluating the prospective
firms from whom he expects to solicit a proposal. The manager must select out

those firms that will be unable to submit a realistic proposal. In addition to identifying the qualified firms, the evaluation process helps to indicate the "most qualified." Selecting the most qualified firms will limit the number of responses and ensure a more realistic analysis of each. The limitation will also make the appraisal process more manageable, expedite the results, and reduce its costs.

The criteria for selection of the most qualified firms are as follows:

1. Type of organization
2. Financial position
3. Experience
4. Personnel proposed
5. Current contracts

1. TYPE OF ORGANIZATION. A manager must be concerned with the stability of the vendor or manufacturer. An organization cannot afford to execute a contract with a firm which will be unable to meet its commitments. In his evaluation, the manager must determine how long a firm has been in business; the number of employees it has; its experience; the location of the sales office; the location of the service office; whether the firm manufactures, designs, and performs its own service or only markets the product or service.

It must be noted that though a firm may be relatively new or small, its capabilities may be strong and effective.

2. FINANCIAL POSITION. The financial stability of an organization is very important. If the firm is in a questionable financial position, it may be unable to complete a contract. Some customers have had to help contracting firms remain solvent in order to complete a project.

Financial data may be secured from annual reports, banks, credit bureaus, and rating organizations such as Dun & Bradstreet.

3. EXPERIENCE. The manager must determine if a potential contractor has the necessary business, technical, functional area, or manufacturing experience to participate in a particular project. The evaluation may help to identify the limitations and capabilities of a firm.

The firm's capabilities in a given project can be ascertained by verifying the references provided to the organization. When verifying the references, the data processing manager should contact the person for whom the contract was performed. This check will enable the manager to secure a description of the project; number of people involved; the approximate man-hours, man-months, or man-years required; and the starting and completion dates for the project.

4. PERSONNEL PROPOSED. This criterion may be used to identify the current limitations and capabilities of a firm. The vendor or manufacturer should provide résumés for the personnel to be involved in the project.

If a firm is new or has not performed on a particular project, the résumés may indicate if the personnel proposed have the necessary background and experience. These people may have performed on a related project while in the employ of another company. To verify these capabilities, the manager should consult previous employers.

5. CURRENT CONTRACTS. During the evaluation process, the manager should request a listing of the contractor's current clients. Armed with this information, a manager should attempt to assess a contractor's current performance and technical capabilities. The assessment is actually made by contacting the various client organizations and soliciting information—the same basic information given above in connection with the experience criterion. The responses will enable a manager to determine if the level of performance and capabilities have remained the same, improved, or regressed. The last situation may occur if a contractor has tried to grow too rapidly or has assumed too many commitments.

The current contracts evaluation offers a manager an excellent opportunity to appraise the abilities of a new organization.

PRELIMINARY EVALUATION OF VENDORS

The manager may evaluate the firms semiannually or annually in order to develop a selected but small "favored suppliers" listing. The listing is generally limited to about ten or twelve firms in each contract type of category—that is, keypunching, software, time-sharing, and so forth. This approach, however, may not be very advantageous because all of the firms on the listing may not be capable of responding to a particular set of specifications. Therefore, it may be more beneficial to retain a somewhat larger listing of firms in each category and then to reevaluate their technical competence prior to each project. To facilitate the reevaluation, the manager supplies the firms with an outline of the task to be performed. This information will enable the firms to respond more specifically to the manager's inquiry.

In either evaluation approach, the manager must ultimately submit the necessary specifications to the selected vendors or manufacturers. This often is referred to as the request for proposal, or RFP process. The number of firms selected for solicitation will depend upon the manager. Many experts feel that from three to ten firms should be approached. Six has been the number cited by many as an optimal figure.

PREPARATION OF SPECIFICATIONS

The requests for proposal, or RFP, must be standardized for each contract category to ensure uniform responses from the potential vendors or manufacturers. The formats for hardware, software, systems, or services will vary somewhat. However, each of these categories is very similar in the following informational areas:

1. General instructions
2. Customer requirements
3. Proposal presentation

General Instructions

The general instructions stipulate the ground rules to be followed in dealing with each and every prospective vendor or manufacturer. The guidelines must be used in order to provide equal opportunity and consideration to all contractors.

a. General objectives
b. Technical coordinator
c. Timetables
d. Benchmarks
e. Method of submission
f. Method of presentation
g. Level of effort expected
h. Required contractual provisions
i. Type of cost proposal desired

1. GENERAL OBJECTIVES. This is a brief statement specifying the desired general objectives of the proposal request. It may also contain a brief description of the task. However, the task will be detailed in the customer requirements segment of the RFP.

2. TECHNICAL COORDINATOR. The manager must select and identify one person to whom all inquiries regarding the request are to be directed.

Due to the complexity and scope of the task, the ground rules may stipulate that all questions must be submitted in writing and properly referenced to the request. Depending upon the nature of the inquiry and the response, copies may be submitted to all other potential contractors. Also, a final date for inquiries may be stipulated here or in the timetable.

3. TIMETABLES. The timetables indicate the dates and times of relevant actions in the request and selection process. This will include dates for briefings, closing date for inquiries, period for benchmark demonstrations, dates for submission of proposals, contractor presentation dates, award date, and desired implementation or installation date.

4. BENCHMARKS. Benchmarks are used to evaluate the ability of a system, software, service, or hardware to perform predefined tasks. When benchmark problems are chosen for evaluation they must be representative of the organization's needs. Generally, they are used to validate any timings or results specified by the contractor. For example, when applied to equipment evaluation, they may measure and analyze the processing capability (e.g., logic, computation); timing needs (e.g., input/output, execution); or equipment requirements (e.g., memory, channels). The benchmark problem or problem mix, and sample or live data, will be submitted to the contractor through the technical coordinator.

The REP may include a request that a presentation be made to demonstrate the capabilities of the hardware, system, software, or service. The timetable will indicate the allowable time period for such presentations. Also, a disclaimer should be included specifying that costs incurred in the preparation and presentation of benchmarks will be borne by the potential vendor or manufacturer.

5. METHOD OF SUBMISSION. The method of submission specifies the number of proposal copies to be submitted and to whom they must be directed. Also, this segment indicates the final data and time for acceptance of proposals. It may also include the statement that no late proposals will be considered.

6. METHOD OF PRESENTATION. Potential contractors are generally invited to make oral presentations. This enables the vendor or manufacturer to point out the significant features of his proposal. Also, it provides the manager with an opportunity to raise any clarifying questions. Presentation dates are stipulated in the timetable.

7. LEVEL OF EFFORT EXPECTED. A brief statement of the level of effort expected can be included in the general instructions. The level can be expressed in terms of man-days, man-months, or dollar value.

Figure 9.1 Sample extract of request for proposal (RFP) general instructions

---

Section I
General Instructions

A. Purpose
   The purpose of this RFP is to solicit proposals for the design and development of an automated Customer Billing and Collection System.

B. Project Coordinator
   All inquiries concerning this RFP are to be directed to:
   Ralph A. Szweda
   Computer Systems Coordinator
   All questions should be submitted in writing, referencing the specific paragraph.

C. Project Timetable
1. Availability of RFP	August 11, 19__
2. Contractors Briefing	August 25, 19__
3. Closing date for inquiries	October 11, 19__
4. Benchmark Presentations	October 2–10, 19__
5. Contractor Proposals Due	November 1, 19__
6. Contractor Presentation	November 6–10, 19__
7. Contract Award	November 22, 19__
8. Desired Installation Date	January 5, 19__

D. Presentations
   Dates for benchmark presentations will be arranged with the Project Coordinator. The bidders are encouraged to make an oral presentation to supplement the written proposal. The dates for such presentations must be arranged with the coordinator.

E. Method of Submission
   The written proposal must be submitted in three bound copies to the Project Coordinator's office before 5 P.M. on November 1, 19__. All supporting graphics and documentation must be included with the proposal.

---

8. Required contractual provisions. A brief statement of the required contractual provisions may be indicated in the general instructions. These should be elaborated upon in the proposed presentation segment. The general instructions may identify the type of provision, such as penalty clauses for late delivery or for nondelivery.

9. Type of cost proposal desired. The type of cost proposal desired should be stipulated in the general instructions to facilitate a contractor's proposed planning. This information may or may not be elaborated upon in the customer requirements segment. The general instructions should stipulate if the proposal should provide for time and expense, fixed price, lease, purchase, etc.

An extract of the general instructions that could be included in an RFP is illustrated in Figure 9.1.

Review Questions: Group 9A

1. Why should the data processing manager be concerned about the financial stability of a potential contractor?
2. What selection criteria would be most applicable to a newly organized software development firm?
3. Who must establish the basis of comparison for vendor proposals?
4. Why is it necessary to formalize the request for proposal?
5. Why should a technical coordinator be named for RFP data dissemination?

Customer Requirements

This section of the RFP provides a statement of the problem; description of the task; or equipment requirements. The actual requirements stipulated will vary depending upon the type of proposal solicited. For example, Figure 9.2 outlines the relevant specifications which may be included in this section of the request for proposal. These specifications are for the acquisition of a complete computer configuration. The specifications may not be as comprehensive for acquisition of individual units such as magnetic disk, data cell, or online terminals.

The requirements in this section of the RFP specify the mandatory and desirable features or characteristics in a proposal. The manager must be certain that what he establishes as a mandatory need is in fact a priority item. There is the danger that by imposing such limitations or constraints one minimizes the probability of soliciting a desired proposal. The vendor or manufacturer must provide for these limitations or constraints in his proposal in order to merit consideration. For example, an organization may stipulate the requirement for an ANSI COBOL capability. If an equipment vendor or manufacturer could not comply with this software requirement, he would be eliminated from the selection process. The imposition of a cost ceiling often inhibits vendors or manufacturers from submitting optimally effective proposals.

Desirable features or characteristics are limitations to a degree. The requirements in this category represent items which would simplify implementation and utilization of the system, software, service, or hardware. Failure by the ven-

General *answers to this comes from functional Specifications.*

These specifications are divided into three parts:

proposal must be divided into these 3 sections.

1. Equipment Specifications
2. Software Specifications
3. Customer Assistance Specifications

1. Equipment Specifications

All responses must be in writing. Supporting technical data and manuals must be included.

identify the hardware

a) Basic desired configuration
b) Optional equipment
c) Software features
d) Data base/teleprocessing features
e) Pricing policy
f) Hardware maintenance provisions
g) Expandability
h) Site engineering
i) Other costs
j) Back-up facilities
k) Error detection, correction and control
l) Installation and delivery dates

optional equipment can also be given.

2. Software Specifications

All responses must be in writing. Supporting technical data and manuals must be included. Include data only on the software and applications packages that are currently available and fully operative. The software must be delivered prior to hardware installation.

What do you expect? What abilities do you want?

a) Operating systems
b) Compiler languages
c) Application packages
d) Utilities

3. Customer Assistance Specifications

All responses must be in writing. Training programs must be adequately described. Résumés of support personnel may be requested.

a) Personnel training
b) Program testing time
c) Systems and programming support

Figure 9.2 RFP customer requirements for hardware acquisition

dor or manufacturer to include a response for a desirable item may or may not result in a penalty. None will result if the potential contractor is able to present an alternative which may better serve the needs of an organization.

The customer requirements section of the RFP may contain the following:

1. Statement of the task or problem
2. Technical requirements

Hardware/Software Specifications and Selection

3. Required cost proposal
4. Compatibility
5. Delivery
6. Customer assistance
7. Reliability

1. STATEMENT OF THE TASK OR PROBLEM. This segment describes the task to be accomplished or the problem to be solved. The manager will have no difficulty in completing this segment for current problems or tasks. However, preparing a statement affecting a future situation may present a more formidable challenge for the manager due to the many uncertainties. The manager must state the task or problem as accurately as possible to ensure the receipt of a proposal which will meet the user's needs efficiently and economically.

2. TECHNICAL REQUIREMENTS. This segment goes beyond the generalized statement of the task or problem. Here the manager delineates the mandatory and desirable characteristics or features to be included in a proposal. The vendor's or manufacturer's responses should indicate the technical characteristics of the hardware; the available software support in the form of operating systems, utility programs, programming languages, and applications packages; and assistance in the form of test time, maintenance, training, documentation, and so forth. The response data becomes an important part of the subsequent cost-performance evaluation.

3. REQUIRED COST PROPOSAL. Preliminary data about the required cost proposal should be included in the ground rules in the general instructions section. This segment will indicate the desired detailed cost breakdown for cost-performance analyses.

4. COMPATIBILITY. Compatibility requirements for hardware, software, or performance may be included in the RFP to ensure interaction with an existing environment. The requirements are an attempt to improve the cost-effectiveness of the potential contractor's proposal. Also, their inclusion may minimize the impact of any change and the time needed to implement the selected proposal. Traditionally, hardware compatibility has been required when acquiring peripherals or upgrading within a given vendor's equipment line. This is somewhat unrealistic because the customer could be certain of securing electronic compatibility and to some degree logical compatibility. The latter could be readily achieved with some additional programming effort. However, the traditional requirements are not entirely valid for plug-to-plug peripherals. The data processing manager must stipulate the necessary hardware, software, and performance compatibility with the existing hardware configuration. The requirements are necessary to secure both electronic and logical compatibility and avoid degradation of the operating characteristics. Hopefully, the manager will secure better performance as a result of faster response times, and improved device reliability at a lower cost.

Software compatibility is often stipulated in order to avoid reprogramming.

Within a vendor's line of computers, the general requirement is for upward compatibility. This mode of compatibility will generally ensure continued use of existing programs without modification. However, this approach may result in underutilization of the proposed hardware. On some occasions, a downward compatibility is sought. This capability will ensure that the existing programs are also processible on the smaller units. The operational flexibility desired actually imposes some severe constraints upon the organization. Downward compatibility can be effective only if the programs can be accommodated within the memory capacity of the smaller machines without modification. Software compatibility may also be desired when considering conversion from one vendor's equipment to that of another. The manager may indicate the specific requirement for a given language such as COBOL, BASIC, or FORTRAN.

Performance requirements may be included in the RFP to indicate that a particular level of operation is desired or that no degradation from an existing level occurs. Compatibility may be stated for such factors as storage capacity, cycle time, recording densities, access time, cost, transfer rates, or reliability. The responses to these requirements may be more difficult to evaluate. However, the cost-effectiveness ratio may prove more beneficial for the organization.

Compatibility should be sought as a means of reducing costs. However, a manager must carefully assess the compatibility requirements. There is the danger that these limitations may hamper an organization from securing an optimally effective approach.

5. DELIVERY. Stipulating a desired delivery date or timetable can be a tricky thing. A manager must forecast when the organization will be ready to accept and utilize the desired hardware, system, software, or service. Where dates are essential, these must be identified as mandatory. The mandatory dates may also be stipulated in one of the required contractual clauses.

6. CUSTOMER ASSISTANCE. Customer assistance is the support provided by the vendor or manufacturer. The assistance may take the form of hardware or software maintenance, user training, or documentation. During the evaluation process the manager will attempt to place a value on each of these characteristics or features. If a contractor's proposal indicates only limited training for users, then the manager must determine the impact on the organization. What costs would be incurred in providing additional training for users? Or, what costs may result from limited training for users? If the manager is willing to accept the contractor's proposal, then he must consider an alternative approach to minimize the negative effects.

7. RELIABILITY. Reliability is a desirable quality control characteristic or feature; it is a requirement that will be critically evaluated in the selection process. For example, in an online real-time application, hardware reliability is essential. Reliability may also be a significant factor when evaluating plug-to-plug peripherals.

Proposal Presentation

This section of the RFP delineates the manner in which a contractor's proposal is to be presented. The prescribed format is designed to ensure uniformity in the presentation and evaluation of information.

The following items may be included:

1. Proposal summary
2. Response to requirements
3. Proposed concept
4. Benchmark results
5. Cost data
6. Facility requirements
7. Supporting documentation

1. PROPOSAL SUMMARY. In this segment the contractor is requested to prepare a summary of his proposal and to list the general recommendations and conclusions. This information serves as an introduction to the contractor's proposal and indicates whether or not the contents are a valid response to the RFP.

2. RESPONSE TO REQUIREMENTS. This segment should contain the vendor's or manufacturer's responses to the mandatory or desirable requirements stipulated in the specifications. This approach helps to highlight the response data and simplifies the selection process.

3. PROPOSED CONCEPT. The proposed concept should be a detailed response by the vendor or manufacturer to the submitted specifications (see Figure 9.2). The concept should also indicate any variations from the RFP proposed by the potential contractor. The variation must be explained to facilitate understanding and to indicate how it will improve upon the original specifications.

The concept may be described as follows:

a) Concept description
b) Technical data
c) Timing tables

a) *Concept description.* The description represents the recommended approach or solution to a problem or task. In addition to detailing the contractor's proposal, the description should identify the concept's advantages and salient attributes. Also, the degree or level, and type of compatibility to the existing environment, should be stipulated. The description may also indicate the expandability of the proposal to the future needs of the organization.

The vendor or manufacturer may be requested to specify where a similar approach has been developed and implemented.

b) *Technical data.* This segment should provide complete technical details to support the proposal previously described. In addition to listing the various operating characteristics, the data should also include summaries derived from the timings to indicate the work load capability. A contractor's hardware proposal will list the operating characteristics of a configuration, the hardware controls, software availability work load estimates, expandability, and reliability. A software proposal may specify such items as the primary programming language, restart and recovery procedures, algorithms utilized, data base organization, etc.

The technical responses will be critically evaluated in the selection process.

c) *Timing tables.* Timing tables requested in the general instructions should be included in this segment of the contractor's proposal. The tables are approximations for an estimated work load. They represent attempts by the vendor or manufacturer to prove that their proposal can meet the customer's requirements efficiently and economically.

Timing for equipment specifications are requested to identify the estimated hours of utilization in relation to available hours. For new hardware acquisition an organization is particularly concerned if the projected work load will exceed the number of available base hours. Any excess requirements above the base may increase the production costs for an organization. Software timings may be requested in order to determine function speeds for such operations as transfer, logic, arithmetic, conversion, etc. The data included in the timing tables may be the result of hand timing, simulation, or benchmark problems.

4. BENCHMARK RESULTS. The data in this segment may contain an outline of the benchmark problems and a report of the test results. Prior to receipt of the contractor's proposal, the manager should have viewed the "live" benchmark demonstrations.

5. COST DATA. The cost information is generally submitted in tabular form in accordance with the specifications included in the general instructions. The cost data may be itemized as follows:

a) One-time
b) Approach cost
c) Customer assistance
d) Supplies
e) Conversion

a) *One-time.* The one-time costs are those incurred by the customer prior to implementation of the proposal. For example, in an equipment proposal the contractor would primarily list the related transportation, insurance, and equipment installation costs.

b) *Approach cost.* The data in this segment must closely abide to the ground rules. These costs will identify the lease, rental, or purchase arrangements, or other cost arrangements such as fixed price, cost plus fixed fee, time and expense, etc. In addition, any maintenance charges involved must be specified.

c) *Customer assistance.* These costs represent those incurred as a result of securing contractor support. They include expenses for such items as training, testing, conversion, documentation, reproduction, etc.

d) *Supplies.* The supplies costs represent those items initially required to develop and implement the proposed concept. Included are such items as magnetic tape, magnetic disks, special forms, etc.

e) Conversion. These costs are incurred in converting from one mode of operation to another. They may include such items as keypunching, program recoding, data coding, parallel testing, etc.

6. FACILITY REQUIREMENTS. Whenever special facilities, such as air-conditioning, power, etc., are required to support the proposal these should be identified in this segment. Also, the specifics such as dimensions, required voltages, temperatures, etc., must be indicated.

7. SUPPORTING DOCUMENTATION. The supporting documentation segment should include relevant technical manuals, configuration drawings, program listings, installation layouts, etc. Generally, these items are necessary to facilitate understanding of the proposed concept and technical data. The specifications are designed to make the selection and evaluation process competitive and objective. This is necessary because of the multiplicity of designs, approaches, and configurations available to the information processor. Also, the specifications form a realistic base for the cost-benefit, cost-effectiveness, and trade-off analyses.

THE VENDOR AND THE RFP

Upon receipt of the request for proposal, the vendor or manufacturer must determine if he is interested in responding to the RFP. For various reasons, a firm may choose not to submit a response. If the firm does decide to respond, then a decision must be made by it to determine the level of effort that will be expended in preparing a response. If the probability of success is very limited, a firm may choose to submit only a very nominal response. This approach is justified because preparing responses can be a very costly item for a contractor. The potential contractor must be concerned with proposing an effective solution or approach within an economical cost range. As a result, the vendor must perform a series of cost-performance trade-offs to recommend an efficient and economical proposal.

Depending upon the type of RFP submitted by the organization, the contractor may choose to simulate the problem or task. A model of the desired approach and its environment must be generated. The problem parameters or constraints are applied against the model and the results are analyzed. The experimentation is continued until an optimal approach is determined.

Equipment vendors have developed configurators to determine the optimal hardware/software mix to meet a user's needs. These configurators select the optimal hardware/software mix only from their own product line. However, this enables a potential contractor to submit a tangible proposal based on fact and not merely rhetoric.

Review Questions: Group 9B

1. What requirements should a customer include in the RFP to ensure that no degradation in system performance will result from implementation of a new approach?

2. Why is it necessary to specify the format for a potential contractor's responses?
3. How are timing tables developed?

VALIDATING THE PROPOSALS

The validation process is one of evaluating and ranking the submitted proposals against the requirements stipulated in the RFP. This process can be difficult and complicated, and often very time-consuming. However, it is necessary if an organization is to determine a proposal's capability to fulfill its needs within a reasonable overall cost constraint. Also, it is essential if an organization is to free itself of the single-vendor procurement concept.

The diversity of designs and approaches to information processing requires consideration of various vendors and manufacturers. In the equipment area, for example, there is a significant trend toward mixing the components in a configuration. This has resulted from the growing number of suppliers offering a variety of freestanding or plug-to-plug peripherals. Experience by a number of organizations has shown that hardware mixing can significantly improve the price-performance ratio in a facility.

This discussion of the validation process will consider the following:

1. Criteria
2. Methods
3. Personnel

Criteria

The proposals submitted by the contractors must be evaluated against a predetermined set of criteria. The criteria are necessary to objectively evaluate a proposal's ability to meet the organization's needs.

The criteria are categorized by mandatory, and desirable, characteristics. If a proposal fails to include a mandatory requirement, then for all practical purposes it is considered to be nonresponsive. The desirable characteristics may be somewhat more difficult to evaluate because the contractor may choose to ignore them, recommend an alternative, or submit as requested. Very often, a proposal will contain a large list of alternative suggestions. The alternatives are included with the hope that the customer will acquire some of the features because their worth may exceed the cost of procurement.

Instead of classifying the criteria, they may be listed in a ranking order. For example, an organization may choose to rank its criteria as follows:

Software performance

Hardware performance

Support availability

Compatibility

Expansion capability

Delivery

Cost

The criteria listed above are too general, however, and each requires sub-definition to identify its relevant desirable characteristics or features. For example, the hardware performance criterion would have to be subdivided into the specific devices (i.e., central processor, input, output, data transmission) and their relevant characteristics. Therefore, the characteristics desired in an input device may include the following:

Medium capacity

Recording rates

Buffering: number, location, operation, restrictions

Channels: number, operation, restrictions

Conversion form and rates

Online/Offline operation switching

Checking features

An analysis of these criteria will help to validate each input device. Subsequently the same process is repeated for each component or feature according to the relevant criteria. Ultimately, the individual evaluations are combined to produce an overall appraisal for the proposed hardware configuration. The criteria for the overall appraisal may include such characteristics as compatibility, reliability, expandability, delivery, throughput capability, etc. These same criteria are then applied against each proposed configuration.

The criteria for evaluating a service such as time-sharing would be quite different. For example, one organization used the following ranking:

System availability

Reliability

Programming languages available

Costs (connect, CPU, storage, minimum, terminal, excess charges, initiation)

Response time

Maximum program size

Maximum storage space

Ease of use

File security

Editing

Formating

Program library

Programming assistance

Documentation

This listing may not be complete or properly ranked for another firm. Each organization must establish its own criteria based on its own needs and desires.

Methods

The selection criteria must be incorporated into a proposed validation method. The method will provide the framework for determining the effectiveness of the vendor's or manufacturer's recommendations, and the related costs.

The validation approach selected may be simple or highly sophisticated. Also, it may be subjective or objective. The level of sophistication and degree of objectivity tend to correlate with the size of the organization. For example, large information processing organizations tend to utilize the more sophisticated and objective approaches. This may be due to their technical competence, or an increased awareness or consciousness of cost-performance. The organization-type may also influence the selection of a validation method. Governmental organizations, for example, attempt to utilize the more sophisticated and objective approaches to proposal validation. This may be due to public scrutiny of their actions.

An organization may choose any one of the following validation methods or combinations thereof:

1. Checklists
2. Criteria tables
3. Published evaluation reports
4. Benchmark problems
5. Test problem
6. Simulation
7. Cost-value analysis

1. CHECKLISTS. The checklist approach is relatively simple and very subjective. The criteria are incorporated into a checklist to be compared against the contractor's responses. Due to the subjective nature of this method, the vendor or manufacturer with the best marketing rhetoric in his proposal will probably secure the contract. This negates the proposition that the user should consider the advantages and disadvantages of each response and determine the cost-benefit relationship of each item in the proposal.

Figure 9.3 illustrates a checklist used by one organization for evaluation of service bureau proposals. The questions are very general and do not clearly define acceptable or desirable characteristics. As a result, the defendability of the final selection is somewhat questionable.

The checklist technique is most effective when the criteria are more detailed and when applied to minor proposals. The detailing of the criteria adds credibil-

1. What are the costs?
2. How will data conversion be handled?
3. What types of input controls will be provided?
4. What types of output controls will be provided?
5. How will data be protected?
6. What is the expected turnaround time?
7. What emergency back-up is available?
8. What type of training will be provided to user personnel?
9. What special reports can be prepared?
10. What documentation will be made available?

Figure 9.3 Example of validation checklist used for service bureau proposals

ity to the selection process. Figure 9.4 illustrates a detailed checklist, developed by an organization for evaluation of proprietary software packages. It provides preliminary data that is subsequently combined with that gathered during the benchmark testing process to produce an overall appraisal.

2. CRITERIA TABLES. The criteria tables use a tabular approach to proposal validation. The desirable characteristics are listed on the table in criteria groupings (hardware, software, vendor support, etc.) by relative importance. The manager assigns a numerical value to each grouping. The sum total of values for all groups does not normally exceed 100. The manager must then appraise

Figure 9.4 Example of software validation checklist

1. What is the package designed to do?
2. Who developed the software package?
3. How is the package organized?
4. Is the package operable?
5. Can the package operate on our hardware configuration?
6. Will the package require modification?
7. Who will modify the package?
8. Can the package be modified if necessary?
9. What are the overall costs?
10. Is thorough and comprehensive documentation available?
11. Who will maintain the package?
12. How long will package maintenance be available?
13. What are the package constraints?
14. Where is the package currently utilized?
15. What is the primary language?
16. What input/output techniques are utilized?
17. What are the required input/output formats?
18. How must the input be organized?
19. What controls are included?
20. What user training is provided?

the desirable characteristics in each grouping and assign them a value. The sum total of values in each group shall not exceed the total allocated to it initially. As the proposals are evaluated, the responses to the desired characteristics are assigned a value ranging from 1 to 10. This response value is multiplied by the characteristics value to determine a vendor score for that item. The vendor scores are then summed to produce a group total and ultimately an overall total for the proposal. For illustration purposes, the software grouping has been extracted from one organization's criteria table (see Table 9.1). The software category has been allocated an overall numerical value of 25. Note that software availability and a data management capability were two very important factors in the evaluation. The software group total indicates a very close score between the two competing vendors. However, the final outcome will be affected by the scores of the other criteria groupings.

Though this approach is regarded as a sophisticated approach to proposal validation, it is not a perfect approach. One of the major difficulties is the assignment of values to groupings and desirable characteristics. The values are assigned on an "objective" basis that for all practical purposes is very subjective. It does force the manager to consider those items that are most important to him and his operation.

3. PUBLISHED EVALUATION REPORTS. Published evaluation reports on hardware and software performance are also used for proposal validation. This approach is often frowned upon because it is regarded as too subjective and not very sophisticated. Yet, many organizations use the published reports in conjunction with other methods to validate the proposals. The Auerbach and Datapro reports, for example, are used frequently for evaluation of hardware devices, and software packages.

A published evaluation report may not be available for a particular hardware configuration, software package, or specific application. Therefore, the organization would be forced to seek an alternative proposal validation method. Also, per-

Table 9.1 Sample extract of criteria table, with weighted values, for a
software comparison

Desirable Characteristics	Criteria Value	Vendor A		Vendor B	
		Response Value	Response Score	Response Value	Response Score
Availability	5	5	25	10	50
Cost	4	6	24	3	12
Reliability	3	6	18	6	18
Documentation	3	5	15	8	24
Maintenance	3	7	21	4	12
Training	2	7	14	5	10
Data Management	5	8	40	5	25
Total	25		157		151

formance reports are not generally available for appraising facilities management proposals, contract programming services, time-sharing services, or service bureau agencies.

However, the reports are an excellent source of information particularly where the information processing staff lacks detailed knowledge of a proposed hardware configuration or device, or software package. Some of the services also include some sections that provide overview information about a particular concept, e.g., minicomputers, data communications, and so forth.

4. BENCHMARK PROBLEMS. Benchmark problems are regarded as one of the more effective ways to validate a proposal. The selected problems are designed to provide the user with a realistic assessment of stated performance. Therefore, the manager must select benchmark problems which are truly representative of the expected workload and the criteria. For example, a manager may choose a job mix that will involve long jobs, short jobs, tape jobs, disk jobs with a required number of seeks, and perhaps a "number cruncher."

The application of these problems against the proposed hardware, system, service, or software will provide the manager with a tangible basis for comparing all contractor proposals. The tests should enable the organization to effectively evaluate gross performance of the system in terms of hardware performance (central processing unit and input/output devices); compiler language and operating system capabilities; diagnostic messages; ability to deal with certain types of data structures; and the effectiveness of software utilities. It may also be possible to test a particular configuration and its ability to interact within a given environment. For example, the ability of a mainframe to interact with a remote batch terminal, several graphic terminals, and a large number of active low-speed terminals.

The decision to utilize benchmark problems for validation purposes must be made prior to dissemination of the RFP. The benchmark documentation should be available to the prospective contractors at the time the RFP specifications are distributed. Prior to preparing the benchmark problems, a manager must determine the expected results. This resolution is necessary in order to minimize the evaluation of unnecessary outputs and facilitate construction of test data. The benchmark documentation will include information about the test data and the specific results required. However, this information should not identify the contents of the actual test data.

Some organizations will provide a vendor with benchmark test data to facilitate a run by the vendor and submission of results to the customer's organization for evaluation. Then, a second more rigorous and extensive benchmark may be processed by the vendor in the presence of representatives from the customer's organization. This does not represent a mistrust of the vendor, but much rather a desire on the part of the customer to make certain that the selected proposal will be the best one for the organization.

This approach to proposal validation requires the existence of operational hardware, software, services, or systems—an obvious disadvantage. However, this could be an advantage because it will ensure that the recommended proposal is functional, not merely marketing rhetoric. Another possible disadvantage is time. But this should not inhibit the manager from developing a problem mix that can be executed within an hour, or slightly longer, and can represent an average day's job mix. The manager can extrapolate from the test results to determine the effectiveness of the vendor's proposal.

Despite the planning and preparation problems and apparent disadvantages, the benchmark approach is very popular.

5. TEST PROBLEMS. The test problems are intended to evaluate the functional effectiveness of a segment of the contractor's proposal. This enables a manager to evaluate the various capabilities of the hardware, software, service, or system without necessarily processing a complete application. Test problems also help to evaluate the truly important capabilities, which are so often overlooked, inadequately measured or evaluated in the benchmark problems.

Test problems may be developed to evaluate the time required to translate source code into object code; response time for two or more jobs in a multiprogramming environment; overheard requirements of the operating system for CPU and channel time in executing a user program; component overlap; length of time required to execute an instruction; etc. The results can be used for cost-performance trade-off judgments. However, the factors or functions tested or measured must be relevant to the proposal's objectives.

The test problems are frequently used to supplement the benchmark evaluations or any other proposal validating method. Often, they are used to give the systems and programming personnel experience in utilizing the hardware, software, service, or system. The testing will provide limited information about the ease of operation and learning.

6. SIMULATION. Simulation is the most sophisticated technique for proposal validation. Properly utilized, this technique can provide meaningful decision-making data to facilitate the optimal selection of a contractor proposal. However, the technique is still not used very much, owing to the costs and efforts required for its implementation. The higher costs result from the construction of one or several mathematical models, development of a data base for the variables, computer utilization, and the number of alternatives desired.

Developing the necessary model or models for proposal validation requires considerable effort (see Figure 9.5). The manager must formulate the primary and secondary objectives, as well as determine the controllable and uncontrollable variables affecting the model. When the model has been developed it must then be tested and debugged. This process may result in changes to the model and some of its parameters.

The tested model is then manipulated and the results analyzed. The variables may then be altered and the model remanipulated to produce another alternative. There is no limitation to the number of iterations that may be performed on a model. However, most users of this validation method prefer to keep the number of iterations to a minimum because of the cost and effort required.

An organization may utilize one of the simulation languages, such as GPSS (General Purpose Systems Simulator), Simscript, or CSS (Computer Systems

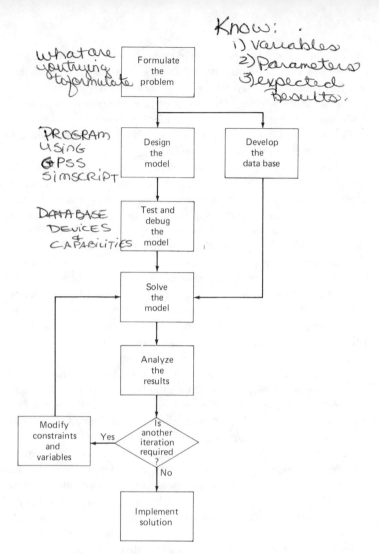

Figure 9.5 Approach to simulation

Simulator), for proposal validation purposes. The manipulation of the model or models can be performed in a batch or online mode. The online mode is more desirable because the vast turnaround facilitates monitoring, evaluation, and modification of the model and results.

An organization may choose to develop a configurator to simulate the best hardware/software mix to meet the organization's needs. The configurator initially translates the user's requirements into one or more models. These models are then processed against the data base containing the hardware/software performance information to produce a number of calculations. These calculations are subsequently outputted in a variety of desired reports.

To construct such a configurator requires a significant investment in time and resources. Therefore, it may be more advantageous for an organization to utilize one of the proprietary packages, such as SCERT.

The configurators are still actually in development. In the future, though, they will undoubtedly be less costly to process and more flexible in operation. They will have the capability to identify optimal hardware/software configurations from the various competitive components.

7. COST-VALUE ANALYSIS. The cost-value technique is used primarily for the evaluation of equipment proposals. The technique may also be referred to as cost-effectiveness analysis. In this method the responses to the mandatory requirements in the RFP are only validated. The premise is that these requirements do not have to be evaluated. The cost-value technique is more concerned with evaluating the worth of a desired feature proposed by the potential contractor.

For example, an organization expresses a desire for an April delivery but a contractor indicates a possible January date. What is the value of the earlier delivery? Or, what would be the value of a delivery in July? The manager must determine if the earlier delivery date would enable him to begin profit-oriented operations sooner. Or, would the later delivery date cause him to seek an alternative processing method, which would increase operating costs? The value or worth in either situation must be determined. Subsequently, the positive or negative worth is subtracted from the total cost of the proposed configuration. The difference represents the total cost required to meet the RFP needs. This is but a calculation and does not lower the actual cost paid to the contractor.

Many organizations argue that the values assigned to the desirable features are very arbitrary and subjective. Consequently, the value attributed may or may not offer a realistic appraisal of actual worth. A counterargument is offered that the assigned values provide the executive committee with some tangible data in assessing a feature's worth to an organization. As a result, there is increased confidence in the proposal finally selected.

The cost-value analysis may also be very helpful in appraising the value of expansion features included in the proposal. The expansion capability may be assessed to determine either the ability of the equipment to assume a larger work load or the ability to interface additional features with the basic configuration. To some degree, the validation technique can also evaluate upgrading within a family of equipment.

The proposal validation method selected will be affected by the time and resources that a manager wishes to expend. It also depends upon whether a manager wishes to be objective or subjective in the selection process. The failure to apply an objective method may only help to increase operating costs needlessly.

Personnel

Prior to submitting the RFP to the vendors or manufacturers, an organization must also determine who will validate and evaluate the submitted proposals.

The selection will depend upon the type of hardware, software, system, or services desired; time available; in-house expertise; and funds availability. The RFP may be issued for such activities as:

Hardware acquisition

Time-sharing services

Distributed processing networks

Application software packages

Contract programming

Facilities management

System studies

Analysis and design services

Service bureau support

Training and education services

Data conversion and preparation services

This variety of activities will force a manager to determine if outside assistance is necessary to validate a contractor's proposal. If a decision is made to use outside assistance, the manager must determine the source of that service. Assistance may be secured from the following:

Independent consultants specializing in data processing

Management consultants offering related services in information processing

Management consultants specializing in information processing services

Accounting firms offering related information processing services

Service bureau organizations offering a variety of services

Computer-related service organizations offering a variety of services and subject matter expertise

Colleges and universities—that is, from research groups and individual faculty members with expertise in information processing services

Governmental organizations tend to utilize outside assistance for proposal validation particularly for hardware selection. Many large organizations secure outside assistance either to verify their findings or to perform the evaluation and validation process. Still others prefer to utilize their own in-house expertise. This is particularly true of organizations with their own information systems planning groups. Many small- and medium-sized organizations tend to favor outside assistance. This is particularly true when an organization is initially becoming involved in automated information processing.

If outside assistance is deemed necessary, a manager should provide the advisory group with the following:

A very specific definition of the objectives

A schedule with checkpoints at which progress reports are due

A description of the interaction required with in-house personnel

Though outside assistance is used in proposal validation, the final responsibility for selection remains with the data processing manager or administrator and with the organization.

NEGOTIATING THE CONTRACT

Upon completion of the validation process, the manager must select the one proposal that best fulfills the organization's present and future needs. This proposal and the RFP specifications must then be converted to contractual terminology. The vendor will offer to simplify this process by tendering a standard contract to the manager. The standard contract can be modified and new provisions added to the document without rewriting the entire document. Obviously, the data processing manager is not responsible for this legalistic conversion. However, he is responsible for articulating the necessary contractual requirements to the legal advisors. The organization must act as an equal party in contract negotiations.

Through the checklist process, the manager ensures that the necessary specifications are included in the legal document. Figure 9.6, for example,

Figure 9.6 Checklist for contract preparation

Site Preparation

1. Time requirements for site preparation must be clearly stated. Sufficient time must be included to provide for construction, if necessary.

2. The site requirements for the following must be specified:
   a) Floor loading needs
   b) Fire detection and protection
   c) Power supply and lighting needs, both regular and emergency
   d) Air-conditioning and air humidification, both regular and emergency
   e) Physical and maintenance space for and around each unit
   f) Service and storage areas for maintenance personnel

3. The space requirements for the following must be specified, if relevant:
   a) Power generator
   b) Air-control equipment
   c) Power rooms
   d) Office space for managers, plus operations, programming, systems, and user personnel
   e) Service and record storage areas

---

illustrates some of the details that may appear on the checklist for ultimate inclusion in the contract. In this example, the information would be incorporated into the contractual clauses under the heading of site preparation.

Contract negotiation and preparation cannot be taken lightly. The vendors or manufacturers will undoubtedly move to protect themselves contractually. The organization must move equally as adroitly to have a well-defined contract prepared—one that will prevent shifting the burden of responsibility to the customer. Items such as standards of performance, delivery dates, installation, testing, system software, training, foreign equipment, remodeling and trade-in, warranty, termination, disputes, confidential information, etc., must be carefully stipulated by the organization in order to minimize the possibility of subsequent litigation for breach of contract, negligence, fraud, misrepresentation, etc.

The termination clause is the most frequently overlooked clause in contracts relating to data processing services. Consequently, there may be no provision for notice of termination, right of access to a customer's property, documentation, control of back-up of files, etc.

If the legal staff or advisors are not very familiar with matters related to information processing contracts, then it may be advisable to call their attention to the American Bar Association's publication entitled "Computers and the Law." Research on reported cases, and articles appearing in the ABA's journal, will also assist them with contractual questions related to information processing.

IMPLEMENTATION PLANNING AND PREPARATION

Following the execution of the contract, the data processing manager must prepare the organization for implementation of the proposal. The planning and readiness process affects the entire organization, not only the information processing activity. It requires involvement by the executive committee, steering committee, user personnel, and information personnel.

This interaction of the concerned parties will help to ensure: a progressive phasing-in of the project; readiness by the users to participate in the inputs and outputs and adjustments by the organization to facilitate success of the new approach. Both the preliminary and final planning to ensure success of implementation and subsequent operation depend on the information gathered during the feasibility study (see chapter 8). The reader will note that the impact upon the organization must have been previously evaluated. As a result, plans now have to be developed and implemented to minimize or eliminate any possible negative effects.

In the planning and preparation for implementation of the project, the manager must consider the following:

1. The conversion approach
2. Planning factors
3. Readiness status

Conversion Approach

The conversion approach to be selected is primarily determined by the project's objectives and the difficulty of integrating this task into the existing framework. The decision may also be influenced by the technical expertise possessed by an organization, as well as factors relating to available resources, time, and cost.

The approach to project implementation may be:

1. Gradual
2. Immediate
3. Overlapping

1. GRADUAL. The gradual approach extends or prolongs the time period allocated to the overall project. It is hoped that by extending the time-frame, an organization can carefully and completely develop and test the new concept before any changes are made. Alternatively, this approach is used in an attempt to minimize or eliminate any negative impact resulting from the transition. In some organizations, the gradual approach is initiated by implementing a pilot installation in order to evaluate the effectiveness and accuracy of the system. Once the system is functioning as desired, additional installations are phased-in. In other organizations, one location is established, then the next is phased-in and the process continues until all of the locations are processing the new approach. The latter may be viewed as a modular or building-block approach to system implementation.

The gradual approach is favored by small organizations that have little or no practical experience in information processing techniques and/or low-volume activities. This approach enables these organizations to wade into the new concept without becoming quickly submerged in a quagmire of problems. The approach is also favored by large organizations for the progressive phasing-in of complex projects. In this case, the project segments are modularized and carefully implemented to ensure user readiness and ultimate success of the new project. The approach may also be favored when converting from a manual to an automated method of processing. To a limited degree, it is also favored by organizations converting from unit-record to computerized equipment. This mode of operation helps to ensure that the existing systems are designed to take advantage of the new equipment.

Before deciding on the gradual approach, the organization must carefully determine the cost-benefit relationship. In some situations, this approach helps to minimize costs because it does not require an immediate investment in a larger staff or more equipment. In other situations, though, costs may be incurred for travel and lodging at test centers, equipment rental, overtime work, data conversion etc.—all because of the lack of an in-house processing capability.

2. IMMEDIATE. The immediate approach implies a relatively instantaneous implementation capability. This presupposes that all of the necessary development, testing, debugging, training, conversion, and documentation has been completed prior to the targeted cutover date. This state of readiness enables an

organization to virtually remove one computer from the area and replace it immediately with another machine. The approach may also be applied successfully when upgrading within a family of computers. The approach is also used very successfully in converting from one information system to another. For example, the new payroll system will be implemented in the first payroll week of July.

For many organizations, the immediate approach to conversion and implementation may appear as radical. This depends on the situation. For example, conversion from one computer configuration to another without allowing for any overlap may be risky. This would require the availability of a well-developed and well-coordinated schedule. But it is also possible to use an emulator that facilitates conversion from one hardware configuration to another without overlap. Though this provides for immediate conversion, it also means an underutilization of the actual processing capability of the hardware if the emulated process continues for an extended period of time. The systems must be redeveloped to make optimal use of the hardware.

Immediate conversion from one system to another also requires some consideration. If the system is very complex or involves many interacting functions, it may not be desirable to attempt to convert from one approach to another on an immediate basis. For example, a large retail establishment decides that all of its stores will convert to point-of-sale operations simultaneously. This type of conversion could prove to be chaotic for the retail firm. But a firm could convert its billing system on an immediate basis without too much difficulty. However, provision must be made for processing transactions that are caught between the old and new system. In one organization, a clerk disposed of $300,000 worth of orders because he did not know how to interject them into the system; the customers used an old order form.

The manager must select the approach that will provide the best results for an organization. There is sometimes a tendency to use the immediate approach in order to impress the executive committee or the steering committee. As a result, a most unrealistic project schedule may be developed and as the end result, a poorly designed and/or poorly tested system.

The immediate approach to conversion and implementation may be possible if an organization uses a turnkey approach. This means that the responsibility for design, development, and implementation is submitted to a contractor who then delivers an operationally ready product to the organization. Though this approach can be very beneficial to an organization, organization supervised testing, prior to actual installation, must be conducted to ensure that no major problems occur following implementation of the turnkey system.

3. OVERLAPPING. The overlapping approach provides a buffer period to facilitate the transition from one method to another. This time interval provides an organization with the ability to conduct additional parallel tests to ensure success of the new approach. The length of the buffer period will vary with the complexity of the project, the time and resources available, the organization size, and the costs. For most organizations, the buffer period ranges from one to

six months. In one organization viewed by this author, the overlap period had been projected for a period of one year. This interval was deemed neccessary to convert to a more sophisticated inventory/production control system utilizing new hardware and software. The system was modularized and allowed for a progressive phasing-in of the completed segments. However, in another organization due to convert to a different hardware vendor and software language, the data processing manager decided upon an open-ended overlap period. He decided to overlap for as long as would be necessary, although the projected period was not to have exceeded nine months. As a result of inaccurate training projections, faulty or inadequate preliminary design data from the feasibility study, poor testing procedures, and poor documentation, the overlap period extended to nearly twenty-two months beyond the equipment delivery date. This overrun proved to be very costly to the overall organization and damaging to the data processing activity.

In conversion from manual to automated processes, overlapping machine costs will not be a factor. However, personnel and supplies costs can be significant. Conversions from unit-record to computing equipment are affected by some level of machine costs, as well as personnel and supplies expenses. In converting from one type of computer to another, the machine costs could be very significant. Even when implementing a software, service, or systems package, the equipment, personnel, and supplies costs can be significant.

For most organizations, the overlapping approach provides the smoothest and most effective transition. An organization selecting this approach should allow for as much overlap as it can afford. This will help to ensure more effective systems and applications, better communications and organized interaction, and more effective documentation. However, the time interval selected should not be open-ended; a time limit must be established for planning, directing, and controlling purposes.

WHICH APPROACH?

In actual operation, many organizations utilize a combination of these approaches to conversion and implementation. The implementation approach selected should be determined only after a cost-benefit analysis has been completed. This analysis must not be restricted to machine, software, service, or system costs. Rather, it must also take into consideration the following factors: resource availability and capability, impact on the organization, and user readiness.

When the approach has been selected, the manager makes his recommendation in the feasibility study. The manager must be prepared to defend his position and provide substantive data to support the stance taken.

Planning Factors

After the approach to conversion and implementation has been determined by the executive committee, data processing manager, and users, the structural framework for its execution must be developed. This framework must be evolved prior to the implementation of the new hardware, software, system, or service. The tasks and activities within the framework constitute the project's implementation plan and schedule. The detailing of the tasks and activities is necessary for direction and control purposes, and subsequently for the readiness status evaluation. A generalized overview of the implementation objectives and related activities is illustrated in Figure 9.7.

The implementation plan can be finalized only after a review of the feasibility study, RFP, accepted vendor's or manufacturer's proposal, and negotiated contract. This review brings into focus all of the necessary tasks, constraints, and parameters affecting project implementation and the schedule. The plan is also affected by the type of project being implemented—hardware, software, system, or service.

The implementation plan and schedule may include the following general factors:

1. Site requirements
2. Communications requirements
3. Organizational manning
4. Information processing personnel requirements
5. System development
6. Program development
7. Data and file conversion
8. Parallel operations
9. Implementation

1. SITE REQUIREMENTS. The site requirements have to be determined in order to facilitate preparation of a safe working environment (see chapter 7). The manager must make certain that he adheres to the requirements stipulated in the negotiated contract; local building, electrical, fire, plumbing, and insurance codes; and organizational policies. Sufficient advanced planning and preparation must be executed to ensure a state of readiness for delivery. This may be a very critical factor where facility construction or renovation is required.

The specific factors that may be included in the consideration of site requirements involve determination or evaluation of:

Overall space requirements

Equipment layout and space requirements for operations and maintenance

Floor loading capacity

Power and lighting requirements, both regular and emergency

Contacting a local moving firm for assistance and/or equipment, if required

Temporary relocation of personnel

Necessary permits secured, and licensing fees paid

Air-conditioning and humidification control requirements, both regular and emergency

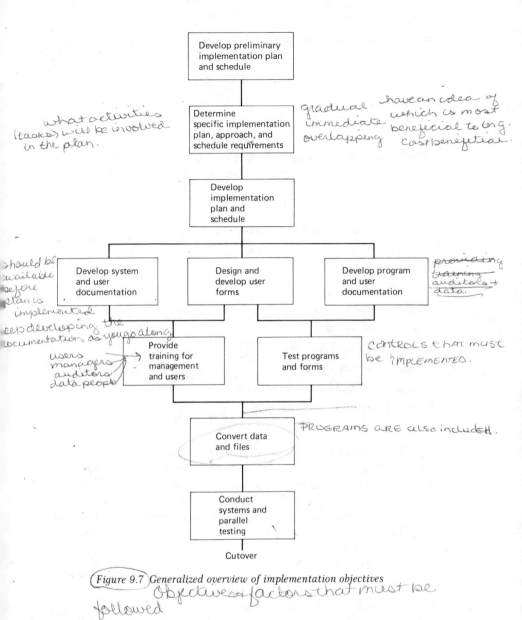

Develop preliminary
implementation plan
and schedule

*what activities
(tasks) will be involved
in the plan.*

Determine
specific implementation
plan, approach, and
schedule requirements

*gradual   have an idea of
immediate   which is most
overlapping   beneficial to org.
cost beneficial.*

Develop
implementation
plan and
schedule

*should be
available
before
plan is
implemented*

Develop system
and user
documentation

*keep developing the
documentation as you go along*

*users
managers
auditors
data people*

Design and
develop user
forms

Develop program
and user
documentation

*providing
training
auditors +
data.*

Provide
training for
management
and users

Test programs
and forms

*CONTROLS THAT MUST
BE IMPLEMENTED.*

Convert data
and files

PROGRAMS ARE ALSO INCLUDED.

Conduct
systems and
parallel
testing

Cutover

Figure 9.7 Generalized overview of implementation objectives

*Objectives & factors that must be
followed*

Raised flooring for cabling and wiring

Smoke-detection and alarm systems

Fire-detection, alarm, and protection systems

Water-detection and damage-control systems

Service and storage areas

Tape and disk library

Environmental security and protection against vandalism or sabotage, or both

Office, work area, and conference room space

Space and positional requirements for materials handling equipment

Scheduled completion dates

Vendor or manufacturer site-acceptance requirements stipulated in the contract

2. COMMUNICATIONS REQUIREMENTS. These factors are relevant to the planning process only if the project involves teleprocessing or data communications equipment or a time-sharing service.

Factors to be considered are:

Equipment layout and space requirements for operation and maintenance

Wiring requirements and limitations *are the lines there? modems.*

Type of circuit required *comm. links, circuits, clean power lines vendors.*

Encryption device requirements *black boxes on lines*

Scheduled installation date

Environmental security

Development of user documentation *how do they communicate? sign on?*

Training of user personnel

Development of management controls

Installation of communications lines

Location of user terminals

must be considered in Imp. plan

3. ORGANIZATIONAL MANNING. During the feasibility study, an evaluation of the proposal's impact upon the organization has to be determined. With the approval of the executive committee, the data processing administrator and manager must now finalize both the organizational structure and manning requirements for the new approach. In all likelihood, the proposed costs and savings are based on changes to the organization chart or manning strengths, or both (see chapters 2 and 3).

Factors to be considered are:

Development of a new organization chart

Development of new job descriptions

Orientation and training of user personnel

Reassignment and retraining of personnel

Scheduled release of personnel

Coordination required with interrelating activities.

4. INFORMATION PROCESSING PERSONNEL REQUIREMENTS. The factors involved in this segment will vary significantly, depending upon the type of infor-

mation processing organization currently in existence. If none exists, then the executive committee must establish such an organization by either appointing a temporary administrator or recruiting an executive to head up the activity (see chapters 2 and 3).

The factors to be considered are:

Review skills inventory for background and experience of personnel *promote from within*

Determine required manning strength prior to installation of the new project *Do you have enough people for the jobs.*
Determine recruitment and selection requirements

Recruit and select personnel

Determine and provide the necessary level of orientation, training, and re-training

5. SYSTEM DEVELOPMENT. This is one of the most difficult parts of the implementation plan and very time-consuming in the schedule. The actual effort and length of time required for the activities in this part of the plan will depend upon the amount of detail previously developed and upon priorities established by the executive committee. The planning for this phase can begin only after the requirements have been finalized (see chapter 8). The requirements must then be correlated with the detailed design information from the feasibility study. The final design process and the interrelated activities can then be initiated (see chapters 3, 4, 5, and 10 regarding the relevant systems development tasks).

The factors that may be included for each system are:

Review of source documents and/or input

Analysis of input, output, working file, and reference data needs

Determination of output and reporting requirements

Analysis of the system flowcharts, logic charts, or decision tables

Development of documentation and performance standards

Preparation of complete documentation for each system

Development and establishment of the necessary management controls

Coordination of system and parallel testing

Determination of the estimated dates of completion

Development of an overall project schedule

6. PROGRAM DEVELOPMENT. As in the case of systems development, this phase of the implementation plan and schedule is an extension of the development work performed in the feasibility study. The preliminary design data developed in the feasibility study is subject to change or modification. The design again is affected by the finalized system's requirements. As a result, some redefinition of the initial design data may be necessary before final design of a program can be initiated (see chapters 3, 4, 5, and 10 regarding the relevant program development tasks).

The factors that may be included in this segment are:

Development or redevelopment of macro- and micro-flowcharts, decision tables, top-down structures, logic outlines, and logic narratives

Analysis of the program specifications

Instruction coding

Desk checking of source programs

Assembly and compilation of source programs

Preparation of test data and test plan

Testing and debugging of the object programs

Preparation of complete program documentation

7. DATA AND FILE CONVERSION. The conversion and purification of data and files may be performed prior to, during, and after implementation. The amount and type of data and files converted and checked prior to implementation will depend upon the priority schedule established for system and program development. This phase of the implementation plan requires a significant amount of control and coordination. One of the problems encountered by the manager during this phase is to secure complete data and files for purification and conversion. As a result, he has to develop and implement numerous management controls (see chapter 10). The availability of the information for conversion is also a problem that requires careful scheduling and coordination.

The factors that may be included in this segment are:

Development of management controls to ensure qualitative conversion

Development of the necessary administrative procedures to ensure correction or validation of exceptions

Coordination of the conversions with the interrelated activities

Development of the necessary procedures for manual transcription of the information to coding sheets

Developing of the necessary transcription forms

Provision for orientation and training on the proper use of transcription codes

8. PARALLEL OPERATIONS. This is one of the most important events in the conversion and implementation cycle. Parallel processing is the simultaneous production of output and reports using the current and proposed approach. This period of dual-system operation enables an organization to test and prove the mathematical and procedural accuracy of the new approach. It also represents an evaluation of the approach's ability to meet the desired objectives.

The parallel-processing phase must not be taken lightly because it entails a complete system's test. This testing requires an effective interaction between the responsible functional activities and the information processing organization. The coordination is required in order to evaluate the source documents, inputs, documentation, management controls, effectiveness of training and orientation, procedures, reports and outputs, and programs. Too frequently, this evaluation is not taken seriously enough; consequently, major problems arise when the new approach is implemented. In one organization, for example, the payroll group considered itself too busy to evaluate the proposed payroll system and its outputs. When the new system was implemented, the users were very unhappy. Despite its earlier agreements and acceptance of the preliminary test outputs, the payroll group suddenly decided it couldn't "live" with the system. As a result, the organization scrapped its new approach and simply computerized the existing unit-record payroll approach. This meant reverting back to processing the payroll and its by-products over a period of four and one-half days instead of one eight-hour shift. This regression resulted in a significant waste of manpower, money, materials, and machine resources, as well as time. Perhaps it could have been prevented by initial executive committee involvement in the project. Alternatively, perhaps more effective coordination by the data processing manager during the feasibility study and subsequent development of the system would have prevented this problem.

The factors that may be included in this segment are:

Coordination of conversion and purification of the necessary data and files *[handwritten: WANT CLEAN ACCURATE COMPLETE DATASET.]* *[handwritten: VALIDATION OF FILES.]*

Coordination of the machine loading for conversion, purification, and testing

Coordination of the checkout of the outputs and reports *[handwritten: USER + AUDITORS TO MAKE SURE DATA IS COMPLETE, ACCURATE, RELIABLE]*

Coordination of the preparation and availability of user and processing documentation

Provision for the necessary orientation and training

Development of the plan and schedule for dual operations

9. IMPLEMENTATION. The implementation phase is concerned with effecting the full operational status of the new project. This may be the culmination of a complete project or the accomplishment of one of a series of goals. The planning within this phase is concerned with determining if the new project can be made fully operational on the desired date. The scheduling is primarily concerned with the actual cutover and, to some degree, with the final details to ensure a successful phasing-in.

The factors in this segment may include: *[handwritten: so problems can be solved so that implementation can go on schedule.]*

A readiness review of the affected activities *[handwritten: must be scheduled, early so make sure people are ready to use the output from the new system.]*

Conducting of orientation seminars on cutover *[handwritten: so people know what to do]*

Conducting of a management presentation for final acceptance *[handwritten: prior to program]*

Each of the factors in the implementation plan must be allocated a time element for scheduling purposes. Both the scheduled activities and the time elements should then be translated to a GANTT chart (see Figure 9.8) or PERT network (see Figure 9.9). The schedule will facilitate the execution of the management functions of planning, organizing, coordinating, directing, and controlling.

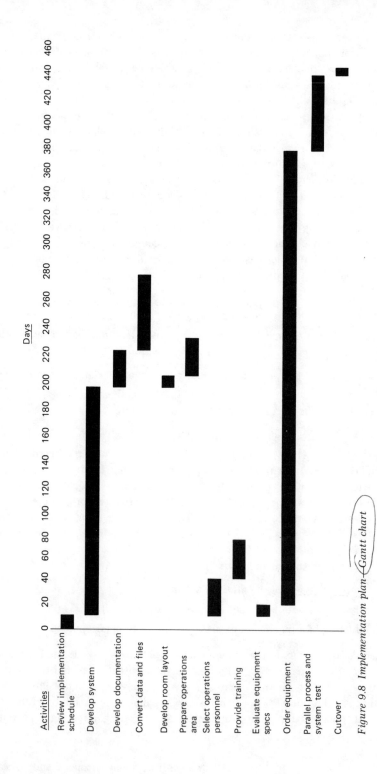

Figure 9.8 Implementation plan—Gantt chart

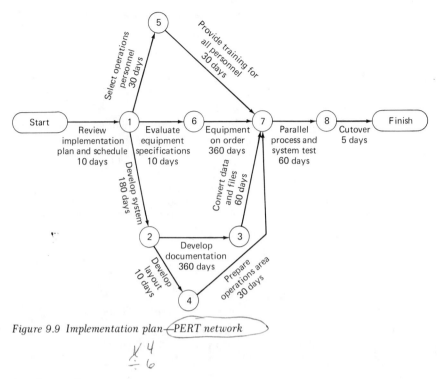

Figure 9.9 Implementation plan—PERT network

Readiness Status

The readiness status evaluation is a formal review of the progress in an implementation plan and schedule. It indicates an organization's preparedness to generate and utilize the project's information products. The review's feedback will enable the manager to develop and initiate appropriate corrective measures or to implement an alternative course of action when necessary.

The target date for a readiness review is generally dependent upon the type of project. The date needs to allow adequate lead time to facilitate implementation of other measures to ensure a reasonable state of readiness or rescheduling of the project cutover. The corrective action should be decided upon only after an analysis of the contractual provisions for delivery and acceptance and/or review of the implementation plan. A contract for hardware acquisition may require that the neccessary environmental facilities be ready at least 30 days prior to project cutover. Alternatively, the implementation plan may require that at least 50 percent of the necessary effort be completed in order to facilitate a significant productive cutover.

The readiness review may utilize an existing GANTT chart or PERT network for status evaluation. Or, instead, a detailed checklist including all of the essential and interacting tasks and steps may be prepared. The status of each key activity is evaluated to determine if any slippage has occurred. Where slippage has occurred, it may be necessary to increase the resources to correct the problem.

However, any proposed changes must be evaluated to determine their effect on the overall project.

THE FOLLOW-UP

After the project has been implemented, a follow-up procedure should be initiated to evaluate its effectiveness. This post-implementation evaluation may be a one-time review or it may be continued for as long a period as is deemed necessary. The follow-up may be conducted to determine the following:

Have desired objectives been achieved?

Have the savings outlined in the feasibility study actually been achieved, surpassed, or negated by increased operating costs?

Is the phase-out timetable being adhered to?

What is the effectiveness of the documentation in the systems, programming, operations, and user organizations?

Are the recommended changes to the organization structure realistic?

Are the personnel duties and responsibilities properly defined and assigned?

Are the management controls effective for capturing, processing, and reporting data?

Has the training been adequate?

Have all of the data and files been converted properly and accurately?

What is the estimated versus actual machine loading?

What are the "before and after" costs for personnel, supplies, and machines?

Does the operations area provide for a safe, secure, and productive working environment?

What is the actual versus authorized personnel strength?

Is user response time satisfactory?

Are there any problems in the implemented system?

Can exceptions to normal processing be handled with ease?

Can corrections to data and information be reentered with ease and accuracy?

If the results of the follow-up are unsatisfactory, it may be necessary to modify or replan the entire project. The follow-up may be conducted by the systems or advanced planning and development personnel. The latter group may be somewhat more impartial in judging the effectiveness of the hardware, software, system, application, service, etc.

The post-implementation evaluation should subsequently be supplemented by an annual systems audit program based on the follow-up principle. The audit may be conducted by the internal or external auditors, advanced planning and development personnel, systems personnel, or management consultants (see chapter 10).

Review Questions: Group 9C

1. How may the proposal validation process be made more objective?
2. What are some of the arguments for and against the use of benchmark problems in proposal validation?
3. Why would it be beneficial for a small organization to utilize a simulator for proposal validation?
4. Why should a data processing manager participate in contract negotiations for the acquisition of data processing services?
5. If an organization was developing a massive management information system, would it be practical for it to utilize a gradual approach to conversion and implementation? Why or why not?
6. If an organization was to utilize an outside optical-scanning service for data conversion, what events would be included in the implementation plan?
7. Why is a readiness review necessary?
8. What factors might be included in a system's follow-up?

SUMMARY

After the need for a new or modified approach to information processing has been justified, the manager must develop the specifications for the request for proposal (RFP). The RFP delineates the organization's required and desired characteristics in the new or modified approach. However, before the specifications can be released, the manager must select the vendors capable of submitting a realistic response. This will require an evaluation of the prospective bidder's organization, financial position, experience, personnel, and technical capability. The manager may perform the contractor evaluations annually, semiannually, or prior to release of the RFP.

The request for proposal will indicate to the prospective bidder the organization's needs and desires. It is a formal document designed to ensure uniform distribution of the specifications, a more uniform response format, and competitive bidding. The RFP are generally divided into three parts: general instructions, customer requirements, and proposal presentation. The general instructions specify the ground rules for the bidder's response; the customer requirements delineate the problem; and the proposal presentation delineates the required responses to the problem.

In order to respond to the RFP, the bidder may perform a series of cost-performance analyses. These may be accomplished by utilizing simulation models or configurators. This process will enable the bidder to submit a meaningful proposal based on fact, rather than marketing rhetoric.

The contractor responses must then be evaluated and ranked by the organization. Though this may be difficult and time-consuming, it is necessary in order to evaluate each proposal's capability. The proposals should initially be compared with the criteria developed by the manager. These criteria are incorporated into a singular or combinatorial validating method. The validating methods include such approaches as checklists, criteria tables, evaluation reports, benchmark problems, test problems, cost-value analysis, and simulation.

The proposals may be validated by the organization's own personnel and/or by an external group of information processing specialists. If an organization chooses to utilize an external group, it must clearly define interaction with in-house personnel.

When a vendor has been selected, a contract must be negotiated. The manager must work closely with the legal staff to ensure that all of the necessary items are included in the agreement. After the terms have been agreed upon, the manager develops an implementation plan and schedule. Both the plan and schedule are affected by the conversion approach selected by the manager and the executive committee. The conversion approach may be gradual, overlapping, or immediate. Following selection of an approach, the manager formulates the actual implementation plan and schedule. An integral part of the plan is a readiness review. This review is necessary to ensure that the organization is capable of generating and utilizing the products of the new information processing approach. When the new approach has been implemented, a follow-up must be initiated to evaluate its effectiveness. The follow-up may be conducted once or it may be continued for as long as is deemed necessary. A follow-up of the implemented system may be performed in order to determine that the desired goals have been achieved, the projected tangible savings have been realized, the phaseout timetable is being adhered to, the user and operation's documentation is effective, and so on. If the results of the follow-up are unsatisfactory, it may be necessary to modify and replan the implemented approach.

CASE STUDY 9.1

Cogency, Consistency, and Clarity College

The director of academic data processing for the college has determined that there exists a need for a new hardware configuration on campus. This new configuration is intended primarily to provide "hands-on" training for students in the data processing curriculum. Some consideration may also be given to utilizing the new configuration as a terminal to an existing in-house IBM 370/148 system.

The director contacted his marketing representative and informed him verbally of his desires. The marketing representative responded with a letter indicating four possible configurations. Each configuration was outlined by machine and model number. In addition, some advantages were listed. Two of the four configurations were recommended as better choices for the college.

In his closing paragraph, the representative extended an invitation to discuss the contents of his letter.

Discussion Questions

1. Is adequate justification for acquiring a new configuration indicated? Explain.
2. Should the director have conducted a feasibility study to provide proper justification?
3. Is the single-vendor contact justified in this instance? Explain.
4. What kind of request for proposal could be developed for the college?
5. How effective is the vendor's response for validation and planning purposes? Explain.
6. What validation approach or approaches might conceivably be applied to this response?
7. Did the director execute his responsibilities as a manager correctly? Explain.

CHAPTER 10

Management Controls for
Information Processing

INTRODUCTION / The conversion to automated processing in accounting, reporting, recordkeeping, and decision-making activities is forcing
changes in the operating procedures for many organizations. Organizations that are upgrading their information systems to make use of teleprocessing and data base technology are forced to review, modify and
even reinforce some of the existing control procedures. New policies and
practices have to be developed and implemented that will effectively
eliminate or minimize the risk of fraud, embezzlement, accidental error,
loss of business and/or customers, law violations, sabotage, and embar-
rassment for an organization. Furthermore, the need to maintain and
improve the reliability of data and/or information means an increasing
emphasis on the development and implementation of procedures for the
prevention, detection, identification, and correction of errors. The failure
to maintain a basic level of reliability results in the loss of user confidence in the data processing function.

Controls are equally important for manual, unit-record, and computer-
based information systems. The controls must be incorporated into every
system during the design and development phases and evaluated during
the system testing, parallel testing, implementation, and follow-up
phases. Controls must never be superimposed on a system; rather, they
must be built in as an integral part of the operation.

The analyst must check with the users and the internal auditors to determine exactly the type and levels of control required. A control procedure adequate for one phase of a system may not be feasible for another.
The analyst must conduct an investigative process that is part of the systems analysis. During this process, the analyst must identify the relation
of the system's inputs and outputs to other systems and the types of controls required, the data flow, the placement of error-detection locations,
and the types of error checking procedures conducted at these points.

The information will enable the analyst to prepare a set of control procedures best suited for the needs of the organization. The systems manager and/or the data processing manager must review the procedures carefully to ensure that the controls are capable of detecting, identifying, and reporting errors, and that there is a capability to correct the error and reenter the correction into the system. Such a sound procedure will help to maintain the confidence of the users and managers and reduce or minimize operating problems and costs.

MANAGEMENT CONTROL OBJECTIVES

The principal objectives of a program of management control for data processing operations are:

To prevent loss of user confidence in the data processing operation

To prevent delays in processing and reporting due to faulty inputs

To minimize file and/or data base maintenance costs and efforts

To ensure that all source data entered into the information processing system are valid

To ensure that all source data entered into the system are transcribed accurately

To ensure that all applicable and pertinent data are included as outputs

To prevent any unauthorized data changes

To ensure that all erroneous data entries in the system are quickly detected and identified as such, and that authorized corrections are made promptly and accurately

To ensure that all processing is accomplished accurately

To prevent the accidental or deliberate alteration of programs, documentation, and files

To prevent the sabotage or destruction of data processing hardware

To protect and preserve the organization's assets

The effective implementation of these control objectives will:

Reduce or eliminate reruns due to errors

Reduce the need for supplementary processing

Reduce or eliminate the wasteful use of manpower, machine, material, and money resources

Enable an organization to continue to transact business despite an accident, disaster, or sabotage

Reduce or eliminate the possibility of fraud and embezzlement

TYPES OF MANAGEMENT CONTROLS

Six basic types of controls are appropriate to data processing operations and systems. These are:

1. Equipment controls
2. Input controls
3. Output controls
4. Program controls
5. External controls
6. Peripheral controls

Equipment Controls

The equipment (hardware) controls are built into the apparatus by the manufacturer to ensure that data is read, processed, transferred, and outputted correctly. The kinds of equipment controls available vary from manufacturer to manufacturer. Consideration of the types of controls available must be included in the feasibility study for both new equipment and systems.

Equipment controls are normally operative as a result of internal machine circuitry and are performed automatically. Whenever available in a hardware configuration, they should not be duplicated by other forms of control. Included in the category of equipment controls are the following:

1. Parity check
2. Echo checking
3. Control lights and indicators
4. File protection
5. Storage protection
6. Automatic retransmission
7. Cryptographic devices

1. PARITY CHECK. The technique is used to ensure the validity of data moved within the computer by verifying the number of binary bits in each code or character.

Character or code representation not meeting the hardware specification will cause a parity check error. A corrective action must then be initiated by the equipment operator. There are several variations on parity bit checking; among the most popular are the block-parity and Hamming code schemes.

2. ECHO CHECKING. Echo checking is a technique used to verify the transmission of data between two points. The data impulses transmitted to an output device are returned to the generating source and compared for accuracy. The original information transmitted should be exactly the same as the information outputted. The comparison is generally performed in a buffering device, with any deviation being indicated on the console for operator or program action.

3. CONTROL LIGHTS AND INDICATORS. Control lights and indicators are used

to alert the equipment operator about such conditions as arithmetic overflows, parity check errors, system interrupts, attempts to violate storage protection, programmable error conditions, faulty or erroneous data, etc. Responding to the indication provided on the console or components of the computing system, the operator takes the appropriate corrective action.

4. FILE PROTECTION. File-protection devices are provided on magnetic tape units and magnetic disk drives to prevent accidental erasure of valid data or master records. On a magnetic tape unit, the protection device is a removable plastic ring. Withdrawing the ring inhibits writing on the tape but allows reading. Inserting the protective ring nullifies the effect of the circuitry and allows both reading and writing on the tape. File protection on a magnetic disk drive is controlled by a control button on the unit. When activated, the button directs the circuitry to inhibit writing on protected records.

5. STORAGE PROTECTION. The storage-protect feature permits the storage or residence of more than one program in the main memory at any one time. It is a hardware feature activated by the executive program to assure correct and continuous operation, with protection against any accidental alteration of the resident programs.

6. AUTOMATIC RETRANSMISSION. Automatic error-detection and retransmission is necessary for data transmitted from an on-line terminal. Some data communications terminals include provision for the automatic retransmission of characters or messages found to be in error—a technique that also involves automatic error-detection. When a character is found to be in error, retransmission of that character, from a buffering device in the terminal, is requested for a given number of times. If the character cannot be correctly reread, an indicator light is turned on at the console of the terminal to signal the need for operator intervention.

7. CRYPTOGRAPHIC DEVICES. These are used to encode and decode sensitive information passing through computers, data communications terminals, and time-sharing terminals. Traditionally, these devices have been used primarily by the military to scramble information. However, many nonmilitary organizations—especially those that are decentralized and those that use public telephone and telegraph lines—are now utilizing such devices to combat the theft or loss of sensitive data.

Review Questions: Group 10A

1. Name the major control categories used in information processing systems.
2. What effect does a cryptographic device have on safeguarding inputs into an information system?

Input Controls

Input controls are primarily well-defined procedures designed to detect the creation, entry, or existence of erroneous or unauthorized data in the input recording, collection, transmittal, and/or transcription process. Their use in the system is intended to ensure that:

All data entering into the system is valid

Source data are received from all points of origin before processing is initiated

Source data are properly and accurately converted from human-sensible to machine-readable form

All original and adjusting entries are made into the system

All transactions are properly recorded at point of origin

The level and extent of input controls implemented in an information processing cycle will be affected by the type of data recorded and/or collected, validation required, the work load, and time available in the processing schedule for their use. The time constraint may be the most significant factor. If more time is available, then the number and type of input controls implemented will be more intense. However, if time is lacking, either fewer controls will be implemented or fewer entries, transactions, or documents will be validated.

Some of the more common kinds of input controls are:

1. Document register
2. Batching
3. Transmittal documents and route slips
4. Document numbering
5. Matching
6. Approvals
7. Verification
8. Self-checking numbers
9. Hash totals
10. Control totals
11. Data checkers
12. Checklists

1. DOCUMENT REGISTER. The document register is one of the oldest forms of input control available. It is primarily used to provide a record of document movement through the information processing cycle. When properly used, it provides an excellent audit trail, although its use may add time to the processing cycle. The register is illustrated in Figure 10.1.

2. BATCHING. A batch is a group or subgroup of transactions affecting a logical file of information. The transactions are ordered or arranged in a manner that gives each group some common identity; for example, a department number or date. The batches are generally limited in size to simplify the error-detecting, -identifying, and -correcting processes.

Each batch is preceded by a batch control record (see Figure 10.2). This contains a serially assigned batch control number, the date of origination, a count of the items included, originating source, hash totals of identifying information,

RECORD OF INVOICES								
DATE OF		SUPPLIER'S INVOICE NUMBER	AMOUNT OF INVOICE	OUR P. O. NUMBER	INVOICE		AUDITOR OR CLERK	REMARKS
INVOICE	PAYMENT				NO. OF ITEMS	TOTAL QUANTITY		

Figure 10.1 Sample document register

and control totals of quantities or amounts. When the documents are transcribed into a machine-readable form and initially machine processed, the batch or item counts and the hash or control totals are checked against the values posted on the batch control record. Any deviation may be isolated by checking the respective totals.

Batches may also be used to reduce keypunching effort, thereby minimizing the possibility of error in the transcription process. Repetitive data for a batch can be automatically duplicated by utilizing program control on the keypunch

RS–64 PAYROLL BATCH CONTROL CARD					
DATE	DEPT.	NO. OF CARDS		BATCH NO.	

FIELD DESCRIPTION	TOTAL HOURS	F R A C.	TOTAL AMOUNTS	D E C.
TIME WORKED AND ADJUSTMENTS				
OVERTIME ALLOWANCES AND ADJUSTMENTS				
OTHER ALLOWANCES AND ADJUSTMENTS				
SUB-TOTAL				
NIGHT BONUS AND ADJUSTMENTS				
GROSS				

DOCUMENT CONTROL		
SEQUENCE	OPERATION	INITIALS
1	LOG IN	
2	KEY PUNCH	
3	KEY VERIFY	
4	PROOF	
5	POST-PAYROLL	

Figure 10.2 Sample form for batch control records

machine. For example, a group of work assignment cards with the same depart-ment number, hours worked, and work order numbers may be batched and duplicated. The keypunch operator would have to punch only the employee number in each card. This type of operation speeds up keypunching and re-duces the possibility of error.

3. TRANSMITTAL DOCUMENTS AND ROUTE SLIPS. Transmittal documents and

TRANSMITTAL DOCUMENT — FORM NO. R5-61

SYSTEM/APPLICATION	IDENTIFICATION NUMBER
ORIGINATOR	LOCATION
TELEPHONE	DATE

TYPE OF DATA TRANSMITTED ▶ — DOCUMENT — CARD — TAPE — DISK

'REQUIRED ENTRY

	DOCUMENT	CARD	TAPE	DISK
BATCH NUMBER(S)	*	*	*	*
DOCUMENT IDENT.	*			
FILE IDENT.		*		
TAPE IDENT.			*	
DISK IDENT.				*
DOCUMENT COUNT	*			
RECORD COUNT		*	*	*
LINE ITEM COUNT				
HASH TOTAL				
QUANTITY TOTAL				
DOLLAR VALUE TOTAL				
NO. OF BOXES/TAPES/DISKS	*	*	*	*

SPECIAL INSTRUCTIONS:

DATA CHECKER	DATE CHECKED	KEYING OPERATOR	DATE KEYED	VERIFIER OPERATOR	DATE VERIFIED	LAST BATCH
	/ /		/ /		/ /	YES / NO

Figure 10.3 Transmittal document form

route slips (see Figure 10.3) establish control over the movement of documents or batches from one location or another. These forms are used to fix responsiblity and accountability for the documents. They are also used to indicate progress or the flow of a document through an operation. In addition to controlling source documents, transmittal documents, as illustrated in Figure 10.3, are used for other machine-readable media, such as cards, paper tape, magnetic tape, diskettes, etc. Furthermore, they can be used for indicating batch or item counts, hash totals, and control totals generated on the input media.

4. DOCUMENT NUMBERING. Assigned-sequence numbers, together with pre-punched and prenumbered forms, may be used to control the number of items or records processed. Running a check on the document numbers ensures inclusion of all documents before, during, and after processing. The control numbers may be stamped or imprinted on the documents; punched into, printed on, or interpreted on the cards; or printed on the output processed on a high-speed printer or tabulator.

Serial numbers may be affixed to the batch record control cards or transmittal slips in order to facilitate document movement control. Soft-paper payroll checks and stock certificates contain numbers imprinted by the forms vendors. Prepunched numbers often appear in punched card drafts or checks to provide an element of document control.

5. MATCHING. In activities where multiple copies of a document are used, it

may be necessary to reassemble and match the documents in the forms set before any processing is initiated.

Matching may also be performed by checking transaction cards against card files, as well as by checking transaction cards against master magnetic tape files. For example, in surveys where a number of forms are mailed out, the responses are matched against a master file for a follow-up on nonresponses.

6. APPROVALS. Approvals are used to regulate the entry of data into a system. These require one or several signatures to effect an input change. The approval procedures must be included in the organizational policies and practices, and in the documentation for a system. Approvals may be required for changes to salary or rate fields on payroll records, credit limits in sales records, commission percentages for salesmen, or inventory safety stock or reorder levels.

7. VERIFICATION. To ensure the accurate transcription of the original data into a machine-sensible form, some type of mechanical or manual verification may be required. In some organizations, a manual verification check is made by visually scanning the source documents, machine-processable input, or a listing of the transcribed input. The verification may be made for completeness of the data elements recorded on the form. This can be accomplished by checking for missing, incomplete, or inaccurate posting. Or, the verification may be made to determine whether the correct form or proper code was used to initiate a desired action.

8. SELF-CHECKING NUMBERS. The self-checking number control is used to prevent or detect the incorrect transcription, transposition, or unauthorized entry of identification numbers, such as account or employee numbers, on data input. The identification numbers are calculated according to a predetermined formula to generate a check digit. The check digit may be subsequently verified within the hardware to ensure that the inputted number is valid. If there is a change in the construction of the identification number, then a change will be reflected in the check-digit value.

There are a number of different check-digit formulae in existence. However, for illustrative purposes, this discussion will be limited to the use of the Modulus 11, because this is a popular system.

The check digit is generated as follows:

Step 1: Assign to each digit in the identification number, beginning with the least significant position, a binary weighting factor beginning with 2.

Step 2: Multiply each digit in the identification number by the assigned weighting factor.

Step 3: Add together all of the products.

Step 4: Divide the sum of the products by 11.

Step 5: Subtract the remainder, from the division in the previous step, from the modulus value of 11.

Step 6: Append the result of the subtraction, which is the check digit, to the identification number.

For example, let us calculate the check digit for the account number 411 42 9285:

Account Number	4	1	1	4	2	9	2	8	5
Weighting Factors: (Powers of Two)	512	256	128	64	32	16	8	4	2
Products:	2048	256	128	256	64	144	16	32	10

Add the Products: $2048 + 256 + 128 + 256 + 64 + 144 + 16 + 32 + 10 = 2954$

Divide Total by 11: $\quad 2954 \div 11 = 268$ Remainder 5
Subtract Remainder: $\quad 11 - 5 = 6$
Check Digit: $\quad\quad\quad$ 6
Account Number with
$\quad$ check digit reads $\quad\quad$ 411 42 9285 6

Alphabetic codes may also be checked by generating the check digit from the numeric characters in each position.

The use of check digits in records obviously increases the size of the record or necessitates restructuring of the record. To some degree, it also increases the possibility of data error. Nevertheless, it is very effective in detecting transcription, transposition, and transmission errors.

The check digit may be calculated manually and appended to the identification numbers on the source documents before they are submitted for transcription or transmittal. Or, the check digit may be generated on the specially equipped keypunch, data recording, or terminal device.

9. HASH TOTALS. A hash total is a sum that results from adding together the contents of a particular data field in all the records in a batch or file. The fields used for hash totals are not normally summed, such as account numbers, invoice numbers, and patient numbers. The totals are generated before processing is initiated and subsequently checked during processing. A missing record may be found by subtracting the current total from the beginning hash total.

Hash totals may be posted on a batch control record, transmittal slip, or route slip in order to provide for document and/or record control. Totals may also be developed for alphabetic fields by summing the numeric portion of each character.

10. CONTROL TOTALS. Control totals are sums generated as a result of accumulating quantity or amount fields in a group of records. As the records are again processed, the fields are accumulated and then compared with the beginning totals as proof that all records have been included.

The beginning totals may be posted on batch control records, transmittal documents route slips, or control logs. For example, a control total may be generated on the number of standard and overtime hours for employees in a given department. These totals will be checked during the processing cycle to detect any possible errors.

To simplify the detection, identification, and correction of errors, the control totals are established by convenient or appropriate organizational groups, such as departments, plants, or branch offices.

11. DATA CHECKERS. Data checkers are the people who validate the source documents and/or input before they are transcribed or processed. The checker manipulates the documents or records according to the procedures developed by the systems analyst. The procedures are established to verify the completeness of a form; the accuracy of calculations; the fact that survey forms have been returned by canvassers; etc. Or, the data checkers may be responsible for performing visual verification checks on the source documents and input.

12. CHECKLISTS. Checklists are prepared by the systems analyst to assist users in the preparation of inputs and to check documents and inputs for completeness and accuracy. The checklists are included in the system's documentation. An example of a checklist procedure is shown in Figure 10.4. The list in this example is used to validate the completeness of an inventory transaction record before it is submitted for keypunching.

Review Questions: Group 10B

1. Why should a data processing manager advocate the use of input controls in an information processing system?
2. How can a self-checking number be used as a form of input control?
3. How can a checklist be an effective form of input control?
4. What input control or controls would you recommend for a system surveying the needs of a day-care center?

Output Controls

Output controls in the information processing cycle are primarily procedural checks. They are more difficult to establish because they are affected by the intermediate processes performed between input and output. For example, an organization may establish calculated payroll tax deductions as one of the output

Figure 10.4 Example of checklist procedure

The stockroom clerk will edit the Stock Transaction Form (RAS-33A) for completeness and accuracy. Check:
    (a) Department Number
    (b) Inventory Class
    (c) Status
    (d) Unit of Issue
    (e) Piece Part Number
    (f) Quantity
    (g) Requisition Number

---

control totals. Initially, this is an unknown value because the only relevant input control total would be the number of tax exemptions. This value becomes the basis for verifying the accuracy of the federal, and possibly the state and local, income tax calculations. The verification is made by subtracting the exemption dollar value from the calculated gross and then applying the respective tax formulae. The payroll clerk performs this calculation for each department to minimize the error-detection problem.

Output controls are developed and implemented to ensure that:

Reports and outputs are accurate

No unauthorized entries to the system have been made

Detected errors and exceptions have been corrected

Outputs and reports are in proper format

Reports appear in human-sensible language

Proper disposition is made of all outputs and reports

These objectives may be attained through the use of the following techniques:

1. Totals
2. Checkpoints and Restart Procedures
3. Setup Procedures
4. Reports Control
5. Console Operating Procedures
6. Distribution Instructions

1. TOTALS. The output total control is determined primarily by the available input control totals. However, as has been stated earlier, the totals generated at the initiation of the information processing cycle may not be identical with those outputted. In a file update process, the input master file record count differs from the updated master file record count because of the inputted add/delete transactions. Therefore, for balancing purposes, separate add/delete item counts and totals have to be generated. These would be intermediate totals used for balancing purposes. For example:

Master File Record Count	4938
Transaction File	
New Records Count	+200
Delete Records Count	−150
Updated Master File Record Count	4988

In the design phase, the systems analyst must develop the necessary output-verification procedures for operations and user personnel. For batch processing, he should establish a procedure to identify each batch, to count the transactions included, and to accumulate the relevant hash and control fields.

If a discrepancy is found in a report, the report should not be released until the cause of the deviation is known. Provision is then made for either correcting the report or producing a supplementary report. In instances where the output becomes input for another program or system, the problem may be more difficult to cope with. Unavailability of time can impose a severe limitation on the problem-correction process. With the advent of more sophisticated management information systems, there is a greater need for maintaining data and informational validity and control. Failure to supply accurate information can only result in faulty and ineffectual decision making.

2. CHECKPOINTS AND RESTART PROCEDURES. Checkpoints are included in a system to determine if processing has been accurately performed up to a given point. The checkpoints have the effect of breaking down a large system into workable and controllable segments. As each segment is correctly processed, the results are recorded on an output medium. Any errors that are detected and identified can be corrected at each checkpoint. The processing is then reiterated from the last checkpoint.

The restart procedures indicate the required corrective action and the steps to reinitiate processing in the system. These procedures must be included in the user and operations documentation for a given system.

The availability of checkpoints and restart procedures helps to reduce the number of reruns, particularly on long runs. Also, they help to minimize the effects that problems and errors can have on the production schedule.

3. SETUP PROCEDURES. The setup procedures are designed to ensure the output of user reports in a proper and meaningful format. The procedures are included as part of the operations documentation.

The operator's manual must include information that enables the operator to set up the hardware for output of the desired report. In addition, a sample of the form is included. This sample should indicate the proper alignment and the fields that are to be outputted.

4. REPORTS CONTROL. A reports control system should be established to bring about the optimal use of resources. This system must be established to ensure the propriety, relevance, clarity, and timeliness of the reports.

Each report should be evaluated according to the checklist shown in Figure 10.5. Reports that do not produce a favorable response to the checklist questions must be further evaluated. Then, if necessary, they must be either redesigned to meet management objectives or deleted from the production schedule to conserve valuable resources.

5. CONSOLE OPERATING PROCEDURES. The console operating procedures for a given system obviously need to provide the necessary operator instructions. This means that operator responses must be carefully tested prior to system implementation and then be monitored during the follow-up. Of particular importance is the instructive output. This segment contains the error messages, oper-

Each report must be evaluated on the basis of the following criteria:
1. Is the report necessary?
2. Does the report contain unnecessary data, which detracts from its clarity?
3. Does the report contain all the necessary data useful for decision-making?
4. Is the report issued when needed?
5. Should the report be condensed?
6. Can the report be combined with another to increase their effectiveness?
7. Does the report contribute to the overall effectiveness of the organization?
8. Is the sequence of the outputted data elements satisfactory?
9. Are those data items most frequently referenced in the proper locations?

Figure 10.5 Checklist for reports control system

ator instructions for checkpoints and restarts, and processing diagnostics. The failure to react properly to these conditions or instructions may result in faulty or inaccurate processing and outputs.

A chart may also be prepared that will identify the relationships between programs in a given job stream. For example, you would identify that the particular program cannot be processed until a previous program has been executed. Or, you may identify that the output of a particular program serves as input to a succeeding program. It is also possible to identify that particular programs can be run at any time without affecting the required processing sequences.

6. DISTRIBUTION INSTRUCTIONS. Data processing has become an invaluable tool in the decision-making process. Consequently, when an output or report is produced, it must be promptly dispatched to the next operation or user after its accuracy has been validated. Dispatching the output that is scheduled to be input to another operation or system is generally less of a problem. Part of this problem is handled by effective documentation. Also, the use of a tape/disk librarian helps to overcome some of the difficulties that may arise.

The system documentation should include instructions for processing the report and for then distributing it. A sample distribution form is given in Figure 10.6. Distribution to a user may be made by special messenger, intra- or inter-plant mail, regular mail, or pickup by functional area. The pickup may be arranged because the distribution schedule does not fit the user's schedule. Distribution by special messenger, though somewhat expensive, may be the most effective method. Intra- or inter-plant mail is frequently the least effective method of distribution, principally because only two pickups and deliveries are possible—one in the morning and the other in the afternoon.

Some organizations are developing special sign-off procedures that require a user's confirmation of receipts of a report. This is being done in order to reduce the number of reruns that are generated as a result of allegedly lost reports.

The method of distribution selected for each system should be tested prior to implementation and should be monitored in the follow-up phase.

DISTRIBUTION PROCEDURE												

DISTRIBUTION PROCEDURE

DATE:_____   PAGE____ OF_____

PROGRAM NO:_____   PROGRAM TITLE:_____

FORM NO:_____   FORM TITLE:_____

STEP NO:_____   DUE OUT:_____
(TIME)   (DATE)

PART NO.	PROCESSING					TO	LOCATION	DISTRIBUTE VIA					
	DECOL	BURST	BIND	TRIM	CFP			SPECIAL MESSEN-GER	INTER-PLANT MAIL	INTRA-PLANT MAIL	U.S. MAIL (REG)	U.S. MAIL (AIR)	PICK UP

SPECIAL INSTRUCTIONS

Figure 10.6 Sample form for distribution procedure

Some of the output controls may overlap or be supplemented by the control techniques in the program, external, and peripheral categories. Furthermore, the output controls may be affected by the output medium, work load, cost, and time. It is the time factor that may have the most significant influence on the level and extent of controls developed and implemented in this category.

1. What are the objectives of an output control program?
2. Why would a data processing manager require the development and implementation of checkpoint and restart procedures in a system?
3. How are console operating procedures used as an output control?
4. What approaches might a manager consider to facilitate distribution of the outputs?

Program Controls

The program controls are an integral part of a computer program or machine operation. Sound planning and effective implementation of these checks provide the user with a series of sophisticated control tools. The checks and their associated procedures enable the user to detect and identify an error condition; they also indicate the necessary remedial action and facilitate reprocessing or prompt error recovery. Also, with some of the techniques, it is possible to develop an audit record of the actions occurring and exercised.

Program controls—sometimes referred to as programming, or processing, checks—are designed principally to ensure that:

All transactions are properly posted

Any lost or nonprocessed data is promptly detected

All codes and conditions are verified prior to processing

The arithmetic and logic checks are peformed accurately

All data has been processed through each program

Failure to achieve these objectives may result in invalid or inaccurate outputs, which, in turn, would invalidate any decisions based on these outputs.

The most common forms of program controls are:

1. Crossfooting
2. Edit checks
3. Zero balancing
4. Existence checks
5. Negative balance test
6. Self-checking number
7. Sequence checks
8. Completeness checks
9. Reasonableness checks
10. Combination checks
11. Range checks
12. Date checks
13. Totals
14. Housekeeping checks
15. Labels

16. Passwords

17. Transaction logs

1. CROSSFOOTING. Crossfooting is a technique that utilizes addition and/or subtraction of a horizontal row or vertical column of factors or elements in order to prove processing and posting accuracy. Crossfooting is used frequently in accounting operations, such as payroll. Here the net pay amounts and individual deductions are accumulated for final totals and then added horizontally to determine if they equal the total gross earnings (see Figure 10.7).

2. EDIT CHECKS. Editing is a common data processing practice utilizing computing or unit-record equipment to test the input or output data against predetermined codes, conditions, or standards. Edit checks are used to ensure data compatibility, not data accuracy. Accuracy must be determined by other means. It is intended that the edit checks performed in the program detect any errors in data elements, data fields, records, and files used in the process. Subsequently, the procedures have to be executed to correct the exceptions or conditions before either processing is continued or output distribution is made; to identify that the error has been detected, process the error and correct later; or provide for automatic correction of the error.

Editing is normally performed for evaluating data item size, mode, and construction. As a result, an edit check is sometimes referred to as a formatting check.

3. ZERO BALANCING. Zero balancing is a technique in which the accumulation of a given quantity or amount field is subtracted from a predetermined beginning balance so as to arrive at a zero balance. Any balance other than a zero will indicate an error condition. The beginning balances are extracted from

Figure 10.7 Example of crossfooting: payroll application

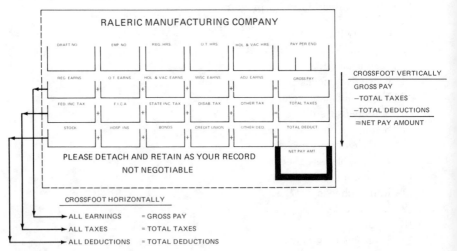

a batch control record, transmittal slip, or control log. These totals will either precede or follow the data. If the totals precede the data, then the method is called the header balancing method; if they follow the data, then this is referred to as the trailer balancing method.

The technique may also be used in a job stream, where the previous programs totals must zero balance before processing of a second program in the sequence is continued.

4. EXISTENCE CHECKS. Existence checks are a form of validity check to determine if a tested code is active, acceptable, or valid. The input may be compared with a deck of master cards, master tape, or reference table to determine its admissability. All unmatched items must then be investigated for cause of the deviation. For example, occupation codes may be compared mechanically with an authorized occupations code file maintained on cards, magnetic tape, or disk, in order to resolve any input errors in the codes prior to processing a manning and authorization listing.

5. NEGATIVE BALANCE TEST. This is a technique used to test the result of an arithmetic operation for a negative balance. In payroll operations, the negative balance test is used to determine if the amount of deductions has exceeded gross pay earnings. In computerized operations, an internal procedure can be initiated to resolve the negative balance. In unit-record, accounting machine operations, a negative balance condition can be signaled by the printing of a CR (credit) or minus sign ($-$) on the print-out.

6. SELF-CHECKING NUMBER. As a program control, the self-checking number is used to validate the identification code for a possible transposition or transcription error. Each time that the equipment processes the identification number, a check digit is computed. The newly calculated digit is then compared with the appended digit in the identification number. If the two digits are not the same, an error-condition signal on the console or other output medium indicates the need for operator or user action.

Another popular self-checking number technique is the Modulus-10 method. The Modulus-10 formula is calculated as follows:

Step 1: Multiply the units position and every alternate digit in the identification number by 2.

Step 2: Crossfoot the digits in the product and those digits in the identification number not multiplied by 2.

Step 3: Subtract the crossfooted total from the next higher number ending in zero.

Step 4: The remainder is the check digit.

Step 5: Append the check digit to the identification number.

Example of Modulus-10:

Identification number	1	2	3	4	5
Alternate digits	1		3		5
Multiple alternate digits by 2					×2

Product	2	7	0
Crossfoot the product (270) and those digits not included in the multiplication (2, 4)			$2+7+0+2+4=15$
Subtract total from the next higher number ending in zero			20
			-15
			5
Check digit			5
Append check digit		12345$\underline{5}$	

As a program control, the self-checking number will help to detect transcription, transposition, and accidental or deliberate alteration errors.

7. SEQUENCE CHECK. Sequence checks are made to ensure that the data is arranged or ordered in an ascending or descending sequence prior to processing. The checks are a very important part of the file update process when the file is organized in a sequential or serial mode.

The sequence check may also be used to select duplicate records from a master or reference file or to assemble data for processing.

8. COMPLETENESS CHECK. A completeness check is made to ensure either that the desired information is included in all of the data fields in a record or that all input is included and in sequence. For example, in an inventory control application, a back-order release record may be checked to determine if it contains a part number, requisition number, and a notation regarding quantity to be released. If the needed information is missing, the record must be identified as incomplete and procedures must then be executed to process this exception.

9. REASONABLENESS CHECK. A reasonableness check is a test made on a field to determine if it has exceeded a predetermined parameter. If it has not exceeded the parameter, then the field is regarded or treated as a normal condition. The check does not ensure that the data is valid, but only that it has not exceeded a stated parameter. Reasonableness checks are used quite frequently in payroll operations, where a parameter has been established on the gross pay figure. Or, they may be used to ensure that a customer has not exceeded a credit limitation on an order.

The reasonableness check is frequently utilized as part of an exception reporting system. This eliminates unnecessary details from reports and indicates only deviations, thereby providing more meaningful data in the decision-making process. An effective reporting system provides the manager only with those situations that cannot be corrected at lower levels in the organizational structure.

10. COMBINATION CHECKS. Combination checks are performed on a record or on several input items to determine their logical relationship and to remove any erroneous combinations of data. Some auditors refer to combination checks as relationship or correlation checks.

Combination checks may be made on medical input, for example, to ensure that a diagnosis code for a pregnancy may be found only in a female patient's record. Or, that a medication dosage does not exceed the allowable tolerances for a given age. Also, the checks may be used to ensure that a requisition for a given stock item can be issued to the requesting unit and in the quantity requested.

11. RANGE CHECK. The range check is a basic validity or admissability test that is most widely used in data validation. The check is applied to a code or data item to determine if it compares to a given set of parameters. The test may be simple or it may be very sophisticated. For example, a simple use of the range check may be an age check for validating records between the ages of 18–30. Records with an age of less than 18 or greater than 30 would be unacceptable. The parameters may also be included in a table to facilitate a table look-up in memory or as master or cross-reference files. For example, the programmer may check the salary parameters (lower and upper) for a given job classification. The programmer would have to check the job classification and the salary to determine if it is included within the prescribed parameters.

Where ranges are changed frequently, it may be more beneficial for an organization to maintain the ranges on an external file rather than incorporate the ranges into the program. Inclusion of the ranges in the programs would require a reassembly or recompilation to effect the change.

12. DATE CHECK. Input records may be checked to determine if they are acceptable on a given date. Date checks can be used to select transactions due for payment in an accounts payable application; to select the effective date of salary increases for employees; to select employees eligible for a merit rating or promotion; or to select inputted items coded with an entry prior to a given date.

Depending on the use made of dates, it may also be necessary to perform a check on the field format and/or logical limits. For example, a calendar date can be only two digits, and a date such as May 42 is unacceptable.

13. TOTALS. Totals may be used to control the number of records processed and the accuracy of processing. The type and level of control established in this category is affected by the input, output, and procedural requirements. The total controls may take the form of batch counts, record counts, hash totals, or control totals.

14. HOUSEKEEPING CHECKS. The housekeeping checks should be part of standard operating procedure in every data processing organization. The housekeeping functions should be performed at the beginning of each computer program to clear buffers, clear registers, reset program switches and bit masks, initialize areas, etc. The checks may be written into the computer program by the

programmer, or he may choose to use the housekeeping capabilities of the IOCS software package.

15. LABELS. A label is an internal identification affixed to a data file on tape or disk to check the file's validity before processing is initiated. The label checking performed in a program ensures that the desired file is actually mounted on a desired unit. For example, a payroll master tape is checked to ensure that it is the current updated file. If it is, then payroll processing is initiated; if it is not, an error indication is signaled to the operator.

16. PASSWORDS. The password is a preestablished key used to identify a user and his right to access a given file. The passwords consist of numbers, letters, and symbols, which identify an authorized user and his terminal location. An authorized user may be given the right to process on the hardware; to enter data changes; or to access data or request a printout. In some organizations, several passwords may be required to effect an operation.

Passwords may have to be changed often to maintain security. Also, procedures must be developed in order to determine a "need-to-know" basis. This step is necessary to limit file access only to authorized users.

17. TRANSACTION LOGS. Transaction logs represent a sophisticated technique for recording events that occur on a computer. The logs may be used to record the users' identification, the files they accessed, and type of inquiry. Subsequently, this information is processed to detect any attempts by unauthorized users to violate file security.

The technique may be further expanded to include a copy of the change transaction, so as to provide an audit trail for the accidental or deliberate entry of erroneous data. This method can be particularly useful for recording data entries from online remote terminals.

The program controls that are implemented may have to be evaluated on a cost-effectiveness basis. It is evident that the implementation of some of the checks, such as transaction logs, may be expensive. The cost is not prohibitive; however, one must determine the worth of the information obtained for this outlay. Also, an organization may not have the personnel resources available to develop and implement some of the checks. Or, the hardware may not have the capacity or the features to implement some of the checks.

Review Questions: Group 10D

1. What type of program control would be used in an inventory control system to ensure numeric data in the part number field of a transaction record?
2. Why would it be advantageous for a manager to advocate the use of a negative balance test in an accounts payable system?
3. If the organization was developing a management information system utilizing terminals, what specific program controls should be considered for application to user personnel?

External Controls

External controls are primarily concerned with providing protection against the entry of unauthorized data into the system—that is, preventing erroneous data from entering the system and unauthorized data from filtering in. These controls are designed to supplement and/or reinforce the controls available in the other categories. As a result, they may overlap, to a limited degree, some of the other controls implemented in an information processing cycle. However, they are a necessary part of the interacting network of controls needed to maintain system reliability.

The external controls are primarily procedural and manual, except for those included in the computer auditing category. Among the more common forms of external control are:

1. Data control
2. Exception processing
3. Administrative procedures
4. Computer audits

1. DATA CONTROL. Data control involves the use of data checkers to validate input and output. The procedures for the controls must be developed by the systems analyst in conjunction with the internal and/or external auditors.

The input validation should be concerned with receipt of inputs, error detection, and data quality. The receipt of inputs must be governed by procedures delineating the schedule, the accountability for and method of movement, and the types and level of control totals. The error-detection and data quality procedures should include such items as checklists to facilitate data preparation and conversion by the data originator or the data transcriber. Also, these two procedures should include methods or steps for reconciling the errors in data or coding or for investigating questionable items.

The output validation procedures are primarily concerned with accuracy, format, and distribution requirements. The specific requirements for each output or report should result from an assessment of user, auditor, and data processing needs. Most organizations consider accuracy to be the prime requirement for evaluating each output or report. The procedures are primarily concerned with balancing the report. These same procedures often do not include any information on how to resolve discrepancies in totals.

The distribution requirements should include the report handling and notification procedures as well. These would include the due-out schedule; special instructions, such as decollation, bursting, or binding; and provision for notifying the user when the report either is complete or has been delayed.

Data control procedures are a must for an organization using an outside service bureau for its processing.

2. EXCEPTION PROCESSING. The systems personnel must develop a procedure for the reporting, handling, correction, and control of data errors and processing exceptions. In many organizations, the errors are flagged and processing of the

job is terminated until the corrections are made and reentered into the input stream. In others, the flagged items are handled separately while the processing continues and then a supplementary run is made. Yet others will flag the errors, continue the process and then hand-correct the report or adjust the output record.

As organizations progress in the use of data processing technology, new data correction procedures are developed. These procedures now focus on identifying the specific error or errors, simplifying the correction process of the user, and providing a means of reentry into the process. Some of the procedures even utilize different options for handling erroneous data, such as rejecting an incorrect data element or field; rejecting the bad record; rejecting a group of transactions or batch; automatically correcting the error; or permitting the error to continue in the process and subsequently make the necessary correction. An organization must consider which of the above options is best suited for a particular application. Rejection of data is generally not suitable for most organizations because it may make reentry difficult. Continuing to process an error requires that the record be flagged in some manner and the correction must be entered as quickly as possible. This may be one of the most difficult procedures to establish and coordinate. The automatic correction of data is possible only where the programmer can be reasonably certain of what the correction should be for a given field. Rejection of a group of records is generally suitable for batch processing, or processing of sequential files.

Where terminal printers and visual display devices are used for identifying error data, the procedures for indicating the errors and causes will have to be abbreviated due to device limitations. However, properly designed systems may make it possible to reenter the daily with some ease and in very timely manner.

Identifying deviations that are detected during processing will not be very unlike the procedures used to handle rejected inputs. The problems are very much the same. Turnaround is a very key factor in the handling and correction process. If the user procedures for handling the erroneous or rejected data are fairly simple, the turnaround time for entering the correction may be kept to a minimum. There is also need to incorporate a feedback procedure to identify that the corrections have been properly executed and are accurate.

Provision must also be made to handle abnormal situations in the processing cycle. Items included in this category are such things as being able to respond to a customer's inquiry regarding his bill, attempting to remove duplicate mailings, or processing inquiries from managers. Very frequently systems are not designed to handle inquiries or questions. Or, situations in which a customer may send an overpayment for an order—$10.70 when the amount was only $10.07. Should the order be returned and the customer requested to submit only the correct amount?

There must also be some form of audit trail included to control the correction process. This procedure is generally established by the systems analyst in cooperation with the internal auditor. A suggested approach may be to identify what correction was made, when, and by whom.

3. ADMINISTRATIVE PROCEDURES. Administrative procedures are concerned with maintaining system accuracy, efficiency, and reliability. Among the primary concerns here are the procedures for distribution, maintenance, and periodic auditing of documentation that affect existing systems. Also, the administrative procedures must be concerned with delineating the personnel authorized to effect a data change as well as the extent of their authority to do so. Inherent in these procedures are the steps and forms to be followed in executing a change transaction. This will help to provide a documented audit trail of the events and activities.

Administrative procedures may also be concerned with the data retention policies and practices. In some organizations, this responsibility may be delegated to the data processing administrator or manager. However, most either leave this responsibility with the internal auditor or follow the guidelines stipulated by the external auditors. Consideration should also be given to policies for the retention of data that may subsequently be used in a legal action. At present, though, there is some legal dispute regarding the admissibility of computer records as legal evidence.

The administrative procedures may also delineate the methods for disposal of sensitive data. This would cover disposing of such items as the contents of wastebaskets, carbons removed from outputs, and reports or records no longer required for retention. The procedures may also govern the practices for deleting sensitive data from such media as magnetic tape, drum, or disk.

The procedures may also govern the safeguards to be followed for online terminal devices at remote locations. For example, the practice may require the removal of a ribbon from a teletypewriter or printer following the processing of sensitive data.

The administrative procedures must also include procedures for trouble reporting. Problems that arise with the software, applications programs, hardware, data, documentation, and so forth must be reported. Though many organizations have such procedures established, many do not follow through on the problems and this ultimately leads to deeper problems.

4. COMPUTER AUDITS. Computer audits—computer-assisted auditing techniques as they are sometimes called—are an effective way of extending audit capability. It is intended that these techniques should reduce the effort required to select and verify the input, output, and processing transactions in a system. These techniques are also intended to determine the effectiveness of the management controls utilized in the system. The audit techniques can be performed with unit-record or computing equipment, although the EAM devices are less flexible.

There are several different computer-auditing techniques, but each of them utilizes the same basic approach. This approach to auditing may be described as:

Identifying the inputs into the system
Identifying the outputs of the system

Determining how the inputs are processed

Testing the efficiency and effect of the system's controls

Among the more common computer auditing techniques are:

a) Detailed testing
b) Sampling
c) Exception analysis
d) Graphic displays
e) Specialized analysis
f) Automated flowcharting
g) Integrated test facility

a) *Detailed testing.* In this technique, the auditor prepares the necessary computer programs and/or control panels to assist in evaluating the system's operation. Either "live" or "artificial" data that is representative of the system's inputs is used in the audit. This will enable the auditor to evaluate the performance of a program, its related subroutines, total controls, and file maintenance procedures.

The detailed testing technique is also used to verify the computational capabilities of a system. If any deviations are found, the auditor will be able to concentrate his attention in that area. The hardware may also be used to simulate the complete processing of a segment of the system. Both of these methods enable the auditor to process a large volume of data in a shorter time span and with only limited clerical effort.

b) *Sampling.* The computer may be used to generate the random numbers, select the sample size within a desired level of confidence, and provide an output of the selected records and/or transactions. The auditor may then follow the processing cycle from input to output in each of the selected items. The processing and outputs may be verified either by utilizing existing printouts and controls or by preparing a series of predetermined results.

The auditor may possibly take the selected items and process them through only a predetermined portion of the system. Very often, the area that is selected either is one that has a high error rate or is one of the key activities in the system.

Sometimes, however, an auditor will select some cases and supervise their manipulation, manually and mechanically, through the processing cycle.

c) *Exception analysis.* Exception analysis is probably the most comprehensive method of auditing because the auditor evaluates an entire file or group of files. The auditor establishes desired exception criteria and applies these to all of the records in the file. Within a relatively short period of time, the auditor may select from a merchandise inventory file, for example, those items that have an unusual cost/price relationship. The exception items may be outputted on a printer for a detailed follow-up. Or, the auditor may take two files and compare items in the records for discrepancies. For example, a cost bulletin file may be compared with the engineering material and layout file concerning standard cost or quantities. Any discrepancies found may be outputted on a printer for reconciliation purposes. This same approach is frequently followed when comparing physical inventory quantities with the on-hand balances in the master inventory file.

d) Graphic displays. Graphic displays are used to evaluate aspects of a single file or multiple files. Generally, a printer or plotter is used. However, it is also feasible and practical to use a cathode-ray tube terminal for this purpose.

The auditor determines the sets of criteria and applies these against a single- or multiple-file application. For example, this technique may be used very effectively in displaying a comparison of current and prior year expense accounts.

e) Specialized analysis. Specialized analysis is an auditing technique that requires the use of special-purpose computer programs. The programs may be written by the auditor or extracted from a program library. Specialized analysis programs may be used for such purposes as cash-flow analysis, portfolio analysis, projected interest income, and evaluation of depreciation schedules. The application of these programs to a large file can significantly reduce the time required for such an analysis.

f) Automated flowcharting. Automated flowcharting is a technique designed to audit an organization's computer programs. The software will automatically block-diagram the instructions in a given program. However, it does not validate program performance.

This technique may be used when an organization's existing documentation is obsolete or unavailable. It is also used to highlight the controls written in the program being evaluated. Furthermore, it is frequently used in comparison with existing documentation to determine its accuracy and relevance. Sometimes, it is used to conduct a surprise audit on an existing operational program to determine if any deliberate alterations had been made.

g) Integrated test facility. The integrated test facility technique was developed by internal auditors to test a system's controls. The technique is sometimes referred to as the mini company or the dummy company technique. The technique operates in conjunction with the normal processing of an information processing system. This means that the auditor and/or a systems analyst establishes a "dummy entity" in the file. The dummy entity may be an employee, customer, account number, product, department, or a small company. The audit process occurs because "live" data are processed against the entity to ensure that the system is functioning correctly. Valid and invalid transactions may be processed concurrently with the system's actual data to determine the data flow through the system from beginning to end.

Because the "test" transactions flow through the system with the "live" data, a decision must be made if the information is to become part of the control totals. It would be much better if the applications programs were modified to inhibit inclusion of the "test" data from the official counts, etc. Also, some consideration should be given to limiting the size or number of entities to prevent the files from becoming cluttered with unofficial data. The identification of the entities must also be kept confidential to provide a meaningful audit trail. Some organizations make their employees aware of the fact that a given system is being intensively audited and that any attempts at fraud or embezzlement will be detected very quickly.

The entity or entities must be reviewed constantly to ensure that the system is functioning correctly.

Review Questions: Group 10E

1. Why must a data processing manager be concerned with the implementation of external controls within the organization?
2. A frequent complaint of magazine subscribers is that they are unable to secure a satisfactory response to their questions about renewals. How can this problem be overcome within the data processing factor?
3. What are some of the different policies and practices that should be incorporated into administrative procedures?
4. If you were asked to select a form of computer auditing for the organization, which technique would you choose? Why?

Peripheral Controls

Peripheral controls, also called supplementary checks, may be described as a series of procedures directly affecting the data processing organization. They are used to direct and control the activities and functions of the data processing personnel, environment, programs, documentation, and files. Unlike the other control categories, peripheral controls are somewhat more general in their context and application.

The peripheral controls are principally concerned with:

a) Environmental security
b) Personnel practices
c) Tape and disk file control

ENVIRONMENTAL SECURITY

Environmental security is concerned with safeguarding the data processing organization's equipment, personnel, sensitive data files, software, programs, and documentation from disasters, acts of sabotage, fraud or embezzlement, mismanagement, and accidents by users, visitors, and operators.

Prevention and contingency plans must be established to cope with the variety of potential hazards previously mentioned. The safeguards must be tailored to meet the needs of the organization yet be realistic. Most organizations do not require a fool-proof security system.

The environmental safeguards may be grouped in the following classifications:

1) Facility security
2) Hardware security

3) Software security

4) Standard operating procedures

5) Data and information protection

1. FACILITY SECURITY. The facility security plan developed by the manager must provide for limited access to the facility and physical security to the area housing the data processing equipment, software, files, and so forth.

Access into the environment may be controlled through many different methods. Some are highly sophisticated and others are quite simple. One of the simplest methods requires recognition of the person seeking admittance by a security guard and/or operating personnel. The identity check may depend on personal recognition, the presence of an authorization card file, an admittance pass, or an identification badge. Identity checks are often supplemented by a sign-in procedure to provide a documented access record. It must be pointed out, though, that these access control methods have not proven entirely successful in every facility.

Some organizations are implementing more sophisticated access controls. One such method involves the use of specially encoded plastic cards that unlock the door when inserted into a reading device mounted outside of the facility. To extend the security capability of such controls, some of these devices require knowledge and manual entry of a predetermined identification code through an attached keyboard. The manually entered code must agree with that encoded in the card or stored in a computer memory bank before the person is allowed to enter.

One important advantage of these devices is that they generally permit the manager to alter the entry codes so that invalid, lost, or stolen cards are ineffective. Often these same devices can activate an automatic reaction to an unauthorized user. This may consist of sounding buzzers or horns, turning on a closed-circuit television camera, alerting the security patrol, etc. In addition, a machine-processible record of the user identification and time entry may be made. Some of the devices also are capable of storing information on entry privileges. These not only control access to an area, but can limit entry by time of day and day of week.

Other measures for limiting access may include such items as not listing the location of the facility in the building directory and eliminating wall direction signs. Also, there is very little purpose in parading visitors through the data processing center to view the hardware. Visitors have been known to pick up cards out of files for samples, push buttons on the hardware, remove protection rings from magnetic tapes, and drop reels or disk packs accidentally. Situations such as these have caused delays in processing.

Physical security must reduce an organization's vulnerability to such hazards as fire, flooding, power failures, and man-made disasters. Fire is the most prevalent threat to an organization. The security plan must emphasize good housekeeping practices to minimize the threat of fire. The plan must also provide for some form of detection, such as smoke and heat detectors. Smoke detectors that are strategically placed in a facility may sound an alarm at first indication of smoke and thereby reduce damage to the hardware and media. Heat detectors will sound the alarm when a high temperature exists in the environment. This arrangement may not be satisfactory because a substantial amount of damage may occur within the environment before an alarm signal is generated by the device. Control of damage is also very important. A facility must be equipped with the proper types of fire extinguishers (see chapter 7), protective covers to minimize smoke and water damage, and emergency shut-off systems for disconnecting the power to the CPU and air-conditioning systems. An emergency storage vault for placement of tape and disk files that are endangered by the smoke, heat, etc., must also be considered. The physical security provisions must be reinforced with the presence of emergency operating procedures and personnel properly trained to execute the procedures.

Flooding also poses a threat to the data processing facility. In multi-storied buildings, for example, the floor above the data processing operations should be reasonably watertight so as to protect the hardware, files, and materials from water damage. Organizations that place their data processing facility in the basement of a building are extremely vulnerable to the flooding threat. The structural floor that supports the raised flooring must provide for good drainage in case of flooding or coolant leakage. The installation of water-detection alarms may prevent serious damage to cabling and wiring beneath the raised floor surface.

Power disruptions are also posing a major threat to many data processing facilities. Blackouts, brownouts, and fluctuations in the voltage and frequency of the incoming power supply pose a threat to the equipment, data, and information. These conditions may cause a computer malfunction, unexplained data errors, reruns, disruptions in the normal operating schedule, and financial losses. Fluctuations can be minimized through the use of a voltage regulator, filter capacitor, or isolation transformer. The power supply problems may be minimized by the use of auxiliary generators, multiple electrical input feeds, an uninterruptible power supply (UPS), or a Power Fail Safe (PFS) feature. The UPS systems are very effective but can be costly. A less costly system is the PFS, which senses power failures and stores the contents of key registers and status words necessary for restarts.

The physical and facility security systems may have to comply with local building and fire protection codes. In some instances, though, the data processing requirements may have to exceed the stipulated building and local regulations.

2. HARDWARE SECURITY. Though many organizations provide security arrangements for the data processing facility, they often fail to protect adequately terminal and communications facilities not included in the centralized data processing area. The terminals are not generally protected from unauthorized personnel and/or theft of sensitive data. Terminals can be tapped; carbon ribbons from the terminals may be used to identify inputs and outputs processed on the device; and the terminal may be used to enter unauthorized and/or faulty

data into a file or computing system. One of the chief needs is to limit access to the terminals by enclosing them in locked rooms or installing lockable covers over the terminals. The software must also be established in such a manner as to accept only authorized users and data. This may be accomplished through the use of an access format and passwords.

The communications lines are also vulnerable to taps. The lines may be protected by installing tap-detection devices to identify any current deviations and insulating the lines to prevent the hook-up of any electromagnetic devices to the lines.

3. SOFTWARE SECURITY. Software security is a general classification, but it includes protection for computer software, applications programs, specialized software packages, documentation, and sensitive data. Most of the protection afforded to these media is through the use of vaults and limited accessability. Some organizations even rotate the use of vaults to add some additional security and reduce vulnerability to sabotage, man-made disasters, natural disasters, fraud and embezzlement, and accidents.

Programs used in processing sensitive data should be classified properly and afforded a high degree of protection. In some organizations, sensitive projects are assigned to a team for design and development to ensure that no one person becomes familiar with the entire project. (The project leader will, of course, be aware of the entire project and the documentation for the system will also provide a complete picture of the application.) Audits applied against the software may also be effective in identifying any discrepancies in the system. The use of the Integrated Test Facility concept could prove most beneficial to an organization because it would constantly monitor the system.

For all of the software identified earlier, a key element of security is back-up. Should any of the items become lost, stolen, and accidentally or deliberately destroyed, the organization would still be able to function with only a disruption.

4. STANDARD OPERATING PROCEDURES. The standard operating procedures must be used to augment the environmental safeguards and to facilitate continued operation. They require preplanning and testing prior to implementation, as well as subsequent evaluation to determine their effectiveness.

Included in this category are the following types of procedures:

a) Back-up
b) Damage control
c) Fire emergency
d) Training

a) *Back-up.* The back-up, or alternate-mode, procedures are developed to facilitate a continuity of operations under other than normal operating conditions. Each sure procedure must be evaluated to determine the cost of delayed processing to an organization (see chapter 5).

The back-up procedures should include the processing documentation; provisions for the transportation of data, personnel, programs, documentation, and supplies; and the agreements for utilization of the alternate facilities. Depending upon organizational security requirements, these procedures may be either included as part of the system's documentation or controlled by the manager.

b) Damage control. To minimize the loss or destruction of the equipment and/or information, damage-control procedures must be established. An important part of these procedures is a determination of record values and the safeguards to be applied to each. The type of damage control to be applied will be affected by the record storage medium. Whenever damage-control equipment is required, its location and application must be documented in the procedures.

One of the items that should be given serious consideration is the use of waterproof covers on the equipment, files, and materials. Such covers are very effective in minimizing the effects of water, smoke, dust, residue, and steam damage.

c) Fire emergency. A written fire-emergency plan must be prepared and documented as part of the standard operating procedures. The installation's personnel should be very familiar with the plan because it delineates their specific responsibilities and actions. The fire-emergency plan must include the location and method for disconnecting the power supply for the data processing equipment and the air-conditioning system. Also, the plan must stipulate the procedures for notifying the internal and/or external firefighting authorities; evacuating personnel; and safeguarding the records. It must also make clear the extent of personnel participation in firefighting and damage control.

d) Training. The training procedures are essential to maintaining an emergency readiness status. The personnel must know the location and proper operation or application of firefighting and damage-control equipment. Their awareness must extend beyond knowledge of the fact that instructions are included in the standard operating procedures. This necessitates the periodic training and testing of the personnel in a simulated emergency operating condition. They should also be trained in the proper use of fire extinguishers in a controlled firefighting environment.

Also, the personnel must be trained in the proper power-disconnect techniques for the data processing and air-conditioning equipment.

5. DATA AND INFORMATION PROTECTION. Measures must be designed to safeguard the data and information used in the information processing systems, documentation, and software. The security procedures in this category affect the following:

 a) Value classification
 b) Storage and protection
 c) Insurance

a) Value classification. A value classification must be applied to the data and information, documentation, and software for management and security purposes. The amount of protection afforded is directly proportional to the value classification—essential, important, beneficial, and nonessential.

Items in the "essential" and "important" classifications must be afforded the highest level of protection. The documentation and software must be maintained in a fire-proof vault; only the operation's copy should be kept in the operations room. The operations copy also must be controlled to prevent loss, sabotage, or an opportunity for fraud and embezzlement. The data and information used in the production runs should be stored in fire-resistant rooms in noncombustible containers. If the data and information records are stored in some other types of containers, an automatic sprinkler system should be available.

To provide greater security, many organizations are storing duplicate key programs, software systems, documentation, and master or sensitive data files at a remote (off-premises) location. Although this procedure may be costly, it provides an organization with a processing capability if its data center and its entire contents are destroyed.

Only those records in the "beneficial" category currently needed for productive processing should be stored in the operations area. The others should be removed from the operations area and either assigned a scratch status, destroyed, or temporarily held in the storage area for salvage purposes.

Diligence must be exercised in removing all unnecessary combustible substances from a storage area in order to minimize the risk of fire.

b) Storage and protection. A security policy must be established to govern the storage of supporting materials and data and information records. Only minimum quantities of cards, printer forms, tapes, and disks should be kept in the processing area. The presence of these items poses a potential fire, safety, and security risk. Many data processing managers do not enforce the policy, and as a result, materials are scattered throughout the processing area, thereby creating potential hazards for an organization. The managers' responsibility is a dual one—providing a secure environment and one that conforms to the guidelines set down by OSHA.

One or more storage areas should be available for the paper- and magnetic-based media. The areas should be surrounded by fire-resistant walls. It is suggested that magnetic-based media be maintained in a separate room. Maximum fire protection must be afforded to these media. Many organizations have equipped these storage areas with automatic carbon-dioxide actuation systems to minimize the damage potential. Also, it is recommended that a storage area for such media be limited to 10,000 cubic feet and that the media be stored in noncombustible containers. Where combustible storage containers are used, the area should be limited to 5,000 cubic feet. In addition to having an automatic firefighting capability, the storage area should be equipped with portable fire extinguishers.

The storage area for paper records and materials can be significantly larger because much more is known about the resistance of these media to fire. It is recommended that the storage area for paper be limited to 50,000 cubic feet. This area must be periodically inventoried to remove records that are no longer useful. Also, where the retention schedule requires continued preservation of paper records, an alternative should be considered—for example, microfilm or magnetic tape storage.

c) Insurance. Insurance has become a means of protecting an organization's investment in data processing. It may be acquired to provide coverage for the damage or destruction of equipment and records. Or, it may be acquired to provide compensation for expenses resulting from the inability to use the available equipment and/or records.

In the former category, there are three standard types of coverage and two that are specifically related to data processing. The standard fire contents, office contents, and valuable papers and records forms provide good coverage for the equipment. However, the media coverage is somewhat limited. Owing to the number of exclusions and limitations in these forms, specialized policies for equipment and records have been developed. However, the equipment and records must be covered in separate policies. The equipment policy may help to cover a lessee's liability for the hardware. The records policy covers the cost of reproduction of the media under emergency conditions and includes some extra expense allowances. The coverage for software systems may be very limited or nonexistent. This is due to the fact that they may be very costly to reproduce.

To cover the loss of equipment and/or records utilization, a data processing extra-expense policy should be considered. This policy helps to minimize the expenses resulting from the replacement of equipment and records. Care must be taken to determine what extra expenses will be incurred. This determination will not be a very simple task, but an organization should attempt to come reasonably close.

PERSONNEL PRACTICES

Safeguards must also be applied to the personnel within the data processing activity. The measures must be designed to minimize the effectiveness of unscrupulous, careless, or incompetent personnel. Indirectly, these practices may also be used to reduce the disruptive effects of employee turnover and to avoid heavy reliance on any one individual.

The personnel safeguards may include the following practices:

1. Code of ethics
2. Nondisclosure agreements
3. Buddy system
4. Rotation
5. Vacations
6. Access control
7. Insurance
8. Authorizations
9. Separation of duties

1. CODE OF ETHICS. A code of ethics is a set of formal or informal rules stipulating a required pattern of conduct. The code is applicable to data processing personnel because they are involved in manipulating sensitive data for various functional activities in the organization. The information they are dealing with should not be divulged, either internally or externally. A copy of the code is usually given to employees when they are hired by the organization. In-

cluded in the code is a statement that the accidental or deliberate disclosure of sensitive data may result in termination of employment. Many organizations require that employees acknowledge receipt of the code by having them sign the form. The carbon copy is then included as a part of the employee's personnel record. The code of ethics should also be applied to service bureau personnel, who are responsible for processing data for a number of different clients, or contractor's personnel employed under a facilities management contract.

The code of ethics may also be applied to those personnel responsible for influencing an order or contract. For example, the code may prohibit the personnel from accepting any gifts from vendors. Or, it may be more comprehensive, requiring the personnel to indicate their financial interests or relationships with vendors of data processing equipment, forms, and supplies in an annual report.

2. NONDISCLOSURE AGREEMENTS. Nondisclosure agreements are legal contracts prohibiting personnel from disclosing information about an organization's systems, programs, simulation models, or other sensitive data to a competitor or other organization. In essence, the agreements state that any techniques developed by employees during the course of employment become property of the organization.

Nondisclosure agreements should also be required of service bureaus and/or consultants performing services for the organization. The agreements may also be utilized when programs are loaned to another organization.

3. BUDDY SYSTEM. The buddy system is a practice requiring the presence of two or more persons in the processing center, particularly on off-shifts, weekends, and holidays. The practice is intended to minimize the opportunity for the deliberate alteration of programs, documentation, and/or data. Many organizations limit this practice to the programming staff. However, some are now extending the practice to the systems and operations personnel. In addition to providing an audit safeguard, the practice increases environmental security and personnel safety.

4. ROTATION. The basic rotation practice is to reassign the personnel periodically to processing different applications. This eliminates the possibility of placing too heavy a reliance upon any one individual for performance of certain jobs. Also, it reduces the opportunities for an unscrupulous employee to deliberately alter programs and/or data.

Many organizations frown upon the rotation practice because it requires better training of the personnel and effective documentation. However, the lack of flexibility in an organization becomes very apparent when a so-called operations specialist is absent, ill, or on vacation. Processing almost grinds to a halt because no other member of the activity is able to maintain a continuity of processing.

Some organizations extend the basic rotation practice to alternating the processing of applications on different shifts. This practice may not be entirely practical for an organization because the schedule may not permit such flexibility. Wherever practical, they attempt to process sensitive data on an abnormal schedule basis. The same approach may be followed in the transmission of sensitive data via communication lines. Alternating operating schedules is a further attempt to minimize the possibility of any theft, fraud, or destructive action.

5. VACATIONS. Few persons would give much consideration to employee vacations as a control technique. However, an organization that can ill afford to have its employees take a vacation can hardly be considered well-managed. This type of situation indicates that a problem exists in the documentation, training methods, personnel, or the manner of assigning and delegating authority and responsibility.

6. ACCESS CONTROL. The limited access practice restricts the use or availability of equipment or information to qualified personnel. This status is allocated to personnel on the basis of "need-to-know." This minimizes the opportunity for the theft or destruction of documentation, programs, sensitive data, or equipment. An additional measure of security is implemented when all accesses are recorded in a log. The log should be audited frequently to detect any unusual activity. For example, access to documentation for a given system should be limited to the systems analyst or programmer assigned to a project. When the documentation is removed from the vault or file, a sign-out record must be completed to maintain accountability for the information.

To ensure that the security is maintained, many organizations are limiting access to documentation storage areas to managerial personnel. Access is also limited to persons who have given notice or who are being discharged. Personnel who are terminated should be given severance pay in lieu of notice. This will prevent unscrupulous persons from committing some form of sabotage.

7. INSURANCE. The insurance safeguards are intended to minimize the losses occurring from the activities of data processing personnel. One of the measures is the bonding of employees by a national insurance company. A second form of insurance is to cover liability for errors and omissions incurred while processing data for other organizations. Also, organizations engaged in providing data processing services for other firms may carry liability insurance to protect them from legal settlements arising from alleged violations of the contract or code of ethics.

8. AUTHORIZATIONS. Written authorizations must be required to effect any change to the software, programs, systems, and/or documentation. The authorizations then become part of the documentation package to provide an audit trail and change history. This practice keeps a manager aware of changes being made, and it will provide a control over the personnel executing the changes.

To minimize the occurrence of accidental or deliberate errors, the changes should be audited by the manager.

9. SEPARATION OF DUTIES. This practice is concerned with separating the duties of the data control clerk, data entry operator, console operator, software personnel, and systems analyst in productive processing. The console operator must not be permitted to modify or change any software and/or program or documentation. The software personnel or systems personnel should not be permitted to function as data control clerks, data entry clerks, or console operators

for any program and/or system designed and developed by them. Some managers justify the latter situation because either the equipment operator has not been properly trained or the documentation has not been completed. Neither of these reasons is acceptable. The operator must be trained prior to cut-over of the system, and the documentation must also be finalized before the system is made fully productive.

Very often the practice of separating duties is ignored in many organizations. Some managers permit their console operators to modify and change programs and consider this an essential part of their training. However, this may be an invitation for an unscrupulous operator to commit fraud very freely. Or, the data and information may be accidentally destroyed or scrambled.

TAPE AND DISK FILE CONTROL

In tape- and disk-oriented hardware systems, there is a need for a file-protection procedure not common to unit-record equipment systems. The digitized information on the tapes and disks is erasable; consequently, valuable information is in danger of accidental and/or deliberate alteration. Therefore, a management control procedure providing maximum protection and utilization of the existing tapes and disks must be developed and maintained.

To provide a measure of protection it is necessary that a media library be established with an effective recordkeeping system. The library system should provide and maintain the following data:

A means of locating any disk or tape in the library files or vault

A record indicating the borrower's name, plus the date and time of issue and return

A means of identifying scratch tapes and disks

A means of identifying tape availability when retention expires

A quality control record indicating the number of read and write errors, length of tape, and date of media test or certification

Available areas on disk for data and/or program storage

A retention control to prevent accidental or deliberate destruction of data and programs

Tape files are much easier to control than those maintained on removable disks. The disks generally, because of their large storage capacity, contain several files. Therefore, availability areas must be carefully controlled to prevent the accidental destruction of data and programs, despite their protection by read-only bits or header and trailer labels. Another problem is that because of their size, disks in many installations are placed on racks or trees near the disk drives or spindles in the computer room. This eliminates some of the physical control which a librarian can exercise over the disks.

The tape and disk file control procedure should consider the following elements:

TITLE		GENERATE DATE	DENSITY
OUTPUT FROM:		INPUT TO:	
RELEASE DATE		REEL	DRIVE	
					OF		

DESCRIPTION			GENERATE DATE
PROGRAM NO.	PHYS. UNIT	FILE NO.	SCRATCH DATE
REEL	DENSITY		
OF	200 556 800 1600		

GENERATION DATE	RETENTION DATE
FILE SYMBOL	
TOTAL RECORDS	NO. PER BLOCK	DENSITY

DESCRIPTION			FILE SYMBOL
DATE WRITTEN	EFFECTIVE DATE	RELEASE DATE	DEVICE
DENSITY	NO. CHANNELS	FOOTAGE	SERIAL NO.

Figure 10.8 Samples of external tape labels

1) An overview of library methods
2) A numbering scheme
3) Recording system
4) Back-up control

1. LIBRARY METHODS. This is an overview of the library function that must identify the security arrangements for the library, an emergency operating procedure for the protection of tapes and disks, testing procedure for tapes and disks, and the processing of new tapes and disks.

2. NUMBERING SCHEME. An organization must have a numbering scheme that will be applied to the external label on the tapes (see Figure 10.8), and disks. The numbering scheme may follow previously established guidelines for identification of systems and/or programs, or it may be a scheme that is used by only the tape and disk librarian for identification and control.

3. RECORDING SCHEME. This segment of the procedure delineates the recordkeeping procedure for controlling the utilization and disposition of the media. An integral part of the recordkeeping involves identification of the media, a historical record of the use made, and the availability of the media for productive purposes. A form, as illustrated in Figure 10.9, may be useful in providing an element of control on utilization and availability.

Figure 10.9 Sample of form for file history

SERIAL NO.	REEL OF	GENERATION			GENERATED ON PROGRAM NO.	EFFECTIVE			SCRATCH			RELEASED			ISSUED TO:			RETURNED		
		MO.	DAY	YR.		MO.	DAY	YR.	MO.	DAY	YR.	MO.	DAY	YR.	DATE MO. DAY		INIT.	DATE MO. DAY		INIT.

FILE HISTORY DATE: PAGE____OF____

APPLICATION NUMBER: APPLICATION TITLE: RETENTION CYCLE:

4. BACK-UP CONTROL. The back-up control is actually established by the systems analyst when the job has been designed and developed. The back-up provides an element of control for reconstruction of file data. The most popular retention scheme is the grandfather-father-son storage scheme. But it is important to note that this scheme is most practical for tape file control. It is not very practical for disk file control.

The grandfather-father-son scheme is illustrated in Figure 10.10. The grandfather is the original or first-generation tape. When the transactions are applied against the grandfather tape in an update process, a tape called the "father" is generated. Subsequently, transactions are applied against the father tape with the new end result being identified as the "son." For back-up control purposes, the grandfather tape is still available along with the transactions activities. Should some questions or problems arise during the generation of the son tape, the original is still available for back-up and regeneration is necessary. Ultimately, the grandfather tape is released as a scratch tape, with the father tape moving up the hierarchical structure as the new grandfather tape, just as the previous son now becomes the father and the new son is generated in the most recent update.

The disk files must also be backed up in some form. Many organizations will copy the contents on another disk pack, whereas in other organizations, the disk is copied on to a tape file for back-up. Dumping the disk file on a printer or typewriter may be acceptable output but would require retranscription to a machine-sensible form to regenerate the original file.

The tape and disk librarian must work in conjunction with the operations manager to determine the number of scratch tapes that will be required each day and to ensure that the necessary master files are available for updating. The librarian must also be concerned with disk space utilization to ensure maximum utilization of the disk space. When a reorganization is necessary, the librarian will notify the operations manager that the process is necessary.

In some organizations, the librarian takes on the additional responsibility for retention of micromedia, such as film, fiche, and/or strips. This presents a different control procedure problem for the data processing manager.

DETERMINATION OF COST-BENEFIT

In this chapter we have discussed a number of different procedures for the prevention, detection, identification, and correction of errors and exceptions from normal processing. Some are very simple and require few resources for actuation. Others are complex and require a greater expenditure of resources for development, implementation, and use.

Therefore, it becomes necessary to determine what price a user should pay for accurate data. Or, what price is a user willing to pay for obtaining accurate data? The greater the need or desire for accuracy, the more costly will be the system because of increased resource needs.

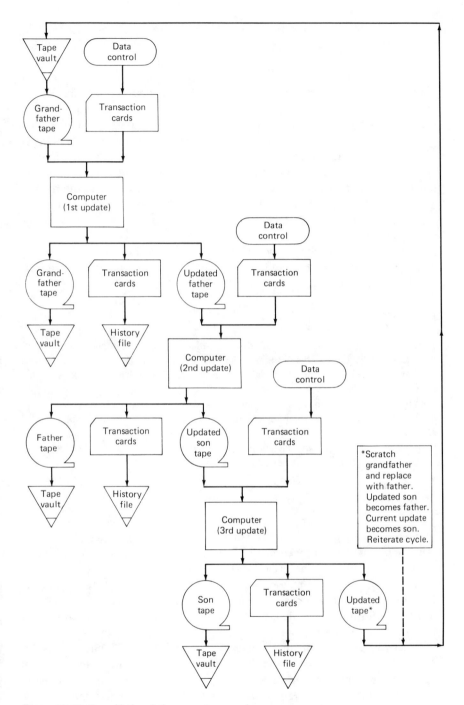

Figure 10.10 Grandfather-father-son storage scheme

In developing or modifying a system, the data processing personnel must determine the cost of supplying a required or desired qualitative level. The cost may be negligible or minimal because the user's requirements can be absorbed within the existing resource structure. It is also possible that the costs may be minimized if greater effectiveness can be achieved from an existing system. However, an additional expenditure may be required if the system's requirements necessitate an increased resource capacity. The user and auditor must then determine if the requirements are justified in light of the additional cost. The data processing personnel should not make the final decision regarding the design and implementation of a management control for a given system and/or program. They must provide the user and auditor with the various alternatives and costs. The user and the auditor must be the final decision makers because they are aware of the environmental constraints that are affecting the organization's needs.

Unfortunately, no blanket policy can be applied to evaluating cost-benefit relationships, because the requirements vary among users and because each data element has a different value.

Review Questions: Group 10F

1. What type of protection can be afforded to the data processing equipment?
2. At the weekly staff luncheon, the president has expressed his concern about the safeguards applied to the organization's accounting records. What suggestions, if any, would you make?
3. What is the value of the buddy system as a personnel safeguard?
4. Why is it necessary to establish a formal recordkeeping system in a tape and disk library?
5. What are the two primary factors in evaluating a user's request for the design and implementation of a particular management control?

SUMMARY

In the management of a data processing organization, it becomes essential to install a series of controls concerned with the protection and production of data in the information processing cycle. These controls are sometimes referred to as audit controls, but they may exceed those normally required by the auditor. Despite the many categories and types of management controls, they are primarily responsible for the quality of the input and output in an organization. In a sense, it may be more practical to regard these as quality controls.

In a dynamic environment, there are a number of interacting influences that may be constant or variable and that have a direct or indirect bearing on the operating procedures of a data processing activity. Therefore, it is essential to the very life of the organization that a series of management controls to maximize the operational effectiveness of the available resources requires that the data be valid, applicable, and processed accurately and quickly. This requires the development and application of equipment, input, output, program, e. nal, and peripheral controls. Some of these controls may be applied simply quickly, but others may require additional time, effort, and expense.

The degree to which controls are applied varies with the system and depen on the equipment, procedures used, cost, and benefits. Good controls must be built into every system during the analysis and design phases of systems planning; they must never be superimposed.

CASE STUDY 10.1

The Raleric Manufacturing Company

The Raleric Manufacturing Company is located in an industrial park on the outskirts of a large metropolitan area. Adjacent to the manufacturing facility is a three-storied building housing the corporate offices. The Computer Center is in the northwest corner of the building. The systems and programming staff are located on the second floor in the southwest corner of the building. The planning group is housed on the third floor in the center of the building.

The Computing Center is on the left side of a main traffic aisle. It houses the keypunch and peripheral equipment operations, in addition to the computer hardware. Also, numerous file cabinets for master files and program data are located in the area. Master tapes, payroll checks, and accounts payable drafts are kept in a vault near the door. The other active and scratch tapes are maintained in a large rack adjacent to the tape drives. Due to a company safety practice restricting weight handling, a considerable quantity of card and forms stock is kept in the processing area.

There is a large storage area adjacent to the Computer Center and to the right of the traffic aisle. This area is used to store all history records except magnetic tape. The records are stored in their original shipping cartons. Also, the card and form stock necessary to support the activity are stored here. The electrical power supply disconnects for the computer, air-conditioning, and peripheral equipment are located near the door of the storage area.

Access to the Computer Center is not limited because the inputs are delivered there by the various clerks and outputs are picked up from the rack located near the door. The storage area also remains unlocked to facilitate easy access to the supplies by the operations personnel. Portable carbon-dioxide extinguishers are located in the Computer Center, and water extinguishers are located in the storage area. An automatic water sprinkler system is located in the Computer Center. However, to minimize water damage to the computer, the water line passing directly over that equipment has been removed.

The company is proud of its Computer Center, so it permits the personnel to bring visitors through the center during the prime shift. Arrangements can also be made for tours during the off-shift hours.

The personnel in the Computer Center like the setting because it is next to a beautiful flower garden. They also like its nearness to an emergency fire-door, which gives them a quick jump on the line heading for the cafeteria at the lunch hour. The off-shift personnel are also pleased, because the center is located near the parking lot. In the summer, the operators use the windows to reach the garden or parking lot. Though this method of exit and entry is frowned upon, it has never been formally discouraged by the data processing manager.

Discussion Questions

1. In your opinion, should the company, which is located in an industrial park, be concerned with environmental safeguards?
2. How would you evaluate the safeguards in effect for the sensitive data and programs in the computer center?
3. Do you feel that the organization's weight handling safety policy is entirely practical? Explain.
4. Should some alternate arrangement be provided for the power-supply disconnect? Or, is it acceptable in its present form?
5. Do you feel any changes are needed in the existing entry access policy for users and visitors? Explain.
6. Does it appear that the organization has an effective firefighting and damage-control procedure? Explain.
7. Should the personnel's informal entry and exit practices continue to be condoned by the data processing manager? What changes, if any, would you recommend to him?
8. What overall plan of safeguards would you recommend for the data processing activity of this organization? Explain.

CASE STUDY 10.2

Eric-Andrea Ice Cream Delights

Your staff is in the process of readying a presentation for management acceptance of a proposed new system. The primary purpose of the system is to reflect employee eligibility and participation in a new group life insurance plan.

The payroll master tape will be used to determine those employees eligible for participation. In the process of determining employee eligibility, the system will compute the amount of coverage an employee qualifies for. It will also compute the monthly premium and prepare a payroll authorization form. The authorization then becomes input for generating records on the group life insurance master tape and the payroll deduction tape. Also, the system must provide for automatic increases in coverage and premiums when an employee's salary increases. Furthermore, the system must provide for cancellation or reduction of coverage and premiums based on employee election for a change.

Provision must also be made to reflect changes in eligibility status when employees are deleted from the master payroll tape due to terminations, leaves of absence, maternity leaves, etc.

As the group life insurance master tape is updated each week, a listing of the coverage will be prepared for the insurance clerk. Also, she would like the following outputs:

Authorizations executed

Authorizations not executed

Cancellations and changes

Additions

Deduction changes

Deduction additions

Deduction deletions

Discussion Questions

1. What general categories of control must be considered in the implementation of the proposed system?
2. What input controls, if any, should be considered for implementation?
3. What program checks would be most appropriate for this system?
4. What controls, if any, would be relevant to safeguarding the outputs?
5. Prepare an argument for or against utilizing a computer audit on this system after it has been implemented.

Narrative Job

Descriptions

In this appendix we have included narrative job descriptions that identify the responsibilities and the duties that may be performed in various occupational positions in the data processing environment. The responsibilities and tasks included in these descriptions are those most commonly assigned; however, the data processing manager may find it necessary to include some additional items or delete some.

As stated in chapter 3, the manager must customize the job descriptions to his specific environment based on organizational objectives, personnel expertise, hardware, software, and budget considerations.

Included are the following:

Manager of Data Processing

Systems Analyst

Data Base Management Analyst/Specialist

Data Communications Analyst/Specialist

Data Processing Training Specialist

Systems Programmer

Applications Programmer

Maintenance Programmer

Programmer Trainee

Computer/Console Operator

Data Control Clerk

Data Entry Operator

Librarian

EAM Equipment Operator

Manager of Data Processing

The manager provides the technical and administrative leadership for all data processing activities in the organization. In this capacity, the manager is responsible for defining the data processing objectives and interrelating them to the overall organizational objectives; developing short- and long-term plans; preparing the required cost estimates and budgets; providing for a communications interface between the data processing function and the upper echelon, and the users of data processing services; projecting and requesting the necessary human, hardware, software, and material resources to provide the required decision-making support; developing activity reports to monitor, evaluate, and report on projects and progress, utilization of resources, and development projects; developing and maintaining data processing documentation and performance standards; organizing career paths and personnel development programs; and developing training programs for data processing, user and managerial personnel.

Systems Analyst

The systems analyst gathers data for analysis of user applications and/or problem areas in order to design and develop new applications or to modify existing applications. In this capacity, the systems analyst analyzes the workflow, forms, files, reports, controls, organizational policies and practices, hardware, software, existing documentation and other applications affecting the application under study; documents existing operations and procedures and evaluates them to determine the operational effectiveness of the existing application and if an alternate approach is necessary; designs new or modified approaches that are technically, economically, and operationally feasible; prepares the necessary flowcharts, decision tables, program specifications, systems test data and plans, user procedures, conversion requirements, time schedules, and cost/savings estimates for new or revised applications; develops the necessary interfaces between data processing and user organizations; monitors the development and implementation process; conducts follow-up sessions to evaluate the effectiveness of recently implemented or revised applications, and prepares project activity reports for the upper echelon and steering committee.

Data Base Management Analyst/Specialist

The data base management analyst/specialist is responsible for maintaining and controlling an operationally effective data base management system that will support the decision-making needs of the overall organization. In this capacity, he defines the content and structure of the data base; establishes and enforces standards for the proper use of the data base; establishes the right of access to various segments of the base; develops and maintains a data element dictionary that will minimize data redundancy and simplify the search for stored elements;

develops training methods and procedures for users on the most efficient methods of inquiry, searching, updating, and retrieving data; maintains records on storage space availability and utilization; establishes procedures for maintaining the integrity and security of the data base; and maintains accurate, current and relevant documentation on the data base management system.

Data Communications Analyst/Specialist

The data communications analyst/specialist is responsible for maintaining an effective data communications network for the organization. In this capacity, he is responsible for designing a basic data communications network that will meet current organizational needs and provide flexibility for change or growth; provides the necessary interfaces with hardware and software vendors to minimize downtime and to resolve or prevent any communications network problems; develops the necessary procedures for data processing and user personnel to make optimal use of the communications hardware and software; develops a feedback reporting system on network and vendor performance; and may be responsible for the supervision of the data communications network.

Data Processing Training Specialist

The data processing training specialist is responsible for developing, coordinating and scheduling all data processing-related training for users, managerial and data processing personnel. In this capacity, the training specialist will prepare and/or review courses that will provide training for an impending conversion, implementation of a given system, use of hardware/software, use of documentation and performance standards, interface with organizational career pathing schemes, and use of performance monitors; either conduct the training sessions personally or will recruit qualified instructors; monitor the effectiveness of organizational and/or vendor sponsored training programs; and develop training objectives and schedules that will concur with organizational objectives.

Systems Programmer

The systems programmer is responsible for the design, development, and maintenance of specialized computer software used in the support of applications programs and control systems. In this capacity, the systems programmer is responsible for maintaining the manufacturer- or vendor-supplied or organization-written operating systems software that is necessary to support the activities of the applications programmers; must install the necessary modifications and enhancements to the operating system software to maintain operational effectiveness; may develop language preprocessors to facilitate the production of applications programs and/or evaluate the effectiveness of such software; develop utility programs that will facilitate the productivity of the applications programmers and/or the operations personnel; prepare cost/benefit analyses on various types of manufacturer- or vendor-supplied software, operating system interfaces with application systems, languages and utility programs; and will develop and conduct training sessions for applications programmers to facilitate optimal use of the existing software.

Applications Programmer

The applications programmer deals primarily with business-oriented, engineering, and scientific applications or problems requiring the use of a computer for processing or problem-solving purposes. In this capacity, the applications programmer is responsible for analyzing user needs based on system objectives specifications, and workflow; designing, developing and implementing computer programs and routines that will facilitate the workflow through a computing system; developing the necessary test data and plans to ensure the processing accuracy of a given program or series of programs; preparing the necessary documentation for user and data processing personnel, and for the systems documentation folder; preparing training material for user and data processing personnel; performing various required trade-off analyses on the use of storage space, processing times, response requirements, and system/program requirements; developing error recovery procedures and routines; and submitting progress reports on current projects.

Maintenance Programmer

The maintenance programmer is responsible for correcting deficiencies and problems that may be present in an existing program, improving the operating performance of an existing computer program, or making the necessary change(s) to an existing program in order to comply with a user request or an internal or external requirement imposed on the system. In executing this responsibility, the maintenance programmer must analyze the requested change(s); review the existing program logic, documentation, and impact on related programs/systems; code the necessary instructions to implement the change(s); prepare test data and plan to ensure the accuracy of the change(s) and correctness of the entire program; analyze the test results to ensure that they meet stated objectives; update the existing program and system documentation; modify the existing user and operations personnel documentation, if necessary; reassemble or recompile the program and insert the production copy in the appropriate library; and submit status reports on progress.

Programmer Trainee

The programmer trainee performs his/her tasks under the direct supervision of an experienced programmer in the applications, systems software or maintenance areas. The trainee analyzes the required program specifications and documentation; illustrates the program logic using flowcharts, decision tables, logic narratives, and/or top-down structures; codes the necessary program steps; prepares test data and plans; verifies test results; designs conversion procedures; develops user and operations personnel documentation; and prepares the necessary system/program documentation.

Computer/Console Operator

The computer/console operator directs and controls the operation of all digital computing equipment. He may also be responsible for the operation of off-line input or output devices and other media conversion devices such as optical scanners. The operator is responsible for the set-up of the computer and associated equipment according to instructions included in the program/system documentation for a given program; mounts the necessary tape, disk, and card files on the various devices and inserts the form(s) into the printer(s); maintains an equipment utilization log; reacts to any corrective action and/or terminating action as described in the operator's documentation; operates the console keyboard, display or control panel in accordance with the documentation for a given program, and standard operating procedures; and notifies the manager of any equipment and/or program malfunctions.

Data Control Clerk

The data control clerk is responsible for performing various quality control functions on the inputs and outputs as defined by the systems personnel. The role of the data control clerk is multi-faceted in many organizations. The data control clerk is responsible for reviewing the inputs received in the operations area and determines its acceptability for processing; contacting various organizational units to ensure that all inputs are submitted prior to processing in order to minimize the need for reruns or supplementary processing; maintaining controls on all inputs received; staging the inputs for subsequent processing by the data entry and/or computer operations personnel; reviewing and checking the accuracy, appearance, and completeness of the outputs, may assist in the breakdown, assembly and distribution of outputs to users; notifying users and operations personnel of any delays in the schedule; and may also be responsible for maintaining an inventory control system for data processing supplies.

Data Entry Operator

The data entry operator may also be identified as a key entry operator. The data entry operator is primarily responsible for the transcription of alphabetic, alphameric, and or numeric data from source documents into an acceptable form for data processing purposes. The responsibilities of a data entry operator may include the following: the entry of data/programs through a keyboard device into a computing system; the keypunching and key verifications of data into a prescribed card format; the use of keyboard devices for entry of data on other media such as magnetic tape, disks, or diskettes; the rejection of source documents that are incomplete or contain inaccurate information; may operate other media conversion devices such as optical scanning or MICR; and may be responsible for maintenance of the tape and disk library, in smaller installations.

Librarian

The librarian is responsible for controlling the data files that are maintained on cards, magnetic tapes, and disks. In addition, the librarian may also be responsible for the control and completion of program maintenance to ensure that the documentation for a given program has been completed and that the program's production copy and back-up copy have been inserted into the appropriate libraries; updating all vendor- or manufacturer-supplied documentation and manuals; coordinating the distribution of all modifications to system/program documentation to appropriate users. In some organizations, the librarian is responsible for staging of all input job streams for processing on the computer system. Also, the librarian may be properly trained to function as a member of the Chief Programmer Team organizational structure.

EAM Equipment Operator

The EAM (electrical accounting machine) operator may also be referred to as the unit-record equipment operator. The EAM operator operates EAM equipment such as sorters, collators, reproducers, tabulators, and interpreters according to a prescribed set of documentation in order to produce a desired end-result; wires the necessary control panels, if none are available, to complete the prescribed tasks; may prepare documentation for EAM equipment operation, when necessary; duplicates mutilated cards and card files; maintains machine utilization records; and notifies the manager of any equipment malfunctions.

Standardized
Charting Symbols

This appendix identifies the various symbols used to represent the functions of an information processing system. They are used in the preparation of system flowcharts, macro-flowcharts, and micro-flowcharts. The charts are used to analyze a problem; to design and implement a solution; and to provide documentation for training, user, operating, and audit personnel.

There are four major symbol-utilization categories. These are:

1. Basic symbols
2. Specialized process symbols
3. Specialized media symbols
4. Additional symbols

BASIC SYMBOLS

The basic symbols are general-purpose symbols established for given functions and are always used to represent that function. They may be used to represent any function in an information processing system. Included in this category are the:

1. Input/output symbol
2. Process symbol
3. Flowline symbol
4. Annotation symbol

1. INPUT/OUTPUT SYMBOL. This symbol represents an input/output function. It is used to represent all data or information available for processing (input); or the recording of processed information (output).

2. Process symbol. This symbol is used to represent any processing function. It may be used to illustrate a single or group of operations; a computer instruction; EAM or EDP equipment, etc.

3. Flowline symbol. This symbol represents the function of linking symbols. It indicates the sequence of available information and executable operations. The flow direction is represented by lines drawn between the symbols. The normal flow of direction is from left to right and top to bottom. Open arrowheads can be placed on the flowlines to ensure understanding of the flow of direction on the chart.

When the flow of direction does not follow the normal direction (left to right and top to bottom), then open arrowheads must be used. Flowlines may cross when they have no logical interrelation. Two or more incoming flowlines may join with one outgoing flowline. Open arrowheads should be placed near the junction points to illustrate flowlines entering and leaving a point.

4. Annotation symbol. This symbol is used to add descriptive comments or explanatory notes to a chart. The annotation symbol is connected to any symbol by a broken line at the point where the comment is most meaningful.

SPECIALIZED PROCESS SYMBOLS

The specialized process symbols are used to provide greater clarity to a flowchart by identifying a specific type of processing operation. These symbols are used in lieu of the basic process symbol. Included in this category are the

1. Decision symbol
2. Predefined process symbol
3. Preparation symbol
4. Auxiliary operation symbol
5. Manual operation symbol

6. Merge symbol
7. Extract symbol
8. Sort symbol
9. Collate symbol

1. Decision symbol. This symbol is used in switching-type and decision operations to determine which alternative or logical path should be followed. The entry into the decision symbol should be from the top. Exits may be made from the bottom point (normal) or either side. Multiple exits may be made from the bottom or sides of the decision symbol.

INCONNECTOR
CONDITION   REFERENCE
A – 001B4
B – 001D5
C – 002A2
D – 003A5
E – 003A3

To identify the alternative paths, some standardized method of identification should be used. A suggested scheme is:

Path Identification			Condition
Y	or	Yes	Condition satisfied
N	or	No	Condition not satisfied
=	or	EQ	Equal
≠	or	UN or NE	Unequal
+	or	POS	Positive
−	or	NEG	Negative
>	or	GR or GT	Greater than
≥	or	GR/E or GE	Greater than or equal to
<	or	L or LT	Less than
≤	or	LE	Less than or equal to
Hi			High
Lo			Low
0	or	Z	Zero

2. PREDEFINED PROCESS SYMBOL. This symbol is used to indicate linkage to a subroutine, subprogram, logical unit, or process. The activity represented by the symbol is not normally represented on this flowchart.

3. PREPARATION SYMBOL. This symbol is used to represent a modification of an instruction or series of instructions, which alter the effect of a program. The modifications include such activities as subroutine initialization; setting an internal switch; initializing, incrementing, or decrementing an index register, etc.

4. AUXILIARY OPERATION SYMBOL. This symbol represents operations performed on equipment that is not under the direct control of the central processing unit. It is normally used to describe equipment which operates at its own speed and is not affected by the speed of its human operator. The symbol may be used to represent such operations as punched card sorting, or punched card collating performed on unit-record equipment.

5. MANUAL OPERATION SYMBOL. This symbol is used to represent any offline input or output producing process geared to the speed of a human being. The symbol may be used to represent such offline keying operations as keypunching, key-to-magnetic tape, and key-to-magnetic disk. Alternatively, it may be used to represent such functions as checking control totals, or logging batch control entries.

6. MERGE SYMBOL. This symbol may be used to represent online or offline operations that generate one set of items from two or more sets—in the same sequence.

7. Extract symbol. This symbol is used for online or offline operations in which two or more sets of items are generated from one set.

8. Sort symbol. This symbol may be used to represent the online or offline sorting operations.

9. Collate symbol. This symbol represents a combination of the merge and extract operations. Two or more sets of items may be generated from two or more other sets. The collate symbol may be used for online or offline operations.

SPECIALIZED MEDIA SYMBOLS

The specialized media symbols are used to specifically identify the media on which the information is recorded for input or output, or both. Included in this category are the following:

1. Punched card symbol
2. Magnetic tape symbol
3. Punched tape symbol
4. Document symbol
5. Online storage symbol
6. Offline storage symbol
7. Display symbol
8. Communication link symbol
9. Manual input symbol
10. Magnetic drum symbol
11. Magnetic disk symbol
12. Core symbol

1. Punched card symbol. Any form of input or output requiring the use of punched cards is represented by this symbol. The symbol is used to represent data in any size or shape of punched card. This includes mark scan cards, mark sense cards, stub cards, partial cards, etc. This symbol may also be used to represent a deck of cards or file of cards. However, there are also specialized symbols to represent both of these functions.

A collection of punched cards may be illustrated utilizing the specialized deck of cards symbols.

A file of related punched cards may be illustrated utilizing the specialized file of cards symbol.

2. Magnetic tape symbol. This symbol is used to represent the use of magnetic tape as an input/output medium. The symbol applies to magnetic tape regardless of type, width, length, or information content.

3. Punched tape symbol. This symbol is used to represent all forms of punched tape used as an input or output medium. The symbol is not limited to punched paper tape; it also applies to such media as punched plastic tape, punched metal tape, etc.

4. DOCUMENT SYMBOL. The document symbol is used to represent printed, handwritten, typed, or optical mark read, documents, or plotter outputs.

5. ONLINE STORAGE SYMBOL. This symbol is a generalized symbol to represent data held on any intermediate or external storage device. The symbol would represent magnetic data cell, magnetic disk, magnetic tapes, magnetic drum, additional magnetic core storage, microfilm, chip or strip systems, etc.

6. OFFLINE STORAGE SYMBOL. This symbol is used to represent data stored offline regardless of the medium or equipment used.

7. DISPLAY SYMBOL. Information which is displayed for manual interpretation at the time of processing is represented by this symbol. This symbol is used for such media as CRT displays, plotters, video devices, online indicators, console printers, time-sharing terminals, etc.

8. COMMUNICATION LINK SYMBOL. This symbol is used to represent the automatic transmission of information from one location to another, from one medium to another, from one type of equipment to another.

The normal flow of direction for the communication link is left to right and top to bottom. An open arrowhead may be used in conjunction with the communications link to improve charting clarity.

The open arrowheads should be used when the flow of direction does not follow the normal path.

The open arrowheads may also be used to indicate a bi-directional flow.

9. MANUAL INPUT SYMBOL. The manual insertion of information into the information processing system via an online device is represented by this symbol. It represents such devices as online keyboards, tag readers, light pens, pushbuttons, transaction recorders, console switch settings, etc.

10. MAGNETIC DRUM SYMBOL. This symbol is a specialized symbol used to represent data stored on a magnetic drum device.

11. MAGNETIC DISK SYMBOL. This symbol is a specialized symbol used to represent data stored on a magnetic disk device.

12. CORE SYMBOL. This symbol is used to represent input or output data stored on magnetic core or a high speed device. The symbol should not be used to represent any form of primary internal storage. It is used to represent a device linked to the primary unit to augment storage capability.

ADDITIONAL SYMBOLS

These symbols are primarily used on a chart to display continuity of functions or operations, and to identify entry and termination points. Included in this category of symbols are the following:

1. Connector
2. Terminal
3. Parallel mode

1. CONNECTOR. The connector symbol is used to maintain a flow of continuity on the flowchart. It may be used to illustrate either a physical break due to paper limitation or an awkward line requirement.

The connectors usually appear in pairs. The inconnector or entry connector has a flowline leaving from it. The outconnector or exit connector has only a flowline entering it.

2. TERMINAL. The terminal or interrupt symbol may be used to illustrate initial starting points, exits from a logical path, interrupts, delay, halts, and returns from an interrupted process.

3. PARALLEL MODE. The parallel mode symbol is used to represent the beginning or end of two or more simultaneous operations.

The symbols in this appendix may be drawn by using a flowcharting template.

GLOSSARY

This glossary is not intended to serve as a dictionary of data terms per se. Rather, it is an example of what an organization may develop for its own personnel.

ABEND. Abnormal end of task. Termination of a task prior to normal completion because of an error condition.

Access method. A technique for moving data between main storage and input/output devices.

Activity. A term to indicate that a record in a master file is used, altered, or referred to.

Activity ratio. The ratio of the number of records in a file which have activity to the total number of records in that file.

Address. A designation that identifies a name, label, register, memory location, location of a station in a communication network, a data source, or a device.

Administrative Terminal System. A system in which terminals are connected by two-way communication lines to a computer under control of a program that allows a typist to type text into the computer, correct and revise text, and have the computer type out the corrected draft.

ALGOL. ALGOrithmic Language. A language primarily used to express computer programs by algorithms.

Algorithm. A prescribed set of well-defined rules or processes for the solution of a problem in a finite number of steps.

American National Standards Institute. ANSI. An organization established for the purpose of establishing voluntary industry standards.

Analysis. The careful investigation of a given problem, and the separation of that problem into its component parts for additional study.

ASCII. American National Standard Code for Information Interchange. The standard code used for information interchange between data processing systems, communications systems, and related equipment.

Assembler language. A source language that includes symbolic machine language statements in which there is a one-to-one relationship with the instruction formats and data formats of the computer.

Attended operation. An application in which individuals are required at both data stations to establish the connection and transfer the data sets from voice mode to data mode.

Background. The environment in a computer system in which low-priority tasks are executed.

BASIC. An algebra-like language used for problem solving by nondata personnel that have access to an interactive computing capability.

BCD. Binary coded decimal notation.

Benchmark problem. A problem or problem mix that is used to evaluate the performance of hardware and/or software.

Cathode-ray tube. CRT. An electronic vacuum tube, such as a television picture tube, that can be used to display graphic images.

Central processor. A unit of the computer that includes the circuits for controlling the interpretation and execution of instructions.

Closed shop. The operation of a data processing facility in which most of the productive problem programming is performed by a group of programming specialists rather than by users.

COBOL. COmmon Business Oriented Language. A business data processing language.

Comment statement. A job control statement used to include information that may be useful in running a job or reviewing a computer program listing.

Compile. To prepare a machine language program from a computer program written in another programming language.

Computer-Assisted Instruction. CAI. A type of data processing application in which a computer is used to assist in the instruction of students.

Computer network. A complex consisting of two or more interconnected computing units.

Computing system. A central processor equipped with main storage, input/output devices, control units, direct-access storage devices, and input/output channels.

Configuration. A group of machines, devices, etc., that make up a data processing system.

Conversational remote job entry. The ability to enter job control language statements and data from a remote data terminal into a computer.

CPU. Central processing unit or processor.

Cursor. A movable spot of light on the cathode-ray tube display that indicates where the next character will be entered.

Data. The basic elements of information represented by numeric, alphabetic, or alphameric characters that are processed on the computing equipment.

Data base management. A software technique for the storage, updating, and retrieval of information stored in a common data bank.

Data collection. The process of gathering data from one or several points to a central location, manually or via a data terminal.

Data communication. The transmission of data from one point to another using such means as telephone and telegraph lines or satellites.

Data conversion. The process of changing data from one form to another form of representation.

Decollate. To separate the plies of a multiple-part form or paper stock.

Dynamic dump. A dump that is performed during the execution of a computer program.

EAM. Electrical accounting machine.

EBCDIC. Extended binary coded decimal interchange code.

EDP. Electronic data processing.

Emulator. A device or computer program that imitates one system with another such that the imitating system accepts the same data, executes the same programs, and achieves the same results as the imitated system.

File maintenance. The activity of keeping file current by adding, changing, or deleting data.

Foreground. The environment within a computing system in which high-priority programs are executed.

FORTRAN. FORmula TRANslating system. A language primarily used to express computer programs by arithmetic formulas.

General-purpose computer. A computer that is designed to handle a wide variety of problems.

Hard copy. A printed copy of machine output in a visually readable form.

Hexadecimal. A number system with a base of sixteen; valid digits range from 0 to F.

IMS. Information Management System. A system designed to organize, catalog, locate, store, retrieve, and maintain information.

Inquiry. A request for information from storage.

Job control statement. A statement in a job that describes its requirements to the operating system.

K. 1,024 bytes; used in referring to storage capacity.

Language. A set of representations, conventions, and rules used to convey information.

Language statement. A statement that may request that a particular operation be performed or may contain data that is to be used by the processing program.

Machine language. A language that is used directly by the computer.

Mainframe. The central processing unit or processor.

Message control program. MCP. A program that is used to control the sending or reception of messages to or from remote terminals.

MODEM. MOdulator-DEModulator. A device that modulates and demodulates a signal transmitted over transmission lines.

Modify. To alter a part of an instruction, routine, or module.

Multiprocessing. The simultaneous execution of two or more computer programs or sequence of instructions by a computer or computer network.

Multiprogramming. The concurrent execution of two or more programs by a computer.

Object code. Output from a compiler or assembler which is itself executable machine code or is suitable for processing to produce executable machine code.

OCR. Optical character recognition.

Offline. Equipment or devices not under the control of the central processing unit.

Online. Equipment or devices under the control of the central processing unit.

Open shop. The operation of a data processing facility in which most of the productive programming is performed by the users rather than by a group of programming specialists.

Optical character recognition. The machine identification of printed characters through use of light-sensitive devices.

Overlay. The technique of repeatedly using the same blocks of internal storage during different stages of a program. When one routine is no longer needed in storage, another routine can replace all or part of it.

Postmortem dump. A static dump, used for debugging purposes, performed at the end of a machine run.

Preventive maintenance. Maintenance specifically intended to prevent faults from occurring during subsequent operation.

Problem-oriented language. A programming language designed for the convenient expression of a given class of problems.

Procedure-oriented language. A programming language designed for the convenient expression of procedures used in the solution of a wide class of problems.

Real time. The performance of a computation during the actual time that the related physical process transpires in order that the results of the computation can be used in guiding the physical process.

Register. A device capable of storing a specified amount of data such as one word.

Remote job entry. Submission of job control language statements and data from a remote data terminal, causing the described jobs to be scheduled and executed as though encountered in the input stream.

Report program generator. A processing program that can be used to generate object programs that produce reports from existing sets of data.

Response time. The time between the submission of an item of work to a computing system and the return of the results.

RPG. Report Program Generator.

Satellite computer. An offline auxiliary computer.

Scheduled maintenance. Maintenance carried out in accordance with an established plan.

Setup time. The time required by an operator to prepare a computing system to perform a job or job step.

Shared file. A direct-access device that may be used by two systems at the same time; a shared file may link two systems.

Simulator. A device, system, or computer program that represents certain features of the behavior of a physical or abstract system.

Snapshot dump. A selective dynamic dump performed at various points in a machine run.

Software. A set of programs, procedures, and possibly associated documentation concerned with the operation of a data processing system.

Sort/merge program. A processing program that can be used to sort or merge records in a prescribed sequence.

Source language. The language from which a statement is translated.

Source program. A computer program written in a source language.

Spooling. The reading and writing of input and output streams on auxiliary storage devices, concurrently with job execution, in a format convenient for later processing or output operations.

Static dump. A dump that is performed at a particular point in time with respect to a machine run, frequently at the end of a run.

Subroutine. A routine that can be part of another routine.

Supervisor. The part of the control program that coordinates the use of the resources and maintains the flow of central processing unit operations.

Syntax. The rules governing the structure of a language.

System generation. The process of using an operating system to assemble and link together all of the parts that constitute another operating system.

Teleprocessing. The processing of data that is received from or sent to remote locations by way of telecommunications lines.

Throughput. The total volume of work performed by a computing system over a given period of time.

Time-sharing. A method of using a computing system that allows a number of users to execute programs concurrently and to interact with the programs during execution.

Tracing routine. A routine that provides a historical record of specified events in the execution of a program.

Update. To modify a master file with current information according to a predefined procedure.

User. Anyone who requires the services of a computer, or anyone who interacts with a computing system.

Utility program. A problem designed to perform an everyday task, such as transcribing data from one storage device to another, e.g., magnetic tape to magnetic disk for back-up purposes.

Verifier. A device similar to the card punch used to check the validity of the transcribed data by rekeying.

X-punch. Same as an eleven-zone punch.

Y-punch. Same as a twelve-zone punch.

Zone punch. A punch in the eleven, twelve, or zero row of a punched card.

BIBLIOGRAPHY

"A Structure for EDP Projects." *EDP Analyzer,* May 1973.

Allen, Brandt. "Embezzler's Guide to the Computer." *Harvard Business Review,* July–August 1975, pp. 79–89.

Amato, Vincent V. "Computer Feasibility Studies: The Do-It-Yourself Approach." *Management Review,* February 1970, pp. 2–9.

Anshen, Melvin. "The Manager and the Black Box." *Harvard Business Review,* November–December 1960, pp. 85–92.

Anderson, William S. "How Managers Can Help Close Systems Expectation Gap." *The Data Communications User,* June 1974, pp. 16–18.

Avots, Ivars. "The Management Side of PERT." *California Management Review,* Winter 1962, pp. 16–27.

Baker, F. Terry. "Chief Programmer Team Management of Production Programming." *IBM Systems Journal* 11:1, pp. 56–73.

Barnett, John H. "Information System Danger Signals." *Management Services,* January–February 1971, pp. 27–30.

Becker, R.T. "Executives Use Computer to Develop EDP Skills." *Administrative Management,* February 1971, pp. 28–29.

Beehler, Paul J. "EDP: Stimulating Systematic Corporate Planning." *Journal of Systems Management,* November 1969, pp. 26–31.

Bellin, Eugene. "Facilities Management, an Approach to Successful Data Processing Management." *Journal of Systems Management,* January 1971, pp. 18–20.

Bellotto, Sam, Jr. "Documentation: EDP's Neglected Necessity." *Administrative Management,* January 1971, pp. 24–26.

Berger, Raymond M. *Computer Programmer Job Analysis.* Montvale, N.J.: AFIPS Press, 1975.

Biesser, James. "Management by Objectives or Appraisal." *Data Management,* April 1970, pp. 24–25.

Bittel, Lester R. *What Every Supervisor Should Know*. New York: McGraw-Hill Book Company, 1959.

Bodenstab, Charles J. "10 Tips for Successful Implementation of Computer Systems." *Financial Executive*, November 1970, pp. 64–66, 68, 70.

Boettinger, Henry M. "Is Management Really an Art?" *Harvard Business Review*, January–February 1975, pp. 54–64.

Boulden, James B. and Elwood S. Buffa. "Corporate Models: On-Line, Real-Time Systems." *Harvard Business Review*, July–August 1970, pp. 65–83.

Brandon, Dick H. and Sidney Segelstein, Esq. *Data Processing Contracts*. New York: Van Nostrand Reinhold Co., 1976.

"Bringing Women into Computing Management." *EDP Analyzer*, August 1976.

Brooks, Frederick P., Jr. "The Mythical Man-Month." *Datamation*, December 1974, pp. 45–52.

Brown, David S. *Delegating and Sharing Work*. Washington, D.C.: Leadership Resources, Inc., 1966.

Burck, Gilbert. *The Computer Age and Its Potential for Management*. New York: Harper & Row, Publishers, 1965.

Burns, Kevin J. "Keys to DBMS Security." *Computer Decisions*, January 1976, pp. 56, 58, 60–62.

Bursk, Edward C. and John F. Chapman (eds.). *New Decision-Making Tools for Managers*. Cambridge, Mass.: Harvard University Press, 1963.

Carr, Peter F. "Poor Security Leaves DP Facilities Ripe for Sabotage." *Computerworld*, June 17, 1970, pp. 1, 4.

Carroll, Archie B. and Hugh J. Watson. "The Computer's Impact upon Management." *Managerial Planning*, May–June 1975, pp. 5–9, 19.

Chapin, Ned. "Flow Chart Packages." *Data Management*, October 1970, pp. 16–17.

————. "Program Documentation—The Valuable Burden." *Software Age*, May 1968, pp. 24–30.

"Charging for Computer Services." *EDP Analyzer*, July 1974.

Charles, P. L. *The Management of Computer Programming Projects*. New York: American Management Association, 1967.

Cheek, Logan M. "Cost Effectiveness Comes to the Personnel Function." *Harvard Business Review*, May–June 1973, pp. 96–105.

Chesebrough, Wilfred C. "Decision Tables as a Systems Technique." *Honeywell Computer Journal*, Fall 1970, pp. 18–25.

Cleff, Samuel H. and Robert M. Hecht. "Computer Man-Job Match." *The Personnel Administrator*, September–October 1970, pp. 3–4, 7–8, 11–12.

Chu, Albert L. C. "Computer Security: Achilles' Heel." *Business Automation*, February 1971, pp. 32–38.

Cleland, David I. "Why Project Management?" *Business Horizons*, Winter 1964, pp. 81–88.

Connally, Gerald E. "Personnel Administration and the Computer." *Personnel Journal*, August 1969, pp. 605–611, 642.

Connolly, James J. "Case Study of a Computer Audit Program." *The Price Waterhouse Review,* Summer 1966, pp. 34–45.

Corsiglia, Jack. "Matching Computers to the Job—First Step Towards Selection." *Data Processing Magazine,* December 1970, pp. 23–27.

Coughlan, Joseph D. and William K. Strand. "Decision-Making and Fallibility." *The Price Waterhouse Review,* Summer 1969, pp. 54–60.

Dahl, O.J., E.W. Dijkstra and C.A.R. Hoare. *Structured Programming.* New York: Academic Press, 1972.

Davis, Ruth M. "Demanding More from Computers." *Computer Decisions,* January 1976, pp. 47–48.

Dean, Neal J. and James W. Taylor. "Managing to Manage the Computer." *Harvard Business Review,* September–October 1966, pp. 98–100.

"Developments in System Analyst Training." *EDP Analyzer,* September 1970, pp. 1–14.

Diebold, John. "Bad Decisions on Computer Use." *Harvard Business Review,* January–February 1969, pp. 14–16, 27–28, 176.

Donelson, William S. "Project Planning and Control." *Datamation,* June 1976, pp. 73–75, 78, 80.

Doney, Lloyd D. and Walter H. Houghton. "Effective Use of Consultants in Operational Areas." *Data Management,* January 1971, pp. 29–31.

Doren, Morris, J. "To get results, tell employee what results you expect." *Modern Hospital,* March 1974.

Dorn, Philip H. "Standards Now!" *Journal of Systems Management,* October 1969, pp. 11–13.

Drucker, Peter F. *The Practice of Management.* New York: Harper and Brothers, Publishers, 1954.

Emery, James C. *Cost/Benefit Analysis of Information Systems.* The Society for Management Information Systems, Chicago, 1971.

Enger, N.L. *Putting MIS to Work.* New York: American Management Association, 1969.

Estes, Neil. "Step-by-Step Costing of Information Systems." *Journal of Systems Management,* October 1969, pp. 20–28.

Ettorre, Anthony F. "Meaningful EDP Appraisal." *The Personnel Administrator,* January–February 1971, pp. 40–41.

Evans, Marshall K. and Lou R. Hague. "Master Plan for Information Systems." *Harvard Business Review,* January–February 1962, pp. 92–103.

Farmer, Jerome. "Auditing and the Computer—A Suggested Program." *Journal of Accountancy,* July 1970, pp. 53–56.

Firnberg, David. "Your Computer in Jeopardy." *Computer Decisions,* July 1976, pp. 28–30.

Fisch, Gerald G. "Line/Staff Is Obsolete." *Harvard Business Review,* September–October 1961, pp. 67–79.

Flannagan, John C. and Robert Miller. *Performance Record Handbook for Supervisors.* Chicago: Science Research Associates, Inc., 1955.

Flippo, Edwin B. *Principles of Personnel Management.* New York: McGraw-Hill Book Company, 1961.

Frazier, Dwight M. "Systems Test." *Computers and Automation,* September 1970, pp. 22–24.

Gibson, Cyrus F. and Richard L. Nolan. "Managing the Four Stages of EDP Growth." *Harvard Business Review,* January–February 1974, pp. 76–88.

Giguere, M. A. "Finding Forms Analysts." *Business Automation,* March 1, 1971, p. 52.

Goetz, Billy E. *Management Planning and Control.* New York: McGraw-Hill Book Company, 1949.

Goldstein, Robert C. and Richard L. Nolan. "Personal Privacy Versus the Corporate Computer." *Harvard Business Review,* March–April 1975, pp. 62–69.

Golgart, Carl W. "Changing Times in Management." *Advanced Management Journal,* January 1970, pp. 33–38.

Gordon, George C. "Putting the Brakes on Turnover." *Personnel Journal,* February 1974, pp. 141–144.

Gottfried, Ira S. "Motivation of Data Processors—Why and How." *Data Management,* September 1970, pp. 104–106.

Gray, Max and Herbert B. Lassiter. "Project Control for Data Processing." *Datamation,* February 1968, pp. 33–38.

Greene, Robert J. "Room at the Top for the DP Manager." *Datamation,* March 1976, pp. 75, 77–78.

Grout, Jarrell C. and Al F. Trussell. "EDP Management Education." *Data Management,* March 1974, pp. 20–23.

Hallinan, Arthur J. and Gilbert A. Mehling. "Internal Audit of a Computer Disaster Plan," *The Internal Auditor,* November–December 1970, pp. 12–16.

Hammond, John S., III. "Do's and Don'ts of Computer Models for Planning." *Harvard Business Review,* March–April 1974, pp. 110–123.

Harrison, William L. "Program Testing." *Data Management,* December 1969, pp. 30–33.

Heath, Frank R. "Guidelines for Identifying High Payoff Applications." *Data Base,* Winter 1976, vol. 7, no. 3, pp. 7–17.

Heeschen, Paul E. "Auditing Data Processing Administratives—Operational Auditing Applied to EDP." *The Internal Auditor,* November–December, 1970, pp. 55–62.

Herzberg, Frederick and Alex Zautra. "Orthodox Job Enrichment: Measuring True Quality in Job Satisfaction." *Personnel,* September–October, 1976.

Hirsch, Rudolph E. "The Value of Information." *The Price Waterhouse Review,* Spring 1968, pp. 22–27.

Hollinger, C. Robert. "Managing the Computer for Competitive Advantage." *Business Horizons,* December 1970, pp. 17–28.

Holton, John B. and Bill Brian. "Structured Top-Down Flowcharting." *Datamation,* May 1975, pp. 80–84.

Horwitz, Geoffrey B. "EDP Auditing—The Coming of Age." *Journal of Accountancy,* August 1970, pp. 48–56.

Howes, Paul R. "EDP Security: Is Your Guard Up?" *The Price Waterhouse Review,* Spring 1971, pp. 46–53.

Jasinski, Frank J. "Adapting Organization to New Technology." *Harvard Business Review,* January–February 1959, pp. 79–86.

Johansen, H. and A. B. Robertson. *Management Glossary.* Edited by E. F. L. Brech. New York: American Elsevier Publishing Co., Inc., 1968.

John, Richard C. and Thomas J. Nissen. "Evaluating Internal Control in EDP Audits." *Journal of Accountancy,* February 1970, pp. 31–38.

Jones, G. Hunter. "You and Your Computers: Who's in Charge Here?" *The Price Waterhouse Review,* 1973, no. 2, pp. 10–16.

"DP Error and Fraud—And What You Can Do About It." *The Price Waterhouse Review,* 1976, no. 2, pp. 3–11.

Joslin, Edward O. "Techniques of Selecting EDP Equipment." *Data Management,* February 1970, pp. 28–30.

Karp, William. "Management in the Computer Age." *Data Management,* November 1970, pp. 23–25.

Karush, Arnold D. "Evaluating Timesharing Systems Using the Benchmark Method." *Data Processing Magazine,* May 1970, pp. 42–44.

Kaufman, Felix. "Data Systems That Cross Company Boundaries." *Harvard Business Review,* January–February 1966, pp. 141–155.

Keider, Stephen P. "Why Projects Fail." *Datamation,* December 1974, pp. 53–55.

Keller, Arnold E. "A Look at the Programming Environment." *Business Automation,* December 1969, pp. 40–45.

Knight, J. B. "A Practical Approach to the Systems Audit." *Journal of Systems Management,* November 1970, pp. 17–18.

Kolence, Kenneth W. "A Software View of Measurement Tools." *Datamation,* January 1, 1971, pp. 32–38.

Kovalcik, Eugene J. "Understanding Systems Engineering." *Journal of Systems Management,* September 1970, pp. 15–21.

Larson, Harry T. "EDP: A 20-Year Ripoff." *INFOSYSTEMS,* November 1974, pp. 26–30.

Laska, Richard M. "Should a Consultant Be Your Guide Through EDP Country?" *Computer Decisions,* January 1971, pp. 26–31.

Leavitt, Harold J. *Managerial Psychology.* Chicago: University of Chicago Press, 1964.

Likert, Renis. *New Patterns of Management.* New York: McGraw-Hill Book Company, 1961.

Lipsett, Laurance, Frank P. Rodgers, and Harold M. Kentner. *Personnel Selection and Recruitment.* Boston: Allyn & Bacon, Inc., 1964.

"Management & the Computer." Wall Street Journal Study, 1969.

"Managing the Programming Effort." *EDP Analyzer,* June 1968.

"Managing the Systems Effort." *EDP Analyzer,* July 1968.

Martino, R. L. *Project Management and Control.* Vols. 1–3. New York: American Management Association, 1964.

Maynard, Jeff. "Objectives of Program Design." *Software Age,* August–September 1970, pp. 13–15.

McFarlan, F. Warren. "Management Audit of the EDP Department." *Harvard Business Review,* May–June 1973, pp. 131–143.

McFarland, Dalton E. *Management: Principles and Practices.* New York: The Macmillan Company, 1964.

McInnis, John W. "An Approach to the Control of Programming Projects." *Computer Services,* March–April 1970, pp. 46–50.

McKinsey & Company, Inc. *Unlocking the Computer's Profit Potential.* 1968.

McNairn, William N. "Objectives." *The Price Waterhouse Review,* Spring 1970, pp. 34–41.

Melitz, Peter W. "Impact of Electronic Data Processing on Managers." *Advanced Management,* April 1961, pp. 4–6.

Menkhaus, Edward J. "EDP: What's It Worth?" *Business Automation,* November 1969, pp. 48–54.

Menkus, Belden. "Management's Responsibilities for Safeguarding Information." *Journal of Systems Management,* December 1976.

Metzger, Philip W. *Managing a Programming Project.* Englewood Cliffs, N.J.: Prentice-Hall, Inc., 1973.

Miller, Lawrence R. "Law and Information Systems." *Journal of Systems Management,* January 1977, pp. 21–29.

Miller, Robert W. "How to Plan and Control with PERT." *Harvard Business Review,* March–April 1962, pp. 93–104.

Mintzberg, Henry. "The Manager's Job: Folklore and Fact." *Harvard Business Review,* July–August 1975, pp. 49–61.

Moore, Michael R. "EDP AUDITS: A Systems Approach." *The Arthur Young Journal,* Winter 1968, pp. 5–15.

Morse, Robert V. "Control Systems for Better Project Management." *Computer Decisions,* July 1971, pp. 28–31.

National Bureau of Standards. "Hazardous Noise Levels in Computer Labs." *NBS Technical News Bulletin,* September 1970, p. 204.

Nelson, E.A. *Management Handbook for the Estimation of Computer Programming Costs.* Commerce Clearinghouse, Springfield, Va., 1967.

Neuschel, Richard F. *Management by System.* New York: McGraw-Hill Book Company, 1960.

Newman, William H. and Charles E. Summer, Jr. *The Process of Management,* Englewood Cliffs, N.J.: Prentice-Hall, Inc., 1961.

Nixon, John W. "Must Data Processing Be Mismanaged." *Data Management,* November 1970, pp. 33–37.

Nolan, Richard L. "Managing the Computer Resource: A Stage Hypothesis." *Communications of the ACM,* July 1973, pp. 399–405.

"Thoughts About the Fifth Stage." *Data Base,* Fall 1975, vol. 7, no. 2, pp. 4–10.

Odeneal, John F. "Top-Down Computer Control." *INFOSYSTEMS*, September 1976, pp. 39–40.

"Overall Guidance of Data Processing." *EDP Analyzer*, August 1968.

Paul, Robert. "What to Expect from a Project Leader." *Computers and Data Processing*, February 1964, pp. 17–20.

Pereson, Lars. "Designing for Minimum Downtime." *Datamation*, November 1974, pp. 51–54.

Perham, John. "The Computer: A Target." *Dun's Review*, January 1971, pp. 34–36.

"Planning for Your New Computer." *Computer Decisions*, December 1970, pp. 10–13.

Porter, W. Thomas, Jr. *Auditing Electronic Systems*. Belmont, Calif.: Wadsworth Publishing Co., Inc., 1966.

"Project Management Systems." *EDP Analyzer*, September 1976.

Redfield, Charles E. *Communication in Management*. Chicago: University of Chicago Press, 1958.

Reisman, David A. "Facilities Planning." *Datamation*, November 1974, pp. 55–59.

Rittersbach, George H. "The Use Side of the New User EDP Interface." *Management Controls*, October–November 1976.

Roodman, F. "Developing an ADP Plan." *Computer Decisions*, January 1975, pp. 2–4.

Ross, Franz E. "Auditing Development and Technical Projects." *Management Review*, September 1976.

Roy, Herbert J. H. "Using Computer-Based Control Systems for Decision-Making." *Advanced Management Journal*, January 1971, pp. 57–62.

Ruth, Marvin S. "EDP Needs More Practitioners." *INFOSYSTEMS*, March 1976, pp. 36–38.

Sampson, Robert C. *Managing the Managers*. New York: McGraw-Hill Book Company, 1965.

Schoderbek, Peter P., and James D. Babcock. "At Last—Management More Active in EDP." *Business Horizons*, December 1969, pp. 53–58.

Schultz, George P. and Thomas L. Whisler (eds.). *Management Organization and the Computer*. Glencoe, Ill.: The Free Press, 1960.

Schwab, Bernhard. "The Economics of Sharing Computers." *Harvard Business Review*, September–October 1968, pp. 61–70.

Scotese, Peter G. "What Top Management Expects of EDP, and Vice Versa." *Business Automation*, February 1971, pp. 48–53.

Scott, William G. *Human Relations in Management*. Homewood, Ill.: Richard D. Irwin, Inc., 1962.

Shannon, Robert E. *Systems Simulation—The Art and Science*. Englewood Cliffs, N.J.: Prentice-Hall, Inc., 1975.

Sharpe, William F. *The Economics of Computers*. New York: Columbia University Press, 1969.

"Skills Inventory Pool Produces 'Man for the Job.'" *Administrative Management*, April 1970, pp. 58–60.

Smith, Paul T. *Computers, Systems, and Profits.* New York: American Management Association, 1969.

Spett, Milton C. "Standards for Evaluating Data Processing Management." *Datamation,* December 1969, pp. 171, 174–178.

Statland, Norman. "Organizing Your Company's EDP: Centralization vs. Decentralization." *The Price Waterhouse Review,* 1975, no. 2, pp. 12–17.

Statland, Norman J., John B. Singel and Fred M. Stiles. "How to Make Your Computer More Productive." *The Price Waterhouse Review,* 1975, no. 2, pp. 36–44.

Stay, J.F. "HIPO and Integrated Program Design." *IBM Systems Journal,* 1976, vol. 15, no. 2, pp. 143–154.

Stevens, D.F. "The Computer Manager's Guide." *Datamation,* June 1976, pp. 88, 90, 94.

Strasser, Charles. "What Management Can Do for EDP." *Advanced Management Journal,* January 1970, pp. 39–43.

Strassman, Paul A. "Managing the Costs of Information." *Harvard Business Review,* September–October 1976.

Szatrowski, Ted. "Rent, Lease, or Buy." *Datamation,* February 1976, pp. 59–62, 64, 68.

Szweda, Ralph A. "An Approach to EDP Documentation." *The Credit Union Executive,* Spring 1970, pp. 11–14.

———. "Audit Controls for Data Processing Operations." *The Credit Union Executive,* Fall 1966, pp. 2–7.

———. "Choosing the Right Computer for Your Credit Union." *The Credit Union Executive,* Fall 1967, pp. 17–25.

———. "Documenting the EDP System." *The Credit Union Executive,* Summer 1970, pp. 18–32.

———. "Studying Proposals from Computer Vendors." *The Credit Union Executive,* Winter 1967, pp. 19–29.

Tagen, Warren B. "Educating the Internal Auditor in EDP." *The Internal Auditor,* January–February 1970, pp. 48–61.

Taylor, James W. and Neal J. Dean. "Managing to Manage the Computer." *Harvard Business Review,* September–October 1966.

"The Configurator: Today and Tomorrow." *Computer Decisions,* February 1971, pp. 38–43.

"The Corporate Data File." *EDP Analyzer,* November 1969.

"The Internal Auditor and the Computer." *EDP Analyzer,* March 1975.

Thorne, Jack F. "Internal Control of Real-Time Systems." *Data Management,* January 1971, pp. 34–37.

Tilles, Seymour. "The Manager's Job—A Systems Approach." *Harvard Business Review,* January–February 1963, pp. 73–81.

Toan, Arthur B., Jr. "Management Information Systems." *The Price Waterhouse Review,* Spring 1970, pp. 42–53.

Van Tassel, Dennie. "Information Security in a Computer Environment." *Computers and Automation,* July 1969, pp. 24–28.

Vergin, Roger C. and Andrew J. Grimes. "Management Myths and EDP." *California Management Review,* Fall 1964, pp. 59–70.

Warner, C. Dudley. "Monitoring: A Key to Cost Efficiency." *Datamation,* January 1971, pp. 40–49.

Warren, Joseph B. "People Problems." *Business Automation,* October 1970, pp. 46–51.

Wasserman, Joseph J. "Plugging the Leaks in Computer Security." *Harvard Business Review,* September–October 1969, pp. 119–129.

Webb, Richard. *"Audassist." The Journal of Accountancy,* November 1970, pp. 53–58.

Weihrich, W. Fred. "Computer Selection." *Data Management,* February 1970, pp. 31–33.

Wessel, Milton R. "Computer Services and the Law." *Business Automation,* November 1970, pp. 48–50.

Whisler, F.L. and S.F. Harper (eds.). *Performance Appraisal Research and Practice.* New York: Holt, Rinehart & Winston, Inc., 1962.

Willoughby, T.C. "Staffing the MIS Function." *Computing Surveys,* December 1972, pp. 241–259.

Withington, F.G. "Five Generations of Computers." *Harvard Business Review,* July–August 1974, pp. 99–108.

Young, Stanley. *Management: A Systems Analysis.* Glenview, Ill.: Scott, Foresman & Company, 1966.

INDEX